# Multi-Regional Input–Output Analysis of the Japanese Economy

Mitsuo Yamada

# Multi-Regional Input–Output Analysis of the Japanese Economy

Springer

Mitsuo Yamada
Institute of Economics
Chukyo University
Nagoya, Aichi, Japan

ISBN 978-981-97-9043-2 ISBN 978-981-97-9041-8 (eBook)
https://doi.org/10.1007/978-981-97-9041-8



This Springer imprint is published by the registered company Springer Nature Singapore Pte Ltd.
The registered company address is: 152 Beach Road, #21-01/04 Gateway East, Singapore 189721, Singapore

# Preface

The input-output table (IOT), developed by Wassily Leontief, is a statistical table that captures the features of economic transactions in a nationwide economy and is a tool to analyze economic interdependence among the sectors in the economy. Currently, it has many applications, such as the evaluation not only of policies and their measurement but also of the economic effects of events by seeking various ripple effects.

Japan has a long history in the construction of IOTs and their application. After 1990, the prefectural IOTs were completed for all forty-seven prefectures. Since then, for every five years, which are the same year of national tables, the prefectural IOTs have been created up to the 2015 table. The prefectural IOTs are currently located as the core of the regional IOTs in Japan, and they have been effectively used for the evaluation of many events, the policy evaluation of local governments, and the economic planning of the region.

Recently, the construction of the IOT for areas smaller than prefectures has gained more interest because of the revitalization of the regional economy. Another trend appears in the interdependency of the regions. The prefectures' tables have been applied to compile them into a multi-regional input-output table (MRIOT). This tendency stems from the recognition that multi-regional input-output analysis becomes more important because regional economies are strongly connected domestically and internationally, and economic transactions are not necessarily limited within a prefecture.

This book focuses on the regional IOT in Japan and its application, especially on the interdependency among regions through MRIOTs. In this book, we discuss issues in constructing MRIOTs and their application to regional interdependency, the economic distance of a metropolitan area, regional revitalization under a declining population, and measuring the economic contribution of specific firms.

The material covered in this book is based on the author's research to date on the MRIOT for Japan. The original papers are as follows:

Chapters 2 and 3: Yamada, Mitsuo (2018), "Construction of 2011 prefectural input-output tables and their comparison," *Economic, Trade and Industry Statistics Study*, 45(4), 23–51 (in Japanese)
Chapters 4 and 8: Yamada, Mitsuo (2018), "Compilation of the 2011 Chubu Region Inter-Regional Input-Output Table," *Sangyo Renkan (Business Journal of PAPAIOS)*, 25(1), 56–73 (in Japanese)
Chapter 5: Yamada, Mitsuo (2013), "Estimation of inter-regional trade using gravity-RAS methods: A case study of the inter-regional input-output table within Aichi Prefecture," Chukyo University, *Institute of Economics Discussion Paper* No. 1301 (in Japanese)
Chapter 6: Yamada, Mitsuo (2020), "Construction of inter-municipal input-output tables and its application–Based on the 2011 Aichi Prefecture input-output table," *Chukyo Economic Review*, 31, 9–36 (in Japanese)
Chapters 7 and 9: Yamada, Mitsuo (2015), "Construction of a Multi-regional Input-Output Table for Nagoya Metropolitan Area, Japan," *Journal of Economic Structures*, 4(11), 1–18
Chapter 10: Yamada, Mitsuo (2022), "Impact of consumption fluctuations under population decline on the municipal economy of Aichi Prefecture," *Sangyo Renkan (Business Journal of PAPAIOS)*, 30(1), 1–15 (in Japanese)
Chapter 11: Yamada, Mitsuo (2020), "Electrification of automobiles and the Aichi Prefecture economy," Chapter 4 in Mitsuo Yamada and Junya Masuda (eds.), *Econometric Modeling of Globalization and Regional Economies*, Keiso Shobo, Tokyo, 119–151 (in Japanese)
Chapter 12: Yamada, Mitsuo (2023), "Inter-regional input-output analysis of the regional contributions of small and medium-sized enterprises: A case study of Nishio City, Aichi Prefecture," *Sangyo Renkan (Business Journal of PAPAIOS)*, 31(1), 42–56 (in Japanese)

I would like to express my gratitude to the Pan Pacific Association of Input-Output Studies, the Economy, the Trade and Industry Statistics Association, Chukyo University School of Economics and Institute of Economics, and Keiso Shobo Publishing, who allowed me to use these original papers for the materials of this book with revisions and data updating. I would also like to thank the Chubu Regional Institute for Social and Economic Research for allowing me to use the Chubu Regional Input-Output Table.

I would like to thank Professor Keiko Nakayama (Chukyo University) and Professor Kiyoshi Fujikawa (Aichi Gakuin University, Emeritus Professor of Nagoya University) for their help in drafting this book, as well as Emeritus Professor Kazuo Inaba (Ritsumeikan University) and Emeritus Professor Taiyo Ozaki (Kyoto Gakuen University, the current Kyoto University of Advanced Science) for their advice on my research. I was able to pursue my research in econometrics, including input-output analysis, thanks to the guidance of Professor Soshichi Kinoshita of (Emeritus Professor of Nagoya University), who was my supervisor during my undergraduate and graduate studies. Unfortunately, Professor Kinoshita passed away in 2017, and

I regret that I cannot present this book to him in person. I would like to take this opportunity to express my gratitude to Profosser Kinoshita.

Finally, I owe my research career to the understanding and support of my wife, Yumi, to whom I dedicate this book in gratitude.

Nagoya, Japan
August 2024

Mitsuo Yamada

# Contents

# About the Author

**Mitsuo Yamada** is an emeritus professor at Chukyo University, Nagoya, Japan, and continues his research activities as a research fellow at the institute of Economics, Chukyo University. He has over 40 years of research experience in the fields of econometric research and input-output analysis in regional and international economics, and energy and environmental economics at Saga University, Mie University, and Chukyo University.

He obtained his Ph.D. degree in economics at Nagoya University. He also served as a visiting researcher at the Economic Research Institute, Economic Planning Agency (currently the Economic and Social Research Institute (ESRI) of the Cabinet Office) and the International Institute for Applied Systems Analysis (IIASA), Austria. He served as President of the Pan Pacific Association of Input-Output Studies (PAPAIOS) and as a board member of the Japan Association for Applied Economics (JAAE). He contributed to the construction of the national input-output tables of Japan as a member of the technical advisory committee, and to the creation of the multi-regional input-output tables of Chubu region as a research advisor of Chubu Region Institute for Social and Economic Research.

# Abbreviations

| | |
|---|---|
| APL | Average propagation length |
| BPO | Business process outsourcing |
| CFS | Commodity flow survey |
| CT | Control total |
| EBPM | Evidence-based policy-making |
| EVs | Electric vehicles |
| FCVs | Fuel cell vehicles |
| HEM | Hypothetical extraction method |
| HEVs | Hybrid vehicles |
| HIM | Hypothetical insertion method |
| IOT | Input-output table |
| JAMA | Japan Automobile Manufacturers Association |
| LQ | Location quotient |
| METI | Ministry of Economy, Trade and Industry |
| MIC | Ministry of Internal Affairs and Communications |
| MITI | Ministry of International Trade and Industry |
| MLIT | Ministry of Land, Infrastructure, Transport and Tourism |
| MRIOT | Multi-regional input-output table |
| NIPSSR | National Institute of Population and Social Security Research |
| NNFFS | Nationwide net freight flow survey (Logistics census) |
| NSFIE | National Survey of Family Income and Expenditure |
| PHVs | Plug-in hybrid vehicles |
| RCA | Revealed comparative advantage |
| REASAS | Regional economic analysis system |
| ROA | Rest of Aichi |
| ROJ | Rest of Japan |
| ROW | Rest of the world |
| SME | Small and medium-sized enterprises |
| SNA | System of National Accounts |
| SUT | Supply and use tables |
| VA | Value added |

# Chapter 1
# Introduction

## 1.1 The Aim of the Book

The input–output table (IOT), developed by Leontief (1936), is a statistical table that captures the features of economic transactions in a nationwide economy and is used as a tool to analyze economic interdependence among the sectors in the economy. Currently, it has many applications, such as the evaluation not only of policies and their measurement but also of the economic effects of events by seeking various ripple effects.

In Japan, the Agency for Economic Investigation and Planning (later the Economic Planning Agency, now the Cabinet Office) and the Ministry of International Trade and Industry (MITI, currently the Ministry of Economy, Trade and Industry or METI), each independently, constructed a trial table for 1951. Since 1955, the input–output table has been constructed every five years as a joint project of related ministries and agencies, which are currently increasing to ten ministries and agencies.[1]

The IOT for each prefecture was also initially developed with Nagano and Aichi Prefecture tables for 1953. The number of prefectures that constructed their input–output tables increased gradually for 1955 and 1960. In 1990, the IOTs for all 47 prefectures of Japan were completed. Since then, for every five years, which are the same year as national tables, the prefectural IOTs have been created up to the 2015 table. The prefectures' input–output tables have been effectively used for the evaluation of many events, the policy evaluation of local governments, and the economic planning of the regions.

[1] The present members are the Ministry of Internal Affairs and Communications (coordinator), the Cabinet Office, the Financial Services Agency, the Ministry of Finance, the Ministry of Education, Culture, Sports, Science and Technology, the Ministry of Health, Labour and Welfare, the Ministry of Agriculture, Forestry and Fisheries, the Ministry of Economy, Trade and Industry, the Ministry of Land, Infrastructure, Transport and Tourism, and the Ministry of Environment (See https://www.soumu.go.jp/english/dgpp_ss/data/io/outline.htm).



M. Yamada, *Multi-Regional Input–Output Analysis of the Japanese Economy*,
https://doi.org/10.1007/978-981-97-9041-8_1

Recently, the construction of the input–output table for areas smaller than prefectures has gained more interest because of the revitalization of the regional economy. Another trend appears in the interdependency of the regions. The prefectures' tables have been applied to compile them into a MRIOT. This tendency stems from the recognition that multi-regional input–output analysis becomes more important because the regional economies are strongly connected domestically and internationally, and economic transactions are not necessarily limited within a prefecture.

The MRIOT is commonly known to have two types: Isard-type and Chenery-Moses-type (Miller and Blair 2009). They differ in the assumption of an interregional trade coefficient. The former requires a complete set of intra- and interregional data, although obtaining such interregional trade coefficients for each sector in each region, especially within a country, is difficult. However, the latter has advantages in compiling the table because of the simplification in applying the common interregional trade coefficient for each sector in each region. For this reason, MRIOTs within a country are usually compiled as the Chenery-Moses type.

Nevertheless, the interregional trade data within a country are still difficult to obtain fully, which forces one to shift from adopting the survey method to some kind of non-survey method in the estimation of the interregional trade coefficients. Location quotient (LQ) techniques, the gravity model, the RAS method, and others have been developed or applied for such estimation. Lahr (1993) reviewed typical regional input–output models from 1963 to 1992 and pointed out the importance of the hybrid approach, both survey-based and non-survey, to construct an accurate IOT with reasonable costs.

Cross-hauling (the simultaneous exporting and importing of the same type of product) is important in interregional trade because ignoring it induces an underestimation of trade and an overestimation of the regional output multiplier (see Kronenberg 2009). LQ techniques are easy to manipulate, at least for two regions, though the techniques have the disadvantage that cross-hauling is inevitably eliminated in interregional trade.

The gravity model, which originally stems from the theory of physics, is applied to explain commodity flows among regions, allowing cross-hauling in interregional trade. The RAS method was originally developed for the estimation of the input–output coefficients, for which only the peripheral information of the column sums and the row sums is known, in an iterative way. This method requires initial values, on which the solution depends. Sargento et al. (2012) compared and assessed the performance of gravity models for explaining interregional trade among regions. Nakano and Nishimura (2013) estimated one type of gravity model with cross-hauling using a survey on interregional transactions and constructed the three-regional IOTs of Japan.

The gravity-RAS method estimates the interregional transaction matrix. If the initial values for the iteration calculation of the RAS method are not obtained by official statistical data or organized survey data, the estimated value by the gravity model is used as the initial value. This method gives consistent values for transactions among regions based on the exports and imports of each region.

This book aims to focus on the regional IOT and its application, especially on the inter-dependency among regions through MRIOTs in Japan. We discuss issues in constructing the MRIOTs and their application to regional interdependency, the economic distance of a metropolitan area, regional revitalization under declining population, and measuring the economic contribution of specific firms.

## 1.2 Outline of the Book

This book, focusing on the Japanese regional IOT, consists of the following two parts: Part one concerns the construction of multi-regional IOTs in Japan, and Part two treats the application of their multi-regional IOTs.

Part one, the construction of interregional IOTs in Japan, consists of six chapters. Chapter 2, Structure of Regional IOTs in Japan, provides an overview of the structure of Japan's IOTs, discusses the positioning of prefectural IOTs, and outlines the estimation methods for regional IOTs. In addition, we give an overview of how to construct the IOTs, both national and regional. The construction of the regional IOT depends on the national IOT.

The structure of Japan's regional IOTs has four layers including national IOT: regional IOTs of the METI below the national IOT, prefectural IOTs below them, and municipal IOTs further below. The METI's regional IOTs had excellent characteristics of aggregation consistency with the national IOT. However, since the METI decided their regional IOTs were no longer to be created after the 2005 table, currently it is reduced to three-tiered structures, including the national table.

Currently, the prefectural IOT is located directly below the national table, but each table is created by each prefecture. Some prefectural IOTs began to be created around the same time as the national IOTs started and have a long history, though IOTs for all 47 prefectures were not completed until 1990. As each prefecture creates its own IOT using information from the same year's national IOT, no guarantee can be offered that its aggregated values will match the corresponding values of the national IOT.

In Chap. 3, we compare prefectural IOTs with the national IOTs. In this chapter, based on the 2011 prefectural IOTs, they were aggregated and compared with the values of the national table after integrating each prefectural table into 80 common sectors. We found that the deviation rate of total production from the national value is less than 1%, the maximum deviation rate by sector is less than 20%, and seven out of 80 sectors exceed 10%, and most of them are within a few percent. As for net exports, including both national and domestic, their sum should be equal to the corresponding values of net exports on the national table. The total deviation divided by the production was less than 1%, but we found that about nine sectors exceeded 10%. The rate of deviation in the goods sector was relatively small, but the rate in the service sector was large. These rates have improved gradually over time.

Chapter 4 discusses the construction of a multi-prefectural IOT. Several inter-prefectural IOTs exist that target specific regions wider than a prefecture. These are the Kansai region IOT for eight prefectures in Kansai (Kansai Institute of Social and Economic Research 2008; Asia Pacific Institute of Research 2012), the Tohoku region IOT for seven prefectures in Tohoku, including Niigata (Tohoku Regional Advancement Center 2011), and the Chubu region interregional IOT covering nine prefectures in the Chubu (central) region (Yamada 2018b; Yamada and Kimura, 2023a, b). Recently, the Kyusyu multi-regional IOT was constructed by the Kyusyu Economic Research Center (Yamada and Kawamura 2024).

In this chapter, we discuss how to create a multi-prefectural IOT, picking up the Chubu region as an example, and discuss the characteristics of each prefecture from the perspective of comparative advantages in production and intraregional dependency due to value-added inducement. For the creation of an inter-prefectural IOT, estimating interregional trade flows among prefectures by sector is important. For this purpose, we can obtain several statistical sources to estimate the interregional trade flow among prefectures that is consistent with the exports and imports of each prefectural IOT.

In Chap. 5, we focus on the estimation of interregional trade with the gravity-RAS method. When creating an intra-regional IOT of one prefecture, estimating the trade among regions is important, one of which, the gravity-RAS method, is examined by applying Aichi prefecture as a case.

The interregional trade data within a country continues to be difficult to obtain completely, which forces one to shift from adopting the survey method to some kind of non-survey method in the estimation of the interregional trade coefficients. LQ techniques, gravity models, the RAS method, and others have been developed or applied for such estimation. Lahr (1993) reviewed typical regional input–output models from 1963 to 1992 and pointed out the importance of the hybrid approach, both survey-based and non-survey, to construct an accurate IOT with reasonable costs.

Cross-hauling (the simultaneous exporting and importing of the same type of product) is important in interregional trade because ignoring it induces an underestimation of trade and an overestimation of the regional output multiplier (see Kronenberg 2009). LQ techniques are easy to manipulate, at least for two regions, though the techniques have the disadvantage of inevitably eliminating cross-hauling in interregional trade. The gravity model, which originally stems from the theory of physics, is applied to explain commodity flows among regions, allowing cross-hauling in interregional trade. The RAS method was originally developed for the estimation of the input–output coefficients, for which only the peripheral information of the column sums and the row sums is known, in an iterative way. This method requires initial values on which the solution depends. Sargento et al. (2012) compared and assessed the performance of some gravity models for explaining interregional trade among regions. Nakano and Nishimura (2013) estimated one type of gravity model with cross-hauling using a survey on interregional transactions and constructed the three-regional IOTs of Japan.

In this chapter, we summarize related preceding research and explain the gravity-RAS method, a method of estimating interregional trade that is considered here. We estimate the model and examine the degree of difference in the IOT of Aichi Prefecture depending on the given conditions.

Chap. 6 discusses the construction of a multi-regional IOT within a prefecture. Compiling IOTs for smaller areas within a prefecture has garnered growing interest. Many studies have examined interregional IOTs within prefectures. Yamada (1995) developed a multi-regional IOT for Mie Prefecture with five regions. Yamada and Horiuchi (2015) conducted a comparative analysis of the interregional IOTs of Mie Prefecture from 1995 to 2010. Tsukamoto et al. (2018) developed an inter-municipal IOT for Aichi Prefecture in 2005.

In this chapter, we estimate an interregional IOT for 54 municipalities based on the 2011 Aichi IOT, in which the 188-sector table is integrated into a 106-sector table. Although the size of the sector is almost half that examined by Tsukamoto et al. (2018), the target year has been updated. We present an outline of the 2011 inter-municipal IOT of Aichi Prefecture, compare the characteristics of municipalities from the estimated IOT, and examine the interdependency among municipalities by the value-added induced by the given final demands.

Chapter 7 focuses on linking adjacent prefectures' multi-regional input–output tables (MRIOTs). In this chapter, using the IOTs for the three prefectures of Aichi, Gifu, and Mie, respectively, we first break down each prefecture's table into the MRIOTs with several small areas for each. Then, we integrate the three MRIOTs into one MRIOT, using the estimated commodity flows among small areas by sector. This MRIOT, with 14 areas and 186 sectors, targets three prefectures, Aichi, Mie, and Gifu, which is called the Tokai region.

Why do we break down the prefecture IOTs into those of several small areas and integrate the small area IOTs into one multi-regional IOT? We think that such a type of IOT makes it possible to solve the analytical problem that a region identified in terms of economic activity is not necessarily the same as the administrative region. We introduce a method to recompile our MRIOT of the Tokai region and discuss the structural characteristics of the Tokai region.

In Part II, which includes five chapters after Chap. 8, we focus on the application of the multi-regional IOTs that we discuss in Part I.

In Chap. 8, we focus on the multiplier decomposition and discuss the regional interdependence in the Chubu region. Understanding the relationships between economic activities among regions is important. As for the Chubu region, it is pointed out that a spatial structure centered on Aichi Prefecture has been formed. Chen et al. (2016) explicitly and quantitatively discuss the interdependent relationship between the Aichi Prefecture, its core, and the eight surrounding prefectures. They focused on the spatial structure of the Chubu region centered on Aichi Prefecture and attempted to quantitatively understand its temporal and spatial transformation processes using the framework of interregional IOTs.

In this chapter, using the Chubu region interregional IOT described in Chap. 4, we examine the mutual relationships between each prefecture in the region by decomposing induced productions of final demands by region. Then, we decompose the secular changes in the induced productions in 2011 and 2015 into technological change and market change factors. Furthermore, in relation to the technological change factors, we apply the multiplier decomposition method proposed by Okamoto

(2012) and Kuwamori (2014) to measure the spillover multiplier and feedback multiplier among the nine prefectures in Chubu region, which reveal changes in the interdependent relationship among Aichi Prefecture, its eight surrounding prefectures, and the rest of Japan (ROJ).

Chapter 9 is titled "Average propagation length and the Economic Zone of the Nagoya Metropolitan Area." Nagoya is the third-largest metropolitan area in Japan, following Tokyo and Osaka. Nagoya City, the capital city of Aichi Prefecture, is the economic center of the Tokai Region, which covers three prefectures: Aichi, Mie, and Gifu. When we focus on the Nagoya metropolitan area, the inter-prefectural IOT like the Chubu region, discussed in Chap. 6, is not a proper tool because prefectures are too large a region to analyze issues in metropolitan areas. Ideally, input–output analysis should be performed based on the municipalities that each prefecture is divided into. However, Aichi Prefecture has 54 municipalities, Mie Prefecture has 29, and Gifu Prefecture has 42, for a total of 125 for the Tokai Region as a whole. An inter-municipal IOT that combines these municipalities would be huge and difficult to handle. Here, we use an interregional IOT that aggregates each municipality into the 14 regions described in Chap. 7.

The closer the distance between areas, the stronger their economic connection. Using the MRIOT for the Tokai region described in Chap. 7, we discuss the structural characteristics of the Nagoya metropolitan area. We apply the Average Propagation Lengths (APL) tool proposed by Dietzenbacher et al. (2005), which is the analytical tool to show the economic distance through the transaction of intermediate goods by sector. We investigate the relationship between the APL distance and physical distance and consider the boundary of the metropolitan area. We then present a way to cope with the various inconsistencies of regional definitions, administrative and economic, in the input–output analysis.

The following three chapters concern the applications of the inter-municipal input–output model, based on the 54 municipalities and 106 sectors of Aichi Prefecture in 2011, which are discussed in Chap. 6.

Chapter 10 discusses the impact of consumption fluctuation caused by a declining population on the regional economy. A declining population, which reduces consumption demand and might bring about the stagnation of the local economy, is one of the critical issues in Japan. Here, by utilizing the projected numbers of population and households in 54 municipalities in the Aichi Prefecture (NIPSSR) and data on consumption expenditure by householder age group (NSFIE), we estimate the future changes in household consumption expenditure. Furthermore, we analyze the impact on production and the value-added to each municipality (inter-municipal IOT for 54 municipalities in Aichi Prefecture).

Here, for the multi-municipal IOT, we applied a consumption endogenous model that considers commuting between the residences and workplaces of employees between municipalities.

We find that as the populations of many municipalities in the Aichi Prefecture continue to decline, their consumption demands also decline alongside their production and value-added. However, in the Nishimikawa area, where the automobile manufacturing industry is vibrant, the population is increasing a little bit, leading to increased consumption and, thereby, increased production and value-added. Owing to the interdependency among the municipalities, production and value-added even in the Nishimikawa area, with its increasing population, are lowered because of the strong spillover effect from other municipalities.

In Chap. 11, we focus on the impact of automobile electrification on the regional economy. The automobile industry has been driving the Japanese economy for a long time. Despite the expanding globalization of automobile production, about half of domestic production is still exported from Japan. However, the Japanese automobile industry has considered changing its production structure in the near future. Of the four so-called "CASE" technologies for automobiles (i.e., connected, autonomous, shared, and electrified capabilities), we focus on electrification. In the wide body of work in this field, both nationally and regionally, no studies have discussed the effect of automobile electrification on municipal economies.

In this chapter, we investigate the impact of automobile electrification on the local economy of Aichi Prefecture, where automobile-related industries are concentrated. The headquarters and main factories of the Toyota Motor Corporation are in Toyota City and the surrounding municipalities in Aichi, which is called the Nishimikawa area. Therefore, by constructing an inter-municipal IOT for 106 sectors and 54 municipalities in Aichi Prefecture for 2011, as stated in Chap. 6, we analyze the municipalities' induced production effects from the electrification of the automobile industry up to 2030.

Several kinds of automobiles are available for electrification: hybrid vehicles (HEVs), plug-in hybrid vehicles (PHVs), electric vehicles (EVs), and fuel cell vehicles (FCVs), each of which has different input structures for production, though the demand is aggregated to one sector that provides the same function of automobiles. This makes the number of rows and columns in the IOT different. Here, we adopted a scenario analysis in which each input structure was aggregated into one, using the given shares of each type of vehicle as a weight. We demonstrate that production in municipal economies that supply more automotive parts is more negatively impacted by electrification; however, a positive effect does exist in the electrical machinery industry.

In Chap. 12, we highlight small and medium-sized enterprises' production and discuss their economic contribution to the regional economy. To revitalize the local economy, leading small and medium-sized enterprises (SMEs) must play an active role. Therefore, calculating and visualizing the economic contribution that these SMEs make to the region and the surrounding areas is important.

The "Hypothetical extraction method (HEM)" is well known as a method measuring the importance of a certain sector's economic activity on the economy. We extend this method to measure the effect of an SME by not extracting but inserting its production activity in the input–output model, which we call the "Hypothetical insertion method (HIM)." This method can be applied in two aspects: the "backward linkage effect" through the procurement of raw materials with the Leontief model and the "forward linkage effect" through the product sales channel with the Ghosh model.

If SME activities exist in the base year of the comparison, the results calculated by the "HIM" might be overestimated unless such activities are eliminated in the base year IOT. Therefore, we discuss the extension of the "HIM."

Citing the example of Nishio City in the Nishimikawa area of Aichi Prefecture, we conducted a questionnaire survey of four SMEs on their production, material, and other costs, as well as regional sales and procurements. We applied the 2011 interregional IOT of Nishio City, with three regions: Nishio City, the rest of Aichi (ROA) Prefecture, and the ROJ, and 106 sectors for each region, based on the multi-municipal IOT in Chap. 6. By measuring the increase in the ripple effects by adding each SME's sector, we obtained the regional contributions of its production in both aspects: the backward and forward linkage effects.

Finally, in Chap. 13, we summarize the conclusions obtained from our research and present the remaining research challenges.

## References


Asia Pacific Institute of Research (former Kansai Institute of Social and Economic Research). 2008. *Compilation of 2000 Kansai interregional input-output table* (in Japanese).

Asia Pacific Institute of Research. 2012. *Compilation and use of the 2005 Kansai interregional input-output table* (in Japanese).

Chen, Y., M. Yamada, and T. Ihara. 2016. Research on spatial interdependence of the Chubu region economy - based on the Chubu region inter-regional input-output table. *Sango Renkan (Business Journal of PAPAIOS)* 23 (3): 88–101 (in Japanese).

Dietzenbacher, E., I. Remero Luna, and N. S. Bosma. 2005. Using average propagation lengths to identify production chains in the Andalusian economy. *Estudios De Economia Aplicada* 23 (2): 405–422.

Kronenberg, T. 2009. Construction of regional input-output tables using nonsurvey methods, The role of cross-hauling. *International Regional Science Review* 32 (1): 40–64.

Kuwamori, Hiroshi. 2014. Decomposition and measurement of international production spillovers. In Chiharu Tamamura, and Hiroshi Kuwamori editors. *International input-output analysis: Theory and applications*, vol. 609, 105–144, Institute of Developing Economies Research Series (in Japanese).

Okamoto, N. 2012. *Regional economies of China: Spatial structure and interdependence.* Ltd, Tokyo (in Japanese): Nippon Hyoron Sha Co.

Leontief, W. 1936. Quantitative input and output relations in the economic system of the united states. *Review of Economics and Statistics, 18* (3): 105–125.

Miller, R.E., and P.D. Blair. 2009. *Input-output analysis: foundations and extensions.* Cambridge University Press.

Nakano, S., and K. Nishimura. 2013. A nonsurvey multiregional input-output estimation allowing cross-hauling: Partitioning two regions into three or more parts. *Annals of Regional Science* 50:935–951.

Sargento, A. L. M., P. N. Ramos, and G. J. D. Hewings. 2012. Inter-regional trade flow estimation through non-survey models: An empirical assessment. *Economic Systems Research* 24 (2): 173–193.

Tohoku Regional Advancement Center. 2011. Report on the Tohoku multi-regional input-output table for 2005 (in Japanese). http://www.kasseiken.jp/association/

Tsukamoto, T., N. Komiyama, and J. Nemoto. 2018. Construction of inter-regional input-output table among all municipalities in Aichi Prefecture and analysis on spatial interdependence between municipalities. *Sango Renkan (Business Journal of PAPAIOS)* 26 (1): 1–20 (in Japanese).

Yamada, M. 1995. Estimation of Mie Prefecture inter-regional input-output table. *Sango Renkan (Business Journal of PAPAIOS)* 5 (4): 52–67 (in Japanese).

Yamada, M. 2018. Compilation of the 2011 Chubu region interregional input-output table. *Sangyo Renkan (Business Journal of PAPAIOS)* 25 (1): 56–73 (in Japanese).

Yamada, M., and Y. Horiuchi. 2015. Comparison of inter-regional input-output tables for Mie Prefecture from 1985 to 2010. *Sango Renkan (Business Journal of PAPAIOS)* 23 (1–2): 15–28 (in Japanese).

Yamada, M., and S. Kawamura. 2024. How to create and use the Kyushu regional input-output table. *Kyushu Economic Survey Monthly* 78:14–23 (in Japanese).

Yamada, Mitsuo, and Shinichiro Kimura. 2023a. Compiling the Chubu region inter-regional input-output table (2015 edition) and preliminary analysis of the regional structure. *Economy, Trade and Industry Statistics Study* 54(1): 1–22 (in Japanese).

Yamada, Mitsuo, and Shinichiro Kimura. 2023b. Analysis of regional economic structure based on the Chubu region inter-regional input-output table (2015 edition)—Characteristics of industries in each prefecture in the Chubu region. *Chubu Research Quarterly 224*: 27–59 (in Japanese).

# Part I
# Construction of Interregional Input–Output Tables in Japan

# Chapter 2
# Structure of Regional Input–Output Tables in Japan

## 2.1 Introduction

The IOT, developed by Wassily Leontief, is a statistical table that captures the features of economic transactions in a nationwide economy and is a tool to analyze economic interdependence among the sectors in the economy. Currently, it is used in many ways, such as the evaluation not only of policies and their measurement but also of the economic effects of events by seeking various ripple effects.

In Japan, the Agency for Economic Investigation and Planning (later the Economic Planning Agency, now the Cabinet Office) and the Ministry of International Trade and Industry (now the Ministry of Economy, Trade and Industry, or METI), each independently, constructed a trial table for 1951. Since 1955, it has been constructed every five years as a joint project of related ministries and agencies, which has been increased to 10 ministries and agencies.[1]

Prefectural IOTs were also created initially with Nagano and Aichi Prefecture tables for 1953 and were increased gradually with the tables for 1955 and 1960. In 1990, the IOTs for all 47 prefectures of Japan were completed. Since then, for every five years, which are the same year as the national tables, the prefectural IOTs have been created up to the 2015 table.

In this chapter, Sect. 2.2 provides an overview of Japan's system of IOTs and discusses the positioning of prefectural IOTs, while Sect. 2.3 outlines the estimation methods for regional IOTs.

[1] The latest published table is the 2015 National Table (Basic Table). Only the previous table covers 2011, not 2010. To use the results of the 2012 economic census survey, which was conducted for the first time in Japan, an IOT corresponding to this survey year was created.

 
M. Yamada, *Multi-Regional Input–Output Analysis of the Japanese Economy*,
https://doi.org/10.1007/978-981-97-9041-8_2

## 2.2 Structure of Input–output Tables in Japan

Figure 2.1 is a systematic diagram depicting the relationships among various IOTs in Japan. There is the national IOT (benchmark tables), which is located at the center (J1) in the figure. The right and left directions correspond to the time axes. Based on the national IOT of J1, an updated IOT exists that is estimated for newer time points with essentially the same concept, definition, and scope as the basic IOT and newly revised values of output, domestic final demand, export, and import for the corresponding year. It is represented by J2 in the figure. On the contrary, J3 are linked tables where possible adjustments of sector, concept, scope, and price fluctuations have been made to the three basic tables for the past ten years.

With the basic IOT of J1 as the starting point, the lower left direction represents the regional axis. It depicts that the unit of the targeting area becomes smaller as it goes to the lower left. Starting with the basic IOT covering the entire country, R1 is the regional table of the METI, P1 is the IOT of each prefecture, and below that is the municipal IOT at C1.

Conversely, the upper direction represents the scope axis of the targeting region. Extending the scope means expanding from a single regional IOT to a multi-regional IOT. For the national IOT J1, inter-national IOTs, M1, which usually link multiple IOTs for nations including Japan with international trade flow, are positioned here. These IOTs capture the interdependence of economic transactions between countries. Examples include the Japan-US IOT (METI 2013a, b) and the Japan–China IOT (METI 2012).

For the regional case of R1, the interregional IOT of METI is positioned in M2 above R1. The table linked each of the nine regional IOTs of METI, which targeted each regional bureau of METI, with the estimated regional trade flows. Additionally,

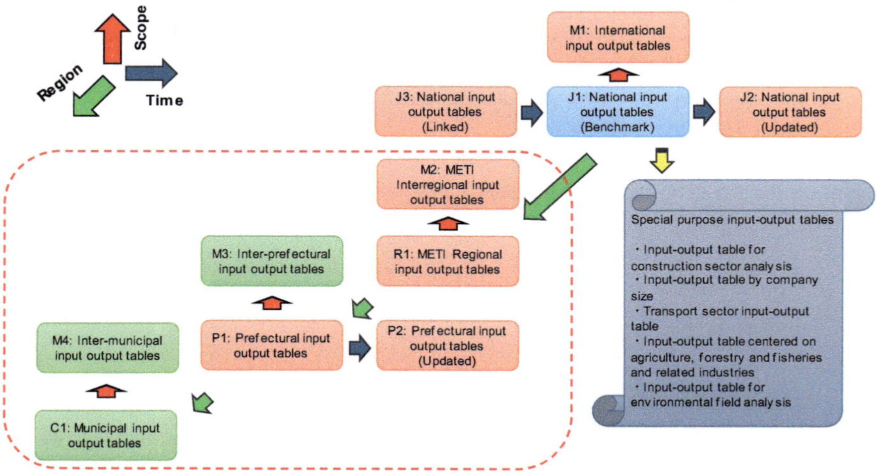


**Fig. 2.1** Structure of IOTs in Japan. *Source* Created by the author

above the prefectural IOT, P1, the inter-prefectural IOTs are located at M3, and above the IOTs for each municipal region, C1, the inter-municipal IOTs are located at M4.

In Fig. 2.1, the national and regional IOTs that are colored orange are mainly constructed by the government—national and local. However, the municipal IOT, C1, and the interregional IOTs for prefecture and municipality, M3 and M4, are usually estimated by not only the local government but also universities and research institutes.

The examples of inter-prefectural IOTs, M3, that cover all of Japan are Ishikawa and Miyagi (2003), Hagiwara (2012), Hitomi (2008), and Arai (2020, 2022). In addition, the Tohoku interregional IOT (Tohoku Regional Advancement Center 2011), Kansai interregional IOT (Kansai institute of social and economic research (current Asia Pacific Institute of Research 2008), Chubu interregional IOT (Chubu Region Institute for Social and Economic Research 2011), and Kyushu region interregional IOT (Yamada and Kawamura, 2024) are concentrated in some regions of Japan.

Other interregional IOTs, M4, also exist that specialize in specific regional areas within a prefecture: interregional IOTs for Hokkaido (Takahata 1992), Ehime (Tsubouchi 1991), Mie (Yamada 1995; Yamada and Horiuchi 2015), and Hyogo (Ashiya and Goto 2015). These tables usually divide the prefecture into several sub-regions.

Recently, in relation to regional revitalization against declining depopulation in Japan, there has been growing interest in the construction of municipal-based IOTs. Larger cities such as Sapporo, Yokohama, Osaka, Nagoya, Fukuoka, etc. have constructed their own IOTs, whereas relatively sixteen municipalities such as Gujo, Kushiro, and others have also constructed their tables.[2]

Another way to construct municipal IOTs is to create inter-municipal IOTs from a prefectural IOT. For the Aichi Prefecture, Tsukamoto et al. (2018) and Yamada (2020a, b) divided each municipal IOT from the Aichi IOT and constructed an interregional IOT for 2005 and 2011, respectively. In this case, all municipal IOTs that have aggregation consistency with prefectural values are created at once.

The national table (benchmark table) plays an extremely important role in the structure of the IOT, as depicted in Fig. 2.1.[3] Furthermore, amid growing interest in the IOTs of smaller regions and the structure of interregional linkages, the METI regional tables and IOTs for each prefecture are second in importance. The tables are constructed by the government—central and local.

An increasing number of attempts have been made to create interregional tables that can grasp the interdependence of the economy in a wider area beyond the administrative boundaries of prefectures. However, IOTs that consider the differences in regional characteristics within prefectures that are not represented by an IOT for the prefecture are becoming necessary.[4] The existence of highly accurate IOTs

---

[2] The website of the PAPAIOS lists sixteen government ordinance-designated cities and sixteen other cities having IOTs (referred to on July 8, 2024) (see https://www.gakkai.ne.jp/papaios/iotable-m.html).

[3] Based on the national IOT, special-purpose IOTs that enable detailed analysis of specific sectors, such as IOTs for the analysis of the construction sector, are also created.

[4] Economic zones with an economic identity are not the same as the prefectures that represent administrative areas but often exceed them as the economy develops. Yamada (2015) decomposes

for each prefecture is the basis for creating IOTs that respond to inter-prefectural interdependence and intra-prefectural diversity.

Nevertheless, creating an IOT takes time. The construction of a national benchmark table takes about three years after the target year. For the prefectural IOT, it takes one or two years after the release of the national benchmark IOT. Furthermore, as it takes five years before the release of the next table, we use the regional IOT that covers the economic structure from no more than nine to ten years prior. This request calls for a reduction in the estimation period of IOTs. Another approach is to use an updated METI table for the national table. Additionally, some prefectures have attempted to create the updated tables.[5]

## 2.3 Overview of the Construction of Regional IOTs

### *2.3.1 Manuals for the Regional IOT*

Table 2.1 presents the manuals for constructing national IOTs (benchmark tables) and regional tables after 2005. For the national IOTs, two types of manuals exist: "Basic Guideline" and "Explanatory Report," which are referred to in constructing regional IOTs.

As a basic manual for regional IOTs, there are two basic guidelines: one is for the regional IOT of METI, and the other is made by the MIC for each prefecture's statistical division in constructing the IOT.

The basic guidelines of the METI's regional table demonstrate how to compile the METI's regional table. As prefecture IOTs are also a type of regional table, although there are differences in target regions, many commonalities exist in the method of constructing a regional IOT. Therefore, each prefecture's statistic division referred to these guidelines and manuals in constructing its IOT. However, as METI decided not to construct their regional IOT for 2011 and thereafter for assorted reasons, the basic guidelines for METI's 2015 regional IOTs were not created. After 2015, the guidelines were no longer applicable in compiling prefectural IOTs.

The MIC created the Basic Guidelines for Creating Regional IOTs to present the guidelines for constructing the prefectural IOTs in 1981. This guideline was revised twice, once in 2001 and then in 2008. In 2014, it was further revised, though it was the unfinished draft version, corresponding to the creation of the 2011 regional IOT as the latest version.

---

the IOTs of the three prefectures in the Tokai Region (Aichi, Gifu, and Mie) into 4–5 sub-regions to analyze the interdependence of these wide-area economic zones. By reconstructing the entire three prefectures as an interregional IOT, he tried to analyze the Nagoya metropolitan area, which is not bound by the administrative boundaries of prefectures, which are referred to in Chaps. 7 and 10 of this book.

[5] It seems necessary to consider the standardization and systemization of the estimation method for regional IOTs, including regionally updated tables.

**Table 2.1** Manuals for input–output tables

| | National table | | METI regional table | Prefecture's table |
|---|---|---|---|---|
| 2005 | *Basic Guidelines for Constructing 2005 Input–Output Tables*, Input–Output Department Director's Meeting, February 2007 | 2005 Input–output Tables, Explanatory Report, MIC, Japan, March 2009 | *Basic Manual for METI 2005 Regional Input–output Tables*, METI, September 2009 | *Basic Guidelines for Creating Regional Input–output Tables*, MIC, Japan, June 2008 |
| 2011 | Basic Guidelines for Constructing 2011 Input–Output Tables, Input–Output Department Director's Meeting, January 2013 | 2011 input–Output Tables, Explanatory Report, MIC, Japan, June 2015 | *Basic Manual for METI 2011 Regional Input–output Tables*, METI, May 2013 | *Basic Guidelines for Creating Regional Input–output tables (unfinished draft)*, MIC, Japan, June 2014 |
| 2015 | Basic Guidelines for Constructing 2015 Input–Output Tables, Input–Output Department Director's Meeting, August 2017 | *2015 Input–output Tables, Explanatory Report*, MIC, Japan, January 2020 | N.A | N.A |

*Source* Created by the author

These manuals and guidelines are referred to in the compilation of prefectural IOTs. Therefore, the prefectural IOTs are essentially based on common sector concepts and definitions of the national IOT, though minor differences appeared in their tables in accordance with their situation.

### *2.3.2 Procedure for the Construction of a National IOT*

Production estimates for the 2011 benchmark IOT began with the reclassification tabulations of the economic census activity survey. Furthermore, the input–output structure surveys were revised to improve the accuracy of estimating the structure of the IOT. In compliance with the 2008 SNA guidelines, the 2015 table includes the in-house-generated software, and research and development were added as part of the investment. In addition, in the 2020 table, a partial shift to Supply and Use tables (SUT) is introduced, resulting in a major change from the conventional method of creating the benchmark IOTs. Currently, the revision in the method of compiling the benchmark IOT is in progress, and the complete revision to the SUT is planned for the 2025 benchmark tables.

Hereafter, we will review the conventional method for constructing the IOTs, as outlined in the "Basic Guidelines for Creating IOTs." Fig. 2.2 depicts the approach for the procedure for the IOT (basic transaction table). Based on (1) the establishment of sectoral classifications, (2) the collection and compilation of statistical data, and (3) the estimation of domestic production values. This involves estimating production values for each sub-item classification (approximately 3400) and integrating them into the sectors of the basic transaction table.

The next step is (4) the estimation of input amounts. Using data obtained from production cost surveys and input–output structure surveys (input surveys), the total amount of production is broken down into the cost of each sector (input amount). However, (5) in estimating the output value, the breakdown of the domestic production value (breakdown of sales destinations) is estimated for each sector using data obtained from surveys related to supply and demand, following which the output value is estimated.

Subsequently, (6) the calculation adjustment of the input and output amounts is performed. The figure of the input value is estimated by the different statistics from those of the output values. Therefore, even in the same cell on the IOT, the amount of the input is generally different from that of the output in the beginning. Therefore, the two values are compared and revised to match a single value by considering which has higher validity.

Source: Quoted from Fig. 2.2, "2015 Basic Outline for the Preparation of Input–Output Tables" by the Input–Output Department Directors' Meeting.

Figure 2.3 presents the procedure flow for estimating figures. Here, as input estimates are based on data in terms of purchaser prices, deducting commercial margins and domestic freight charges from them is necessary to estimate input values in terms of producer prices. However, the data underlying output values were originally based on producer prices and do not require such adjustments. After these adjustments to the price evaluation, modifications will be made to ensure the input and output of a specific cell match on a producer price basis.

### *2.3.3 Procedure for the Construction of Regional IOTs*

IOTs for each prefecture are essentially estimated using information from the national table (basic transaction table), with reference to the METI's regional tables and the method used to create past tables for each prefecture, though the METI's tables were not compiled after the 2005 tables.

According to the MIC's "Basic Manual for Compiling Regional Input–Output Tables," the procedure for creating regional IOTs generally follows steps (1) to (7) below:

(1) Establishment of the basic framework, such as sector classification
(2) Collection of basic statistics
(3) Estimation of regional production values for each sector
(4) Estimation of input amount (including gross value-added sector)
(5) Estimation of the final demand sector (including imports)

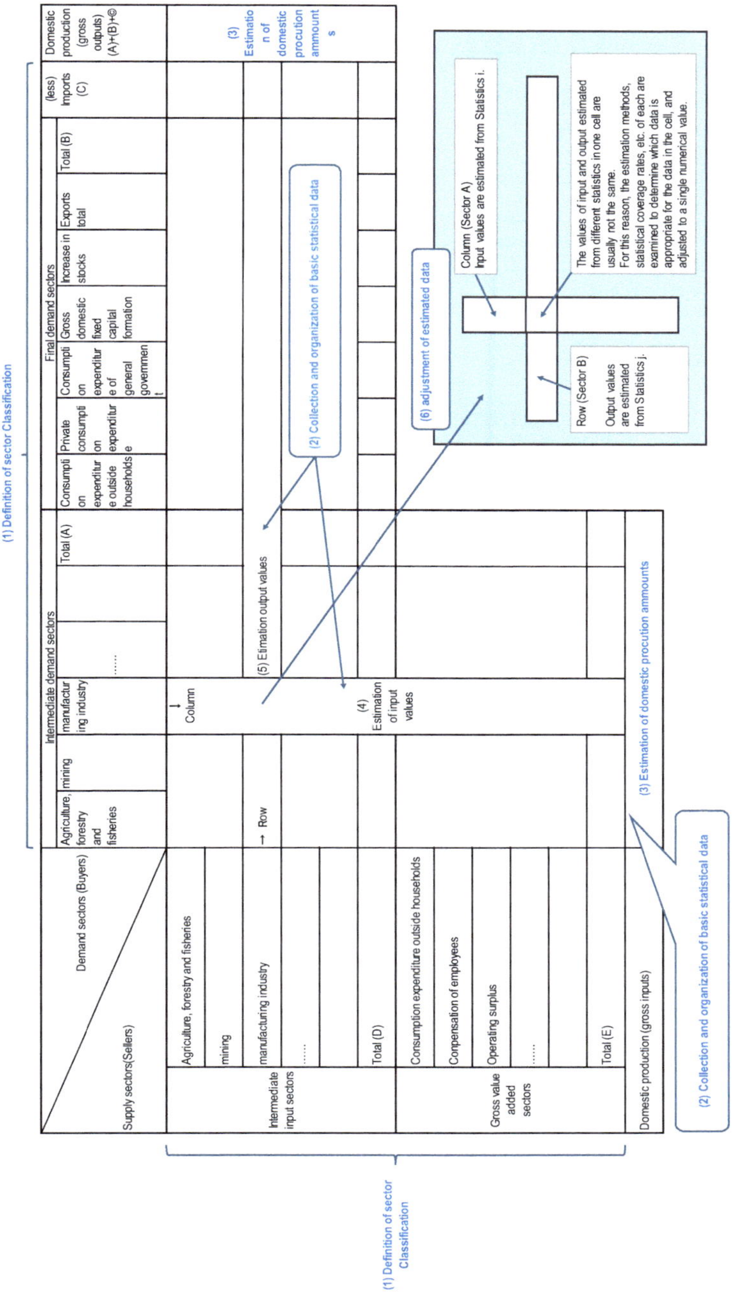


**Fig. 2.2** Outline of the procedure for creating an input–output table (basic table). *Source* Created by the author, based on Figure 2-1 of the Basic Guidelines for Constructing 2015 Input-Output Table

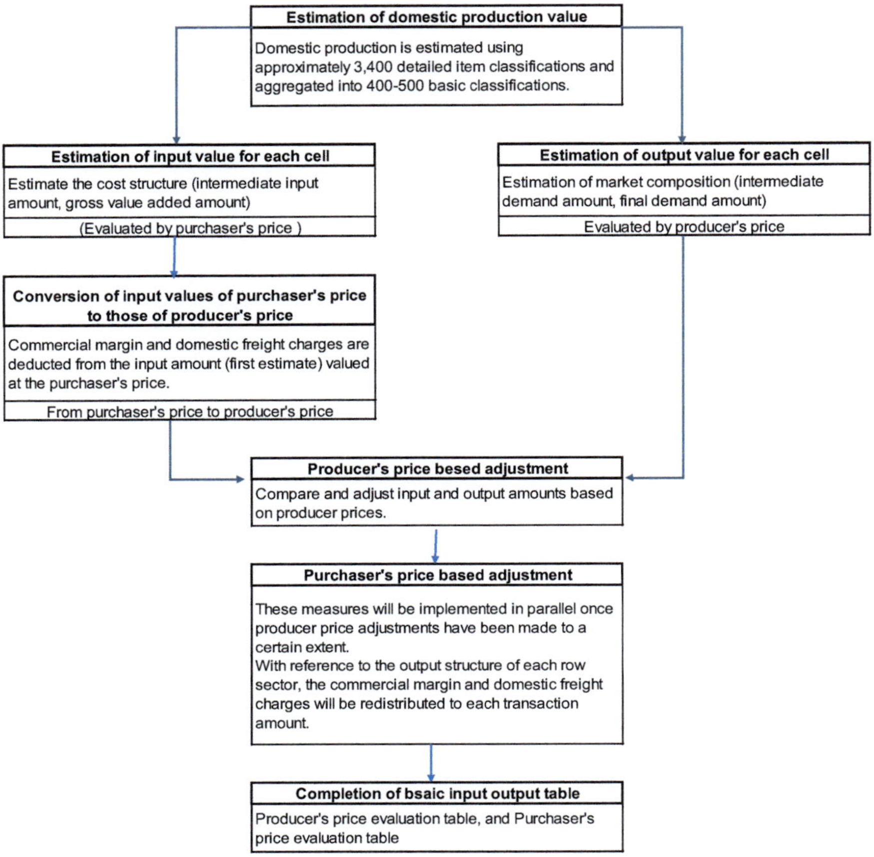


**Fig. 2.3** Estimation procedure for IOT. *Source* Created by the author, based on Figure 2.2 of the Basic Guidelines for Constructing 2015 Input-Output Table

(6) Calculation of balance adjustment
(7) Summary of estimation results.

For the regional IOT, an essentially similar procedure is applied as for the national table: based on the collection of basic statistical data, the production value is estimated, the input amount for each sector (including the value-added sector) is estimated, the output amount for each sector (including the final demand) is estimated, and these values are finally adjusted for the calculation balance.

(1) In setting the basic framework, the definition and scope of sector classifications as per the guidelines of the national IOT (basic transaction table) are determined.
(2) In collecting basic statistics, the reclassified compilation of the economic census and trade statistics and input coefficients for the national table are provided to the local government by the central government. Each prefecture-specific survey,

such as the "Commodity Flow Survey (CFS) in Manufacturing Sectors" and the "Sales Survey of the Service Industry Outside the Prefecture," is conducted in addition to specific interviews with industry groups and individual businesses.

(3) Estimating regional production value is the key to the regional IOTs. Using sector classifications that are as detailed as possible will ultimately represent clear regional characteristics.

(4) When estimating input values (including the gross value-added), two options are available: estimating them by the input coefficients of the corresponding national tables and by the input coefficients in the previous prefectural table multiplied by the rate of change in the national input coefficients. A trial calculation of input values will be created using one of these options, and further modifications will be made to reflect the characteristics of the region.

However, unlike the national table, no international trade statistics by prefecture exist except for the aggregation by regional customs. The export of a regional custom does not indicate that of the prefecture where the regional custom is located. Therefore, estimating the amounts of exports and imports by region is not easy. Several pieces of information are used to estimate exports and imports: the export ratio to production in the manufacturing sectors, the import coefficient in the national table, the previous prefectural table, etc.

Furthermore, estimating domestic imports and exports with other prefectures is limited. In METI's regional IOT, they conducted a special survey called the "Product Distribution Survey" to estimate interregional commodity flow. The statistics were used for the estimation of domestic exports and imports for each prefecture. However, the statistics may have been interrupted because METI decided not to construct the regional IOT of 2011 and after. Another source is MLIT's "Nationwide net freight flow survey (Logistics Census)," which provides data on the flow rate between prefectures by an item on a weight basis, though it is essentially a three-day survey.

Therefore, in the case of the regional IOT, input amounts are estimated in advance, final demand sectors (including imports and exports) are estimated for each sector, and the figures are adjusted in the direction of the output. Finally, the following consistency checks are performed:

1) Both productions in the row and column are set with the same values for each sector (if the correspondence between sectors is one-to-many or many-to-one, the sum of multiple sectors).
2) The total value of non-household consumption expenditure in the final demand sector is the same as the sum of non-household consumption expenditure in the gross value-added sector.
3) Products produced within the region are exported unless they are demanded within the region or added to the net increase in inventories. In addition, all imported goods are demanded within the region.
4) Consequently, the following constraints hold:

- Exports, international and interregional $\leq$ production; a net increase in inventories of products; a net increase in inventories of semi-finished products and work-in-progress.
- Imports, international and interregional $\leq$ intermediate demand within the region + final demand within the region; a net increase in inventories of products; a net increase in inventory of semi-finished products and work-in-progress.

5) "Imports (direct purchases)" are included in "household consumption expenditure" because their definition and scope are "direct transactions of goods or services with foreign markets by resident households." Therefore, the amount of household consumption expenditure will never be smaller than the absolute value of "imports (direct purchases)."
6) For sectors that have sub-item classifications related to "semi-finished products/ work-in-progress" among the sub-categories that make up the basic classification, the values are assigned to the sector of the "semi-finished products and work-in-progress inventory."
7) The total of the gross value-added sectors is coincident with the total of the final demand sector (excluding imports), which establishes two-sided equivalence.
8) The amount of each sector's "government consumption expenditure (social capital depletion)" in the final demand sector matches the corresponding sector's amount of "capital depreciation provision (social capital depreciation)" in the gross value-added sector.

### *2.3.4 Points to Keep in Mind When Constructing Regional IOTs*

The estimation of the sectoral production value, called control total (CT), is the most important in compiling national IOTs, and the same is true in compiling regional tables. Here, in addition to that, we summarize two points that should be kept in mind when creating regional production tables.

1) Estimation of imports and exports

First, estimates of imports and exports, international and interregional, are another critical issue for creating regional IOTs. International exports consist of three items: ordinary trade, special trade, and direct purchases.

For the estimation of ordinary trade, regional customs trade statistics, CFS, and the economic census are used. However, as the trade statistics by the local customs office do not correspond to the imports and exports by prefecture except for Hokkaido and Okinawa, both of which correspond to the region to aggregate the statistics, some revisions or estimations are necessary.

Exports and imports of goods sectors among prefectures are estimated using the "CFS," and the trade and transport sectors are calculated by multiplying the amount of exported and imported goods by the freight and margin rates. Furthermore, the service sector mainly deals with consumption activities associated with the cross-movement of population and head office expenses. The former are the interregional traveler's expenses and the cross-regional commuter's expenses, both of which are calculated based on the number of people and the amount spent per person. The latter is based on the prefectural total of head office expenses, which is obtained by multiplying the head office expenses per person from the "Survey on Activities at Head Offices" and the head office employees in the prefecture. The import and export of head office expenses by prefecture are calculated based on the ratio of employees at branch offices in other prefectures, which is obtained from the Economic Census.

Though the METI's regional IOT only estimates the import and export of employee income for commuters, the Tokyo metropolitan IOT, which contains the head office sector as one sector, also includes consumption activities outside the region by commuters. In that case, a separate survey will be conducted on out-of-prefecture purchases by item for commuters.

The "CFS" conducted by the METI was extremely important in estimating imports and exports among regions in the METI's regional IOTs, and it is also important for prefectural IOTs. Therefore, whether this statistical survey can be maintained even after the METI withdraws from constructing regional IOTs will determine the accuracy of prefectural IOTs in Japan.

Therefore, establishing a system for maintaining and implementing this statistical survey as soon as possible is considered necessary. In addition, no sufficient surveys on cross-regional trade in the service sector exist, which requires the enhancement, standardization, and organization of surveys related to the cross-regional trade of services, such as the "out-of-prefecture sales survey of the service industry."[6]

2) Handling of head office expenses

The second point concerns the head office expenses.

In the national IOT, production inputs are estimated by dividing them into inputs related to product manufacturing and indirect inputs such as head office expenses. The former is estimated based on input surveys for each sector, such as the "Mining and Manufacturing Input Survey," and the latter is estimated based on the "Survey on Corporate Management Activities."

In the case of regional IOTs, inputs are generally estimated using the input coefficients in the national table; however, the production activities are not actually located in the same region as the head office. If head office services received from other regions are not recorded as imports, they are supplied from their own area, which induces overestimation in the spillover analysis. Conversely, if head office services are exported but are not taken into consideration, their activities will not be sufficiently reflected in production. To avoid such problems, explicitly dealing with head office expenses becomes necessary.

[6] Tanigawa (2012) discusses estimates of imports and exports based on the METI's regional IOTs.

If the production activity and the head office activity do not exist in the same area, there are two ways to grasp it: a) the method of importing expenses for the head office, and b) the method of setting up the head office sector.[7]

a) Method of importing expenses from the head office

Suppose a production activity and head office activity are in different regions. The input amount in the location of the production includes overhead expenses of the head office not located in the area, and the employee income includes not only the wages of the factory employees but also the wages of the head office employees. The other expenses in the value-added sector are the same. Therefore, the factory location can import these goods and services related to the headquarters and employee income of the headquarters location, and the headquarters location can balance them by exporting them to the factory location. The METI's regional IOTs adopted this method to evaluate head office expenses.

This method allows the factory location to avoid the problem of overestimating the ripple effect by importing the head office service. However, in areas such as Tokyo, where head office functions are concentrated, even though many workers work and a large number of goods and services are input to carry out "head office activities," it is not recorded in the area concerned as production value because the head office service is not treated as a sector-specific activity. For this reason, the IOT does not adequately reflect the activities of the head office, and the ripple effects cannot be analyzed effectively. The Osaka prefectural IOT adopted this method.

b) Method of setting up headquarters as one sector

If the ratio of imports and exports for headquarters services is large, establishing a separate sector for the headquarters' expenses is desirable. There are two methods: (1) the head office of all sectors is consolidated into one dummy sector; (2) separating the head office for each production sector; and (3) consolidating several sectors into a group (with a similar input structure) and establishing that as the head office. The 2011 Tokyo IOT adopted method (1).

The production value at the location of the factory includes head office expenses, and they are newly recorded as the production at the location of the head office; hence, when aggregated by region, it will be larger than the production value in the national table. In terms of inputs, inputs for head office activities are collectively expressed as head office services in the activities of the corresponding production factory, and inputs for producing head office services are independently included in a dummy sector called "head office."

Currently, except for the Tokyo IOT, no prefectural IOT exists that explicitly includes the headquarters office as a sector, though the recent IOT of Nagoya City included the headquarters office as one sector.

[7] The concept and estimation method are summarized in MIC (2014).

## 2.4 Concluding Remarks

In this chapter, we first observed various IOTs in Japan as a system, in which, setting the national IOT (benchmark table) at the origin, each IOT was positioned by three coordinate axes: time, scope, and region. Consequently, we found the following:

- Regional IOTs are created using information from national tables, which is the core of the structure.
- In recent years, based on the prefectural IOTs, attempts have been made to develop further interregional IOTs connecting the adjacent prefectures and interregional IOTs within a prefecture.

These are caused by the increasing interest in regional revitalization in a society with a declining population, but more fundamentally, there is a difference between the administrative division of prefectures and the economic unit to be analyzed, which is related to the issue of setting the scope of the targeting area. To solve the discrepancies, it is possible to form targeting regions by disassembling and reconfiguring the IOTs of prefectures as administrative regions. This trend does not mean that prefectural IOTs are becoming unnecessary. Conversely, prefectural IOTs can be viewed as becoming increasingly important as a benchmark for creating IOTs for smaller regions.

Next, we outlined the characteristics of regional IOTs. First, we outlined the procedure for creating the basic national table and compared it to that for creating the regional table. The initial and most important step in creating regional tables is to estimate the production value of CT, followed by an estimate of interregional trade. Therefore, we demonstrated the key elements that should be considered while dealing with these matters.

Furthermore, with respect to handling head office expenses, which are important in regional IOTs but have not yet been sufficiently covered, we have presented an outline of their significance, how to handle them in IOTs, and how to estimate them.

Headquarters are concentrated in Tokyo and Osaka. Although these prefectures provide headquarters services to other regions, their production and exports are not explicitly represented in the usual regional IOTs. Consequently, production (and therefore added value) is underestimated in the exporting region, ignoring production. Furthermore, in many prefectures that have imported head office services, the production inducement effect will be overestimated, ignoring the imports. Such biases need to be avoided.[8]

**Appendix: A Brief Survey of the Multi-regional Input-Output Tables in Japan**

Several MRIOT-based prefecture tables exist in Japan. Table 2.2 presents the typical experiences related to such issues that are categorized into three groups.

The first group is the inter-prefectural MRIOT covering all 47 prefectures in Japan, including Ishikawa and Miyagi (2003) for the 1995 Table, Hitomi (2008) for the 2000

[8] For this reason, the IOT for Tokyo, where head offices are concentrated, has a structure that explicitly represents the activities of the head office as one sector.

**Table 2.2** Multi-regional input–output tables in Japan

| Types of RIO | Authors | Target Year | Target regions | Sector Size | Estimation of Commodity flow |
|---|---|---|---|---|---|
| (1) Inter-prefectural MRIOT covering Japan overall | Ishikawa and Miyagi (2003) | 1995/ | 47 prefectures in Japan | 45 sectors | RAS method with the survey statistics of domestic net freight flows (MLIT) |
| | Hitomi (2008) | 2000 | 47 prefectures in Japan | 59 sectors | Gravity model using the freight flow data of MLIT and the commodity flow data of METI |
| | Hagiwara (2012) | 1990–2000–2005-linked MRIOT | 47 prefectures in Japan | 59 sectors | Extended-RAS method with the net freight flow of MLIT, employees' commuting flow of the Census, and the communication traffic data of MIC |
| | Arai (2020, 2022) | 2005, 2011 | 47 prefectures in Japan | 77 sectors, including a sector of headquarters activity | RAS method with the commodity flow data of METI and other sources |
| (2) Inter-prefectural MRIOT for the specific region within Japan | Kansai Institute for Social and Economic Research (2008) | 2000 | 7 prefectures in the Kansai region | 100 sectors | Special survey data on commodity flow (METI) |

(continued)

**Table 2.2** (continued)

| Types of RIO | Authors | Target Year | Target regions | Sector Size | Estimation of Commodity flow |
|---|---|---|---|---|---|
| | Asia Pacific Institute of Research (2012) | 2005 | 7 prefectures in the Kansai region | 104 sectors | RAS method with the survey statistics of domestic net freight flows (MLIT) and employees' commuting flow from the Census (MIC), and others |
| | Tohoku Regional Advancement Center (2011) | 2005 | 7 prefectures in the Tohoku region | 43 sectors | Special survey data on commodity flow (METI) |
| | Yamada (2010) | 2000 | 3 prefectures in the Tokai region | 185 sectors | The RAS method with the special commodity flow (METI) survey data |
| | Chubu Region Institute for Social and Economic Research (2011) | 2005 | 9 prefectures in the Chubu region | 95 sectors | The RAS method with the survey statistics of domestic net freight flows (MLIT) |
| | Yamada (2018b), Yamada and Kimura (2023a, b) | 2011/2015 | 9 prefectures in the Chubu region | 104 sectors | The RAS method with the survey statistics of domestic net freight flows (MLIT) |
| | Ishiro (2011), Ishiro (2014) | 2000/2005 | 11 prefectures in the Kanto region | 28 sectors | The RAS method with the survey statistics of domestic net freight flows (MLIT) |

(continued)

**Table 2.2** (continued)

| Types of RIO | Authors | Target Year | Target regions | Sector Size | Estimation of Commodity flow |
|---|---|---|---|---|---|
| | Suhara, Guo, and Ishiro (2020) | 2011 | 4 prefectures in the Shikoku region | 37 sectors | Balanced after estimating exports with the survey statistics of domestic net freight flows (MLIT) |
| | Yamada and Kawamura (2024) | 2015 | 9 prefectures in the Kyushu region | 100 sectors | The RAS method with the survey statistics of domestic net freight flows (MLIT) |
| (3) Intra-prefectural MRIOT for the specific prefecture | Tsubouchi (1991) | 1988 | 6 areas in Ehime Prefecture | 50 sectors | Special survey data on the commodity flow in Ehime |
| | Takahata (1992) | 1985 | 4 areas in Hokkaido | 61 sectors | Statistics on freight flow and passenger flow |
| | Yamada (1996) Chen and Yamada (2015), Yamada and Horiuchi (2015) | 1985/1990/ 1995/2000/ 2005/2010 | 5 areas in Mie Prefecture | 84 sectors | RAS method with the survey data on freight flows |
| | Ishikawa (2004) | 1995 | 3 areas in Aichi Prefecture | 46 sectors | LQ method |
| | Nakano and Nishimura (2007) | 2000 | 3 areas in Aichi Prefecture | 46 sectors | The gravity model estimated using the commodity flows of METI MRIOT |
| | Nomura et al. (2011) | 2000 | 3 areas in Yamaguchi Prefecture | 104 sectors | LQ method |

(continued)

**Table 2.2** (continued)

| Types of RIO | Authors | Target Year | Target regions | Sector Size | Estimation of Commodity flow |
|---|---|---|---|---|---|
| | Yamada and Owaki (2012), Yamada (2013) | 2005 | 4 areas in Aichi Prefecture | 186 sectors | Gravity-RAS method |
| | Tsukamoto, Komiyama, and Nemoto (2018) | 2005 | 67 municipalities in Aichi Prefecture | 189 sectors | Gravity-RAS method |
| | Yamada (2020) | 2011 | 54 municipalities in Aichi Prefecture | 106 sectors | Gravity-RAS method |
| | Takeda (2020) | 2011 | 3 areas in Kumamoto Prefecture | 104 sectors | Production-demand share method |

*Source* Created by the author

Table, and Hagiwara (2012) for the 1990–2000–2005-linked MRIOT. Because the number of prefectures has increased, the sector size has been reduced to around fifty. The estimation of commodity flows among prefectures essentially depends on the RAS method.[9] As the initial values of the RAS method, the authors used the data from the survey statistics of domestic net freight flows (MLIT),[10] the commodity flow data of METI,[11] the employees' commuting flow of the Census, and the communication traffic data of MIC.[12] Unfortunately, these tables are not publicly available, though Arai (2020, 2022) constructed and released 2005 and 2011 MRIOTs with 77 sectors, including one sector for headquarters activity.

The second group is the inter-prefectural MRIOTs focusing on the specific regions in Japan, which includes the Kansai region MRIOT (Kansai Institute for Social and Economic Research 2008), the Tohoku region MRIOT (Tohoku Regional Advancement Center 2011), the Tokai region MRIOT (Yamada 2010), and the Chubu region MRIOT (Chubu Region Institute for Social and Economic Research 2011; Yamada 2018b; Yamada and Kimura 2023a, b). These tables were made to investigate some regions in Japan, and their sector size is commonly about ninety. The commodity flows between prefectures were estimated essentially by the RAS method with different statistical sources for the initial values. The Kansai and Chubu region MRIOTs have a relatively long history in the revision of their tables. Shikoku region and Kyushu region have recently joined in constructing their MRIOT.

The third group is the intra-prefectural MRIOT for a specific prefecture. The Ehime Prefecture MRIOT (Tsubouchi 1991), Hokkaido Prefecture MRIOT (Takahata 1992), and Mie Prefecture MRIOT (Yamada 1996) were the pioneering studies. After 2000, several new studies appeared, such as the 1995 Aichi Prefecture MRIOT (Ishikawa 2004), the 2000 Aichi Prefecture MRIOT (Nakano and Nishimura 2007), the Yamaguchi Prefecture MRIOT (Nomura et al. 2011), and the 2005 Aichi Prefecture MRIOT (Yamada and Owaki 2012; Yamada 2013; Tsukamoto et al. 2018). In recent works, the 2011 Aichi Prefecture MRIOT (Yamada 2020a, b) and the 2011 Kumamoto Prefecture MRIOT (Takeda 2020) were added. The Hokkaido Prefecture MRIOTs are continuously constructed by the local government.

For the estimation of commodity flows within a prefecture, the pioneering works depended on the statistics regarding the freight flow and passenger flow within the prefecture or on special surveys conducted on the commodity flow of the goods produced if there were no statistics for flows within the prefecture. In the case of Mie Prefecture, Yamada (1996) applied the RAS method with the survey data of freight flow as the initial values of the iterations. Nakano and Nishimura (2007) applied the gravity model. Ishikawa (2004) and Nomura et al. (2011) used the LQ method, which

---

[9] The RAS method is a commonly used procedure for bi-proportionally balancing a matrix of SUT or IOT. The RAS method is an iteratively revised method of input coefficient matrix **A**, multiplying two diagonalized matrices, R and S, from both sides, as $\mathbf{R} \cdot \mathbf{A^0} \cdot \mathbf{S} \rightarrow \mathbf{A^1}$. R and S denote substitution effects and fabrication effects, respectively. The RAS is named after the economist Richard Stone (1919–1991) who was a pioneer in this field (Miller and Blair 2009).

[10] Ministry of Land, Infrastructure, Transport and Tourism, Japan.

[11] Ministry of Economy, Trade, and Industry, Japan.

[12] Ministry of Internal Affairs and Communications, Japan.

estimates the net transaction between two areas by the relative advantage measures.[13] Yamada (2013) developed the gravity-RAS method, in which a gravity model was used to obtain the initial values of the RAS iterations.

## References

Arai, Sonoe. 2020. Compilation of the 2005 prefectural input-output table and its overview. In *RIETI discussion paper* 20-J-009. Research institute of economy, trade and Industry (in Japanese).

Arai, Sonoe. 2022. Compilation of the 2011 prefectural input-output table and its overview. In *RIETI discussion paper* 22-J-003. Research Institute of Economy, Trade and Industry (in Japanese).

Ashiya, Tsunenori, and Hiroshi Goto. 2015. Analysis of the economic ripple effects of regional economic zones based on the inter-regional input-output table estimated for the seven-regions in Hyogo Prefecture. *Sango Renkan (Business journal of PAPAIOS) 22* (3), 106–114 (in Japanese)

Asia Pacific Institute of Research (former Kansai Institute of Social and Economic Research). 2008. *Compilation of 2000 Kansai interregional input-output table* (in Japanese).

Asia Pacific Institute of Research. 2012. *Compilation and use of the 2005 Kansai interregional input-output table* (in Japanese).

Chubu Region Institute for Social and Economic Research (Former Chubu Industrial and Regional Revitalization Center). 2011. *Chubu Region Inter-regional input-output table (2005 edition)* (in Japanese).

Hagiwara, Taiji. 2012. Compilation of 47-prefectures' interregional input-output table and its application. *Kobe University Economic Review* 58: 33–46 (in Japanese).

Hitomi, Kazumi. 2008. *Development of multi-regional input-output table for 47 prefectures in Japan. —Analysis of inter-prefectural production inducement structure using internal and external multipliers* CRIEPI Research Report Y07035 (in Japanese).

Ishikawa, Yoshifumi. 2004. A three-region interregional input-output model using non-survey technique. *Journal of Japan Society of Civil Engineers* 758 (4–63): 45–55 (in Japanese).

Ishikawa, Yoshifumi, and Toshihiko Miyagi. 2003. Analysis of the input-output structure using multi-prefectural input-output table of Japan. *Studies in Regional Science* 34 (1): 139–152 (in Japanese).

Ishiro, Taku. 2011. Water footprint analysis of the Kanto River basin: Through the compilation of the Kanto inter-regional input-output table and water use data. *Sango Renkan (Business Journal of PAPAIOS)* 19 (2): 56–66 (in Japanese).

Ishiro, Taku. 2014. The Analysis of interregional specialization of Kanto Region in 2005: the compilation of kanto interregional input-output table in 2005 and the comparative analysis of 2005 and 2000. *Ryutsu Keizai University Review* 48 (4): 19–39 (in Japanese).

METI. 2012 Japan-China input-output table for 2007. http://www.meti.go.jp/statistics/tyo/kokusio/nittyuu/2007nen/gaiyou.html

METI. 2013. *Basic manual for METI 2011 regional input-output tables* (in Japanese).

METI. 2013. Japan-US input-output table for 2005. http://www.meti.go.jp/statistics/tyo/kokusio/result/result_15.html

MIC. 2014. *Basic guidelines for creating regional input-output tables (unfinished draft)* (in Japanese).

Miller, R.E., and P.D. Blair. 2009. *Input-output analysis: Foundations and extensions.* Cambridge University Press.

[13] There are several variations of the LQ model for the estimation of the export and import of the region (See Miller and Blair 2009).

Nakano, Satoshi, and Kazuhiko Nishimura. 2007. Estimation of interregional trade in partitioning regional input-output tables. *Sango Renkan (Business Journal of PAPAIOS)* 15 (3): 44–53 (in Japanese).

Nomura, Junichi, Makoto Kinoshita, Hidetomo Saito, and Sachiyo Asahi. 2011. Economic impacts of trans-regional tourists' expenditures utilizing multiregional I-O table of Yamaguchi Prefecture, Japan. *Sangyo Renkan (Business Journal of PAPAIOS) 19* (3): 72–93 (in Japanese).

Suhara, Natsumi, Jianing Guo, and Taku Ishiro. 2020. Measurement of interdependence within Shikoku region: Creation and analysis of the 2011 Shikoku interregional input-output table. *Yokohama Journal of Social Sciences* 24 (4): 71–90 (in Japanese).

Takahata, Yoshihiro. 1992. Interregional input-output table of Hokkaido Prefecture. *Sango Renkan (Business Journal of PAPAIOS)* 3 (3): 24–29 (in Japanese).

Takeda, Kenta. 2020. Construction an inter-regional input-output table for Kumamoto Prefecture and its analysis. *Sango Renkan (Business Journal of PAPAIOS)* 28 (1): 21–38 (in Japanese).

Tanigawa, Takamichi. 2012. On the estimation of regional trade in the METI's regional input-output table. *Sango Renkan (Business Journal of PAPAIOS)* 20 (2): 147–164 (in Japanese).

Tohoku Regional Advancement Center. 2011. *Report on the Tohoku multi-regional input-output table for 2005* (in Japanese). http://www.kasseiken.jp/association/

Tsubouchi, Takehiro. 1991. On the interregional input-output table of Ehime prefecture. *Sangyo Renkan (Input-Output Analysis) 2* (1): 35–42 (in Japanese).

Tsukamoto, Takahiro, Naoko Komiyama, and Jiro Nemoto. 2018. Construction of inter-regional input-output table among all municipalities in Aichi Prefecture and analysis on spatial interdependence between municipalities. *Sango Renkan (Business Journal of PAPAIOS)* 26 (1): 1–20 (in Japanese).

Yamada, Mitsuo. 1995. Estimation of Mie Prefecture inter-regional input-output table. *Sango Renkan (Business Journal of PAPAIOS)* 5 (4): 52–67 (in Japanese).

Yamada, Mitsuo. 1996. An interregional input-output table of Mie Prefecture, Japan: Estimation and applications. *Journal of Applied Input-Output Analysis* 5 (4): 52–67.

Yamada, Mitsuo. 2010. Compilation of 2000 inter-regional input-output table for Tokai Region. *Chukyo Economic Review, Chukyo University* 21: 59–82 (in Japanese).

Yamada, Mitsuo. 2015. Construction of a Multi-regional Input-Output Table for Nagoya Metropolitan Area, Japan. *Journal of Economic Structures* 4 (11): 1–18.

Yamada, Mitsuo. 2018b. Compilation of the 2011 Chubu region interregional input-output table. *Sangyo Renkan (Business Journal of PAPAIOS)* 25 (1): 56–73 (in Japanese).

Yamada, Mitsuo. 2020a. Construction of inter-municipal input-output tables and its application–Based on the 2011 Aichi Prefecture input-output table. *Chukyo Economic Review, 31*, 9–36 (in Japanese).

Yamada, Mitsuo. 2020b. Construction of inter-municipal input-output tables and its application–Based on the 2011 Aichi Prefecture input-output table. *Chukyo Economic Review, 31*, 9–36 (in Japanese).

Yamada, Mitsuo, and Yukio Horiuchi. 2015. Comparison of inter-regional input-output tables for Mie Prefecture from 1985 to 2010. *Sango Renkan (Business Journal of PAPAIOS)* 23 (1–2): 15–28 (in Japanese).

Yamada, Mitsuo, and Soei Kawamura. 2024. How to create and use the Kyushu regional input-output table. *Kyushu Economic Survey Monthly* 78: 14–23 (in Japanese).

Yamada, Mitsuo, and Shinichiro Kimura. 2023b Analysis of regional economic structure based on the Chubu region inter-regional input-output table (2015 edition)—Characteristics of industries in each prefecture in the Chubu region. *Chubu Research Quarterly 224*, 27–59 (in Japanese).

Yamada, Mitsuo, and Yuichi Owaki. 2012. Estimation of 2005 inter-regional input-output table of four-regions within Aichi Prefecture. *Institute of economics discussion paper* No. 1205. Chukyo University (in Japanese).

Yamada, Mitsuo, and Shinichiro Kimura. 2023a. Compiling the Chubu region inter-regional input-output table (2015 edition) and preliminary analysis of the regional structure. *Economy, Trade and Industry Statistics Study 54* (1): 1–22 (in Japanese).
Yamada, Mitsuo. 2013. Estimation of inter-regional trade using gravity–RAS methods: a case study of the inter-regional input-output table within Aichi Prefecture. *Institute of economics discussion paper* No.1301. Chukyo University (in Japanese).

# Chapter 3
# Comparison of Prefectural Input–Output Tables in Japan

## 3.1 Introduction

In the previous chapter, we discussed the structure of Japan's input–output tables. Limited to domestic regional IOTs, below the national IOT there used to be regional IOTs of the METI, below that there were prefectural IOTs, and further below that there were municipal IOTs. It had a four-layered structure, including the national IOT. However, as the METI's Regional IOTs were no longer created continuously after the 2005 table, a three-tiered structure excluding that table is available now.

Currently, the prefectural IOT is located below the national table, but this table is created by each prefecture. Prefectural IOTs began around the same time as the national IOTs and have a long history, but it was not until 1990 that IOTs for all 47 prefectures were completed. However, since each prefecture creates its own IOTs using information from the same year's national IOTs, there is no guarantee that the aggregated values of them will match the corresponding values of the national input–output table.

In this chapter, based on the 2011 Prefectural Input–Output Tables, we examine the accuracy of the Prefectural IOTs by comparing them with the values in the National IOT for the same year and examining the degree of deviation. In Sect. 3.2, we will summarize the characteristics of the prefectural IOTs, and in Sect. 3.3, we will examine the accuracy of the correction of the 47 prefectural IOTs to the national IOTs. Section 3.4 summarizes the results of the study.

## 3.2 Comparison of 2011 Prefectural Input–Output Tables

Table 3.1 presents a comparison of the 2011 prefectural IOT. Since 2011, the national table was published in June 2015, and there has been a gap of about two years, with prefectures that published the table earlier in January 2016 and the last one in January



M. Yamada, *Multi-Regional Input–Output Analysis of the Japanese Economy*,
https://doi.org/10.1007/978-981-97-9041-8_3

2018. The 2011 IOTs underwent a major change in estimation, using production value estimates from the newly introduced Economic Census. In addition, as the METI's regional IOT has not been developed after the 2005 table, the government's support for the construction of the prefectural IOT has reduced, and consequently, the estimation period was extended in some prefectures compared to the previous table.

Looking at the number of sectors in the released IOTs, Okinawa is the only prefecture that publishes the basic classifications; 26 prefectures publish in integrated minor classifications (approximately 190 sectors), and 20 prefectures publish in intermediate classifications (approximately 108 sectors). Figure 3.1 depicts its regional distribution. The prefectures that published in the minor classification are concentrated in the Kanto, Chubu, and Kinki areas, which have relatively large economic scales.

As for the dummy sector, all prefectures have set up "office supplies," but almost all prefectures except Hokkaido, Mie, Hyogo, and Okinawa have a sector of "self-transportation." As for imports and exports, 31 prefectures make separate estimates for international and domestic exports (and imports), respectively, and 16 prefectures make estimates collectively for exports (and imports). Figure 3.2 displays its regional distribution. Prefectures for which separate estimates of international and domestic exports (imports) have not been made are concentrated in the Tohoku, Hokuriku, Chugoku, and Kyushu regions.

There are 45 prefectures that estimate social capital depletion. Miyagi and Kyoto do not explicitly present the values of social capital depletion in the value-added sector and general government consumption expenditure (social capital depletion) in the final demand sector, whereas Iwate and Okinawa do not estimate them. There are 17 prefectures where the same amount is not recorded in the same sector for social capital depreciation in the column and general government consumption expenditure (social capital depreciation) in the row. Only Tokyo estimated head office activities as an independent sector, and Osaka Prefecture records head office expenses as part of export and import domestically. Other prefectures do not include head office expenses in their IOTs.

Regarding employment tables, Saitama and Hyogo published in the minor classification, 42 prefectures published in the middle classification, and Shimane and Okinawa published in the major classification. In addition, although not explicitly depicted in Table 3.1, some estimates of domestic trade with the other prefectures in the service sector are estimated as net exports and net immigration. Their table shows "domestic exports = 0, domestic imports = net exports" when net exports < 0.

**Table 3.1** Characteristics of the 2011 prefectural input-output tables

| Prefecture | | Input-output transaction table | | | | Employment table | | | |
|---|---|---|---|---|---|---|---|---|---|
| | | Basic table | Minor classification | Middle classification | Major classification | Basic table | Minor classification | Middle classification | Major classification |
| | Japan | 518/397 | 190 | 108 | 37 | 393 | 190 | 108 | 37 |
| 1 | Hokkaido | – | – | 104/64 | 33 | – | – | 104/64 | 33 |
| 2 | Aomori | – | – | 108 | 40 | – | – | 108 | 40 |
| 3 | Iwate | – | 189 | 103 | 36 | – | – | 103 | 36 |
| 4 | Miyagi | – | – | 110 | 37 | – | – | 110 | 37 |
| 5 | Akita | – | – | 108 | 39 | – | – | 108 | 39 |
| 6 | Yamagata | – | – | 108 | 34 | – | – | 108 | 37 |
| 7 | Fukushima | – | – | 107 | 39 | – | – | 107 | 39 |
| 8 | Ibaragi | – | 190 | 108 | 37 | – | – | 108 | 37 |
| 9 | Tochigi | – | – | 103 | 37 | – | – | 103 | 37 |
| 10 | Gunma | – | – | 108 | 37 | – | – | 108 | 37 |
| 11 | Saitama | – | 190 | 108 | 37 | – | 190 | 108 | 37 |
| 12 | Chiba | – | 190 | 108 | 37 | – | – | 108 | 37 |
| 13 | Tokyo | – | 191 | 111 | 38 | – | – | 111 | 38 |
| 14 | Kanagawa | – | 190 | 108 | 37 | – | – | 108 | 37 |
| 15 | Niigata | – | 178 | 108 | 37 | – | – | 108 | 37 |
| 16 | Toyama | – | 190 | 108 | 37 | – | – | 108 | 37 |
| 17 | Ishikawa | – | 190 | 108 | 37 | – | – | 108 | 37 |

(continued)

**Table 3.1** (continued)

| Prefecture | | Input-output transaction table | | | | Employment table | | | |
|---|---|---|---|---|---|---|---|---|---|
| | | Basic table | Minor classification | Middle classification | Major classification | Basic table | Minor classification | Middle classification | Major classification |
| 18 | Fukui | – | – | 104 | 37 | – | | 104 | 37 |
| 19 | Yamanashi | – | 190 | 108 | 37 | – | – | 108 | 37 |
| 20 | Nagano | – | 190 | 109 | 37 | – | | 109 | 37 |
| 21 | Gifu | – | 190 | 108 | 37 | – | – | 108 | 37 |
| 22 | Shizuoka | – | 190 | 109 | 37 | – | – | 109 | 37 |
| 23 | Aichi | – | 188 | 110 | 43 | – | – | 110 | 43 |
| 24 | Mie | – | 188 | 107 | 39 | – | – | 107 | 39 |
| 25 | Shiga | – | 190 | 108 | 37 | – | – | 108 | 37 |
| 26 | Kyoto | – | 180 | 105 | 37 | – | | 105 | 37 |
| 27 | Osaka | – | 190 | 108 | 37 | – | – | 108 | 37 |
| 28 | Hyogo | – | 188 | 107 | 39 | – | 188 | 107 | 39 |
| 29 | Nara | – | – | 108 | 37 | – | – | 108 | 37 |
| 30 | Wakayama | – | 190 | 108 | 37 | – | – | 108 | 37 |
| 31 | Tottori | – | – | 108 | 39 | – | | 108 | 39 |
| 32 | Shimane | – | – | 98 | 39 | – | – | – | 39 |
| 33 | Okayama | – | – | 108 | 37 | – | – | 108 | 37 |
| 34 | Hiroshima | – | – | 108 | 45 | – | – | 108 | 45 |

(continued)

**Table 3.1** (continued)

| Prefecture | | Input-output transaction table | | | | Employment table | | | |
|---|---|---|---|---|---|---|---|---|---|
| | | Basic table | Minor classification | Middle classification | Major classification | Basic table | Minor classification | Middle classification | Major classification |
| 35 | Yamaguchi | – | – | 108 | 37 | – | | 108 | 37 |
| 36 | Tokushima | – | – | 108 | 37 | – | – | 108 | 37 |
| 37 | Kagawa | – | – | 108 | 37 | – | – | 108 | 37 |
| 38 | Ehime | – | 178 | 105 | 39 | – | – | 105 | 39 |
| 39 | Kochi | – | – | 108 | 40 | – | – | 108 | 40 |
| 40 | Fukuoka | – | 189 | 107 | 39 | – | – | 107 | 39 |
| 41 | Saga | – | – | 108 | 37 | – | – | 108 | 37 |
| 42 | Nagasaki | – | – | 108 | 40 | – | – | 108 | 40 |
| 43 | Kumamoto | – | – | 104 | 37 | – | – | 101 | 36 |
| 44 | Oita | – | – | 104 | 36 | – | – | 104 | 36 |
| 45 | Miyazaki | – | – | 108 | 40 | – | – | 108 | 40 |
| 46 | Kagoshima | – | – | 106 | 39 | – | – | 106 | 39 |
| 47 | Okinawa | 401/343 | * | * | 15 | – | – | – | 35 |
| | | 1 | 23 | 47 | 47 | 0 | 2 | 45 | 47 |

(continued)

**Table 3.1** (continued)

| Prefecture | | Input-output transaction table | | | | | |
|---|---|---|---|---|---|---|---|
| | | Dummy sectors | | | Social capital | | Separeation of international/ internal transaction in export/ import |
| | | Private transport | Office supplies | Head office expesses | Calculated | Row/Column consistency | |
| | Japan | ✓ | ✓ | | ✓ | ✓ | - |
| 1 | Hokkaido | ✓ | ✓ | - | ✓ | ✓ | ✓ |
| 2 | Aomori | ✓ | ✓ | - | ✓ | ✓ | ✓ |
| 3 | Iwate | ✓ | ✓ | - | - | ✓ | - |
| 4 | Miyagi | ✓ | ✓ | - | ✓[a] | ✓[a] | - |
| 5 | Akita | ✓ | ✓ | - | ✓ | ✓ | - |
| 6 | Yamagata | ✓ | ✓ | - | ✓ | - | - |
| 7 | Fukushima | ✓ | ✓ | - | ✓ | ✓ | ✓ |
| 8 | Ibaragi | ✓ | ✓ | - | ✓ | ✓ | ✓ |
| 9 | Tochigi | ✓ | ✓ | - | ✓ | - | ✓ |
| 10 | Gunma | ✓ | ✓ | - | ✓ | - | ✓ |
| 11 | Saitama | ✓ | ✓ | - | ✓ | ✓ | ✓ |
| 12 | Chiba | ✓ | ✓ | - | ✓ | - | ✓ |
| 13 | Tokyo | ✓ | ✓ | - | ✓ | ✓ | ✓ |
| 14 | Kanagawa | ✓ | ✓ | - | ✓ | ✓ | ✓ |

(continued)

**Table 3.1** (continued)

| Prefecture | | Input-output transaction table | | | | | |
|---|---|---|---|---|---|---|---|
| | | Dummy sectors | | | Social capital | | Separeation of international/ internal transaction in export/ import |
| | | Private transport | Office supplies | Head office expesses | Calculated | Row/Column consistency | |
| 15 | Niigata | ✓ | ✓ | - | ✓ | ✓ | ✓ |
| 16 | Toyama | ✓ | ✓ | - | ✓ | ✓ | - |
| 17 | Ishikawa | ✓ | ✓ | - | ✓ | ✓ | - |
| 18 | Fukui | - | ✓ | - | ✓ | - | ✓ |
| 19 | Yamanashi | ✓ | ✓ | - | ✓ | - | ✓ |
| 20 | Nagano | ✓ | ✓ | - | ✓ | ✓ | ✓ |
| 21 | Gifu | ✓ | ✓ | - | ✓ | ✓ | ✓ |
| 22 | Shizuoka | ✓ | ✓ | - | ✓ | - | ✓ |
| 23 | Aichi | ✓ | ✓ | - | ✓ | - | ✓ |
| 24 | Mie | ✓ | ✓ | - | ✓ | ✓ | ✓ |
| 25 | Shiga | ✓ | ✓ | - | ✓ | - | ✓ |
| 26 | Kyoto | ✓ | ✓ | - | ✓[a] | ✓[a] | ✓ |
| 27 | Osaka | ✓ | ✓ | ✓[b] | ✓ | - | ✓ |
| 28 | Hyogo | ✓ | ✓ | - | ✓ | - | ✓ |
| 29 | Nara | ✓ | ✓ | - | ✓ | ✓ | ✓ |
| 30 | Wakayama | ✓ | ✓ | - | ✓ | ✓ | - |
| 31 | Tottori | ✓ | ✓ | - | ✓ | ✓ | - |

(continued)

**Table 3.1** (continued)

| Prefecture | | Input-output transaction table | | | | | |
|---|---|---|---|---|---|---|---|
| | | Dummy sectors | | | Social capital | | Separeation of international/ internal transaction in export/ import |
| | | Private transport | Office supplies | Head office expesses | Calculated | Row/Column consistency | |
| 32 | Shimane | ✓ | ✓ | - | ✓ | ✓ | - |
| 33 | Okayama | ✓ | ✓ | - | ✓ | ✓ | - |
| 34 | Hiroshima | ✓ | ✓ | - | ✓ | ✓ | - |
| 35 | Yamaguchi | ✓ | ✓ | - | ✓ | ✓ | - |
| 36 | Tokushima | ✓ | ✓ | - | ✓ | - | ✓ |
| 37 | Kagawa | ✓ | ✓ | - | ✓ | - | ✓ |
| 38 | Ehime | ✓ | ✓ | - | ✓ | ✓ | ✓ |
| 39 | Kochi | ✓ | ✓ | - | ✓ | - | ✓ |
| 40 | Fukuoka | ✓ | ✓ | - | ✓ | - | - |
| 41 | Saga | ✓ | ✓ | - | ✓ | - | - |
| 42 | Nagasaki | ✓ | ✓ | - | ✓ | ✓ | ✓ |
| 43 | Kumamoto | ✓ | ✓ | - | ✓ | ✓ | ✓ |
| 44 | Oita | ✓ | ✓ | - | ✓ | ✓ | - |
| 45 | Miyazaki | ✓ | ✓ | - | ✓ | ✓ | - |
| 46 | Kagoshima | ✓ | ✓ | - | ✓ | - | ✓ |
| 47 | Okinawa | - | ✓ | - | - | - | ✓ |
| | | 43 | 47 | 2 | 45 | 28 | 30 |

[a]The estimated transaction values included in the other sectors: depreciation of fixed capital and consumption expenditure of the general government
[b]The activity of the head office sector is estimated, which is included in the internal transaction with the other prefectures and is not treated as a dummy sector
*Source* Created by the author

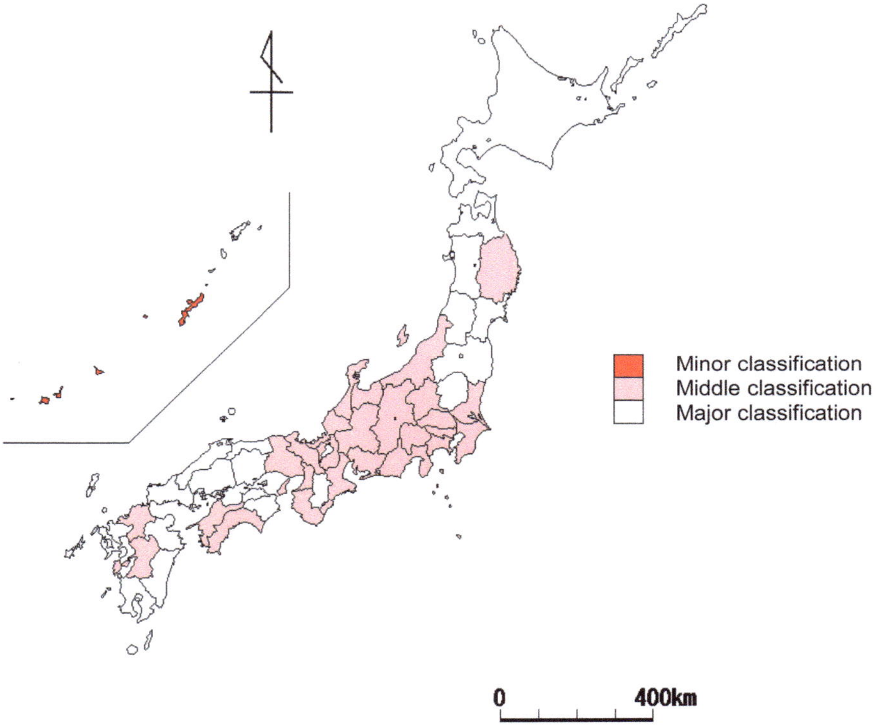


**Fig. 3.1** Number of sectors in prefectural input–output tables. *Source* Created by the author using the geographic information analysis support system "MANDARA"

## 3.3 Aggregation Consistency Between Prefectural Tables and National Tables

The prefectural IOTs for 1990 were completed for all 47 prefectures. Ohira et al. (1997) compared these tables with the national table and indicated a deviation of 4.27% in the production value. Regarding the 1995 table, we also indicated a deviation rate of 2.99%. Asahi and Yamada (2008) confirmed a 2.89% gap in the 2000 table, and Yamada (2011) revealed a 2.66% gap in the 2005 table. Thus, the divergence between the aggregated production of each prefecture and national value tends to narrow; however, differences in the sectors and the concepts in each IOT do exist, and an adjustment in comparing the prefectural IOTs is necessary. By sector, the divergence tends to be larger in the service sector than in the goods sector. However, after the 2011 IOT, the data from the economic census survey were available, which was expected to improve the accuracy of the prefectural IOT.

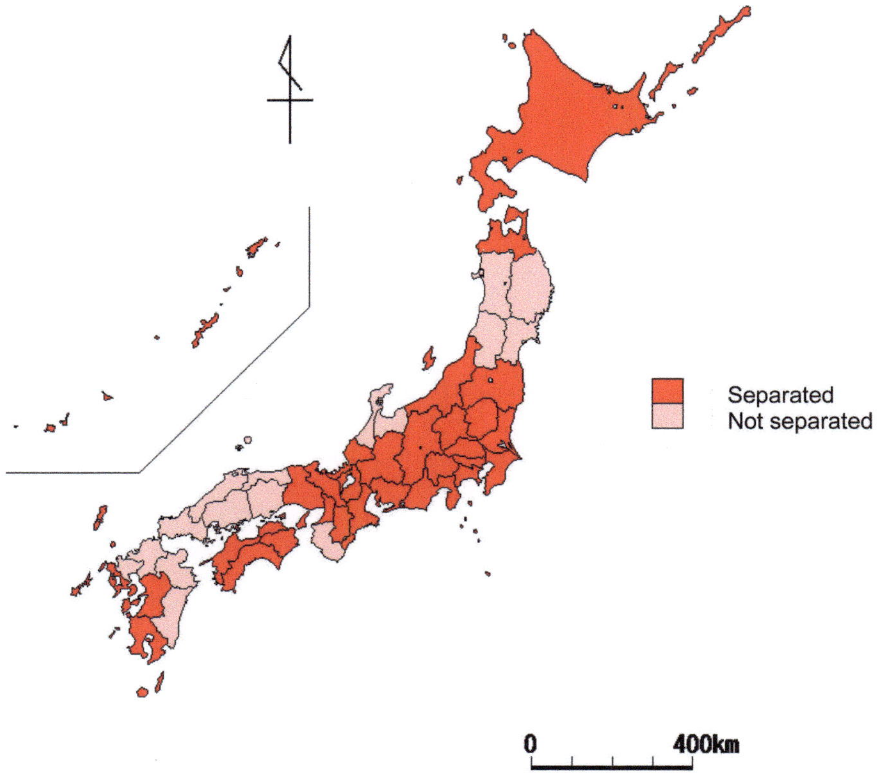


**Fig. 3.2** Separation of international/internal trades in exports/imports in prefectural input–output tables. *Source* Created by the author using the geographic information analysis support system "MANDARA"

### *3.3.1 Sector Definition and Adjustment of the Prefecture Table for the Comparison*

Although prefectural IOTs are constructed by using sector classifications and statistical information from the national IOT, they are not necessarily estimated by using common sector classifications and regional statistics for each prefecture. The unit of most of the released tables is the same as the national IOT, one million yen, though some are different, such as a thousand yen or ten thousand yen, because their economic scale is small. Furthermore, as depicted in Table 3.1, the handling of the self-transport sector, social capital depletion, and head office sector are different. Therefore, when aggregating IOTs for each prefecture to compare them with the national IOT, these differences need to be removed.

First, we compared the sectors defined by each prefecture in the 2011 IOT, defined the 80 sectors in Table 3.2 as common sectors, and integrated the IOTs of each

**Table 3.2** Definition of common sectors

| Middle classification of National table (108 sectors) | | | Common classification (80 sectors) | |
|---|---|---|---|---|
| No. | Code | Sector name | No. | Sector name |
| 1 | 011 | Crop cultivation | 1 | Crop cultivation |
| 2 | 012 | Livestock | 2 | Livestock |
| 3 | 013 | Agricultural services | 3 | Agricultural services |
| 4 | 015 | Forestry | 4 | Forestry |
| 5 | 017 | Fishery | 5 | Fishery |
| 6 | 061 | Metallic ores | **6** | **Metallic ores, and non-metallic ores** |
| 7 | 062 | Coal mining, crude petroleum and natural gas | 7 | Coal mining, crude petroleum and natural gas |
| 8 | 063 | Non-metallic ores | **6** | **Metallic ores, and non-metallic ores** |
| 9 | 111 | Foods | *8* | *Food, veverage, feeds and organic fertilizer, n.e.c., and tobacco* |
| 10 | 112 | Beverage | 9 | Beverage |
| 11 | 113 | Feeds and organic fertilizer, n.e.c | *8* | *Food, veverage, feeds and organic fertilizer, n.e.c., and tobacco* |
| 12 | 114 | Tobacco | | |
| 13 | 151 | Textile products | 10 | Textile products |
| 14 | 152 | Wearing apparel and miscellaneous ready-made textile products | 11 | Wearing apparel and miscellaneous ready-made textile products |
| 15 | 161 | Lumber and wood products | 12 | Lumber and wood products |
| 16 | 162 | Furniture and fixtures | 13 | Furniture and fixtures |
| 17 | 163 | Pulp, paper, paperboard and building paper | 14 | Pulp, paper, paperboard and building paper |
| 18 | 164 | Paper products | 15 | Paper products |
| 19 | 191 | Printing, plate making and book binding | 16 | Printing, plate making and book binding |
| 20 | 201 | Chemical fertilizer | 17 | Chemical products |
| 21 | 202 | Industrial inorganic chemicals | | |
| 22 | 203 | Petrochemical basic products | | |
| 23 | 204 | Organic chemical products (except petrochemical basic products) | | |
| 24 | 205 | Synthetic resins | | |
| 25 | 206 | Synthetic fibers | | |

(continued)

**Table 3.2** (continued)

| Middle classification of National table (108 sectors) | | | Common classification (80 sectors) | |
|---|---|---|---|---|
| No. | Code | Sector name | No. | Sector name |
| 26 | 207 | Medicaments | | |
| 27 | 208 | Final chemical products (except medicaments) | | |
| 28 | 211 | Petroleum refinery products | 18 | Petroleum and coal products |
| 29 | 212 | Coal products | | |
| 30 | 221 | Plastic products | 19 | Plastic products |
| 31 | 222 | Rubber products | 20 | Rubber products |
| 32 | 231 | Leather, fur skins and miscellaneous leather products | 21 | Leather, fur skins and miscellaneous leather products |
| 33 | 251 | Glass and glass products | ***23*** | ***Glass and glass products, potter, china and earthenware, miscellaneous ceramic, stone and clay products*** |
| 34 | 252 | Cement and cement products | 22 | Cement and cement products |
| 35 | 253 | Pottery, china and earthenware | ***23*** | ***Glass and glass products, potter, china and earthenware, miscellaneous ceramic, stone and clay products*** |
| 36 | 259 | Miscellaneous ceramic, stone and clay products | | |
| 37 | 261 | Pig iron and crude steel | 24 | Iron and steel |
| 38 | 262 | Steel products | | |
| 39 | 263 | Cast and forged steel products | | |
| 40 | 269 | Miscellaneous iron or steel products | | |
| 41 | 271 | Non-ferrous metals | 25 | Non-ferrous metals |
| 42 | 272 | Non-ferrous metal products | 26 | Non-ferrous metal products |
| 43 | 281 | Metal products for construction and architecture | 27 | Metal products for construction and architecture |
| 44 | 289 | Miscellaneous metal products | 28 | Miscellaneous metal products |
| 45 | 291 | General-purpose machinery | 29 | General-purpose machinery |
| 46 | 301 | Production machinery | 30 | Production machinery |
| 47 | 311 | Business oriented machinery | 31 | Business oriented machinery |
| 48 | 321 | Electronic devices | 32 | Electronic devices |

(continued)

**Table 3.2** (continued)

| Middle classification of National table (108 sectors) | | | Common classification (80 sectors) | |
|---|---|---|---|---|
| No. | Code | Sector name | No. | Sector name |
| 49 | 329 | Miscellaneous electronic components | 33 | Miscellaneous electronic components |
| 50 | 331 | Electrical devices and parts | 34 | Electrical devices and parts |
| 51 | 332 | Household electric appliances | 35 | Household electric appliances |
| 52 | 333 | Applied electronic equipment and electric measuring instruments | 36 | Applied electronic equipment, electric measuring instruments, and miscellaneous electrical machinery |
| 53 | 339 | Miscellaneous electrical machinery | | |
| 54 | 341 | Household electronics equipment | 37 | Information and communication electronics equipment |
| 55 | 342 | Electronic computing equipment and accessory equipment of electronic computing equipment | | |
| 56 | 351 | Passenger motor cars | 38 | Automobile, and motor vehicle parts and accessories |
| 57 | 352 | Miscellaneous cars | | |
| 58 | 353 | Motor vehicle parts and accessories | | |
| 59 | 354 | Ships and repair of ships | 39 | Ships, and miscellaneous transportation equipments |
| 60 | 359 | Miscellaneous transportation equipment and repair of transportation equipment | | |
| 61 | 391 | Miscellaneous manufacturing products | 40 | Miscellaneous manufacturing products, reuse and recycling |
| 62 | 392 | Reuse and recycling | | |
| 63 | 411 | Building construction | 41 | Building construction |
| 64 | 412 | Repair of construction | 42 | Repair of construction |
| 65 | 413 | Public construction | 43 | Civil engineering construction |
| 66 | 419 | Miscellaneous civil engineering and construction | | |
| 67 | 461 | Electricity | 44 | Electricity, gas and heat supply |
| 68 | 462 | Gas and heat supply | | |
| 69 | 471 | Water supply | 45 | Water supply |
| 70 | 481 | Waste management service | 46 | Waste management service |

(continued)

**Table 3.2** (continued)

| Middle classification of National table (108 sectors) | | | Common classification (80 sectors) | |
|---|---|---|---|---|
| No. | Code | Sector name | No. | Sector name |
| 71 | 511 | Commerce | 47 | Commerce |
| 72 | 531 | Finance and insurance | 48 | Finance and insurance |
| 73 | 551 | Real estate agencies and rental services | 49 | Real estate agencies and rental services |
| 74 | 552 | House rent | 50 | House rent |
| 75 | 553 | House rent (imputed house rent) | 51 | House rent (imputed house rent) |
| 76 | 571 | Railway transport | 52 | Railway transport |
| 77 | 572 | Road transport (except self-transport) | 53 | Road transport (except self-transport) |
| 78 | 573 | Self-transport | 54 | Self-transport |
| 79 | 574 | Water transport | 55 | Water transport |
| 80 | 575 | Air transport | 56 | Air transport, and freight forwarding |
| 81 | 576 | Freight forwarding | | |
| 82 | 577 | Storage facility service | 57 | Storage facility service |
| 83 | 578 | Services relating to transport | 58 | Services relating to transport |
| 84 | 579 | Postal services and mail delivery | 59 | Postal services and mail delivery |
| 85 | 591 | Communications | 60 | Communications |
| 86 | 592 | Broadcasting | 61 | Broadcasting |
| 87 | 593 | Information services | 62 | Information services |
| 88 | 594 | Internet based services | | |
| 89 | 595 | Image information, sound information and character information production | | |
| 90 | 611 | Public administration | 63 | Public administration |
| 91 | 631 | Education | 64 | Education |
| 92 | 632 | Research | 65 | Research |
| 93 | 641 | Medical service | 66 | Medical, health and hygiene |
| 94 | 642 | Health and hygiene | | |
| 95 | 643 | Social insurance and social welfare | 67 | Social insurance and social welfare |
| 96 | 644 | Nursing care | 68 | Nursing care |
| 97 | 659 | Miscellaneous non-profit services | 69 | Miscellaneous non-profit services |

(continued)

**Table 3.2** (continued)

| Middle classification of National table (108 sectors) | | | Common classification (80 sectors) | |
|---|---|---|---|---|
| No. | Code | Sector name | No. | Sector name |
| 98 | 661 | Goods rental and leasing services | 70 | Goods rental and leasing services |
| 99 | 662 | Advertising services | 71 | Advertising services |
| 100 | 663 | Motor vehicle maintenance and machine repair services | 72 | Motor vehicle maintenance and machine repair services |
| 101 | 669 | Miscellaneous business services | 73 | Miscellaneous business services |
| 102 | 671 | Hotels | 74 | Hotels |
| 103 | 672 | Eating and drinking services | 75 | Eating and drinking services |
| 104 | 673 | Cleaning, barber shops, beauty shops and public baths | 76 | Cleaning, barber shops, beauty shops and public baths |
| 105 | 674 | Amusement and recreational services | 77 | Amusement and recreational services |
| 106 | 679 | Miscellaneous personal services | 78 | Miscellaneous personal services |
| 107 | 681 | Office supplies | 79 | Office supplies |
| 108 | 691 | Activities not elsewhere classified | 80 | Activities not elsewhere classified |
| 109 | 700 | Total of intermediate sectors | 81 | Total of intermediate sectors |

*Source* Created by the author

prefecture according to these 80 sectors. At that time, the tables with different units were corrected to one million yen. Table 3.2 shows the correspondence between the middle classification of national table and the common classification defined here. In mots cases, adjacent sectors have been integrated, but there are three cases where non-adjacent sectors have been combined into one, which are distinguished by the Italic, Gothic, and Italic-Gothic styles.

According to Table 3.1, there were four prefectures: Hokkaido, Mie, Hyogo, and Okinawa, where the self-transportation sector was not defined. Defining a dummy sector of self-transport increases its production value. Without adjusting for this difference in comparing each prefectural IOT with the national table, the sum of prefectural IOTs will be underestimated by that amount.

Iwate and Okinawa prefectures do not consider the depletion of social capital. When capital depreciation provisions (social capital depletion) and its general government consumption expenditure are recorded, the amount of production increases accordingly. Therefore, directly comparing it with the national table will result in an underestimation.

There are differences in the estimates for exports and imports. Some prefectures estimate exports and imports separately from international and domestic transactions, and others estimate only their sum. However, when comparing regional tables with national tables, separating each of the exports and imports into international and domestic is necessary. The sum of international exports and imports ought to have the same values as the national table, respectively. The sum of domestic exports and imports, which are the transactions among prefectures, must cancel each other when aggregated nationwide. It is important whether the total net exports in the national table are the same as the total net exports in the prefectural table.

Unlike other prefectural tables, the Tokyo IOT explicitly deals with the head office sector. Characteristically, the Tokyo table is an interregional IOT with two regions—Tokyo and the ROJ. For the comparison, we reduced the Tokyo interregional IOT to an intra-regional IOT of Tokyo. Then we reorganized the table in which the amount of expense incurred by the headquarters was returned to each sector and then aggregated it.[1] Because of such adjustments, the total production is smaller than the value of the original IOT of Tokyo.

### *3.3.2 Comparison of Total Amount by Item*

Tables 3.3 and 3.4 present the aggregated values for each row and column of the input–output table: the value of the national table, the aggregated values of prefecture tables, the amount of deviation, and the rate of deviation.

The rate of divergence between the production values in the national and prefectural tables displays a slight underestimation of prefectures' tables at 0.97%; however, the intermediate input total (endogenous sector total (rows)) is 3.70% underestimated, and the gross value-added sector total is 1.68% overstated. However, to eliminate the difference in the treatment of self-transportation and social capital depletion, the deviation rate between the two is 0.52% underestimated when the corrected production value is compared by excluding that production value.

The deviation rate for each item in the gross value-added sector is as follows: non-household consumption expenditure (row) is 1.03%; employee income is – 1.28%; the operating surplus is 10.31%; provision for capital depreciation is 6.00%; indirect tax (including tariffs and import goods excluding) is 1.35%; and (excluding) ordinary subsidies is – 2.93%. The deviation rate of operating surplus and allowance for capital depreciation is slightly larger among them.

Regarding the divergence of final demand items, non-household consumption expenditure (column) differs by 1.03%, private consumption expenditure differs by – 0.39%, general government consumption expenditure by 3.74%, gross domestic fixed capital formation (public) by 3.21%, gross domestic fixed capital formation

[1] Here, in the Tokyo table, the input amount of the head office sector is returned to each sector, and the row balance is achieved by including non-household consumption expenditure (column) generated by production related to the export of head office expenses in the export.

**Table 3.3** Comparison of aggregated values for each of the endogenous and value-added sectors

| | Japan | Prefecture, total | Deviation amount | Deviation rate |
|---|---|---|---|---|
| | Billion Yen | Billion Yen | Billion Yen | % |
| Total of intermediate sectors | 462,770 | 445,636 | −17,134 | − 3.70 |
| Consumption expenditure outside households (column) | 13,633 | 13,774 | 141 | 1.03 |
| Compensation of employees | 248,421 | 245,237 | −3 ,185 | − 1.28 |
| Operating surplus | 86,806 | 95,759 | 8,953 | 10.31 |
| Depreciation of fixed capital | 85,690 | 90,829 | 5,139 | 6.00 |
| Depreciation of fixed capital (Social fixed capital depreciation) | 14,018 | 10,640 | −3 ,378 | − 24.10 |
| Indirect taxes (except custom duties and commodity taxes on imported goods) | 31,934 | 32,367 | 433 | 1.35 |
| (less) Current subsidies | −3 ,597 | −3 ,492 | 105 | −2.93 |
| Total of gross value added sectors | 476,905 | 484,939 | 8,034 | 1.68 |
| **Domestic production (gross outputs)** | **939,675** | **930,575** | **−9 ,100** | **−0.97** |
| Self-transport | 8,933 | 7,959 | −973 | −10.90 |
| Depreciation of fixed capital (Social fixed capital depreciation) | 14,018 | 10,640 | −3 ,378 | −24.10 |
| **Domestic production (gross outputs) modified** | **916,724** | **911,975** | **−4 ,749** | **−0.52** |

*Source* Created by the author

(private) by 0.45%, and net increase in inventory differs by 3.94%. Their deviation rates are within 4%. General government consumption expenditure (social capital depletion), which is treated differently among prefectures, has a larger divergence. However, the deviation rate of net exports is extremely large, at − 70.46%.

### *3.3.3 Comparison of Production Value by Sector*

Figure 3.3 is a bar graph comparing production values by sector in the national and prefectural tables aggregated. In general, the values of all goods and services sectors are remarkably close to each other. Table 3.5 displays the production value by sector in the national table and the prefectural table aggregated, as well as the amount and rate of deviation between the two. In this table, the sectors are sorted in ascending order of the deviation rate.

Over 10.0% tend to be underestimated compared to the national table in the sectors of "construction repair," "water transportation," "automobile maintenance/

**Table 3.4** Comparison of aggregated values for each of the endogenous and final demand sectors

| | Japan | Prefecture, total | Deviation amount | Deviation rate |
|---|---|---|---|---|
| | Billion Yen | Billion Yen | Billion Yen | % |
| Total of intermediate sectors | 462,770 | 445,636 | −17,134 | −3.70 |
| Consumption expenditure outside households (column) | 13,633 | 13,774 | 141 | 1.03 |
| Consumption expenditure (private) | 282,821 | 281,733 | −1,089 | −0.39 |
| Consumption expenditure of general government | 84,718 | 87,890 | 3,172 | 3.74 |
| Consumption expenditure of general government (social fixed capital depreciation) | 14,018 | 10,638 | −3,380 | −24.11 |
| Gross domestic fixed capital formation (public) | 20,401 | 21,055 | 654 | 3.21 |
| Gross domestic fixed capital formation (private) | 70,983 | 71,305 | 322 | 0.45 |
| Increase in stocks | 980 | 1,018 | 39 | 3.94 |
| Balancing sector | 1,563 | 1,133 | −430 | −27.51 |
| Total domestic final demand | 489,119 | 489,186 | 68 | −0.12 |
| Total domestic demand | 951,888 | 934,822 | −17,066 | −1.86 |
| Exports, international and domestic | 70,945 | 346,753 | – | – |
| Total Final demand | 560,063 | 835,300 | 275,237 | 49.14 |
| **Total demand** | **1,022,833** | **1,280,937** | **258,104** | **25.23** |
| (less) Imports, international and domestic | − 83,158 | −350,362 | – | – |
| Net exports | − 12,213 | *−3,608* | 8,605 | −70.46 |
| Total of final demand sectors | 476,905 | 484,939 | 8,034 | 1.68 |
| **Domestic production (gross outputs)** | **939,675** | **930,575** | **−9,100** | **−0.97** |

*Source* Created by the author

mechanical repair," and "self-transportation." Additionally, the sectors of "other business services," "broadcasting," "petroleum and coal products," "livestock," "non-ferrous metal smelting and refining," "industrial electrical equipment," "other services for individuals," "forestry," and "non-ferrous metal processed products" exceed 5.0%. Of these, the fact that there are prefectures that do not estimate "self-transportation" is related. If they are estimated, the deviation will be a little smaller.

Conversely, the sectors that tend to be overestimated compared to the national table are "residential rent (imputed rent)," "metallic minerals/non-metallic minerals," and "electronic devices," and the deviation rate for these exceeds 10%. In addition, the deviation rate of "hotels," "air transportation/freight transportation," "housing rent,"

**Fig. 3.3** Production value of the national table and aggregate values of the prefecture's tables. *Source* Created by the author

"research," "waste treatment," "commercial machinery," "tanned leather, fur, and related products," "electricity/gas/heat supply," and "warehouse" exceeded 5%

**Table 3.5** Comparison of production value by sector

| | | Production | | | |
|---|---|---|---|---|---|
| | | Japan | Prefecture, total | Deviation amount | Deviation rate |
| | | Billion Yen | Billion Yen | Billion Yen | % |
| 42 | Repair of construction | 9,773 | 8,128 | −1 ,645 | −16.83 |
| 55 | Water transport | 5,196 | 4,470 | −726 | −13.97 |
| 72 | Motor vehicle maintenance and machine repair services | 12,589 | 11,132 | −1 ,457 | −11.58 |
| 54 | Self-transport | 8,933 | 7,959 | −973 | −10.90 |
| 73 | Miscellaneous business services | 37,706 | 34,109 | −3 ,597 | −9.54 |
| 61 | Broadcasting | 3,561 | 3,222 | −338 | −9.50 |
| 18 | Petroleum and coal products | 19,857 | 18,121 | −1 ,736 | −8.74 |
| 2 | Livestock | 2,931 | 2,703 | −229 | −7.80 |
| 25 | Non-ferrous metals | 3,120 | 2,915 | −205 | −6.56 |
| 34 | Electrical devices and parts | 7,181 | 6,723 | −459 | −6.38 |
| 78 | Miscellaneous personal services | 8,127 | 7,621 | −506 | −6.22 |
| 4 | Forestry | 776 | 732 | −43 | −5.59 |
| 26 | Non-ferrous metal products | 5,942 | 5,644 | −298 | −5.01 |
| 52 | Railway transport | 6,331 | 6,051 | −280 | −4.42 |
| 9 | Beverage | 6,699 | 6,416 | −283 | −4.23 |
| 49 | Real estate agencies and rental services | 12,276 | 11,769 | −507 | −4.13 |
| 67 | Social insurance and social welfare | 7,847 | 7,526 | −321 | −4.09 |
| 14 | Pulp, paper, paperboard and building paper | 4,305 | 4,154 | −152 | −3.52 |
| 39 | Ships, and miscellaneous transportation equipments | 6,627 | 6,401 | −227 | −3.42 |
| 47 | Commerce | 93,656 | 90,546 | −3 ,110 | −3.32 |
| 16 | Printing, plate making and book binding | 5,113 | 4,956 | −157 | −3.08 |

(continued)

**Table 3.5** (continued)

| | | Production | | | |
|---|---|---|---|---|---|
| | | Japan | Prefecture, total | Deviation amount | Deviation rate |
| | | Billion Yen | Billion Yen | Billion Yen | % |
| 63 | Public administration | 39,405 | 38,370 | −1 ,035 | −2.63 |
| 60 | Communications | 17,669 | 17,209 | −459 | −2.60 |
| 41 | Building construction | 23,663 | 23,073 | −590 | −2.49 |
| 75 | Eating and drinking services | 25,256 | 24,643 | −614 | −2.43 |
| 29 | General-purpose machinery | 9,425 | 9,197 | −228 | −2.42 |
| 43 | Civil engineering construction | 19,078 | 18,635 | −443 | −2.32 |
| 58 | Services relating to transport | 6,004 | 5,866 | −137 | −2.28 |
| 24 | Iron and steel | 30,487 | 29,791 | −696 | −2.28 |
| 69 | Miscellaneous non-profit services | 5,166 | 5,051 | −114 | −2.21 |
| 37 | Information and communication electronics equipment | 7,902 | 7,741 | −161 | −2.04 |
| 36 | Applied electronic equipment, electric measuring instruments, and miscellaneous electrical machinery | 5,297 | 5,202 | −95 | −1.80 |
| 17 | Chemical products | 27,634 | 27,192 | −442 | −1.60 |
| 53 | Road transport (except self-transport) | 15,449 | 15,252 | −197 | −1.28 |
| 1 | Crop cultivation | 6,043 | 5,970 | −73 | −1.21 |
| 70 | Goods rental and leasing services | 9,788 | 9,675 | −113 | −1.16 |
| 76 | Cleaning, barber shops, beauty shops and public baths | 5,851 | 5,787 | −64 | −1.09 |

(continued)

**Table 3.5** (continued)

| | | Production | | | |
|---|---|---|---|---|---|
| | | Japan | Prefecture, total | Deviation amount | Deviation rate |
| | | Billion Yen | Billion Yen | Billion Yen | % |
| **81** | **Total of intermediate sectors** | **939,675** | **930,575** | **−9 ,100** | **−0.97** |
| 66 | Medical, health and hygiene | 44,190 | 43,890 | −299 | −0.68 |
| 5 | Fishery | 1,435 | 1,426 | −9 | −0.61 |
| 80 | Activities not elsewhere classified | 5,010 | 4,980 | −30 | −0.60 |
| 68 | Nursing care | 8,238 | 8,192 | −46 | −0.56 |
| 38 | Automobile, and motor vehicle parts and accessories | 38,944 | 38,838 | −106 | −0.27 |
| 59 | Postal services and mail delivery | 1,405 | 1,403 | −2 | −0.14 |
| 45 | Water supply | 4,567 | 4567 | 0 | −0.01 |
| 7 | Coal mining, crude petroleum and natural gas | 196 | 196 | 0 | 0.04 |
| 15 | Paper products | 3,109 | 3,116 | 7 | 0.23 |
| 8 | Food, veverage, feeds and organic fertilizer, n.e.c., and tobacco | 28,842 | 28,973 | 131 | 0.45 |
| 19 | Plastic products | 9,984 | 10,058 | 74 | 0.74 |
| 3 | Agricultural services | 851 | 859 | 8 | 0.91 |
| 28 | Miscellaneous metal products | 7,026 | 7,108 | 83 | 1.18 |
| 40 | Miscellaneous manufacturing products, reuse and recycling | 4,510 | 4,568 | 58 | 1.28 |
| 22 | Cement and cement products | 2,303 | 2,335 | 32 | 1.37 |
| 33 | Miscellaneous electronic components | 7,316 | 7,420 | 104 | 1.42 |

(continued)

**Table 3.5** (continued)

| | | Production | | | |
|---|---|---|---|---|---|
| | | Japan | Prefecture, total | Deviation amount | Deviation rate |
| | | Billion Yen | Billion Yen | Billion Yen | % |
| 64 | Education | 22,711 | 23,056 | 345 | 1.52 |
| 30 | Production machinery | 14,359 | 14,600 | 241 | 1.68 |
| 62 | Information services | 24,931 | 25,406 | 475 | 1.91 |
| 20 | Rubber products | 2,922 | 2,983 | 61 | 2.08 |
| 71 | Advertising services | 6,078 | 6,217 | 138 | 2.28 |
| 79 | Office supplies | 1,325 | 1,357 | 32 | 2.38 |
| 13 | Furniture and fixtures | 1,734 | 1,778 | 44 | 2.54 |
| 11 | Wearing apparel and miscellaneous ready-made textile products | 2,029 | 2,088 | 59 | 2.89 |
| 35 | Household electric appliances | 2,564 | 2,646 | 82 | 3.19 |
| 77 | Amusement and recreational services | 8,938 | 9,228 | 290 | 3.24 |
| 27 | Metal products for construction and architecture | 3,105 | 3,214 | 108 | 3.48 |
| 23 | Glass and glass products, potter, china and earthenware, miscellaneous ceramic, stone and clay products | 4,136 | 4,285 | 149 | 3.60 |
| 48 | Finance and insurance | 32,094 | 33,338 | 1,244 | 3.88 |
| 12 | Lumber and wood products | 1,920 | 1,997 | 76 | 3.98 |
| 10 | Textile products | 1,325 | 1,380 | 55 | 4.14 |
| 74 | Hotels | 4,582 | 4,811 | 230 | 5.01 |
| 56 | Air transport, and freight forwarding | 3,150 | 3,314 | 164 | 5.20 |

(continued)

**Table 3.5** (continued)

| | | Production | | | |
|---|---|---|---|---|---|
| | | Japan | Prefecture, total | Deviation amount | Deviation rate |
| | | Billion Yen | Billion Yen | Billion Yen | % |
| 50 | House rent | 12,472 | 13,137 | 665 | 5.33 |
| 65 | Research | 12,126 | 12,788 | 662 | 5.46 |
| 46 | Waste management service | 3,765 | 3,991 | 225 | 5.99 |
| 31 | Business oriented machinery | 6,434 | 6,830 | 396 | 6.15 |
| 21 | Leather, fur skins and miscellaneous leather products | 333 | 354 | 21 | 6.34 |
| 44 | Electricity, gas and heat supply | 21,187 | 22,600 | 1,412 | 6.67 |
| 57 | Storage facility service | 1,767 | 1,902 | 135 | 7.67 |
| 51 | House rent (imputed house rent) | 46,440 | 51,491 | 5,051 | 10.88 |
| 6 | Metallic ores, and non-metallic ores | 564 | 632 | 68 | 12.01 |
| 32 | Electronic devices | 6,092 | 7,273 | 1,181 | 19.38 |

*Source* Created by the author

### *3.3.4 Comparison of Net Exports and Exports by Sector*

Figure 3.4 is a bar graph comparing net exports by sector in the national and prefectural tables aggregated. Although there are many sectors in which the values are relatively close to each other, some sectors, such as "commerce" and "automobile maintenance/machine repair," have large discrepancies. Table 3.6 presents the net exports by sector in the national table and the aggregate prefectural table, and the amount and rate of deviation between the two, the sectors of which are in ascending order of the deviation rate. As net exports are the difference between exports and imports, the rate of deviation here is not defined as the rate of deviation of net exports of the prefecture aggregated divided by the net export of the national value, but as their ratio to the production value of the corresponding sector in the national table.

Net exports tend to be smaller than the national table: "broadcasting," "automobile maintenance/mechanical repair," "other business services," "education," "forestry," "fisheries," and "livestock." These divergence rates exceed 5%, and only "broadcasting" among them accounts for over 10%. These sectors underestimate their exports relative to their imports, which we must consider when estimating exports and imports in the prefectural IOT.

**Fig. 3.4** Net exports comparison of Japan and prefectural tables. *Source* Created by the author

However, the sectors whose net exports tend to be excessive compared to the national table are "Coal/Crude Oil/Natural Gas," "Metallic Minerals/Nonmetallic Minerals," "Electronic Devices," "Wood/Wood Products," "Textile Products," "Warehousing," and "Advertisement," all of which have deviation rates of more than 10%.

Among them, "coal, crude oil, and natural gas" have a relatively small production scale, and the deviation rate from the production value is large at 706.95%.

Additionally, the sectors of "commercial machinery," "consumer electrical equipment," "glass/ceramics/and related products," "cement/cement products," "rubber products," and "construction/architectural metal products," "air transport/freight

**Table 3.6** Comparison of net exports by sector

| | | Production | Net exports | | | |
|---|---|---|---|---|---|---|
| | | Japan | Japan | Prefecture, total | Deviation amount | Deviation rate |
| | | Billion Yen | Billion Yen | Billion Yen | Billion Yen | % |
| 61 | Broadcasting | 3,561 | 0 | −364 | −364 | −10.22 |
| 72 | Motor vehicle maintenance and machine repair services | 12,589 | 2 | −1 ,112 | −1 ,114 | −8.85 |
| 73 | Miscellaneous business services | 37,706 | −393 | −3 ,381 | −2 ,987 | −7.92 |
| 64 | Education | 22,711 | −55 | −1 ,581 | −1 ,526 | −6.72 |
| 4 | Forestry | 776 | −125 | −170 | −45 | −5.85 |
| 5 | Fishery | 1,435 | −203 | −282 | −79 | −5.48 |
| 2 | Livestock | 2,931 | −39 | −187 | −148 | −5.06 |
| 55 | Water transport | 5,196 | 1,444 | 1,187 | −257 | −4.94 |
| 78 | Miscellaneous personal services | 8,127 | 18 | −373 | −391 | −4.81 |
| 18 | Petroleum and coal products | 19,857 | −2 ,268 | −3 ,149 | −881 | −4.44 |
| 69 | Miscellaneous non-profit services | 5,166 | −35 | −224 | −190 | −3.68 |
| 36 | Applied electronic equipment, electric measuring instruments, and miscellaneous electrical machinery | 5,297 | 834 | 667 | −167 | −3.15 |
| 34 | Electrical devices and parts | 7,181 | 1,335 | 1,197 | −138 | −1.92 |
| 9 | Beverage | 6,699 | −483 | −607 | −125 | −1.86 |
| 38 | Automobile, and motor vehicle parts and accessories | 38,944 | 9,923 | 9,204 | −719 | −1.85 |
| 25 | Non-ferrous metals | 3,120 | −1 ,488 | −1 ,541 | −52 | −1.68 |
| 80 | Activities not elsewhere classified | 5,010 | −36 | −115 | −79 | −1.58 |

(continued)

**Table 3.6** (continued)

| | | Production | Net exports | | | |
|---|---|---|---|---|---|---|
| | | Japan | Japan | Prefecture, total | Deviation amount | Deviation rate |
| | | Billion Yen | Billion Yen | Billion Yen | Billion Yen | % |
| 37 | Information and communication electronics equipment | 7,902 | −2 ,350 | −2 ,432 | −82 | −1.03 |
| 45 | Water supply | 4,567 | 8 | −20 | −28 | −0.61 |
| 39 | Ships, and miscellaneous transportation equipments | 6,627 | 2,060 | 2,043 | −18 | −0.27 |
| 24 | Iron and steel | 30,487 | 2,223 | 2,166 | −57 | −0.19 |
| 52 | Railway transport | 6,331 | 22 | 17 | −5 | −0.08 |
| 68 | Nursing care | 8,238 | 0 | −5 | −5 | −0.06 |
| 66 | Medical, health and hygiene | 44,190 | −3 | −8 | −5 | −0.01 |
| 67 | Social insurance and social welfare | 7,847 | 0 | 0 | 0 | 0.00 |
| 41 | Building construction | 23,663 | 0 | 0 | 0 | 0.00 |
| 43 | Civil engineering construction | 19,078 | 0 | 0 | 0 | 0.00 |
| 63 | Public administration | 39,405 | 0 | 0 | 0 | 0.00 |
| 51 | House rent (imputed house rent) | 46,440 | 0 | 15 | 15 | 0.03 |
| 3 | Agricultural services | 851 | 0 | 1 | 1 | 0.10 |
| 16 | Printing, plate making and book binding | 5,113 | −14 | −3 | 11 | 0.21 |
| 76 | Cleaning, barber shops, beauty shops and public baths | 5,851 | −3 | 15 | 17 | 0.30 |

(continued)

**Table 3.6** (continued)

| | | Production | Net exports | | | |
|---|---|---|---|---|---|---|
| | | Japan | Japan | Prefecture, total | Deviation amount | Deviation rate |
| | | Billion Yen | Billion Yen | Billion Yen | Billion Yen | % |
| 53 | Road transport (except self-transport) | 15,449 | 849 | 899 | 50 | 0.33 |
| 75 | Eating and drinking services | 25,256 | −211 | −107 | 104 | 0.41 |
| 30 | Production machinery | 14,359 | 4,766 | 4,844 | 78 | 0.54 |
| 42 | Repair of construction | 9,773 | 0 | 70 | 70 | 0.72 |
| 81 | Total of intermediate sectors | 939,675 | −12,213 | −3 ,608 | 8,605 | 0.92 |
| 50 | House rent | 12,472 | 18 | 139 | 121 | 0.97 |
| 14 | Pulp, paper, paperboard and building paper | 4,305 | −168 | −126 | 42 | 0.98 |
| 60 | Communications | 17,669 | −16 | 163 | 180 | 1.02 |
| 70 | Goods rental and leasing services | 9,788 | 252 | 360 | 108 | 1.10 |
| 48 | Finance and insurance | 32,094 | −68 | 330 | 398 | 1.24 |
| 40 | Miscellaneous manufacturing products, reuse and recycling | 4,510 | −1 ,193 | −1 ,133 | 60 | 1.32 |
| 54 | Self-transport | 8,933 | 0 | 136 | 136 | 1.53 |
| 17 | Chemical products | 27,634 | −952 | −481 | 471 | 1.71 |
| 46 | Waste management service | 3,765 | 3 | 69 | 66 | 1.76 |
| 74 | Hotels | 4,582 | −223 | −140 | 83 | 1.80 |
| 29 | General-purpose machinery | 9,425 | 2,030 | 2,200 | 170 | 1.80 |

(continued)

**Table 3.6** (continued)

| | | Production | Net exports | | | |
|---|---|---|---|---|---|---|
| | | Japan | Japan | Prefecture, total | Deviation amount | Deviation rate |
| | | Billion Yen | Billion Yen | Billion Yen | Billion Yen | % |
| 33 | Miscellaneous electronic components | 7,316 | 1,022 | 1,197 | 175 | 2.39 |
| 26 | Non-ferrous metal products | 5,942 | 98 | 267 | 169 | 2.85 |
| 58 | Services relating to transport | 6,004 | 473 | 644 | 171 | 2.85 |
| 47 | Commerce | 93,656 | 6,603 | 9,306 | 2,704 | 2.89 |
| 19 | Plastic products | 9,984 | 514 | 832 | 318 | 3.18 |
| 59 | Postal services and mail delivery | 1,405 | −2 | 42 | 45 | 3.19 |
| 15 | Paper products | 3,109 | −54 | 46 | 100 | 3.21 |
| 11 | Wearing apparel and miscellaneous ready-made textile products | 2,029 | −3 ,401 | −3 ,332 | 68 | 3.37 |
| 65 | Research | 12,126 | 5 | 466 | 461 | 3.80 |
| 8 | Food, veverage, feeds and organic fertilizer, n.e.c., and tobacco | 28,842 | −5 ,684 | −4 ,553 | 1,131 | 3.92 |
| 13 | Furniture and fixtures | 1,734 | −400 | −328 | 72 | 4.14 |
| 49 | Real estate agencies and rental services | 12,276 | 2 | 556 | 554 | 4.52 |
| 79 | Office supplies | 1,325 | 0 | 67 | 67 | 5.05 |
| 1 | Crop cultivation | 6,043 | −2 ,148 | −1 ,836 | 312 | 5.16 |
| 77 | Amusement and recreational services | 8,938 | −127 | 341 | 468 | 5.23 |
| 44 | Electricity, gas and heat supply | 21,187 | 25 | 1,141 | 1,115 | 5.26 |

(continued)

**Table 3.6** (continued)

| | | Production | Net exports | | | |
|---|---|---|---|---|---|---|
| | | Japan | Japan | Prefecture, total | Deviation amount | Deviation rate |
| | | Billion Yen | Billion Yen | Billion Yen | Billion Yen | % |
| 21 | Leather, fur skins and miscellaneous leather products | 333 | −742 | −725 | 18 | 5.36 |
| 62 | Information services | 24,931 | −409 | 941 | 1,350 | 5.42 |
| 28 | Miscellaneous metal products | 7,026 | 8 | 396 | 388 | 5.52 |
| 56 | Air transport, and freight forwarding | 3,150 | −595 | −408 | 187 | 5.94 |
| 20 | Rubber products | 2,922 | 229 | 405 | 176 | 6.03 |
| 22 | Cement and cement products | 2,303 | 5 | 145 | 140 | 6.07 |
| 23 | Glass and glass products, potter, china and earthenware, miscellaneous ceramic, stone and clay products | 4,136 | 296 | 582 | 286 | 6.93 |
| 35 | Household electric appliances | 2,564 | −465 | −261 | 204 | 7.97 |
| 31 | Business oriented machinery | 6,434 | −68 | 510 | 578 | 8.98 |
| 71 | Advertising services | 6,078 | −151 | 499 | 650 | 10.69 |
| 57 | Storage facility service | 1,767 | 107 | 300 | 192 | 10.89 |
| 10 | Textile products | 1,325 | 61 | 211 | 151 | 11.36 |
| 12 | Lumber and wood products | 1,920 | −952 | −728 | 224 | 11.66 |
| 27 | Metal products for construction and architecture | 3,105 | −166 | 259 | 425 | 13.68 |
| 32 | Electronic devices | 6,092 | 1,518 | 2,734 | 1,216 | 19.96 |

(continued)

**Table 3.6** (continued)

| | | Production | Net exports | | | |
|---|---|---|---|---|---|---|
| | | Japan | Japan | Prefecture, total | Deviation amount | Deviation rate |
| | | Billion Yen | Billion Yen | Billion Yen | Billion Yen | % |
| 6 | Metallic ores, and non-metallic ores | 564 | −3,133 | −2 ,749 | 384 | 68.06 |
| 7 | Coal mining, crude petroleum and natural gas | 196 | −20,141 | −18,756 | 1,385 | 706.95 |

*Source* Created by the author

transportation," "other metal products," "information services," "leather, fur, and similar products," "Electricity/gas/heat supply," "Entertainment services," "Cultivated agriculture," and "office supplies" have a deviation rate that exceeds 5%. In these sectors, exports are overestimated compared to imports.

The net exports of "self-transportation" and "office supplies" are positive in the prefectural aggregates, partly because the head office sector in the Tokyo IOT is returned to each sector. As for the "office supplies" sector, it is not zero in Osaka, Tottori, Saga, and Okinawa. Additionally, Kagawa accounts for the non-zero net exports as positive exports of "housing rent (imputed rent)."

### *3.3.5 Relationship Between the Rate of Divergence Between Production and the Values of Major Items*

The five graphs in Figs. 3.5, 3.6, 3.7, 3.8 and 3.9 present scatter diagrams of the deviation rate of the prefectural production values aggregated from national production values by 80 sectors with the following five items: the deviation rate of the intermediate input total, the deviation of the gross value-added total, the deviation rate of the intermediate demand total, the deviation rate of the regional final demand total, and the deviation rate of net exports, respectively.

However, in the scatter diagrams, both the intermediate demand total in Fig. 3.6 and the net exports in Fig. 3.9 show that the production values of "metallic minerals/nonmetallic minerals" and "coal, crude oil, and natural gas" are small, and their deviation rates are large. Therefore, we excluded these two sectors in the figures.

Both the total intermediate input in Fig. 3.5 and the total gross value-added in Fig. 3.6 have a strong positive correlation with the divergence rate of the corresponding sectoral production value. Sectors with large discrepancies in production values have large discrepancies in intermediate inputs and the gross value-added.

In the prefectural table, after estimating the production value, CT, by sector, on the premise of the similarity of the input structure and value-added structure of the

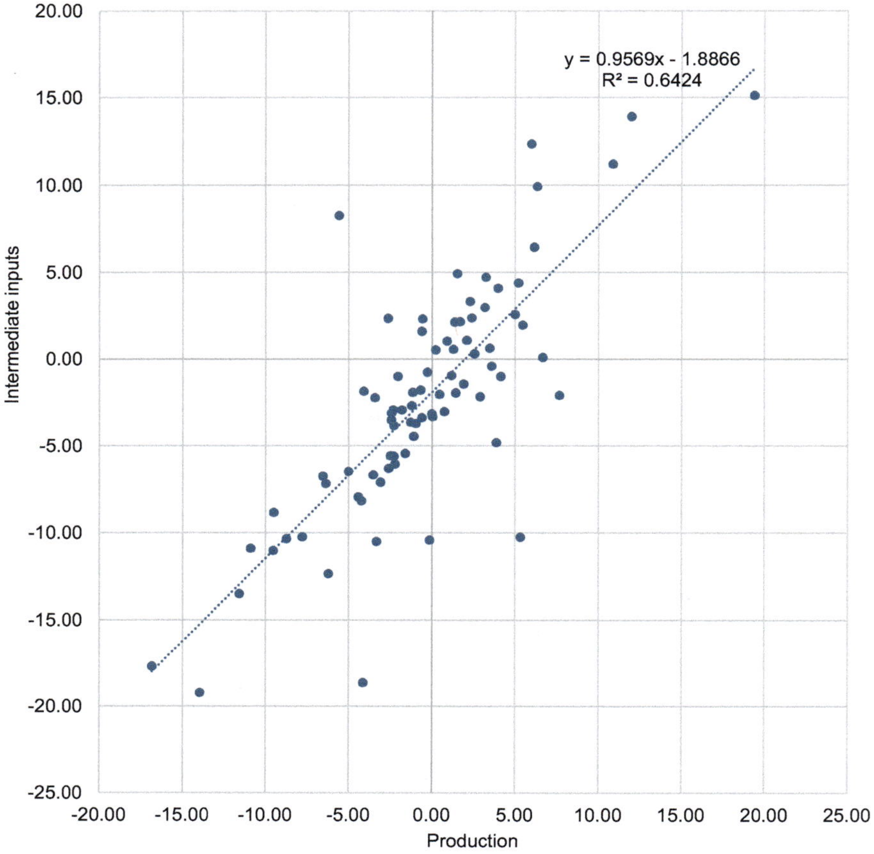


**Fig. 3.5** Deviation rates of production and intermediate inputs. *Source* Created by the author

prefecture to those of the nation, we estimated values for intermediate input and gross value-added in the prefecture. If there is a large deviation for CT, it means that the value of intermediate input and gross value-added will be affected accordingly.

In contrast, the discrepancies between the intermediate demand total in Fig. 3.7 and the regional final demand total in Fig. 3.8 do not have a strong positive relationship with the output deviation rate. The positive and negative discrepancies that occur in the column direction may be offset to some extent in the row direction aggregation. Additionally, the final demand in the region is unlikely to be affected by the value of production by sector because it is estimated independently; hence, the correlation is thought to be low.

Finally, if we look at the rate of deviation of net exports in Fig. 3.9, the strength of the positive correlation is second only to that of the intermediate input total and the gross value-added total, although it is not as strong. As there is a tendency to adjust net exports, especially imports, when it is necessary to adjust the horizontal

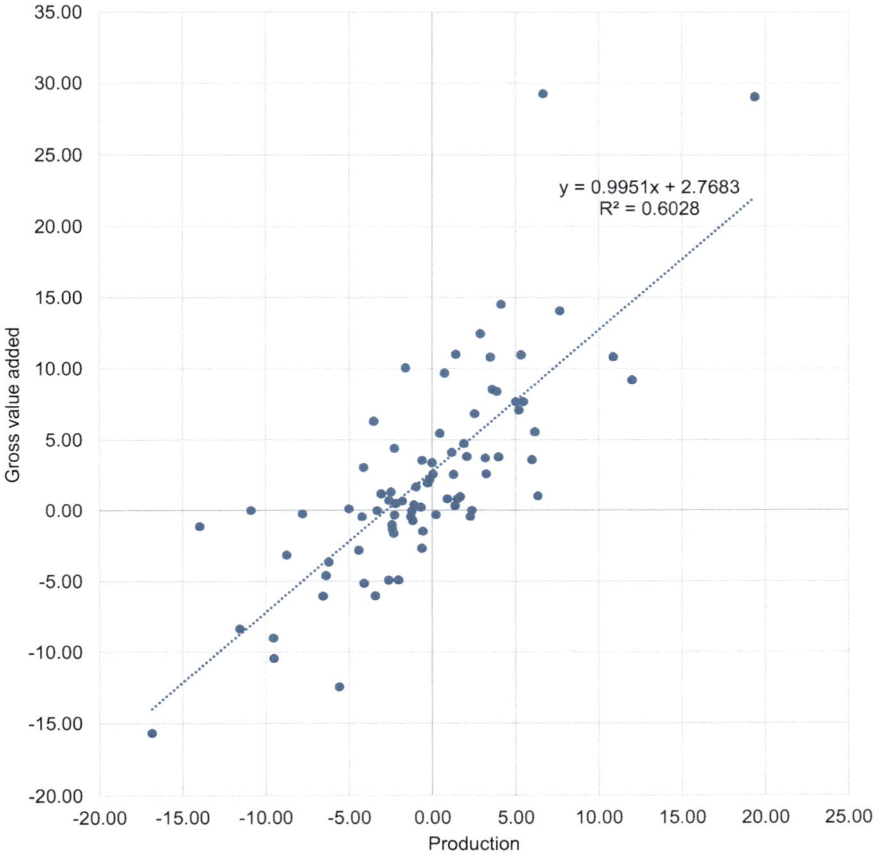


**Fig. 3.6** Deviation rates of production and gross value-added. *Source* Created by the author

balance, the sector with a large deviation rate of production is expected to have a large deviation rate of net exports. Looking at it this way, in constructing prefectural IOTs, accurately estimating the sectoral production value, CT, is important.

## 3.4 Concluding Remarks

In this chapter, we summarized the state of publication of prefectural IOTs in 2011 and sorted out the characteristics of each prefectural IOT and the employment table that was published. Furthermore, after integrating each prefectural table into 80 common sectors, they were aggregated and compared with the values of the national table.

In terms of the total amount of production, the deviation rate is less than 1%, the maximum deviation rate by sector is less than 20%, seven sectors out of 80 sectors

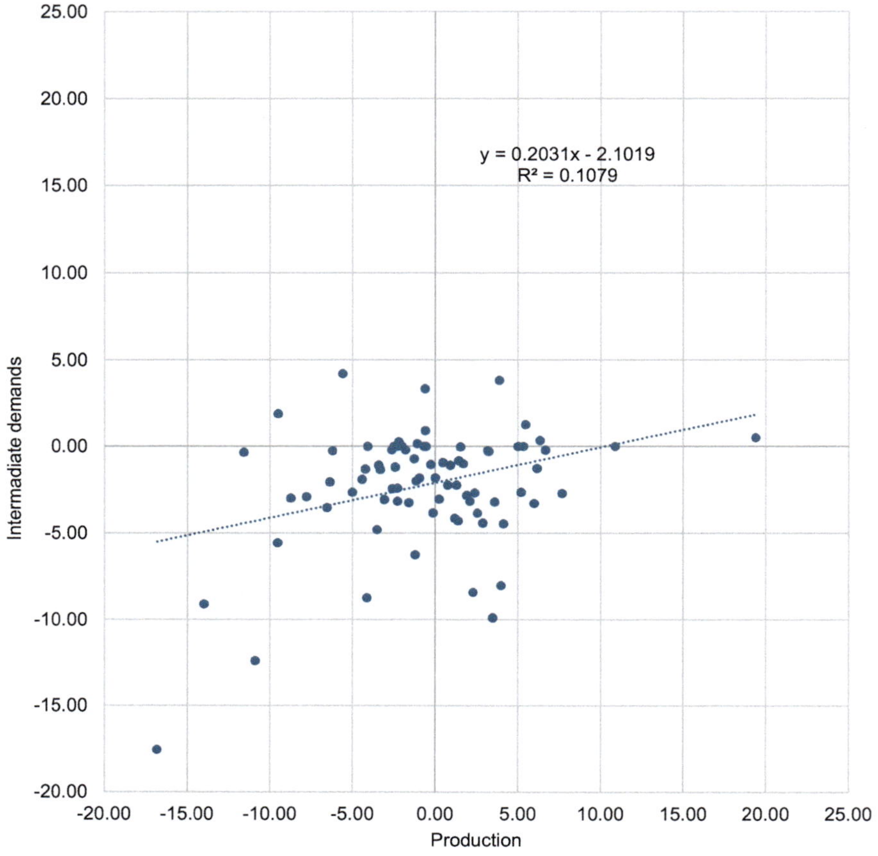


**Fig. 3.7** Deviation rates of production and intermediate demands. *Source* Created by the author

exceed 10%, and most of them are within a few percent. As for net exports, the total deviation from production is less than 1%, but we found that there are about nine sectors with deviation rates exceeding 10%. In the earlier tables, the rate of deviation in the goods sector was relatively small, but the rate of deviation in the service sector was large. The rate of divergence has also improved considerably, and the introduction of the economic census seems to have had an effect.

In the column direction, the sectoral deviation rate of intermediate inputs and gross value-added has a positive correlation with the sectoral deviation rate of production value. In the horizontal direction, intermediate demand totals and domestic final demand totals have a low correlation with the production value in their deviation rate. However, a positive correlation exists between net exports and the production value in their deviation rate. Hence, this means that the accuracy of the sectoral output estimation, CT, is extremely important in developing regional IOTs.

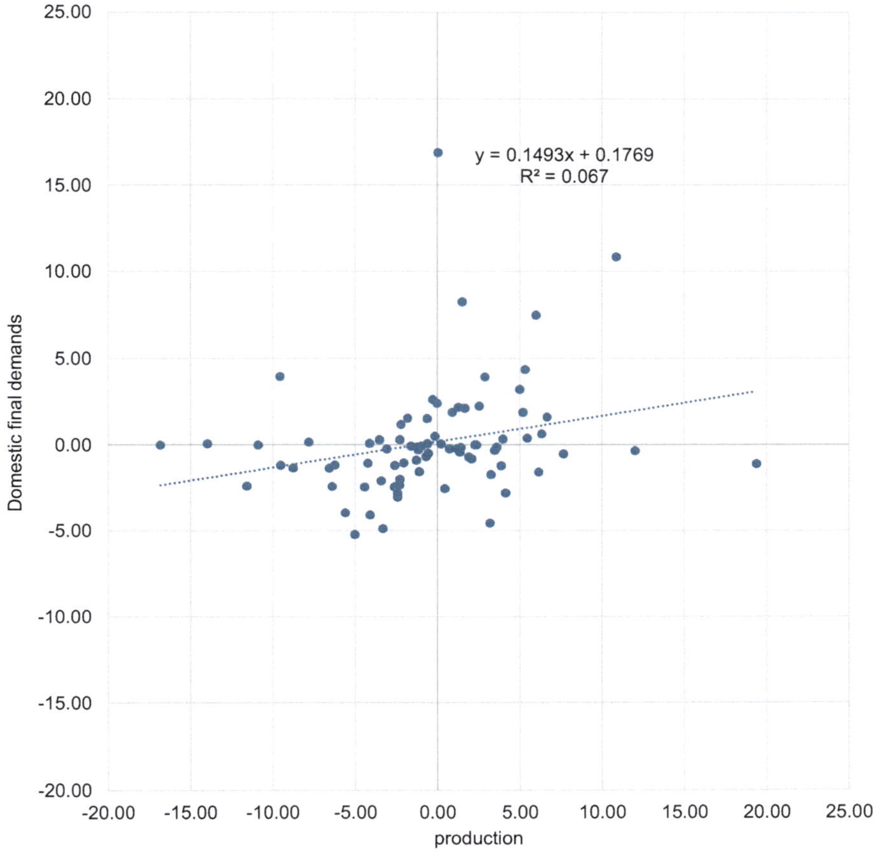


**Fig. 3.8** Deviation rates of production and domestic final demands. *Source* Created by the author

The regional IOT of the METI was consistent with the national IOT and was a highly exact IOT in which not only the production value but also interregional trade were estimated based on primary statistics. However, METI decided not to construct this regional IOT after 2005.

Consequently, prefectural IOTs became more important. The comparative study of the prefectural IOTs and the national IOTs examined in this chapter is important in not only evaluating the accuracy of regional tables but also revealing potential issues.

To improve the accuracy of regional-level IOTs and make them easier to use, there needs to be interaction not only between national and local government statisticians but also between statisticians and their users.

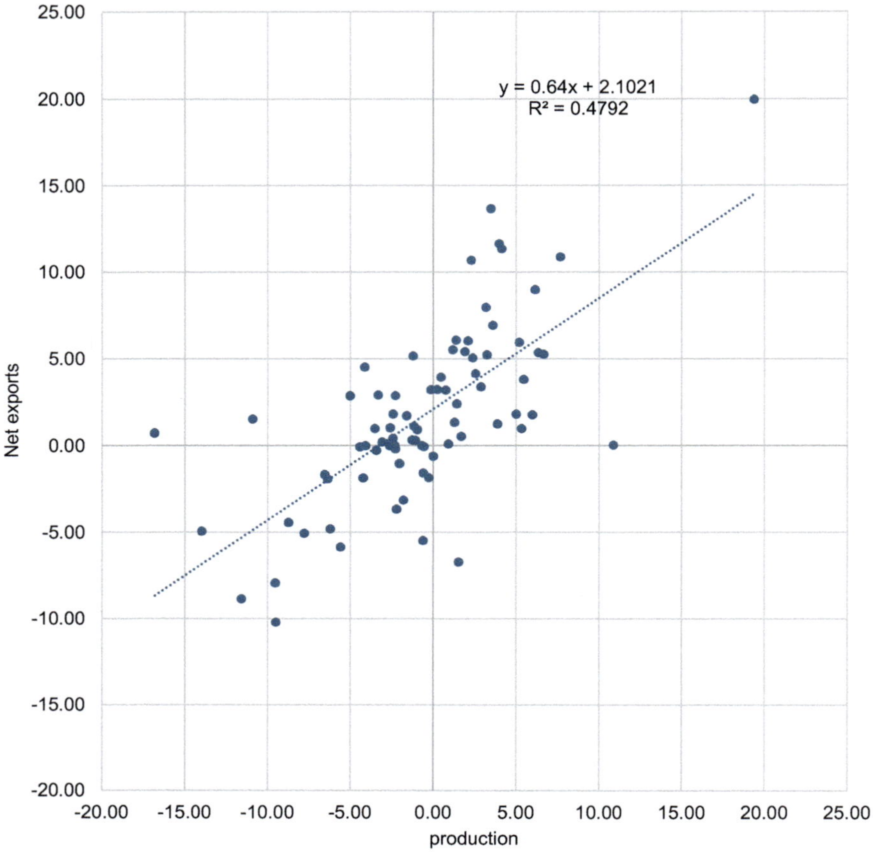


**Fig. 3.9** Deviation rates of production and net exports. *Source* Created by the author

# References


Asahi, Sachiyo, and Mitsuo Yamada. 2008. Comparison and evaluation of regional input-output tables for 2000. *Sango Renkan (Business Journal of PAPAIOS)* 16 (1): 3–16 (in Japanese).

Ohira, Sumihiko, Taiji Yoshida, and Toshihiko Nakagawa. 1997. Evaluation and analysis of the prefectural input-output tables for 1990. *Sango Renkan (Business Journal of PAPAIOS)* 7 (3): 55–64 (in Japanese).

Yamada, Mitsuo. 2011. Comparison and evaluation of regional input-output tables for 2005. *Sango Renkan (Business Journal of PAPAIOS)* 19 (1): 64–79 (in Japanese).

# Chapter 4
# Construction of the Multi-Prefectural Input–Output Table

## 4.1 Introduction

The Chubu Region Institute of Social and Economic Research started with the construction of the Chubu Region Interregional Input–Output Table (2005 Edition) in 2011 covering nine prefectures in the Chubu (central) region,[1] developed various IOTs as IOT (Updated Table 2010 Edition) in 2013 and "Chubu region IOT (Linked Tables 1995–2000–2005)" in 2014, and analyzed the regional structure of the Chubu region and various ripple effects.[2]

Several inter-prefectural IOTs exist that target specific, wide areas based on prefectural IOTs. Kansai Region Input–Output Table (Asia Pacific Institute of Research 2008, 2012), Tohoku Region Input–Output Table for seven prefectures in Tohoku, including Niigata (Tohoku Regional Advancement Center 2011), and an interregional IOT for the three prefectures of Tokai Region (Yamada 2010).

As IOT for 2011 and 2015 in each prefecture was released, we could develop the Chubu region interregional IOTs for each year, which were developed by estimating newly interregional trade coefficients and linking each prefectural IOT with the interregional trade. In this chapter, we summarize the method of creating the IOT and discuss the characteristics of the regional structure that can be seen from the IOT.

Below, in Sect. 4.2, we explain how to create the Chubu region interregional table for 2011 and 2015. Section 4.3 discusses the interregional/sectoral dependencies in terms of the average spillover length, and Sect. 4.4 concludes.

---

[1] The nine prefectures in the Chubu region—Toyama, Ishikawa, Fukui, Nagano, Gifu, Shizuoka, Aichi, Mie, and Siga—are defined by the Chubu Area Development and Improvement Act (1966).

[2] Ihara et al. (2015) introduced the method to construct the Chubu Region interregional IOT.



M. Yamada, *Multi-Regional Input–Output Analysis of the Japanese Economy*,
https://doi.org/10.1007/978-981-97-9041-8_4

## 4.2 Estimation Method for the Chubu Region Interregional Input–Output Tables

### 4.2.1 *Estimation of Interregional Input–Output Tables*

Figure 4.1 depicts the procedure for constructing the Chubu region interregional IOT. First, while considering regional characteristics and the sector definitions in the available prefecture IOTs, we define the common sector definitions and concepts and convert each prefecture's IOTs into such a common format. Second, we estimate the interregional trade matrix within and outside the Chubu region according to the defined common sectors. The third is to develop a single interregional IOT using the interregional trade matrix and the IOT of each prefecture.

First, we describe the definition of the common sector. The definition of sectors in each prefecture's IOT differs in the size of the classification. The actual sector definition may differ even if the number of sectors is the same. Therefore, comparing the sector definitions of each prefecture to decide the number of sectors and their correspondence as common sectors is necessary. Additionally, although the monetary unit of the released IOTs is roughly the same as the National Basic Tables, which is 1 million yen, it may be different in some prefectures, such as 10,000 yen; therefore, it is necessary to adjust the unit as well.

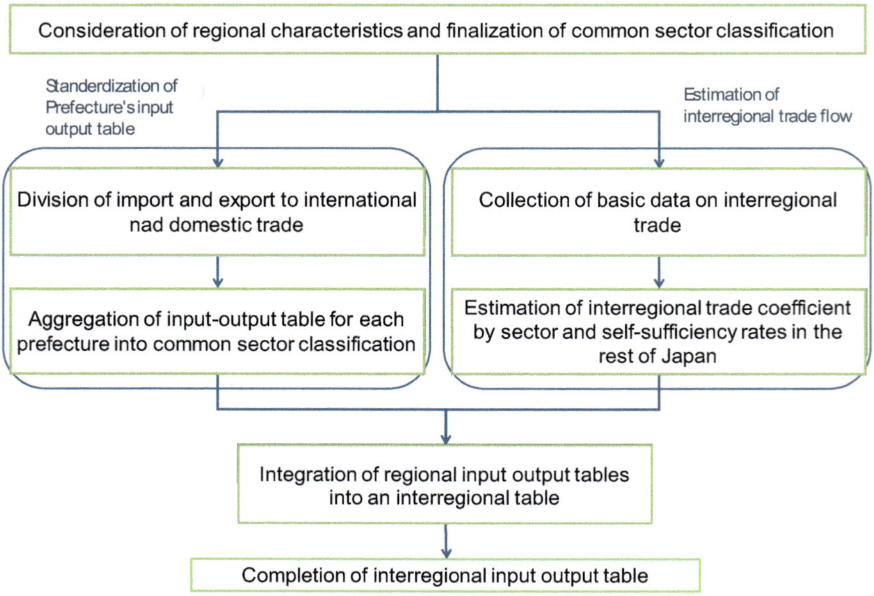


**Fig. 4.1** Procedure for creating the Chubu region interregional IOT. *Source* Based on Fig. 2 by Ihara et al. (2015) with partial modification

Table 4.1 presents the characteristics of nine prefectures' IOT in the Chubu region. The size of the 2011 IOTs obtained was approximately 190 sectors. After comparing these sector definitions and the sector definitions in the 2005 Chubu region IOTs, we decided to adopt 108 sectors, as depicted in Table 4.2, which correspond roughly to the integrated middle classifications of the national table. However, our definition of 108 sectors differs from that of the national table of 108 sectors in the following ways:

We integrated two sectors of "Chemical fertilizers" and "Inorganic chemical products" and two of "Iron and steel/crude steel" and "Steel materials" as one sector, respectively. We also separated one sector of "Other transport machinery/repair" into two sectors of "Railway vehicles/repair" and "Aircraft/aircraft," and a sector of "commerce" into two of "wholesale" and "retail." In addition, we adjusted the

**Table 4.1** Characteristics of 2011 IOT for nine prefectures in the Chubu region

| Prefecture | No. of Sectors | Unit | Separation of trade, international and domestic | Self-transport | Social capital depreciation | Iron scrap and non-ferrous scrap |
|---|---|---|---|---|---|---|
| 1. Toyama | 190 | Million yen | No | Yes | Yes | Yes |
| 2. Ishikawa | 190 | Ten thousand yen | No | Yes | Yes | Yes |
| 3. Fukui[a] | 161 | Ten thousand yen | Yes | Yes | Yes | Yes |
| 4. Nagano | 190 | Million yen | Yes | Yes | Yes | Yes |
| 5. Gifu | 190 | Million yen | Yes | Yes | Yes | Yes |
| 6. Shizuoka | 190 | Million yen | Yes | Yes | Yes | Yes |
| 7. Aichi | 188 | Million yen | Yes | Yes | Yes | Yes |
| 8. Mie | 188 | Million yen | Yes | No | Yes | Yes |
| 9. Shiga[a] | 190 | Million yen | Yes | Yes | Yes | Yes |
| 10. ROJ | – | – | – | – | – | – |
| 11. Japan | 190 | Million yen | Yes | Yes | Yes | Yes |
| 12. Chubu region IO | 108 | Million yen | Yes | No | No | Exogenous |

[a] Obtained detailed tables from each prefecture

*Source* Created by the author

**Table 4.2** Definition of 2011 the Chubu region interregional input–output table

| National input output table | | | Chubu region input output table | | | |
|---|---|---|---|---|---|---|
| Middle classification (108 sectors) | | | 108 Sectors | | 40 Sectors | |
| No. | Code | Sector name | Code | Sector name | Code | Sector name |
| 1 | 011 | Crop cultivation | 01 | Crop cultivation | 1 | Agriculture, forestry and fishery |
| 2 | 012 | Livestock | 02 | Livestock | | |
| 3 | 013 | Agricultural services | 03 | Agricultural services | | |
| 4 | 015 | Forestry | 04 | Forestry | | |
| 5 | 017 | Fishery | 05 | Fishery | | |
| 6 | 061 | Metallic ores | 06 | Metallic ores | 2 | Mining |
| 7 | 062 | Coal mining, crude petroleum and natural gas | 07 | Coal mining, crude petroleum and natural gas | | |
| 8 | 063 | Non-metallic ores | 08 | Non-metallic ores | | |
| 9 | 111 | Foods | 09 | Foods | 3 | Beverages and Foods |
| 10 | 112 | Beverage | 10 | Beverage | | |
| 11 | 113 | Feeds and organic fertilizer, n.e.c. | 11 | Feeds and organic fertilizer, n.e.c. | | |
| 12 | 114 | Tobacco | 12 | Tobacco | | |
| 13 | 151 | Textile products | 13 | Textile products | 4 | Textile products |
| 14 | 152 | Wearing apparel and miscellaneous ready-made textile products | 14 | Wearing apparel and miscellaneous ready-made textile products | | |
| 15 | 161 | Lumber and wood products | 15 | Lumber and wood products | 5 | Pulp, paper and wooden products |
| 16 | 162 | Furniture and fixtures | 16 | Furniture and fixtures | | |
| 17 | 163 | Pulp, paper, paperboard and building paper | 17 | Pulp, paper, paperboard and building paper | | |
| 18 | 164 | Paper products | 18 | Paper products | | |
| 19 | 191 | Printing, plate making and book binding | 19 | Printing, plate making and book binding | 17 | Miscellaneous manufacturing products |
| **20** | **201** | **Chemical fertilizer** | **20** | **Chemical fertilizer, and industrial inorganic chemicals** | 6 | Chemical products |
| **21** | **202** | **Industrial inorganic chemicals** | | | | |
| 22 | 203 | Petrochemical basic products | 21 | Petrochemical basic products | | |

(continued)

**Table 4.2** (continued)

| National input output table | | | Chubu region input output table | | | |
|---|---|---|---|---|---|---|
| Middle classification (108 sectors) | | | 108 Sectors | | 40 Sectors | |
| No. | Code | Sector name | Code | Sector name | Code | Sector name |
| 23 | 204 | Organic chemical products (except petrochemical basic products) | 22 | Organic chemical products (except petrochemical basic products) | | |
| 24 | 205 | Synthetic resins | 23 | Synthetic resins | | |
| 25 | 206 | Synthetic fibers | 24 | Synthetic fibers | | |
| 26 | 207 | Medicaments | 25 | Medicaments | | |
| 27 | 208 | Final chemical products (except medicaments) | 26 | Final chemical products (except medicaments) | | |
| 28 | 211 | Petroleum refinery products | 27 | Petroleum refinery products | 7 | Petroleum and coal products |
| 29 | 212 | Coal products | 28 | Coal products | | |
| 30 | 221 | Plastic products | 29 | Plastic products | 17 | Miscellaneous manufacturing products |
| 31 | 222 | Rubber products | 30 | Rubber products | | |
| 32 | 231 | Leather, fur skins and miscellaneous leather products | 31 | Leather, fur skins and miscellaneous leather products | | |
| 33 | 251 | Glass and glass products | 32 | Glass and glass products | 8 | Ceramic, stone and clay products |
| 34 | 252 | Cement and cement products | 33 | Cement and cement products | | |
| 35 | 253 | Pottery, china and earthenware | 34 | Pottery, china and earthenware | | |
| 36 | 259 | Miscellaneous ceramic, stone and clay products | 35 | Miscellaneous ceramic, stone and clay products | | |
| **37** | **261** | **Pig iron and crude steel** | **36** | **Pig iron, crude steel, and steel products** | **9** | Iron and steel |
| **38** | **262** | **Steel products** | | | | |
| 39 | 263 | Cast and forged steel products | 37 | Cast and forged steel products | | |
| 40 | 269 | Miscellaneous iron or steel products | 38 | Miscellaneous iron or steel products | | |
| 41 | 271 | Non-ferrous metals | 39 | Non-ferrous metals | 10 | Non-ferrous metals |

(continued)

**Table 4.2** (continued)

| National input output table | | | Chubu region input output table | | | |
|---|---|---|---|---|---|---|
| Middle classification (108 sectors) | | | 108 Sectors | | 40 Sectors | |
| No. | Code | Sector name | Code | Sector name | Code | Sector name |
| 42 | 272 | Non-ferrous metal products | 40 | Non-ferrous metal products | | |
| 43 | 281 | Metal products for construction and architecture | 41 | Metal products for construction and architecture | 11 | Metal products |
| 44 | 289 | Miscellaneous metal products | 42 | Miscellaneous metal products | | |
| 45 | 291 | General-purpose machinery | 43 | General-purpose machinery | 12 | General-purpose machinery, and production machinery |
| 46 | 301 | Production machinery | 44 | Production machinery | | |
| 47 | 311 | Business oriented machinery | 45 | Business oriented machinery | | |
| 48 | 321 | Electronic devices | 46 | Electronic devices | 13 | Electronic components |
| 49 | 329 | Miscellaneous electronic components | 47 | Miscellaneous electronic components | | |
| 50 | 331 | Electrical devices and parts | 48 | Electrical devices and parts | 14 | Electrical machinery |
| 51 | 332 | Household electric appliances | 49 | Household electric appliances | | |
| 52 | 333 | Applied electronic equipment and electric measuring instruments | 50 | Applied electronic equipment and electric measuring instruments | | |
| 53 | 339 | Miscellaneous electrical machinery | 51 | Miscellaneous electrical machinery | | |
| 54 | 341 | Household electronics equipment | 52 | Household electronics equipment | 15 | Information and communication electronics equipment |
| 55 | 342 | Electronic computing equipment and accessory equipment of electronic computing equipment | 53 | Electronic computing equipment and accessory equipment of electronic computing equipment | | |

(continued)

**Table 4.2** (continued)

| National input output table | | | Chubu region input output table | | | |
|---|---|---|---|---|---|---|
| Middle classification (108 sectors) | | | 108 Sectors | | 40 Sectors | |
| No. | Code | Sector name | Code | Sector name | Code | Sector name |
| 56 | 351 | Passenger motor cars | 54 | Passenger motor cars | 16 | Transportation equipment |
| 57 | 352 | Miscellaneous cars | 55 | Miscellaneous cars | | |
| 58 | 353 | Motor vehicle parts and accessories | 56 | Motor vehicle parts and accessories | | |
| 59 | 354 | Ships and repair of ships | 57 | Ships and repair of ships | | |
| *60* | *359* | *Miscellaneous transportation equipment and repair of transportation equipment* | *58* | *Rolling stock and repair of rolling stock* | | |
| | | | *59* | *Aircrafts and repair of air crafts* | | |
| | | | *60* | *Miscellaneous transport equipment* | | |
| 61 | 391 | Miscellaneous manufacturing products | 61 | Miscellaneous manufacturing products | 17 | Miscellaneous manufacturing products |
| 62 | 392 | Reuse and recycling | 62 | Reuse and recycling | | |
| 63 | 411 | Building construction | 63 | Building construction | 18 | Construction |
| 64 | 412 | Repair of construction | 64 | Repair of construction | | |
| 65 | 413 | Public construction | 65 | Public construction | | |
| 66 | 419 | Miscellaneous civil engineering and construction | 66 | Miscellaneous civil engineering and construction | | |
| 67 | 461 | Electricity | 67 | Electricity | 19 | Electricity, gas and heat supply |
| 68 | 462 | Gas and heat supply | 68 | Gas and heat supply | | |
| 69 | 471 | Water supply | 69 | Water supply | 20 | Water supply, and waste management service |
| 70 | 481 | Waste management service | 70 | Waste management service | | |
| *71* | *511* | *Commerce* | *71* | *Wholesale trade* | *21* | *Commerce* |

(continued)

**Table 4.2** (continued)

| National input output table | | | Chubu region input output table | | | |
|---|---|---|---|---|---|---|
| Middle classification (108 sectors) | | | 108 Sectors | | 40 Sectors | |
| No. | Code | Sector name | Code | Sector name | Code | Sector name |
| | | | *72* | *Retail trade* | | |
| 72 | 531 | Finance and insurance | 73 | Finance and insurance | 22 | Finance and insurance |
| 73 | 551 | Real estate agencies and rental services | 74 | Real estate agencies and rental services | 23 | Real estate |
| 74 | 552 | House rent | 75 | House rent | | |
| 75 | 553 | House rent (imputed house rent) | 76 | House rent (imputed house rent) | | |
| 76 | 571 | Railway transport | 77 | Railway transport | 24 | Railway transport |
| 77 | 572 | Road transport (except self-transport) | 78 | Road transport (except self-transport) | 25 | Road Transport |
| 78 | 573 | Self-transport | – | – | | |
| 79 | 574 | Water transport | 79 | Water transport | 26 | Water transport |
| 80 | 575 | Air transport | 80 | Air transport | 27 | Air transport |
| 81 | 576 | Freight forwarding | 81 | Freight forwarding | 28 | Other stansport service |
| 82 | 577 | Storage facility service | 82 | Storage facility service | | |
| 83 | 578 | Services relating to transport | 83 | Services relating to transport | | |
| 84 | 579 | Postal services and mail delivery | 84 | Postal services and mail delivery | | |
| 85 | 591 | Communications | 85 | Communications | 29 | Information and communications |
| 86 | 592 | Broadcasting | 86 | Broadcasting | | |
| 87 | 593 | Information services | 87 | Information services | | |
| 88 | 594 | Internet based services | 88 | Internet based services | | |
| 89 | 595 | Image information, sound information and character information production | 89 | Image information, sound information and character information production | | |

(continued)

**Table 4.2** (continued)

| National input output table | | | Chubu region input output table | | | |
|---|---|---|---|---|---|---|
| Middle classification (108 sectors) | | | 108 Sectors | | 40 Sectors | |
| No. | Code | Sector name | Code | Sector name | Code | Sector name |
| 90 | 611 | Public administration | 90 | Public administration | 30 | Public administration |
| 91 | 631 | Education | 91 | Education | 31 | Education and research |
| 92 | 632 | Research | 92 | Research | | |
| 93 | 641 | Medical service | 93 | Medical service | 32 | Medical, health care and welfare |
| 94 | 642 | Health and hygiene | 94 | Health and hygiene | | |
| 95 | 643 | Social insurance and social welfare | 95 | Social insurance and social welfare | | |
| 96 | 644 | Nursing care | 96 | Nursing care | | |
| 97 | 659 | Miscellaneous non-profit services | 97 | Miscellaneous non-profit services | 33 | Miscellaneous non-profit services |
| 98 | 661 | Goods rental and leasing services | 98 | Goods rental and leasing services | 34 | Business services |
| 99 | 662 | Advertising services | 99 | Advertising services | | |
| 100 | 663 | Motor vehicle maintenance and machine repair services | 100 | Motor vehicle maintenance and machine repair services | | |
| 101 | 669 | Miscellaneous business services | 101 | Miscellaneous business services | | |
| 102 | 671 | Hotels | 102 | Hotels | 35 | Hotels |
| 103 | 672 | Eating and drinking services | 103 | Eating and drinking services | 36 | Eating and drinking services |
| 104 | 673 | Cleaning, barber shops, beauty shops and public baths | 104 | Cleaning, barber shops, beauty shops and public baths | 38 | Miscellaneous personal services |
| 105 | 674 | Amusement and recreational services | 105 | Amusement and recreational services | 37 | Amusement and recreational services |
| 106 | 679 | Miscellaneous personal services | 106 | Miscellaneous personal services | 38 | Miscellaneous personal services |
| 107 | 681 | Office supplies | 107 | Office supplies | 39 | Office supplies |

(continued)

**Table 4.2** (continued)

| National input output table | | | Chubu region input output table | | | |
|---|---|---|---|---|---|---|
| Middle classification (108 sectors) | | | 108 Sectors | | 40 Sectors | |
| No. | Code | Sector name | Code | Sector name | Code | Sector name |
| 108 | 691 | Activities not elsewhere classified | 108 | Activities not elsewhere classified | 40 | Activities not elsewhere classified |
| 109 | 700 | Total of intermediate sectors | 109 | Total of intermediate sectors | 41 | Total of intermediate sectorsn |

*Source* Created by the author

input values of "self-transportation" to be returned to the input of their respective sectors. Furthermore, the sectors of "iron scrap" and "non-ferrous metal scrap" were set as exogenous sources, and we omitted the values of the sectors in "social capital depletion" in the value-added sector and the final demand sector.

As exports and imports are not separated into two sectors of international and domestic trade in Toyama and Ishikawa's IOTs, we estimated exports (imports) by multiplying the corresponding nationwide sectoral export/production ratios (sectoral import coefficients) by the value of production (domestic total demand) in the original IOT and subtracted it from the total exports (imports) to obtain the domestic exports (imports). After the estimation, we integrated them into 108 sectors, which is a common sector classification.

The IOT for "The ROJ" region was obtained by subtracting the table values for the nine prefectures in the Chubu region from the 108-sector national table corresponding to the common sector.[3]

### 4.2.2 *Estimation of the Interregional Trade Flow*

Next, we discuss the estimation of interregional trade by sector. There are two sets of information from the METI's Commodity Distribution Survey and the MLIT's Survey of Net Cargo Flow in Japan to estimate interregional trade flows in each sector. The commodity distribution survey provides the "regional composition ratio by consumption area" and "composition ratio by sales destination industry" by 46 sectors of the manufacturing sectors for nine regions nationwide defined by the METI. On the contrary, the Survey of Net Cargo Flow in Japan provides the volume of trade between 47 prefectures for nine categories and 85 items on a physical volume basis. Here, we used data from the Survey of net cargo flow in Japan, which provides more detailed trade information between nine prefectures in the Chubu region.

[3] It is necessary to estimate the domestic exports and imports in the "The rest of Japan" IOT separately.

Corresponding the basic classification sector of the 2011 National IOT to the 85-sector classification of the logistics census, we estimated the inter-prefectural trade value (value basis) by sector by taking the weighted sum of the inter-prefectural trade volume (based on physical quantity) with the weight of the corresponding production value of national data. Then we aggregated it for the nine prefectures in the Chubu region and the ROJ to obtain a value for the inter-prefectural trade matrix for the Chubu region. However, as this amount of trade is not consistent with the exports and imports of each prefecture's IOT, the RAS method is used to estimate the amount of trade that is consistent with these imports and exports.

Inter-prefectural trade in a certain sector is expressed as depicted in Table 4.3. Here, we set the value of trade from prefecture $i$ to prefecture $j$ as $T_{ij}$, the domestic export of prefecture $i$ as $E_i$, and the domestic import of prefecture $j$ as $M_j$ then we obtain $\sum_{j=1}^{10} T_{ij} = E_i$, and $\sum_{i=1}^{10} T_{ij} = M_j$. As the sum of the domestic exports equals that of the domestic imports, then $\sum_{i=1}^{10} \sum_{j=1}^{10} T_{ij} = \sum_{i=1}^{10} E_i = \sum_{j=1}^{10} M_j$.

Though we are able to obtain the value of the domestic export and import from each IOT, the domestic export and import in the "ROJ" region, $E_{10}$ and $M_{10}$, were not obtained by subtracting the corresponding values of nine prefectures from that of the national table. However, with the domestic total demand $D_{10}$ and the self-sufficiency rate $\tau_{10}$, we are able to obtain domestic imports in the "ROJ" region from $M_{10} = (1 - \tau_{10})(D_{10} - M_{10}^W)$, where $X_{10}$ is the production, $E_{10}^W$ presents the international export, and $M_{10}^W$ the international import. The domestic export is reduced as $E_{10} = \sum_{j=1}^{10} M_j - \sum_{i=1}^{9} E_i$.

The self-sufficiency rate $\tau_{10}$ is obtained from the estimated trade values of the Chubu Region, including the trade within each prefecture. However, some of them do not satisfy the following condition:

$$\sum_{i=1}^{9} E_i - M_{10} = \sum_{j=1}^{9} M_j - E_{10} \geq 0.$$

In such cases, we adjust the rate to meet the condition. Table 4.4 shows the initial value for the RAS estimation of the trade matrix by sector and the self-sufficiency rates that are used.

Finally, IOTs with common sectors for each prefecture and interregional trade matrices by sector are used to integrate into a single regional IOT of the Chubu Region.

### *4.2.3 Employment Table Estimates*

The employment tables for the nine prefectures in the Chubu region are released at the middle classification level; therefore, we can basically use these values as they are. However, as there are differences between the 108 sectors defined as our common

**Table 4.3** The inter-prefectural trade flow by sector

| From \To | 1: Toyama | 2: Ishikawa | 3: Fukui | 4: Nagano | 5: Gifu | 6: Shizuoka | 7: Aichi | 8: Mie | 9:Shiga | 10: The rest of Japan | Domestic exports, total |
|---|---|---|---|---|---|---|---|---|---|---|---|
| 1: Toyama | – | $T_{1,2}$ | $T_{1,3}$ | $T_{1,4}$ | $T_{1,5}$ | $T_{1,6}$ | $T_{1,7}$ | $T_{1,8}$ | $T_{1,9}$ | $T_{1,10}$ | $E_1$ |
| 2: Ishikawa | $T_{2,1}$ | – | $T_{2,3}$ | $T_{2,4}$ | $T_{2,5}$ | $T_{2,6}$ | $T_{2,7}$ | $T_{2,8}$ | $T_{2,9}$ | $T_{2,10}$ | $E_2$ |
| 3: Fukui | $T_{3,1}$ | $T_{3,2}$ | – | $T_{3,4}$ | $T_{3,5}$ | $T_{3,6}$ | $T_{3,7}$ | $T_{3,8}$ | $T_{3,9}$ | $T_{3,10}$ | $E_3$ |
| 4: Nagano | $T_{4,1}$ | $T_{4,2}$ | $T_{4,3}$ | – | $T_{4,5}$ | $T_{4,6}$ | $T_{4,7}$ | $T_{4,8}$ | $T_{4,9}$ | $T_{4,10}$ | $E_4$ |
| 5: Gifu | $T_{5,1}$ | $T_{5,2}$ | $T_{5,3}$ | $T_{5,4}$ | – | $T_{5,6}$ | $T_{5,7}$ | $T_{5,8}$ | $T_{5,9}$ | $T_{5,10}$ | $E_5$ |
| 6: Shizuoka | $T_{6,1}$ | $T_{6,2}$ | $T_{6,3}$ | $T_{6,4}$ | $T_{6,5}$ | – | $T_{6,7}$ | $T_{6,8}$ | $T_{6,9}$ | $T_{6,10}$ | $E_6$ |
| 7: Aichi | $T_{7,1}$ | $T_{7,2}$ | $T_{7,3}$ | $T_{7,4}$ | $T_{7,5}$ | $T_{7,6}$ | – | $T_{7,8}$ | $T_{7,9}$ | $T_{7,10}$ | $E_7$ |
| 8: Mie | $T_{8,1}$ | $T_{8,2}$ | $T_{8,3}$ | $T_{8,4}$ | $T_{8,5}$ | $T_{8,6}$ | $T_{8,7}$ | – | $T_{8,9}$ | $T_{8,10}$ | $E_8$ |
| 9: Shiga | $T_{9,1}$ | $T_{9,2}$ | $T_{9,3}$ | $T_{9,4}$ | $T_{9,5}$ | $T_{9,6}$ | $T_{9,7}$ | $T_{9,8}$ | – | $T_{9,10}$ | $E_9$ |
| 10: The rest of Japan | $T_{10,1}$ | $T_{10,2}$ | $T_{10,3}$ | $T_{10,4}$ | $T_{10,5}$ | $T_{10,6}$ | $T_{10,7}$ | $T_{10,8}$ | $T_{10,9}$ | – | $E_{10}$ |
| Domestic imports, total | $M_1$ | $M_2$ | $M_3$ | $M_4$ | $M_5$ | $M_6$ | $M_7$ | $M_8$ | $M_9$ | $M_{10}$ | - |

*Source* Created by the author

**Table 4.4** Initial value and self-sufficiency rate for RAS estimation of each sectoral trade

| Code | Sector name | Information for initial values of RAS | Self-sufficiency rate |
|---|---|---|---|
| 01 | Crop cultivation | 2010 Net freight Flow Census | 0.979 |
| 02 | Livestock | 2010 Net freight Flow Census | 0.984 |
| 03 | Agricultural services | Demand and supply ratio | 0.990 |
| 04 | Forestry | 2010 Net freight Flow Census | 0.993 |
| 05 | Fishery | 2010 Net freight Flow Census | 0.963 |
| 06 | Metallic ores | 2010 Net freight Flow Census | 1.000 |
| 07 | Coal mining, crude petroleum and natural gas | 2010 Net freight Flow Census | 1.000 |
| 08 | Non-metallic ores | 2010 Net freight Flow Census | 0.996 |
| 09 | Foods | 2010 Net freight Flow Census | 0.905 |
| 10 | Beverage | 2010 Net freight Flow Census | 0.906 |
| 11 | Feeds and organic fertilizer, n.e.c | 2010 Net freight Flow Census | 0.930 |
| 12 | Tobacco | 2010 Net freight Flow Census | 0.800 |
| 13 | Textile products | 2010 Net freight Flow Census | 0.500 |
| 14 | Wearing apparel and miscellaneous ready-made textile products | 2010 Net freight Flow Census | 0.910 |
| 15 | Lumber and wood products | 2010 Net freight Flow Census | 0.941 |
| 16 | Furniture and fixtures | 2010 Net freight Flow Census | 0.704 |
| 17 | Pulp, paper, paperboard and building paper | 2010 Net freight Flow Census | 0.848 |
| 18 | Paper products | 2010 Net freight Flow Census | 0.839 |
| 19 | Printing, plate making and book binding | 2010 Net freight Flow Census | 0.954 |
| 20 | Chemical fertilizer, and industrial inorganic chemicals | 2010 Net freight Flow Census | 0.975 |
| 21 | Petrochemical basic products | 2010 Net freight Flow Census | 0.988 |

(continued)

**Table 4.4** (continued)

| Code | Sector name | Information for initial values of RAS | Self-sufficiency rate |
|---|---|---|---|
| 22 | Organic chemical products (except petrochemical basic products) | 2010 Net freight Flow Census | 0.880 |
| 23 | Synthetic resins | 2010 Net freight Flow Census | 0.880 |
| 24 | Synthetic fibers | 2010 Net freight Flow Census | 0.700 |
| 25 | Medicaments | 2010 Net freight Flow Census | 0.700 |
| 26 | Final chemical products (except medicaments) | 2010 Net freight Flow Census | 0.889 |
| 27 | Petroleum refinery products | 2010 Net freight Flow Census | 0.981 |
| 28 | Coal products | 2010 Net freight Flow Census | 0.960 |
| 29 | Plastic products | 2010 Net freight Flow Census | 0.800 |
| 30 | Rubber products | 2010 Net freight Flow Census | 0.800 |
| 31 | Leather, fur skins and miscellaneous leather products | 2010 Net freight Flow Census | 0.990 |
| 32 | Glass and glass products | 2010 Net freight Flow Census | 0.712 |
| 33 | Cement and cement products | 2010 Net freight Flow Census | 0.960 |
| 34 | Pottery, china and earthenware | 2010 Net freight Flow Census | 0.450 |
| 35 | Miscellaneous ceramic, stone and clay products | 2010 Net freight Flow Census | 0.700 |
| 36 | Pig iron, crude steel, and steel products | 2010 Net freight Flow Census | 0.953 |
| 37 | Cast and forged steel products | 2010 Net freight Flow Census | 0.900 |
| 38 | Miscellaneous iron or steel products | 2010 Net freight Flow Census | 0.953 |
| 39 | Non-ferrous metals | 2010 Net freight Flow Census | 0.990 |
| 40 | Non-ferrous metal products | 2010 Net freight Flow Census | 0.862 |
| 41 | Metal products for construction and architecture | 2010 Net freight Flow Census | 0.800 |
| 42 | Miscellaneous metal products | 2010 Net freight Flow Census | 0.934 |

(continued)

**Table 4.4** (continued)

| Code | Sector name | Information for initial values of RAS | Self-sufficiency rate |
|---|---|---|---|
| 43 | General-purpose machinery | 2010 Net freight Flow Census | 0.847 |
| 44 | Production machinery | 2010 Net freight Flow Census | 0.847 |
| 45 | Business oriented machinery | 2010 Net freight Flow Census | 0.800 |
| 46 | Electronic devices | 2010 Net freight Flow Census | 0.750 |
| 47 | Miscellaneous electronic components | 2010 Net freight Flow Census | 0.833 |
| 48 | Electrical devices and parts | 2010 Net freight Flow Census | 0.833 |
| 49 | Household electric appliances | 2010 Net freight Flow Census | 0.500 |
| 50 | Applied electronic equipment and electric measuring instruments | 2010 Net freight Flow Census | 0.833 |
| 51 | Miscellaneous electrical machinery | 2010 Net freight Flow Census | 0.833 |
| 52 | Household electronics equipment | 2010 Net freight Flow Census | 0.900 |
| 53 | Electronic computing equipment and accessory equipment of electronic computing equipment | 2010 Net freight Flow Census | 0.833 |
| 54 | Passenger motor cars | 2010 Net freight Flow Census | 0.600 |
| 55 | Miscellaneous cars | 2010 Net freight Flow Census | 0.700 |
| 56 | Motor vehicle parts and accessories | 2010 Net freight Flow Census | 0.846 |
| 57 | Ships and repair of ships | 2010 Net freight Flow Census | 0.861 |
| 58 | Rolling stock and repair of rolling stock | 2010 Net freight Flow Census | 0.960 |
| 59 | Aircrafts and repair of air crafts | 2010 Net freight Flow Census | 0.700 |
| 60 | Miscellaneous transport equipment | 2010 Net freight Flow Census | 0.700 |
| 61 | Miscellaneous manufacturing products | 2010 Net freight Flow Census | 0.800 |
| 62 | Reuse and recycling | Demand and supply ratio | 0.980 |
| 63 | Building construction | – | 1.000 |

(continued)

**Table 4.4** (continued)

| Code | Sector name | Information for initial values of RAS | Self-sufficiency rate |
|---|---|---|---|
| 64 | Repair of construction | – | 1.000 |
| 65 | Public construction | – | 1.000 |
| 66 | Miscellaneous civil engineering and construction | – | 1.000 |
| 67 | Electricity | Demand and supply ratio | 0.960 |
| 68 | Gas and heat supply | Demand and supply ratio | 0.990 |
| 69 | Water supply | – | 1.000 |
| 70 | Waste management service | Demand and supply ratio | 0.970 |
| 71 | Wholesale trade | Estimated interregional trade in goods sector | 0.990 |
| 72 | Retail trade | Estimated interregional trade in goods sector | 0.980 |
| 73 | Finance and insurance | Demand and supply ratio | 1.000 |
| 74 | Real estate agencies and rental services | Demand and supply ratio | 1.000 |
| 75 | House rent | – | 1.000 |
| 76 | House rent (imputed house rent) | – | 1.000 |
| 77 | Railway transport | 2010 Net freight Flow Census | 0.900 |
| 78 | Road transport (except self-transport) | 2010 Net freight Flow Census | 0.926 |
| 79 | Water transport | 2010 Net freight Flow Census | 0.931 |
| 80 | Air transport | Interregional transportation of domestic air passengers and cargo | 0.999 |
| 81 | Freight forwarding | Interregional trade estimates of transport sectors | 0.980 |
| 82 | Storage facility service | Interregional trade estimates of transport sectors | 0.980 |
| 83 | Services relating to transport | Interregional trade estimates of transport sectors | 0.950 |
| 84 | Postal services and mail delivery | Demand and supply ratio | 0.995 |
| 85 | Communications | Demand and supply ratio | 0.995 |
| 86 | Broadcasting | Demand and supply ratio | 0.995 |
| 87 | Information services | Demand and supply ratio | 0.998 |
| 88 | Internet based services | Demand and supply ratio | 0.999 |
| 89 | Image information, sound information and character information production | Demand and supply ratio | 0.999 |

(continued)

**Table 4.4** (continued)

| Code | Sector name | Information for initial values of RAS | Self-sufficiency rate |
|---|---|---|---|
| 90 | Public administration | – | 1.000 |
| 91 | Education | 2010 population census: Interregional school commuters | 0.995 |
| 92 | Research | Demand and supply ratio | 1.000 |
| 93 | Medical service | 2010 population census: Interregional commuters | 0.998 |
| 94 | Health and hygiene | 2010 population census: Interregional commuters | 1.000 |
| 95 | Social insurance and social welfare | 2010 population census: Interregional commuters | 0.998 |
| 96 | Nursing care | - | 1.000 |
| 97 | Miscellaneous non-profit services | Estimated interregional trade in goods sector | 0.999 |
| 98 | Goods rental and leasing services | Estimated interregional trade in goods sector | 0.999 |
| 99 | Advertising services | Estimated interregional trade in goods sector | 0.999 |
| 100 | Motor vehicle maintenance and machine repair services | Estimated interregional trade in goods sector | 1.000 |
| 101 | Miscellaneous business services | Estimated interregional trade in goods sector | 1.000 |
| 102 | Hotels | Number of domestic overnight travelers between regions | 0.950 |
| 103 | Eating and drinking services | Interregional domestic travel consumption | 0.995 |
| 104 | Cleaning, barber shops, beauty shops and public baths | 2010 population census: Interregional commuters | 0.990 |
| 105 | Amusement and recreational services | 2010 population census: Interregional commuters | 0.998 |
| 106 | Miscellaneous personal services | 2010 population census: Interregional commuters | 0.998 |
| 107 | Office supplies | – | 1.000 |
| 108 | Activities not elsewhere classified | – | 1.000 |
| 109 | Total of intermediate sectors | | – |

*Source* Created by the author

sector classification and the definitions of the middle classification divisions of each prefecture, some modifications are necessary.

For all prefectures, "other transport" is divided into "railway vehicles and repairs," "aircraft and repairs,"[4] and "other transportation machinery," and "commerce" is separated into "wholesale" and "retail." For Fukui Prefecture, "automobiles" is separated into "other automobiles" and "automobile parts and accessories." For Aichi Prefecture, "road transportation" is divided into "road transportation (excluding private transportation)" and "freight forwarding." Regarding the separation of "wholesale" and "retail" sectors, the number of employees in the 2012 Economic Census Activity Survey is used as a proportional division index, and the separation estimation of other sectors is based on the multiplied values of the employment coefficient of the national employment table by the production value of each prefecture. Additionally, in calculating the numbers for the ROJ by the difference between the national employment table and the sum of the nine prefectures' employment tables, negative values were obtained in some sectors, which were corrected for consistency.[5]

## 4.3 Comparison of Regional Structures

### *4.3.1 Comparative Advantage in Production and Employment*

The 2011 Chubu region interregional IOT has 108 sectors in each of the nine prefectures and 1080 sectors in total, including the "ROJ" region. Here, to compare the regional structure of the nine prefectures in the Chubu region, we pick up comparative advantage indicators for production and employment by sector to examine their characteristics.

Table 4.5 depicts the comparative advantage index of production by sector for each prefecture after integrating the values of the 108 sectors into those of the 40 sectors. The values exceeding 2 or those less than 0.5 are shown in bold and italics, respectively.[6]

As for manufacturing, Toyama Prefecture is highly competitive in non-ferrous metals, metal products, chemical products, and electronic components. Ishikawa Prefecture is highly competitive in textile products, electronic components, general machinery, and information and communication electronics equipment. Fukui Prefecture has competitiveness in textile products, electronic components, and non-ferrous metals. Nagano Prefecture has electronic components as well as information and communication electronics equipment; wooden products, electrical machinery,

---

[4] For Aichi Prefecture, "aircraft and repairs" is listed separately.

[5] These are values for self-employed and family employees, and values that are not consistent with the national values are set at 0.

[6] Here, we have given a value close to the 100th quantile, which corresponds to approximately 10–15% of the top and bottom, respectively.

**Table 4.5** Comparative advantages of production value

| Sector name | | Toyama | Ishikawa | Fukui | Nagano | Gifu | Shizuoka | Aichi | Mie | Shiga | ROJ | Total |
|---|---|---|---|---|---|---|---|---|---|---|---|---|
| 1 | Agriculture, forestry and fishery | 0.88 | 0.87 | 0.86 | 1.61 | 0.87 | 0.69 | *0.41* | 0.80 | 0.52 | 1.08 | 1.00 |
| 2 | Mining | **3.50** | 0.81 | 0.99 | 1.77 | 1.31 | 0.73 | *0.29* | 0.85 | 0.69 | 1.04 | 1.00 |
| 3 | Beverages and foods | 0.61 | 0.61 | *0.38* | 1.45 | 0.78 | **2.11** | 0.72 | 0.76 | 0.83 | 1.00 | 1.00 |
| 4 | Textile products | 1.50 | **4.11** | **10.64** | 0.51 | **3.29** | 0.64 | 1.22 | *0.49* | **2.95** | 0.83 | 1.00 |
| 5 | Pulp, paper and wooden products | 1.88 | 1.07 | 1.13 | 0.77 | **2.32** | **2.99** | 0.76 | 0.69 | 1.33 | 0.91 | 1.00 |
| 6 | Chemical products | **2.70** | 0.59 | 1.83 | *0.47* | 0.84 | 1.20 | 0.52 | **2.27** | 1.49 | 0.99 | 1.00 |
| 7 | Petroleum and coal products | *0.03* | *0.03* | *0.03* | *0.05* | *0.04* | *0.04* | 0.59 | **2.42** | *0.03* | 1.13 | 1.00 |
| 8 | Ceramic, stone and clay products | 1.37 | 0.93 | 1.44 | 1.57 | **3.56** | 0.75 | 1.34 | **2.04** | **6.64** | 0.80 | 1.00 |
| 9 | Iron and steel | 0.75 | *0.16* | *0.10* | *0.09* | *0.39* | *0.16* | 1.61 | *0.12* | *0.25* | 1.06 | 1.00 |
| 10 | Non-ferrous metals | **5.40** | 0.52 | **2.36** | 0.63 | 0.87 | 1.06 | 0.89 | **2.52** | 0.98 | 0.92 | 1.00 |
| 11 | Metal products | **2.98** | 1.08 | 1.02 | 1.81 | **2.71** | 1.17 | 1.20 | 1.29 | **2.18** | 0.88 | 1.00 |
| 12 | General-purpose machinery, and production machinery | 2.00 | **2.68** | 0.52 | 1.87 | 1.75 | 1.35 | 1.35 | 1.20 | **3.10** | 0.86 | 1.00 |
| 13 | Electronic components | **2.65** | **3.58** | **3.80** | **3.31** | 1.10 | *0.42* | 0.82 | **7.01** | **2.00** | 0.77 | 1.00 |

(continued)

**Table 4.5** (continued)

| Sector name | | Toyama | Ishikawa | Fukui | Nagano | Gifu | Shizuoka | Aichi | Mie | Shiga | ROJ | Total |
|---|---|---|---|---|---|---|---|---|---|---|---|---|
| 14 | Electrical machinery | *0.32* | 0.72 | 0.99 | 1.29 | 1.13 | **2.82** | 1.40 | 1.56 | **3.95** | 0.83 | 1.00 |
| 15 | Information and communication electronics equipment | *0.08* | **2.01** | *0.14* | **2.93** | 1.19 | 1.50 | 0.65 | 1.06 | 0.51 | 0.98 | 1.00 |
| 16 | Transportation equipment | *0.26* | *0.42* | *0.27* | 0.72 | 1.23 | **2.48** | 3.76 | 2.48 | 1.26 | 0.66 | 1.00 |
| 17 | Miscellaneous manufacturing products | 1.45 | 0.87 | 1.44 | 1.38 | 1.85 | 1.42 | 1.40 | 1.49 | **3.22** | 0.87 | 1.00 |
| 18 | Construction | 1.17 | 1.04 | 1.35 | 0.96 | 1.14 | 0.76 | 0.84 | 0.68 | 0.90 | 1.03 | 1.00 |
| 19 | Electricity, gas and heat supply | 1.19 | 1.70 | **4.46** | 0.91 | 0.95 | 0.50 | 1.05 | 1.70 | 0.53 | 0.97 | 1.00 |
| 20 | Water supply, and waste management service | 1.06 | 1.02 | 0.94 | 1.08 | 1.00 | 1.10 | 0.83 | 0.97 | 0.69 | 1.02 | 1.00 |
| 21 | Commerce | 0.74 | 0.91 | 0.73 | 0.86 | 0.81 | 0.71 | 0.94 | *0.43* | *0.45* | 1.05 | 1.00 |
| 22 | Finance and insurance | 0.85 | 0.98 | 0.86 | 0.89 | 1.14 | 0.98 | 0.64 | 0.71 | 0.66 | 1.05 | 1.00 |
| 23 | Real estate | 1.29 | 0.91 | 1.00 | 0.98 | 0.95 | 0.70 | 0.83 | 0.72 | 0.81 | 1.04 | 1.00 |
| 24 | Railway transport | *0.22* | *0.26* | *0.17* | *0.49* | *0.37* | **3.09** | 0.91 | 0.63 | 0.59 | 0.98 | 1.00 |
| 25 | Road Transport | 0.94 | 1.40 | 1.14 | 0.87 | 1.29 | 0.95 | 1.11 | 1.01 | 0.70 | 0.99 | 1.00 |
| 26 | Water transport | *0.24* | *0.23* | *0.35* | *0.00* | *0.00* | *0.46* | 1.02 | 1.09 | *0.01* | 1.09 | 1.00 |

(continued)

**Table 4.5** (continued)

| | Sector name | Toyama | Ishikawa | Fukui | Nagano | Gifu | Shizuoka | Aichi | Mie | Shiga | ROJ | Total |
|---|---|---|---|---|---|---|---|---|---|---|---|---|
| 27 | Air transport | *0.25* | 1.23 | *0.00* | *0.03* | *0.00* | *0.12* | 0.64 | *0.00* | *0.00* | 1.16 | 1.00 |
| 28 | Other stansport service | 0.52 | 0.77 | 0.66 | 0.85 | 0.78 | 1.04 | 0.96 | 0.48 | 1.11 | 1.03 | 1.00 |
| 29 | Information and communications | *0.46* | 0.83 | 0.56 | 0.67 | 0.52 | *0.46* | 0.63 | *0.37* | *0.40* | 1.11 | 1.00 |
| 30 | Public administration | 0.61 | 1.04 | 1.20 | 0.94 | 0.98 | 0.67 | 0.55 | 0.62 | 0.76 | 1.07 | 1.00 |
| 31 | Education and research | 0.89 | 1.21 | 0.95 | 1.06 | 0.97 | 1.03 | 0.92 | 0.60 | 1.25 | 1.01 | 1.00 |
| 32 | Medical, health care and welfare | 0.96 | 1.19 | 1.05 | 1.10 | 1.07 | 0.83 | 0.67 | 0.72 | 0.79 | 1.04 | 1.00 |
| 33 | Miscellaneous non-profit services | 1.06 | 1.30 | 1.54 | 1.70 | 1.23 | 0.91 | 0.62 | 0.96 | 1.40 | 1.01 | 1.00 |
| 34 | Business services | 0.59 | 0.80 | 0.64 | 0.91 | 0.61 | 0.70 | 0.68 | *0.47* | 0.45 | 1.08 | 1.00 |
| 35 | Hotels | 0.84 | **2.29** | 1.17 | **2.85** | 1.44 | 1.42 | *0.44* | 1.13 | 0.74 | 0.98 | 1.00 |
| 36 | Eating and drinking services | 0.70 | 1.11 | 0.79 | 0.94 | 0.95 | 0.84 | 0.81 | 0.59 | 0.68 | 1.05 | 1.00 |
| 37 | Amusement and recreational services | 0.66 | 0.96 | 0.63 | 0.86 | 1.14 | 0.76 | 0.72 | 0.63 | 0.76 | 1.06 | 1.00 |
| 38 | Miscellaneous personal services | 0.97 | 0.96 | 0.93 | 1.06 | 1.01 | 0.98 | 0.80 | 0.54 | 0.64 | 1.04 | 1.00 |
| 39 | Office supplies | 0.92 | 0.95 | 0.94 | 1.06 | 1.16 | 0.95 | 0.84 | 0.99 | 0.91 | 1.02 | 1.00 |

(continued)

**Table 4.5** (continued)

| Sector name | | Toyama | Ishikawa | Fukui | Nagano | Gifu | Shizuoka | Aichi | Mie | Shiga | ROJ | Total |
|---|---|---|---|---|---|---|---|---|---|---|---|---|
| 40 | Activities not elsewhere classified | 0.95 | 1.07 | 0.94 | 1.00 | 0.97 | 1.56 | 0.77 | 0.99 | 0.91 | 1.00 | 1.00 |
| | Total of intermediate sectors | 1.00 | 1.00 | 1.00 | 1.00 | 1.00 | 1.00 | 1.00 | 1.00 | 1.00 | 1.00 | 1.00 |

*Source* Created by the author

transportation equipment, and food and beverages are highly superior. Aichi Prefecture has a high advantage in transportation equipment, in which the competitiveness is concentrated. Mie Prefecture has comparative advantages in electronic components, nonferrous metals, transportation equipment, petroleum and coal products, chemical products, ceramics, as well as stone and clay products, while Shiga Prefecture has an advantage in ceramics, stone and clay products, electrical machinery, miscellaneous manufacturing products, general-purpose machinery and production machinery, textile products, metal products, and electronic components.

In addition to the manufacturing industry, comparative advantages are also observed in Toyama Prefecture's mining industry, Fukui Prefecture's electricity, gas, and heat supply, Shizuoka Prefecture's rail transportation, as well as Ishikawa Prefecture and Nagano Prefecture's hotels.

Table 4.6 depicts the comparative advantage index by region and sector based on employment. In this table, values above 2 and below 0.5 are shown in bold and italics, respectively. In general, the same tendency is observed in the comparative advantage index on production value. In Toyama Prefecture, mining, iron and steel, electricity, gas, and heat supply are added as sectors with comparative advantages. In Ishikawa Prefecture, information and communications disappear, and in Fukui Prefecture, the superiority of non-ferrous metals weakens slightly. Conversely, other miscellaneous nonprofit services and hotels join the competitive sector.

General-purpose machinery and production machinery are newly added to Nagano Prefecture, and the superiority of metal products declines in Gifu Prefecture. In Shizuoka Prefecture, food and beverages as well as rail transport dropped, and in Aichi Prefecture, the steel industry joined. In Mie Prefecture, mining and electrical machinery joined, and non-ferrous metals dropped. In Shiga Prefecture, chemical products were added, and the superiority of metal products declined.

### 4.3.2 Intra-Regional Dependency Due to Value-Added Inducement

Figure 4.2 is a stacked bar graph depicting the amount of value-added induced in its own prefecture by a one-unit increase in each final demand by prefecture and sector in the Chubu region. Apart from the office supplies sector, the amount of value-added induced is low in agriculture, forestry and fisheries, manufacturing, construction, electricity, gas and heat supply, water transportation, and air transportation, while it is large in many tertiary industries such as water supply, and waste disposal, commerce, finance and insurance, real estate, rail transport, road transport (excluding private transport), other transport services, information and communications, public administration, education and research, medical, health care and welfare, miscellaneous non-profit services, business services, hotel, eating and drinking services, amusement and recreational services, and miscellaneous personal services.

**Table 4.6** Comparative advantages of employment

| Sector name | | Toyama | Ishikawa | Fukui | Nagano | Gifu | Shizuoka | Aichi | Mie | Shiga | ROJ | Total |
|---|---|---|---|---|---|---|---|---|---|---|---|---|
| 1 | Agriculture, forestry and fishery | 0.88 | *0.41* | 1.12 | 1.37 | *0.42* | 1.17 | 0.53 | 0.60 | *0.46* | 1.05 | 1.00 |
| 2 | Mining | 1.97 | 1.15 | 0.58 | 0.69 | 1.93 | 1.32 | 0.60 | **2.18** | 0.57 | 0.98 | 1.00 |
| 3 | Beverages and foods | 0.94 | 0.98 | 1.14 | 1.22 | 0.92 | 1.36 | 0.86 | 1.15 | 0.81 | 0.99 | 1.00 |
| 4 | Textile products | 1.38 | **4.05** | **8.20** | *0.41* | **3.09** | 0.74 | 1.33 | 0.63 | **2.86** | 0.85 | 1.00 |
| 5 | Pulp, paper and wooden products | 1.70 | 0.94 | 1.64 | 0.95 | **2.64** | **2.68** | 1.17 | 1.31 | 1.42 | 0.87 | 1.00 |
| 6 | Chemical products | **3.49** | 0.68 | 1.55 | *0.29* | 1.05 | 1.90 | 0.67 | **2.00** | **2.23** | 0.94 | 1.00 |
| 7 | Petroleum and coal products | *0.40* | *0.45* | *0.36* | *0.38* | 0.98 | *0.10* | 0.85 | **3.14** | 0.71 | 1.05 | 1.00 |
| 8 | Ceramic, stone and clay products | 1.27 | 1.51 | 1.24 | 1.02 | 5.07 | 0.85 | 1.86 | **2.16** | **3.91** | 0.80 | 1.00 |
| 9 | Iron and steel | **2.76** | 0.76 | *0.34* | *0.47* | 0.68 | *0.31* | **2.18** | 0.80 | 0.79 | 0.95 | 1.00 |
| 10 | Non-ferrous metals | **5.00** | 0.79 | 1.54 | 1.40 | 1.70 | **2.35** | 1.10 | 1.82 | 1.83 | 0.85 | 1.00 |
| 11 | Metal products | **3.21** | 1.15 | 0.94 | 1.26 | 1.99 | 1.46 | 1.51 | 1.59 | 1.74 | 0.87 | 1.00 |
| 12 | General-purpose machinery, and production machinery | 1.53 | **2.09** | 0.64 | **2.10** | 1.76 | 1.63 | 1.55 | 1.44 | **2.31** | 0.86 | 1.00 |
| 13 | Electronic components | **2.45** | **2.45** | **3.43** | **3.56** | 1.52 | 0.82 | 0.51 | **2.66** | **3.61** | 0.87 | 1.00 |

(continued)

**Table 4.6** (continued)

| Sector name | | Toyama | Ishikawa | Fukui | Nagano | Gifu | Shizuoka | Aichi | Mie | Shiga | ROJ | Total |
|---|---|---|---|---|---|---|---|---|---|---|---|---|
| 14 | Electrical machinery | 0.61 | 0.95 | 1.00 | 1.64 | 1.46 | **2.81** | 1.49 | **2.55** | **3.68** | 0.82 | 1.00 |
| 15 | Information and communication electronics equipment | *0.18* | 1.30 | *0.33* | 3.41 | 0.69 | 1.03 | 0.57 | 0.68 | 0.75 | 1.01 | 1.00 |
| 16 | Transportation equipment | *0.45* | *0.42* | 0.52 | 0.72 | 1.78 | **2.99** | **4.31** | **2.63** | 1.25 | 0.64 | 1.00 |
| 17 | Miscellaneous manufacturing products | 1.57 | 1.06 | 1.83 | 1.11 | 1.36 | 1.44 | 1.38 | 1.39 | **2.20** | 0.91 | 1.00 |
| 18 | Construction | 1.28 | 0.85 | 0.99 | 1.07 | 0.80 | 0.90 | 0.96 | 0.91 | 0.71 | 1.01 | 1.00 |
| 19 | Electricity, gas and heat supply | **2.06** | 0.79 | **2.11** | 1.09 | 0.77 | 0.98 | 1.16 | 0.97 | 0.77 | 0.98 | 1.00 |
| 20 | Water supply, and waste management service | 0.99 | 0.89 | 0.87 | 1.07 | 1.03 | 1.14 | 0.88 | 1.46 | 0.91 | 1.00 | 1.00 |
| 21 | Commerce | 0.83 | 1.03 | 0.85 | 0.93 | 1.02 | 0.85 | 1.00 | 0.93 | 0.79 | 1.01 | 1.00 |
| 22 | Finance and insurance | 0.96 | 1.08 | 1.02 | 0.96 | 1.00 | 0.71 | 0.86 | 0.78 | 0.93 | 1.03 | 1.00 |
| 23 | Real estate | *0.47* | 0.83 | *0.49* | *0.48* | 0.56 | 0.68 | 0.88 | 0.54 | 0.75 | 1.06 | 1.00 |
| 24 | Railway transport | 0.96 | 0.77 | 1.04 | 1.04 | 1.03 | 0.82 | 0.97 | 1.00 | 1.46 | 1.00 | 1.00 |
| 25 | Road Transport | 0.94 | 1.02 | 0.86 | 0.91 | 0.93 | 1.03 | 1.06 | 1.08 | 0.81 | 1.00 | 1.00 |
| 26 | Water transport | *0.49* | *0.47* | *0.16* | *0.07* | *0.11* | *0.40* | 0.52 | 1.01 | *0.19* | 1.12 | 1.00 |

(continued)

**Table 4.6** (continued)

| Sector name | | Toyama | Ishikawa | Fukui | Nagano | Gifu | Shizuoka | Aichi | Mie | Shiga | ROJ | Total |
|---|---|---|---|---|---|---|---|---|---|---|---|---|
| 27 | Air transport | *0.08* | *0.14* | *0.00* | *0.07* | *0.09* | *0.21* | 0.67 | *0.02* | *0.00* | 1.15 | 1.00 |
| 28 | Other stansport service | 0.73 | 1.05 | 1.18 | 0.54 | 0.98 | 1.10 | 1.15 | 1.26 | 1.16 | 0.99 | 1.00 |
| 29 | Information and communications | *0.38* | 0.72 | *0.38* | *0.49* | *0.31* | *0.39* | 0.76 | 0.65 | *0.36* | 1.09 | 1.00 |
| 30 | Public administration | 0.53 | 1.13 | 1.17 | 0.93 | 0.99 | 0.83 | 0.69 | 0.96 | 0.98 | 1.04 | 1.00 |
| 31 | Education and research | 1.04 | 1.22 | 0.93 | 0.93 | 0.99 | 0.96 | 0.82 | 0.95 | 1.29 | 1.01 | 1.00 |
| 32 | Medical, health care and welfare | 1.00 | 1.11 | 1.11 | 0.87 | 1.06 | 0.83 | 0.81 | 1.03 | 1.16 | 1.02 | 1.00 |
| 33 | Miscellaneous non-profit services | 1.00 | 1.61 | **2.15** | 1.04 | 1.43 | 0.85 | 0.77 | 1.32 | 1.50 | 0.99 | 1.00 |
| 34 | Business services | 0.70 | 0.81 | 0.64 | 0.74 | 0.67 | 0.91 | 1.02 | 0.79 | 0.77 | 1.03 | 1.00 |
| 35 | Hotels | 1.25 | **2.02** | **2.26** | **2.51** | 2.00 | 1.43 | 0.54 | 1.36 | 1.34 | 0.93 | 1.00 |
| 36 | Eating and drinking services | 0.93 | 0.98 | 0.78 | 0.84 | 0.95 | 0.89 | 1.09 | 1.00 | 0.92 | 1.01 | 1.00 |
| 37 | Amusement and recreational services | 0.71 | 1.11 | 0.88 | 0.86 | 1.77 | 0.76 | 0.95 | 1.16 | 1.41 | 1.00 | 1.00 |
| 38 | Miscellaneous personal services | 1.06 | 1.04 | **0.70** | 1.08 | 1.02 | 0.85 | 0.95 | 0.61 | 0.59 | 1.02 | 1.00 |
| 39 | Office supplies | – | – | – | – | – | – | – | – | – | – | – |

(continued)

**Table 4.6** (continued)

| | Sector name | Toyama | Ishikawa | Fukui | Nagano | Gifu | Shizuoka | Aichi | Mie | Shiga | ROJ | Total |
|---|---|---|---|---|---|---|---|---|---|---|---|---|
| 40 | Activities not elsewhere classified | 1.01 | 0.98 | 7.70 | 1.01 | *0.25* | *0.48* | 1.21 | 1.03 | 0.97 | 0.96 | 1.00 |
| | Total of intermediate sectors | 1.00 | 1.00 | 1.00 | 1.00 | 1.00 | 1.00 | 1.00 | 1.00 | 1.00 | 1.00 | 1.00 |

*Source* Created by the author

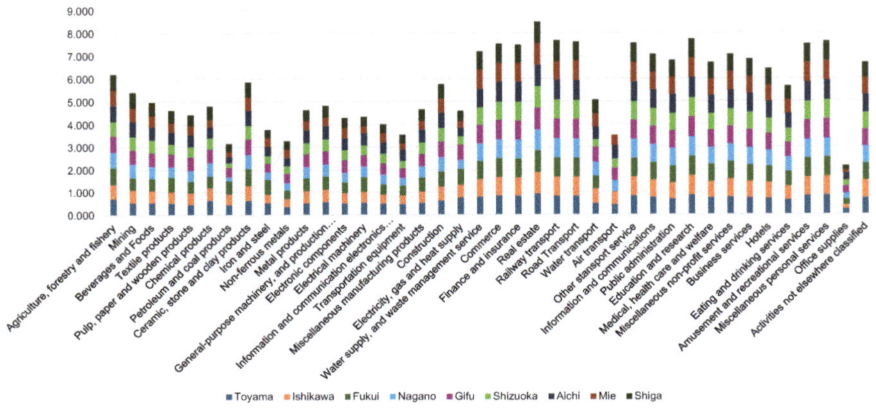


**Fig. 4.2** Value-added induced in its own prefecture by a one-unit increase in each final demand by prefecture in the Chubu Region. *Source* Created by the author

Figure 4.3 depicts the difference between the amount of value-added induced in each prefecture and Aichi Prefecture, which is also represented by a stacked bar graph. Compared to Aichi Prefecture, which has the largest economy in the Chubu region, the amount of value-added induced by its own prefecture is generally small in almost all sectors. This is thought to reflect the fact that prefectures with smaller economies procure more goods and services from other prefectures. However, there are some exceptions, such as chemical products, petroleum, coal products, iron and steel, electric power, gas, water supply, and water transportation, where the amount of value-added induced to the own region is greater than that of Aichi Prefecture. As for air transportation, many prefectures have a larger negative difference with Aichi Prefecture, the demand for which leaks out of the other prefectures into prefectures without airports.

Figure 4.4 compares the amount of value-added induced in the Chubu Region excluding the own prefecture and the amount of value-added induced outside the Chubu Region ("ROJ") brought about by a one-unit increase in the final demand by sector and prefecture. In the figure, the sum of the nine cases is presented.

The dependence on both the Chubu region and outside the Chubu area is strong in the manufacturing sector. In particular, the sector that has the strongest relationship with the Chubu region is transportation machinery, which is followed by textile products, pulp, paper, wood products, general-purpose machinery and production machinery, electronic components, electrical machinery, as well as information and communication electronics equipment. These sectors have almost the same strength as their dependence outside the Chubu Region.

Conversely, sectors that have stronger dependency outside the Chubu region than those within the Chubu region are iron and steel, chemical products, and metal products. These sectors procure intermediate goods in a wider area.

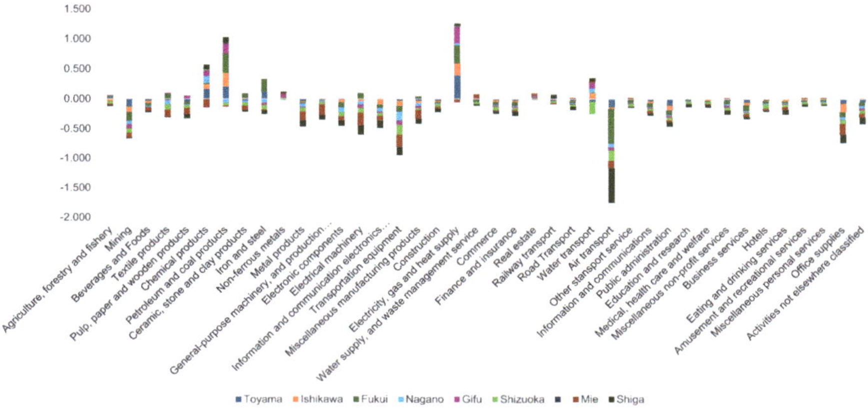


**Fig. 4.3** The difference between the amount of value-added induced in each prefecture and Aichi Prefecture. *Source* Created by the author

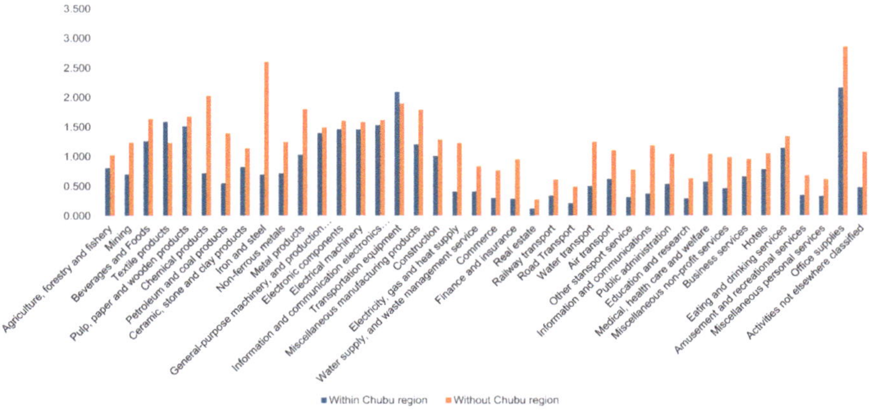


**Fig. 4.4** Comparison of value-added induced within the Chubu Region, excluding the own prefecture, and that outside the Chubu Region. *Source* Created by the author

The ripple effects in the tertiary sectors are relatively smaller compared to those in the manufacturing sectors, and the ripple effect is smaller inside the Chubu region than outside the Chubu region. Among them, hotels and restaurant services have a relatively large ripple effect, to which tourism contributes.

## 4.4 Concluding Remarks

This chapter discusses how to construct the 2011 Chubu Region interregional IOT and the employment table for the nine prefectures of the Chubu Region. Then, based on the interregional table that was constructed, we calculated the comparative advantage index of production and employment and demonstrated which industry led the region from the aspect of production and employment. Furthermore, based on the amount of value-added induced, we examined interdependence in the Chubu Region. In the Chubu Region, there is a significant impact among prefectures within the region, mainly in transportation equipment, textile products, pulp, paper, wooden products, metal products, general purpose and production machinery, electronic components, electrical machinery, information and communication electronics equipment, and miscellaneous manufacturing products. It became clear that the ripple effect on areas outside the Chubu area is also large. Yamada and Kimura (2023) constructed the 2015 Chubu Region interregional IOT with almost the same construction method. Further discussion on the Chubu Region using both IOTs is provided in Chapter 8.

## References

Asia Pacific Institute of Research (former Kansai Institute of Social and Economic Research). 2008. *Compilation of 2000 Kansai interregional input-output table* (in Japanese).

Asia Pacific Institute of Research (2012) *Compilation and use of the 2005 Kansai interregional input-output table* (in Japanese).

Chubu Region Institute for Social and Economic Research. 2013a. *Chubu region input-output table (Updated Table 2010 Edition)* (in Japanese)

Chubu Region Institute for Social and Economic Research (Former Chubu Industrial and Regional Revitalization Center). 2011. *Chubu region inter-regional input-output table (2005 Edition)* (in Japanese).

Chubu region Institute for Social and Economic Research. 2014. *Chubu region interregional input-output table (Linked Tables 1995–2000–2005)* (in Japanese).

Ihara, Takeo, Shen Xuemei, and Chen Yantian. 2015. On the construction of the Chubu region inter-regional input-output table. *Sango Renkan (Business journal of PAPAIOS) 22* (3): 91–105 (in Japanese).

MIC. 2015. *2011 input-output tables, explanatory report* (in Japanese).

Tohoku Regional Advancement Center. 2011. *Report on the Tohoku multi-regional input-output table for 2005* (in Japanese). http://www.kasseiken.jp/association/

Yamada, M. 2010. Compilation of 2000 inter-regional input-output table for Tokai Region. *Chukyo Economic Review, Chukyo University* 21:59–82 (in Japanese).

Yamada, Mitsuo, and Shinichiro Kimura. 2023b. Analysis of regional economic structure based on the Chubu region inter-regional input-output table (2015 edition)—Characteristics of industries in each prefecture in the Chubu region. *Chubu Research Quarterly 224,* 27–59 (in Japanese).

Yamada, Mitsuo, and Shinichiro Kimura. 2023a. Compiling the Chubu region inter-regional input-output table (2015 edition) and preliminary analysis of the regional structure. *Economy, Trade and Industry Statistics Study 54* (1): 1–22 (in Japanese)

# Chapter 5
# Estimating Interregional Trade by the Gravity-RAS Method

## 5.1 Introduction

IOT is a statistical table and an economic analytical tool that was developed by Wassily Leontief. In Japan, the Economic Deliberation Agency (later the Economic Planning Agency, currently the Cabinet Office) and the Ministry of International Trade and Industry (MITI, currently the Ministry of Economy, Trade and Industry, or METI), have independently made trial versions of the IOT of Japan with 1951 as the target year. After the trial tables were created, it has been created every five years as a joint project of related ministries and agencies[1] since 1955.

Additionally, the Ministry of International Trade and Industry (MITI, currently the Ministry of Economy, Trade and Industry) divided the country into nine regions for the year 1960 and created nine intra-regional IOTs that were consistent with the national table. Then the MITI created a non-competitive IOT (interregional table) for nine regions and released the table at the end of fiscal 1966. Since then, two types of regional input–output tables, intra-regional tables and interregional tables, have been created every five years in accordance with the year in which the national table was created.[2]

Pioneering works of the prefectural IOTs were the tables of Nagano and Aichi Prefectures for 1953, followed increasingly by the 1955 and 1960 tables. In the 1990 tables, all 47 prefectures of Japan began to create them, and by aggregating them,

---

[1] Currently, it is a joint project of ten ministries and agencies.

[2] Each regional IOT of METI covers an area under the jurisdiction of each regional bureau of METI, and all of them cover the entire country. It is consistent with the national IOT when each table is aggregated by region. In the interregional IOT of METI, a special survey called the "Commodity Distribution Survey" is conducted to survey the shipping destinations of businesses involved in the production of each region and industry, and the interregional trade matrices for each sector are estimated based on that information.



M. Yamada, *Multi-Regional Input–Output Analysis of the Japanese Economy*,
https://doi.org/10.1007/978-981-97-9041-8_5

it became possible to compare them with the values of the national IOT and the regional IOT of the METI.[3]

Because of the development of prefectural IOTs in Japan, there has recently been growing interest in creating interregional IOTs that combine these IOTs and in applying IOTs to smaller regions within a prefecture. This research also fills the gap between the input–output table, which treats administrative units as regions due to the limitations of statistical data, and the actual regional economies that operate beyond that. In addition, the growing interdependence between regions has brought about the importance of interregional input–output tables.

In this chapter, when creating an intra-regional IOT of a prefecture, it is necessary to estimate the trade among regions, one of which, the gravity-RAS method, is examined by applying the Aichi Prefecture as a case. The next section summarizes related preceding research, and Sect. 5.3 explains the gravity-RAS method, a method of estimating interregional trade that is taken up here. Section 5.4 summarizes the estimation results of the model; Sect. 5.5 examines the degree of difference in the IOT of Aichi Prefecture depending on the given conditions; and finally, it summarizes the results of this research.

## 5.2 Preceding Research

With the development of regional IOTs for METI and prefectural IOTs, attempts to construct interregional IOTs linking each prefectural table have increased. Furthermore, interregional IOTs within a prefecture, targeting small regions within prefectures and linking them, have increased.

Examples of interregional IOTs at the prefectural level are the interregional IOT of Tokyo (Ishida et al. 1996) targeting Tokyo and the ROJ, Osaka Prefecture's interregional IOT, which includes three regions: Osaka Prefecture, the rest of Kinki region, and the ROJ (Ito et al. 1997), and Mie Prefecture's interregional IOT, which includes two regions of Mie Prefecture and the ROJ (Yamada and Asahi 1999). These tables focus on one prefecture and aim to analyze the interdependence between the prefecture and the ROJ.

Interregional IOTs that concentrate on relations among the neighboring prefectures also exist. The Kansai interregional IOT targets seven prefectures in the Kansai Region (Asia Pacific Institute of Research (former Kansai Institute of Social and Economic Research) 2008; Asia Pacific Institute of Research 2012), and the Tohoku interregional IOT focuses on the six prefectures of Tohoku and Niigata prefectures (Tohoku regional Advancement Center 2011). The Tokai interregional IOT covers three prefectures of the Tokai region and the ROJ (Yamada 2010), the Chubu interregional IOT covers nine prefectures in the Chubu Region and the ROJ (Chubu

[3] Ohira et al. (1997) conducted a comparison of the 1990 prefectural IOTs for the first time. Furthermore, the 1995 table was conducted by Yamada and Asahi (2002), the 2000 table by Asahi and Yamada (2008), the 2005 table by Yamada (2011), and the 2011 table by Yamada (2018a).

Industrial and Regional Revitalization Center 2011, 2012) are other examples. These IOTs have the advantage of being able to analyze in detail the interdependence of target neighboring prefectures while simultaneously being able to evaluate the effects nationwide.

Several inter-prefectural IOTs cover all 47 prefectures of Japan. Ishikawa and Miyagi (2003) were pioneers who created the 1995 table of 47 prefectures and 45 sectors. Regarding inter-prefectural trade, while utilizing the MLIT's "National Freight Net Flow Survey," they adjusted to balance the imports and exports with the regions of the nine interregional IOTs of the METI to achieve higher-level consistency.

Hitomi (2008) used the IOT of 47 prefectures to construct an inter-prefectural IOT with 48 sectors in 2000. Based on the MLIT's "National Freight Net Flow Survey," he estimated interregional trade in the goods sector. For the service sector, he estimated the gravity model by using the regional trade data of METI's interregional input–output table.

Furthermore, Hagiwara (2012) constructed an interregional IOT for the period 1990–2005 for 59 sector tables in 47 prefectures, enabling analysis of changes over time. The imports and exports are based on the method proposed by Miyagi et al. (2003). For trade, Hagiwara used the MLIT's "National Freight Net Flow Survey" for the interregional movement of workers from the population census and telecommunications traffic data as initial values. He also used the trade data from METI's nine-region IOT as a restriction when he applied the extended RAS method to estimate inter-prefectural trade.

Regarding the interregional IOT within a prefecture, the IOT of Ehime Prefecture is available, which divides the prefecture into six regions and 50 sectors for each region (Tsubouchi 1991), the IOT of Hokkaido Prefecture, which divides Hokkaido into four regions and 61 sectors for each region (Takahata 1992), and the IOT of Mie Prefecture (Yamada 1995), which divides Mie into five regions and 84 sectors for each region.

In the case of Hokkaido, trade is estimated using the "Freight Regional Flow Survey" and "Passenger Regional Flow Survey" of MLIT.[4] As these surveys essentially did not provide information on intra-prefectural trade, Ehime and Mie Prefectures estimated their interregional trade using their own survey data on trade among the regions within the prefecture. These three tables commonly depend on the survey data for the estimation of their trade among the regions within the prefecture.

In addition, Ishikawa (2004) focused on Aichi Prefecture and constructed the interregional IOTs in 1995 for three regions: Nagoya City, Aichi Prefectures, and other regions. Nakano and Nishimura (2007) presented an interregional IOT for 46 sectors in three regions: Nagoya City, other prefectures, and the region outside the prefecture. Nomura et al. (2011) conducted an interregional IOT of 104 regional sectors, and they divided Yamaguchi Prefecture into three regions: Yamaguchi City, Hagi City, and the other regions within the prefecture.

[4] From these surveys, the trade flow between 47 prefectures was obtained, but Hokkaido is divided into seven regions: Sapporo, Asahikawa, Muroran, Kushiro, Obihiro, and Kitami.

In estimating interregional trade, Yamada (1995) used the RAS method with initial values based on the logistics survey data within Mie Prefecture. Nakano and Nishimura (2007) used the gravity method, and Ishikawa (2004) and Nomura et al. (2011) used the LQ method. As the LQ method is a method of estimating trade based on the comparative advantage between two regions, Nomura et al. (2011) dealt with three regions in the prefecture and devised a two-stage application of the LQ method.

In general, interregional trade involves transactions in both directions; however, the estimation of imports and exports by the LQ method estimates only one direction, either exports or imports, and the rest is 0. On the contrary, the RAS and gravity methods do not eliminate the bi-directionality of imports and exports; hence, this difference also affects the size of the production spillover effect.[5]

Yamada and Owaki (2012), based on the 2005 Aichi Input–Output Table, estimated the interregional IOT for four regions: Nagoya City, the Owari region, the Nishimikawa region, and the Higashimikawa region. This estimate is based on the 186-sector table, which was partially adjusted from the 190-sector table of Aichi Prefecture.

Here, they used an estimation method that combines the gravity model and the RAS method for the interregional transactions within the prefecture. However, there was a problem because they set a priori values for the parameters of the gravity model. Here, by replacing the parameter values of the gravity model with the estimated values using the trade flow data from the 2005 interregional IOT of METI, we newly estimate interregional trade and compare how interregional trade changes with the case of a priori parameter setting.

## 5.3 Estimation Method of the Interregional Trade

In this section, we discuss the method of estimating the interregional trade, after dividing the prefectural IOT of Aichi Prefecture into four regions within the prefecture (Yamada and Owaki 2012).

At the beginning of the estimation, we have the prefectural IOT, the Aichi Prefecture in our case. First, we divide the value of each item of the IOT into the values of four regions: Nagoya City, Owari Region, Nishimikawa Region, and Higashimikawa Region.

The supply and demand balance formula for sector i in region R is expressed as follows:

$$\sum X_{ij}^R + FD_i^R + E_i^R - M_i^R + \Delta N_i^R = X_i^R$$

$$D_i^R + E_i^R - M_i^R + \Delta N_i^R = X_i^R$$

[5] In general, if the import that originally exists is assumed to be 0, which is assumed to be produced within the region, then the production ripple effect becomes large.

**Table 5.1** The trade of sector i among four regions

| From\To | Nagoya City | Owari | Nishimikawa | Higashimikawa | Total |
|---|---|---|---|---|---|
| Nagoya city | $T_i^{11}$ | $T_i^{12}$ | $T_i^{13}$ | $T_i^{14}$ | $T_i^{1\cdot}$ |
| Owari | $T_i^{21}$ | $T_i^{22}$ | $T_i^{23}$ | $T_i^{24}$ | $T_i^{2\cdot}$ |
| Nishimikawa | $T_i^{31}$ | $T_i^{32}$ | $T_i^{33}$ | $T_i^{34}$ | $T_i^{3\cdot}$ |
| Higashimikawa | $T_i^{41}$ | $T_i^{42}$ | $T_i^{43}$ | $T_i^{44}$ | $T_i^{4\cdot}$ |
| Total | $T_i^{\cdot 1}$ | $T_i^{\cdot 2}$ | $T_i^{\cdot 3}$ | $T_i^{\cdot 4}$ | $T_i^{\cdot\cdot}$ |

*Source* Created by the author

Here, $\sum X_{ij}^R$ is the intermediate demand of the commodity i, $FD_i^R$ is the final demand of the commodity i, $E_i^R$ is the export of the commodity i, $M_i^R$ is the import of the commodity i, $\Delta N_i^R$ is the net export of the commodity i within Japan, $X_i^R$ is the product of the commodity i. $D_i^R = \sum X_{ij}^R + FD_i^R$ means the total demand of commodity i within the region. The exports and imports include not only international transactions but also trade outside the prefectures in Japan.

Yamada and Owaki (2012) estimated the intermediate demand, the final demand within the region, the export, and the import independently and obtained net exports within the prefecture as the difference. The trade among the four regions within the prefecture must be determined in a manner that is consistent with this difference.

The trade between the four regions of sector i is depicted in Table 5.1.

Here, $T_i^{RS}$ is the value of sector i trade from region R to region S, $T_i^{R\cdot}$ is the total value of sector *i* trade from region *R* to all of Aichi Prefecture, and $T_i^{\cdot S}$ is the value of the total trade value of sector *i* that region *S* receives from all of Aichi Prefecture.

The total amount of trade from a certain area to the entire Aichi Prefecture equals the amount of production in that area minus exports outside the prefecture. Additionally, the total trade amount from the whole of Aichi Prefecture to that area equals the intra-regional demand of that area minus the imports outside the prefecture.

$$T_i^{R\cdot} = X_i^R - E_i^R \tag{5.1}$$

$$T_i^{\cdot R} = D_i^R - M_i^R \tag{5.2}$$

Here, $T_i^{R\cdot}$ obtained by subtracting the exports outside the prefecture $E_i^R$ from the production in R region $X_i^R$ represents the amount of supply within the prefecture. Furthermore, $T_i^{\cdot R}$ after deducting the import, $M_i^R$ represents the amount of demand in the prefecture. Although $T_i^{R\cdot} \neq T_j^{\cdot R}$ means not balanced for each region,[6] their aggregate value is balanced, i.e.

[6] From the supply and demand balance formula for R region i sector,
$D_i^R - M_i^R + \Delta N_i^R = X_i^R - E_i^R$
Then,
$T_i^{\cdot R} + \Delta N_i^R = T_i^{R\cdot}$
$T_i^{R\cdot} \neq T_i^{\cdot R}$.

$$\Sigma T_i^{R\cdot} = \Sigma T_j^{\cdot R} \tag{5.3}$$

Here,

$$\sum T_i^{RS} = T_i^{R\cdot} \tag{5.4}$$

$$\sum T_i^{RS} = T_i^{\cdot S} \tag{5.5}$$

We need to estimate $T_i^{RS}$ that satisfies the above equation as well as the restrictions. Here, we use the RAS method, which uses initial information from the gravity model (hereinafter referred to as the gravity-RAS method) to estimate interregional trade within the prefecture.

### *5.3.1 Gravity Model*

The gravity model tries to apply the law of universal gravitation[7] to the problem of economic transactions between regions. It attempts to explain the number of transactions between regions in terms of three factors: the supply potential of the exporting region, the demand potential of the importing region, and the distance between the two regions. If we establish that the amount of transactions from region R to region S is $T_i^{RS}$, the total amount of movement from region R is $T_i^{R\cdot}$, the total amount of movement toregion S is $T_i^{\cdot S}$, and the distance between regions R and S is $\overline{L}^{RS}$, then the gravity model is expressed as follows:

$$T_i^{RS} = k_{RS} \frac{\left(T_i^{R\cdot}\right)^{\alpha} \left(T_i^{\cdot S}\right)^{\beta}}{\left(\overline{L}^{RS}\right)^{\gamma}} \tag{5.6}$$

Here, α, β, and γ are parameters to be estimated from the transaction amounts, total volume amount, and distance.

However, as the amount of transaction $T_i^{RS}$ from region R to region S is a variable to be estimated here, estimating the parameter value based on the data is not possible. Therefore, Yamada and Owaki (2012) used the gravity model given a priori as $\alpha = \beta = 1$ and $\gamma = 2$. That is,

$$T_i^{RS} = k_{RS} \frac{\left(T_i^{R\cdot}\right)\left(T_i^{\cdot S}\right)}{\left(\overline{L}^{RS}\right)^{2}} \tag{5.7}$$

[7] Newton's law of universal gravitation states that the force of attraction between two bodies is proportional to their mass and inversely proportional to the square of their distance.

Even so, the parameter $k_{RS}$ is undecided; therefore, interregional trade cannot be estimated as it is. Therefore, assuming $k_{RS} = k_{\cdot S}$, the import rate is calculated as follows from the amount of transaction $T_i^{RS}$, the total amount of transaction at the origin $T_i^{R\cdot}$, and the distance between two points $\overline{L}^{RS}$:

$$t_i^{RS} = \frac{T_i^{RS}}{\sum_R T_i^{RS}} = \frac{k_{\cdot S} \frac{T_i^{R\cdot} T_i^{\cdot S}}{\left(\overline{L}^{RS}\right)^2}}{\sum_R k_{\cdot S} \frac{T_i^{R\cdot} T_i^{\cdot S}}{\left(\overline{L}^{RS}\right)^2}} = \frac{\frac{T_i^{R\cdot}}{\left(\overline{L}^{RS}\right)^2}}{\sum_R \frac{T_i^{R\cdot}}{\left(\overline{L}^{RS}\right)^2}} \tag{5.8}$$

The gravity model essentially explains the amount of transaction between two regions and generally does not explain the transaction within a region that corresponds to the diagonal elements in Table 5.1. However, we must estimate the transaction amount within each region. Hence, we extend the usual gravity model by including the transaction within each region, whose distance is set as a non-zero value. The estimated amounts of transactions between regions and within regions are used as an initial value for estimating the trade amount $T_i^{RS}$ by the RAS method. Therefore, we consider that the extended gravity model can be similarly applied by measuring the non-zero average distance for the transaction within the area.

### 5.3.2 *Average Distance Between Regions*

Distance between regions includes physical distance, time distance, and cost distance. Yamada and Owaki (2012) used physical distance. As for measuring the distance, first, the distance $L^{rs}$ between each municipality in Aichi Prefecture is obtained using a Google map search. Here, r and s represent the municipalities in Aichi Prefecture and the wards of Nagoya City. Then, the average distance between the four regions is calculated, weighted by the daytime population $E^r$ by municipality.

$$\overline{L}^{RS} = \frac{\sum_{r \in R} \sum_{s \in S} L^{rs} E^r E^s}{\sum_{r \in R} \sum_{s \in S} E^r E^s} \tag{5.9}$$

Table 5.2 presents the average distances between the four regions obtained in this way.

## 5.4 Parameter Estimation of the Gravity Model

In the previous section, I described the method of estimating interregional trade by using the gravity-RAS method based on the a priori parameter setting used by Yamada and Owaki (2012). This method has an advantage because it can estimate

**Table 5.2** The average distances between the four regions (km)

| From\To | Nagoya City | Owari | Nishimikawa | Higashimikawa | Average |
|---|---|---|---|---|---|
| Nagoya city | 8.6 | 21.4 | 32.7 | 67.7 | 24.7 |
| Owari | 21.4 | 28.7 | 41.0 | 75.9 | 33.8 |
| Nishimikawa | 32.7 | 41.0 | 19.1 | 42.4 | 33.9 |
| Higashimikawa | 67.7 | 75.9 | 42.4 | 20.1 | 61.0 |
| Average | 24.7 | 33.8 | 33.9 | 61.0 | 33.4 |

*Source* Created by the author

intra-prefectural IOTs even if there is no information on the trade among regions within a prefecture. However, the results vary depending on the values of a priori parameters. Furthermore, there is a problem because it is not possible to verify whether the given value is appropriate or not.

Here, we estimated the parameters of the gravity model based on the trade data between the nine regions nationwide obtained from the 2005 interregional IOT of METI and used the parameters to estimate the trade of the interregional IOT within Aichi Prefecture.

### *5.4.1 Specification of the Model*

In the previous section, we applied the gravity model to the trade data between the nine regions in Japan in Table 5.3. The data were obtained from the 2005 interregional IOT of METI.

$$T_i^{RS} = k_{RS} \frac{\left(T_i^{R\cdot}\right)^{\alpha} \left(T_i^{\cdot S}\right)^{\beta}}{\left(\overline{L}^{RS}\right)^{\gamma}} \tag{5.10}$$

Taking the logarithm of the above equation, the following equation is reduced:

**Table 5.3** The nationwide nine regional trade in sector i

| From\To | Hokkaido | Tohoku | … | Okinawa | Total |
|---|---|---|---|---|---|
| Hokkaido | $T_i^{11}$ | $T_i^{12}$ | … | $T_i^{19}$ | $T_i^{1\cdot}$ |
| Tohoku | $T_i^{21}$ | $T_i^{22}$ | … | $T_i^{29}$ | $T_i^{2\cdot}$ |
| : | : | : | | : | : |
| Okinawa | $T_i^{91}$ | $T_i^{42}$ | … | $T_i^{99}$ | $T_i^{9\cdot}$ |
| Total | $T_i^{\cdot 1}$ | $T_i^{\cdot 2}$ | … | $T_i^{\cdot 9}$ | $T_i^{\cdot\cdot}$ |

*Source* Created by the author

**Table 5.4** Three variations of the gravity model estimation

| | Model 1 | Model 2 | Model 3 |
|---|---|---|---|
| Trade within a region | Excluded | Excluded | Included |
| Distance data | Km | Time | Km |
| Sectors without trade | 30 | 30 | 30 |
| Estimated sectors | 153 | 153 | 153 |
| Not estimated Sectors | 3 | 3 | 3 |

*Source* Created by the author

$$\log(T_i^{RS}) = \log(k_{RS}) + \alpha \log(T_i^{R\cdot}) + \beta \log(T_i^{\cdot S}) - \gamma \log(\overline{L}^{RS}) \quad (5.11)$$

Here, the purpose is to estimate interregional trade within the prefecture using the gravity-RAS method. In our case, as it is necessary to determine the values of both intra-regional and interregional trade within the prefecture, we have to obtain the parameter values of the gravity model and calculate the initial value from the gravity model to use them as initial information for the RAS estimation. For this purpose, we estimated the parameters for the extended gravity model that includes trade within each region. For comparison, we also estimated the models that do not include intra-regional trade and examined the differences among them. Table 5.4 presents the variations.

Here, for the trade data, we used an integrated table corresponding to the 186 sectors of the 2005 interregional IOT of METI to obtain the trade matrix data among nine regions by sector.[8] Additionally, for the distance data, we calculated the average distance[9] among the nine regions based on the distance and required time for each prefecture obtained by Google search.

Models 1 and 2 represent estimates based on data excluding intra-regional trade, and Model 3 represents estimates based on data including intra-regional trade. In addition, Models 1 and 3 estimate when physical distance is used for distance data, and Model 2 estimates when time-distance is used. There are 33 sectors without trade; 153 of the remaining 156 sectors can be estimated, and the remaining 3 sectors cannot be estimated.[10]

[8] The sector of the 2005 regional IOT of METI conforms to the national IOT of the (row) 520 and (column) 407 sector, but the definition of the sector is slightly different: (row) 404 and (column) 350 sectors. Here, we integrated the METI regional IOT into 186 sectors-squared table.

[9] The distance within the area was substituted by the average distance from the center of a circular area equivalent to the area of the prefecture. The distances of the nine regions nationwide were obtained as the weighted average of the distances between prefectures based on daytime population weights.

[10] Sectors with no trade are all sourcing from within the region. The three sectors for which estimates could not be made were "coal/oil/natural gas," "iron scrap," and "non-ferrous metal scrap.".

### 5.4.2 Estimation Results

Table 5.5 summarizes the estimation results for 153 sectors for the three variations. The distributions of the four-parameter estimates of the constant term, the total amounts of transactions on the origin and destination sides, and the distance can be seen. Estimated values are significant in most sectors for all models, but there are variations between sectors. Regarding the trade amounts of origin and destination, Models 1 and 2, which exclude intra-regional trade, have larger variations than Model 3, which includes them. Conversely, the distance parameter of Model 3 is larger than that of Models 1 and 2.

**Table 5.5** Estimated results of the gravity models

| Model 1 | Const | Log E | Log M | Log D |
|---|---|---|---|---|
| Maximum | 10.11 | 3.55 | 1.55 | 0.71 |
| Minimum | −37.52 | 0.47 | −0.19 | −2.17 |
| Average | −9.37 | 1.05 | 0.96 | −0.66 |
| Av. of goods sector | −10.15 | 1.05 | 1.00 | −0.60 |
| Av. Of service sector | −7.19 | 1.04 | 0.86 | −0.82 |
| St. Dev | 6.24 | 0.27 | 0.23 | 0.44 |
| Number significantly estimated | 107 | 152 | 151 | 110 |
| Model 2 | Const | Log E | Log M | Log D |
| Maximum | 5.60 | 3.84 | 15.4 | 0.74 |
| Minimum | −37.74 | 0.42 | −0.46 | −2.28 |
| Average | −11.79 | 1.03 | 0.92 | −0.56 |
| Av. of goods sector | −12.28 | 1.04 | 0.96 | −0.52 |
| Av. of service sector | −10.41 | 1.03 | 0.83 | −0.69 |
| St. Dev | 5.31 | 0.29 | 0.25 | 0.42 |
| Number significantly estimated | 134 | 152 | 149 | 100 |
| Model 3 | Const | Log E | Log M | Log D |
| Maximum | 8.48 | 1.92 | 1.27 | −0.20 |
| Minimum | −18.89 | −0.02 | −0.08 | −3.08 |
| Average | −4.06 | 0.99 | 0.74 | −1.29 |
| Av. of goods sector | −4.38 | 0.96 | 0.75 | −1.12 |
| Av. of service sector | −3.13 | 1.06 | 0.70 | −1.77 |
| St. Dev | 4.47 | 0.28 | 0.23 | 0.57 |
| Number significantly estimated | 73 | 150 | 149 | 149 |

*Source* The author's estimates
*Note* Log E is the logarithmic variable of the total amount of transactions on the origin side; log M is for the destination; and log D is the logarithmic variable of the distance data

Comparing Models 1 and 2, the difference in physical and time distance data does not bring about a significant difference in parameter values. Rather, as can be seen by comparing Models 1 and 3, a larger difference is brought by the condition of whether intra-regional trade is included or not.

Comparing the parameters between the goods and service sectors, all models display a smaller elasticity value for the distance parameter of the goods sector. Looking at this with Model 3, the average of the goods sectors was −1.12, and that of the service sectors was −1.77. In addition, the elasticity of the total transaction amount on the origin side was 0.99, and that of the destination side was 0.74.

Figure 5.1 depicts the distribution of estimated values of the distance parameter. Models 1 and 2, which exclude intra-regional trade, are located at an average of −0.6, and some sectors have positive values. Conversely, Model 3, which includes intra-regional trade, is located at an average of −1.12, and it can be seen that all sectors give negative values.

Yamada and Owaki (2012) set the parameters of the total amount of trade on the origin and destination sides to 1, respectively, and the distance parameters to −2. However, assuming that the nationwide interregional gravity model can also be applied to interregional trade within Aichi Prefecture, the estimation results here reveal that the distance parameter value given a priori is somewhat excessive, especially for the goods sector.

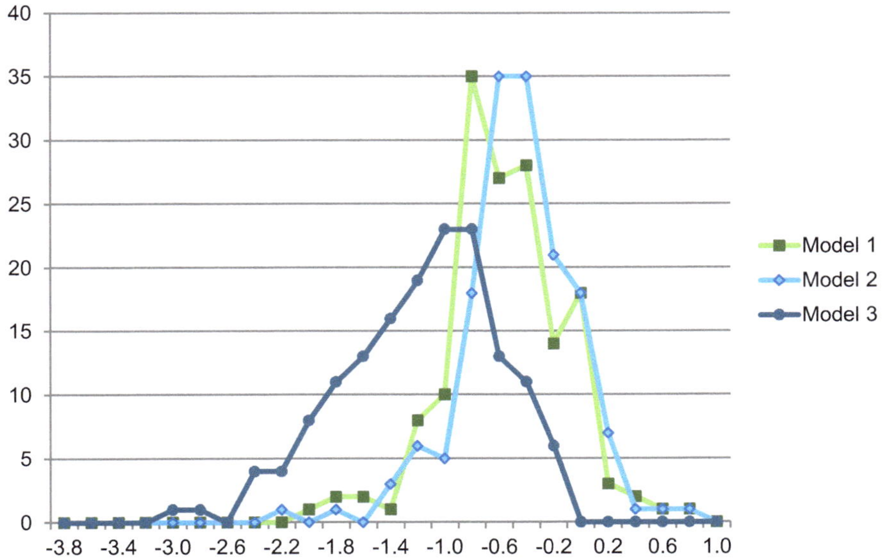


**Fig. 5.1** Distribution of the distance parameter estimates. *Source* Estimated and drawn by the author

**Table 5.6** Comparison of three input–output tables

| | IOT-A | IOT-B |
|---|---|---|
| Estimation method | Gravity-RAS method | Gravity-RAS method |
| Distance parameter | −2 | Estimated values of regression |
| Trade parameters of origin and destination | 1 | Estimated values of regression |
| Reference | Yamada and Owaki (2012) | Model 3 in our estimation |

*Source* Created by the author

## 5.5 Application to the Aichi Prefecture's Interregional Input–output Table

In the previous section, we estimated three variations of the gravity model and compared the results. Although good statistical results were obtained for all models, there were cases in which a positive value of the elasticity was estimated for the distance parameter in Models 1 and 2.

In this section, based on the estimation results of Model 3, where there are no negative values in distance parameters and there is a difference in elasticity between the goods and service sectors, the gravity-RAS method is used to estimate the trade coefficient by sector for the construction of an interregional IOT within Aichi Prefecture. In addition, we will conduct a comparison of our IOT with the IOT of Yamada and Owaki (2012), which was estimated using a priori parameters.

The following two IOTs are compared: IOT-A in Table 5.6 were those of Yamada and Owaki (2012). In this input–output table, a distance parameter of −2 and a total transaction parameter of 1 are given a priori. IOT-B is an interregional IOT that estimates trade by sector using the gravity model estimated from the 2005 interregional IOT of METI. Here, we use an extended gravity model (Model 3) that includes intra-regional trade. All these tasks are essentially carried out in 186 sectors.

After integrating each of the interregional IOTs with 186 sectors by four regions into 40 sectors by four regions, the trade coefficients for interregional trade within the prefecture are calculated.[11]

Table 5.7 presents the difference in IOT-C based on IOT-A. IOT-C estimates of the interregional trade are based on regression estimates. Therefore, the value of the distance parameter varies by sector; however, the average for the goods sector is −1.12, and the average for the service sector is −1.77. Therefore, there are many sectors whose elasticity values are smaller than the value of −2 assumed in IOT-A. If a smaller elasticity of the distance reduces the varied cost of the longer interregional trade, then it is expected to increase the amount of the trade.

In the sector, the demand of Nagoya City decreased by 1.9%, the Owari region by 2.4%, the Nishimikawa region by 4.2%, and the Higashimikawa region by 7.6%. The

[11] Here, the trade coefficients mean the trade shares against the domestic demand of each region within the prefecture.

**Table 5.7** Difference of the trade coefficients between IOT-A and IOT-B

| | | Nagoya City | | | | Owari | | | |
|---|---|---|---|---|---|---|---|---|---|
| | | Nagoya to Nagoya | Owari to Nagoya | Nishi-mikawa to Nagoya | Higashi-mikawa to Nagoya | Nagoya to Owari | Owari to Owari | Nishi-mikawa to Owari | Higashi-mikawa to Owari |
| 01 | Agriculture | −0.8 | −2.4 | 0.5 | 2.7 | 0.2 | −1.5 | 0.5 | 0.9 |
| 02 | Forestry | 0.0 | −0.1 | 0.2 | −0.1 | 0.0 | 0.0 | 0.5 | −0.5 |
| 03 | Fishery | 0.0 | −6.6 | 3.8 | 2.9 | 0.0 | −6.3 | 3.2 | 3.0 |
| 04 | Mining | −0.8 | −1.7 | 0.7 | 1.8 | 0.3 | −1.8 | 0.5 | 1.0 |
| 05 | Food and beverage | −5.5 | 0.0 | 3.4 | 2.1 | 2.0 | −6.2 | 2.3 | 1.9 |
| 06 | Textile products and apparel | −10.2 | −1.9 | 6.4 | 5.7 | 1.4 | −8.7 | 3.2 | 4.1 |
| 07 | Pulp, paper, wood products | −3.6 | −0.3 | 2.2 | 1.8 | 1.3 | −4.8 | 1.7 | 1.8 |
| 08 | Chemical products | −11.1 | 3.8 | 5.1 | 2.2 | 1.2 | −6.8 | 3.8 | 1.8 |
| 09 | Petroleum and coal products | −0.1 | −0.3 | 0.4 | 0.0 | 0.1 | −0.4 | 0.4 | 0.0 |
| 10 | Plastic products | −8.5 | −1.4 | 6.5 | 3.3 | 0.1 | −9.5 | 5.7 | 3.7 |
| 11 | Ceramics | −10.9 | 9.4 | 1.0 | 0.5 | 1.9 | −3.5 | 1.1 | 0.6 |
| 12 | Other ceramics, stone and clay products | −5.4 | 0.9 | 4.0 | 0.5 | 0.6 | −4.7 | 3.4 | 0.7 |
| 13 | Iron and steel | −5.5 | 1.6 | 3.2 | 0.7 | 0.2 | −3.0 | 2.3 | 0.5 |
| 14 | Nonferrous metals | −15.5 | 3.9 | 5.1 | 6.5 | −4.0 | −7.2 | 5.0 | 6.1 |
| 15 | Metal products | −6.4 | 1.0 | 4.0 | 1.3 | 1.3 | −6.5 | 3.7 | 1.5 |
| 16 | General machinery | −9.4 | 2.3 | 4.9 | 2.3 | 3.2 | −8.9 | 3.4 | 2.3 |
| 17 | Electric machinery | −13.0 | 0.6 | 9.0 | 3.5 | 1.3 | −12.7 | 7.8 | 3.6 |

(continued)

**Table 5.7** (continued)

| | | Nagoya City | | | | Owari | | | |
|---|---|---|---|---|---|---|---|---|---|
| | | Nagoya to Nagoya | Owari to Nagoya | Nishi-mikawa to Nagoya | Higashi-mikawa to Nagoya | Nagoya to Owari | Owari to Owari | Nishi-mikawa to Owari | Higashi-mikawa to Owari |
| 18 | Information and communication equipment | −2.6 | −11.3 | 11.4 | 2.5 | 0.9 | −11.1 | 8.0 | 2.2 |
| 19 | Electronic components | −3.7 | −17.1 | 19.5 | 1.3 | −0.1 | −16.7 | 15.7 | 1.2 |
| 20 | Auto and motor vehcle parts | −10.3 | −5.8 | 13.3 | 2.9 | −2.7 | −14.3 | 14.2 | 2.7 |
| 21 | Aircraft | −8.1 | 8.1 | 0.0 | 0.0 | 4.8 | −4.8 | 0.0 | 0.0 |
| 22 | Other transport equipment | −3.1 | −3.5 | 3.8 | 2.8 | 1.2 | −6.5 | 2.9 | 2.4 |
| 23 | Precision machinery | −3.1 | −3.8 | 3.2 | 3.6 | 1.7 | −3.7 | 0.6 | 1.4 |
| 24 | Miscellaneous manufacturing products | −1.0 | −0.6 | 0.7 | 0.9 | 0.2 | −2.9 | 1.4 | 1.3 |
| 25 | Construction | 0.4 | −0.3 | −0.1 | 0.0 | 0.0 | 0.2 | −0.2 | 0.0 |
| 26 | Electricity, gas, and heat supply | 8.3 | −5.2 | −2.7 | −0.4 | −1.2 | 6.6 | −4.3 | −1.1 |
| 27 | Water supply and waste treatment | 3.2 | −0.4 | −2.1 | −0.7 | −1.7 | 4.7 | −2.0 | −1.0 |
| 28 | Commercial | −5.2 | 2.3 | 1.7 | 1.1 | −0.2 | −3.0 | 2.0 | 1.2 |

(continued)

**Table 5.7** (continued)

| | | Nagoya City | | | | Owari | | | |
|---|---|---|---|---|---|---|---|---|---|
| | | Nagoya to Nagoya | Owari to Nagoya | Nishi-mikawa to Nagoya | Higashi-mikawa to Nagoya | Nagoya to Owari | Owari to Owari | Nishi-mikawa to Owari | Higashi-mikawa to Owari |
| 29 | Finance and Insurance | −8.0 | 1.6 | 3.9 | 2.5 | 1.8 | −5.3 | 1.5 | 2.0 |
| 30 | Real estate | 0.3 | −0.2 | −0.1 | 0.0 | −0.1 | 0.3 | −0.1 | −0.1 |
| 31 | Ttransportation | −4.3 | 2.6 | 1.1 | 0.6 | 1.4 | −3.7 | 1.3 | 1.0 |
| 32 | Telecommunications | 0.0 | −0.1 | 0.1 | 0.1 | 0.1 | 0.0 | −0.1 | 0.1 |
| 33 | Public administration | 0.0 | 0.0 | 0.0 | 0.0 | 0.0 | 0.0 | 0.0 | 0.0 |
| 34 | Education and Research | −2.4 | −0.4 | 2.2 | 0.6 | 0.0 | −4.3 | 3.1 | 1.2 |
| 35 | Medical, Healthcare, Social Security, and Nursing | 0.0 | 0.0 | 0.0 | 0.0 | 0.0 | 0.0 | 0.0 | 0.0 |
| 36 | Other public services | 0.3 | −0.1 | −0.1 | 0.0 | −0.1 | 0.2 | −0.1 | −0.1 |
| 37 | Business services | 0.5 | −0.2 | −0.3 | 0.0 | −0.7 | 1.2 | −0.4 | −0.1 |
| 38 | Personal service | 0.0 | 0.0 | 0.0 | 0.0 | 0.0 | 0.0 | 0.0 | 0.0 |
| 39 | Office supplies | 0.0 | 0.0 | 0.0 | 0.0 | 0.0 | 0.0 | 0.0 | 0.0 |
| 40 | Activities not elsewhere classified | 6.1 | −7.9 | −0.5 | 2.2 | −7.5 | 11.6 | −4.9 | 0.7 |
| | Total of intermediate sectors | −1.9 | 0.1 | 1.2 | 0.6 | 0.0 | −2.4 | 1.7 | 0.7 |

(continued)

**Table 5.7** (continued)

| | | Nishi-mikawa | | | | Higashi-mikawa | | | |
|---|---|---|---|---|---|---|---|---|---|
| | | Nagoya to Nishi-mikawa | Owari to Nishi-mikawa | Nishi-mikawa to Nishi-mikawa | Higashi-mikawa to Nishi-mikawa | Nagoya to Higashi-mikawa | Owari to Higashi-mikawa | Nishi-mikawa to Higashi-mikawa | Higashi-mikawa to Higashi-mikawa |
| 01 | Agriculture | 0.3 | 3.8 | −3.4 | −0.7 | 0.3 | 2.2 | 2.1 | −4.6 |
| 02 | Forestry | 0.0 | 0.0 | 0.0 | 0.0 | 0.0 | 0.0 | −0.3 | 0.3 |
| 03 | Fishery | 0.0 | 10.9 | −14.2 | 3.4 | 0.0 | 13.1 | 3.9 | −17.0 |
| 04 | Mining | 0.2 | 4.4 | −6.0 | 1.3 | 0.1 | 3.0 | 8.1 | −11.2 |
| 05 | Food and beverage | 3.5 | 6.7 | −11.5 | 1.3 | 2.8 | 8.5 | 3.5 | −14.8 |
| 06 | Textile products and apparel | 3.7 | 5.6 | −13.9 | 4.7 | 3.5 | 10.9 | 11.6 | −26.0 |
| 07 | Pulp, paper, wood products | 2.1 | 5.3 | −7.4 | 0.1 | 1.7 | 9.1 | 2.4 | −13.2 |
| 08 | Chemical products | 4.4 | 4.7 | −11.3 | 2.2 | 6.0 | 8.5 | 0.2 | −14.8 |
| 09 | Petroleum and coal products | 0.1 | 1.1 | −1.2 | 0.0 | 0.1 | 0.4 | −0.5 | 0.0 |
| 10 | Plastic products | 1.7 | 4.5 | −9.0 | 2.9 | 1.8 | 9.8 | 7.7 | −19.3 |
| 11 | Ceramics | 2.8 | −2.0 | −1.4 | 0.6 | 4.3 | 4.4 | 0.1 | −8.8 |
| 12 | Other ceramics, stone and clay products | 1.5 | 2.5 | −5.1 | 1.2 | 1.4 | 3.5 | 0.3 | −5.2 |
| 13 | Iron and steel | 1.5 | 2.8 | −5.1 | 0.7 | 2.1 | 3.7 | 1.2 | −7.0 |

(continued)

**Table 5.7** (continued)

| | | Nishi-mikawa | | | | Higashi-mikawa | | | |
|---|---|---|---|---|---|---|---|---|---|
| | | Nagoya to Nishi-mikawa | Owari to Nishi-mikawa | Nishi-mikawa to Nishi-mikawa | Higashi-mikawa to Nishi-mikawa | Nagoya to Higashi-mikawa | Owari to Higashi-mikawa | Nishi-mikawa to Higashi-mikawa | Higashi-mikawa to Higashi-mikawa |
| 14 | Nonferrous metals | 6.1 | 1.5 | −7.4 | −0.2 | 10.3 | 7.6 | 7.4 | −25.3 |
| 15 | Metal products | 2.7 | 4.5 | −8.8 | 1.5 | 2.9 | 8.6 | 4.2 | −15.7 |
| 16 | General machinery | 4.8 | 3.7 | −9.9 | 1.4 | 8.6 | 13.7 | 2.0 | −24.4 |
| 17 | Electric machinery | 5.1 | 5.6 | −13.8 | 3.1 | 6.4 | 13.4 | 6.9 | −26.7 |
| 18 | Information and communication equipment | 1.1 | 11.2 | −13.4 | 1.0 | 1.1 | 11.2 | −1.7 | −10.6 |
| 19 | Electronic components | 0.7 | 12.4 | −14.1 | 1.0 | 0.7 | 12.7 | 4.9 | −18.3 |
| 20 | Auto and motor vehcle parts | 0.8 | 1.9 | −6.0 | 3.2 | 1.0 | 2.8 | 10.6 | −14.3 |
| 21 | Aircraft | 5.8 | −5.7 | −0.1 | 0.0 | 7.4 | −6.4 | −0.1 | −0.9 |
| 22 | Other transport equipment | 1.7 | 7.3 | −10.9 | 1.9 | 1.1 | 6.1 | 8.6 | −15.8 |
| 23 | Precision machinery | 2.0 | 7.4 | −11.2 | 1.8 | 1.5 | 7.3 | 16.2 | −25.0 |
| 24 | Miscellaneous manufacturing products | 0.5 | 1.8 | −3.8 | 1.5 | 0.7 | 6.3 | 4.2 | −11.2 |
| 25 | Construction | −0.3 | 0.0 | 0.4 | −0.1 | −0.4 | 0.0 | 0.0 | 0.4 |
| 26 | Electricity, gas, and heat supply | −5.2 | −2.2 | 10.1 | −2.8 | −4.6 | −4.2 | −4.3 | 13.0 |

(continued)

**Table 5.7** (continued)

| | | Nishi-mikawa | | | | Higashi-mikawa | | | |
|---|---|---|---|---|---|---|---|---|---|
| | | Nagoya to Nishi-mikawa | Owari to Nishi-mikawa | Nishi-mikawa to Nishi-mikawa | Higashi-mikawa to Nishi-mikawa | Nagoya to Higashi-mikawa | Owari to Higashi-mikawa | Nishi-mikawa to Higashi-mikawa | Higashi-mikawa to Higashi-mikawa |
| 27 | Water supply and waste treatment | −2.1 | −4.6 | 8.4 | −1.7 | −1.3 | −4.9 | −3.6 | 9.8 |
| 28 | Commercial | 3.2 | 0.5 | −5.5 | 1.8 | 8.1 | 2.0 | 2.2 | −12.3 |
| 29 | Finance and Insurance | 8.9 | 2.3 | −11.9 | 0.7 | 9.9 | 5.6 | 4.1 | −19.6 |
| 30 | Real estate | −0.4 | 0.0 | 0.5 | −0.1 | −0.3 | −0.2 | −0.1 | 0.6 |
| 31 | Ttransportation | 3.1 | 0.2 | −4.6 | 1.3 | 4.9 | 3.1 | 1.6 | −9.6 |
| 32 | Telecommunications | −0.2 | 0.2 | −0.1 | 0.0 | 0.1 | 0.4 | 0.1 | −0.7 |
| 33 | Public administration | 0.0 | 0.0 | 0.0 | 0.0 | 0.0 | 0.0 | 0.0 | 0.0 |
| 34 | Education and Research | 1.3 | 3.1 | −6.0 | 1.7 | 1.0 | 3.6 | 4.9 | −9.5 |
| 35 | Medical, Healthcare, Social Security, and Nursing | 0.0 | 0.0 | 0.0 | 0.0 | 0.0 | 0.0 | 0.0 | 0.0 |
| 36 | Other public services | −0.3 | −0.1 | 0.5 | −0.1 | −0.2 | −0.2 | −0.2 | 0.6 |
| 37 | Business services | −0.2 | −0.9 | 1.2 | −0.1 | 0.6 | −0.5 | −0.8 | 0.7 |
| 38 | Personal service | 0.0 | 0.0 | 0.0 | 0.0 | 0.0 | 0.0 | 0.0 | 0.0 |
| 39 | Office supplies | 0.0 | 0.0 | 0.0 | 0.0 | 0.0 | 0.0 | 0.0 | 0.0 |

(continued)

**Table 5.7** (continued)

| | | Nishi-mikawa | | | | Higashi-mikawa | | | |
|---|---|---|---|---|---|---|---|---|---|
| | | Nagoya to Nishi-mikawa | Owari to Nishi-mikawa | Nishi-mikawa to Nishi-mikawa | Higashi-mikawa to Nishi-mikawa | Nagoya to Higashi-mikawa | Owari to Higashi-mikawa | Nishi-mikawa to Higashi-mikawa | Higashi-mikawa to Higashi-mikawa |
| 40 | Activities not elsewhere classified | −0.7 | −3.2 | 6.0 | −2.1 | 1.7 | 0.8 | 4.6 | −7.1 |
| | Total of intermediate sectors | 1.2 | 1.6 | −4.2 | 1.3 | 2.0 | 2.4 | 3.3 | −7.6 |

*Source* Calculated and created by the author

decrease in local procurement in Nagoya City and the Owari region was covered by imports from the Nishimikawa region, and the decrease in the Nishimikawa region was mainly compensated by the supply from the Owari region. The decrease in the Higashimikawa region was covered by the imports from the Owari region and the Nishimikawa Region. Moreover, in the tertiary sectors, the commercial sector and the transportation sector, which have a relation to the commodity sectors with their margin, had similar tendencies in the difference, though the other sectors have no significant difference between the models.

## 5.6 Concluding Remarks

In this chapter, we examined the gravity-RAS method that is necessary for the construction of an interregional IOT within the prefecture, taking Aichi Prefecture as an example. Originally, trade among small regions within the prefecture should have been estimated based on the data from statistical surveys, but if such primary statistics cannot be obtained, a non-survey method using some model will be useful.

The RAS method, the LQ method, and the gravity model are considered. Yamada and Owaki (2012) estimated interregional trade using the gravity-RAS method, which combines the gravity model and the RAS method. At that time, the parameter values of the gravity model are given as a priori values. Here, we estimated the parameter values by using the nationwide trade data of the 2005 interregional IOT of METI, then applied the values to estimate the trade among smaller regions in Aichi Prefecture to construct an interregional IOT of Aichi Prefecture. We examined the extent to which the revised IOT is corrected by using the regression estimates of the gravity model, which is considered an alternative method for applying a priori values to the gravity model.

Regarding the estimation of the gravity model, we estimated three variations. Comparing the model that does not include local trade and the model that includes local trade, the former has smaller variations in the estimated elasticity, while the latter has larger variations. Regarding the elasticity of the distance parameter, the former gives a smaller value, while the latter has an average value close to 1 in the goods sector and an average value close to 2 in the service sector. Here, we used the parameter estimates of the extended gravity model, including the own region, according to our purpose of use.

In addition, we constructed two different interregional IOTs of Aichi Prefecture using different parameter values as the initial values of the gravity-RAS method and compared the differences in the trade coefficients in the interregional IOTs. Regarding the distance parameter, it has been determined that the lower the elasticity value, the more active the trade between regions. In fact, compared to the IOT used by Yamada and Owaki (2012), the newly estimated IOT has a smaller value for the distance parameter and has been revised so that trade between regions within the prefecture is more active.

As the way the elasticity value is presented affects the results of tabulation, it is preferable to have a clearer basis for the given value. Here, as one of them, we propose to use the gravity-RAS method for estimating interregional trade within a prefecture. Of course, it should be added that nothing beats the effort of getting survey data directly.

## References

Asahi, S., and M. Yamada. 2008. Comparison and evaluation of regional input-output tables for 2000. *Sango Renkan (Business Journal of PAPAIOS)* 16 (1): 3–16 (in Japanese).

Asia Pacific Institute of Research (former Kansai Institute of Social and Economic Research). 2008 *Compilation of 2000 Kansai interregional input-output table* (in Japanese)

Asia Pacific Institute of Research. 2012. *Compilation and use of the 2005 Kansai interregional input-output table* (in Japanese).

Chubu Region Institute for Social and Economic Research (Former Chubu Industrial and Regional Revitalization Center). 2011. *Chubu region inter-regional input-output table (2005 Edition)* (in Japanese).

Hagiwara, T. 2012. Compilation of 47-prefectures' interregional input-output table and its application. *Kobe University Economic Review* 58:33–46 (in Japanese).

Hitomi, Kazumi. 2008. *Development of multi-regional input-output table for 47 prefectures in Japan.—Analysis of inter-prefectural production inducement structure using internal and external multipliers.* CRIEPI Research Report Y07035 (in Japanese).

Ishida, K., M. Shimizu, M. Arai, and H. Sakuramoto. 1996. Analysis of the economic structure of megacities VI -Characteristics of the Tokyo economy as seen in the Tokyo interregional input-output tables for 1985 and 1990-. *Sango Renkan (Business Journal of PAPAIOS)* 7 (1): 31–46 (in Japanese).

Ishikawa, Yoshifumi. 2004. A three-region interregional input-output model using non-survey technique. *Journal of Japan Society of Civil Engineers* 758(4–63): 45–55 (in Japanese).

Ishikawa, Y., and T. Miyagi. 2003. Analysis of the input-output structure using multi-prefectural input-output table of Japan. *Studies in Regional Science* 34 (1): 139–152 (in Japanese).

Ito, S., K. Hashi, N. Taira, and Y. Minamino. 1997. Economic analysis using the 1990 Osaka inter-regional input-output table: Comparison between regions and interdependence. *Sango Renkan (Business Journal of PAPAIOS)* 7 (3): 73–82 (in Japanese).

Miyagi, Toshihiko, Yoshifumi Ishikawa, Miho Shimizu, and Masahira Yuri. 2003. Creating of inter-prefectural input-output tables using each regional input-output tables and its application. In *Paper presented at the 26th civil engineering planning research conference* (in Japanese).

Nakano, S., and K. Nishimura. 2007. Estimation of interregional trade in partitioning regional input-output tables. *Sango Renkan (Business Journal of PAPAIOS)* 15 (3): 44–53 (in Japanese).

Nomura, J., M. Kinoshita, H. Saito, and S. Asahi. 2011. Economic impacts of trans-regional tourists' expenditures utilizing multiregional I-O table of Yamaguchi Prefecture, Japan. *Sangyo Renkan (Business Journal of PAPAIOS)* 19 (3): 72–93 (in Japanese).

Ohira, S., T. Yoshida, and T. Nakagawa. 1997. Evaluation and analysis of the prefectural input-output tables for 1990. *Sango Renkan (Business Journal of PAPAIOS)* 7 (3): 55–64 (in Japanese).

Takahata, Y. 1992. Interregional input-output table of Hokkaido Prefecture. *Sango Renkan (Business Journal of PAPAIOS)* 3 (3): 24–29 (in Japanese).

Tohoku regional advancement center. 2011. Report on the Tohoku multi-regional input-output table for 2005, (in Japanese). http://www.kasseiken.jp/association/

Tsubouchi, Takehiro. 1991. On the interregional input-output table of Ehime Prefecture. *Sangyo Renkan (Input-Output Analysis)* 2(1): 35–42 (in Japanese).

Yamada, M. 1995. Estimation of Mie Prefecture inter-regional input-output table. *Sango Renkan (Business Journal of PAPAIOS)* 5 (4): 52–67 (in Japanese).
Yamada, Mitsuo. 2010. Compilation of 2000 inter-regional input-output table for Tokai Region *Chukyo Economic Review*, Chukyo University 21: 59–82 (in Japanese).
Yamada, M. 2011. Comparison and evaluation of regional input-output tables for 2005. *Sango Renkan (Business Journal of PAPAIOS)* 19 (1): 64–79 (in Japanese).
Yamada, M. 2018. Construction of 2011 prefectural input-output tables and their comparison. *Economic, Trade and Industry Statistics Study* 45 (4): 23–51 (in Japanese).
Yamada, M., and S. Asahi. 2002. Comparison and evaluation of regional input-output tables for 1995. *Sango Renkan (Business Journal of PAPAIOS)* 10 (3): 47–64 (in Japanese).
Yamada, Mitsuo, and Yuichi Owaki. 2012. Estimation of 2005 inter-regional input-output table of four-regions within Aichi Prefecture, Chukyo University, *Institute of economics discussion paper* No. 1205 (in Japanese).

# Chapter 6
# Construction of a Multi-Regional Input–Output Table within a Prefecture

## 6.1 Introduction

There has been a growing interest in compiling IOTs for smaller areas within prefectures. Many studies have examined interregional IOTs within prefectures. Yamada (1995) studied Mie Prefecture, which consists of five regions. Yamada and Horiuchi (2015) conducted a multi-point comparative analysis of the interregional IOTs of Mie Prefecture from 1995 to 2010. Ishikawa (2004) estimated the interregional IOT of two regions within Aichi Prefecture and the ROJ, applying the LQ method to trade transactions. Yamada and Owaki (2012) used the gravity-RAS method for transactions among four regions in Aichi Prefecture. Yamada (2015) analyzed the regional interdependency of 14 regions in three adjacent prefectures, Aichi, Mie, and Gifu, in an interregional IOT. Tsukamoto et al. (2018) used the 2005 Aichi prefectural IOT (189 section tables) to create the 2005 inter-municipal IOT for 67 municipalities in the prefecture.

In this chapter, we estimate an interregional IOT for 54 municipalities based on the 2011 Aichi IOT, in which the 188-sector table is integrated into a 106-sector table. Although the size of the sector is almost half that examined by Tsukamoto et al. (2018), the target year has been updated. We have attempted to improve the estimation of the table.

In Sect. 6.2, we present an outline of the 2011 inter-municipal IOT of Aichi Prefecture. In Sect. 6.3, we compare the characteristics of municipalities with the estimated IOT. Section 6.4 examines the interdependency among municipalities based on the value-added induced by given final demands. Finally, Sect. 6.5 summarizes the results.

 
M. Yamada, *Multi-Regional Input–Output Analysis of the Japanese Economy*,
https://doi.org/10.1007/978-981-97-9041-8_6

## 6.2 Constructing an Inter-municipal Input–output Table

In this section, we describe how to construct our MRIOT for Aichi Prefecture. First, the IOT for each of the 54 municipalities in Aichi Prefecture was estimated from the 2011 Aichi Prefecture IOT released by the prefecture (see Table 6.1 for the municipalities of Aichi Prefecture). Next, the trade flow among municipalities in Aichi Prefecture was estimated for each sector using the gravity-RAS method. The IOT is based on the 106-sector table (see Table 6.2 for a list of the sectors).[1] In addition, as the IOT includes the ROJ as an endogenous region, the inter-municipal IOT of Aichi Prefecture has 5,830 endogenous sectors (55 regions by 106 sectors).

The Aichi prefectural IOT has been divided into IOTs for each municipality using the following procedure (see Fig. 6.1):

(1) Estimate the product value (Control Total (CT), $X_i^r$) by sector in each municipality by multiplying the product value $X_i^A$ by sector in Aichi Prefecture by the division index of product $\omega_i^r$.

$$X_i^r = X_i^A \cdot \omega_i^r \tag{6.1}$$

(2) Multiply the estimated municipal product $X_j^r$ with the input coefficient $a_{ij}$ and the value-added coefficient $v_{ij}$ of the Aichi prefectural IOT to estimate the intermediate input $X_{ij}^r$ and the value-added $V_{ij}^r$ of the municipal IOT.

$$X_{ij}^r = a_{ij} X_j^r \tag{6.2}$$

$$V_{ij}^r = v_{ij} X_j^r \tag{6.3}$$

(3) Estimate the final demand $F_{ij}^r$ within each municipality using the municipal division index $\upsilon_{ij}^r$ for each final demand $F_{ij}^A$ in the Aichi Prefecture IOT.

$$F_{ij}^r = F_{ij}^A \cdot \upsilon_{ij}^r \tag{6.4}$$

(4) Exports to the ROJ $E_i^{rJ}$ and to the ROW $E_i^{rW}$ are estimated by multiplying the export ratio of the Aichi Prefecture $e_i^{AJ} = E_i^{AJ}/X_i^A$ and $e_i^{AW} = E_i^{AW}/X_i^A$ with the municipal product $X_i^r$, respectively.

$$E_i^{rJ} = e_i^{AJ} \cdot X_i^r \tag{6.5}$$

[1] The 2011 IOT of Aichi Prefecture has 188 sectors, which are compiled into 106 sectors. At that time, we combined two sectors, “3511 passenger cars” and “3521 trucks, buses, and other automobiles,” into one sector “automobiles,” and returned the activity of “573 self-transport” to the input of each sector. Additionally, the sectors “2612 iron scrap” and “2712 non-ferrous metal scrap” were moved to exogenous sectors.

**Table 6.1** Areas and associated municipalities within Aichi Prefecture

| No. | Area name | Municipalities of Aichi Prefecture | | | | |
|---|---|---|---|---|---|---|
| 1 | Nagoya city | Nagoya city | | | | |
| 2 | Owari area | Ichinomiya city | Seto city | Kasugai city | Inuyama city | Konan city |
| | | Komaki city | Inazawa city | Owariasahi city | Iwakura city | Toyoake city |
| | | Nishin city | Kiyosu city | Kitanagoya city | Nagakute city | Togo town |
| | | Toyoyama town | Oguchi town | Fuso town | | |
| 3 | Ama area | Tsushima city | Aisai city | Yatomi city | Ama city | Oharu town |
| | | Kanie town | Tobishima village | | | |
| 4 | Chita area | Handa city | Tokoname city | Tokai city | Obu city | Chita city |
| | | Agui town | Higashiura town | Minamichita town | Mihama town | Taketoyo town |
| 5 | Nishimikawa area | Okazaki city | Hekinan city | Kariya city | Toyota city | Anjo city |
| | | Nishio city | Chiryu city | Takahama city | Miyoshi city | Koda town |
| 6 | Higishimikawa area | Toyohashi city | Toyokawa city | Gamagori city | Shinshiro city | Tahara city |
| | | Shidara town | Toei town | Toyone village | | |

*Source* Prepared by the author, based on the regional classification provided on the Aichi Prefecture website (https://www.pref.aichi.jp/site/userguide/link-citytown.html)

$$E_i^{rW} = e_i^{AW} \cdot X_i^r \tag{6.6}$$

Furthermore, imports from the ROJ $M_i^{rJ}$ and from the ROW $M_i^{rW}$ are estimated by multiplying the import coefficients of the Aichi Prefecture $m_i^{AJ} = M_i^{AJ}/D_i^A$ and $m_i^{AW} = M_i^{AW}/D_i^A$ with the municipal domestic demand $D_i^r$, respectively.

$$M_i^{rJ} = m_i^{AJ} \cdot D_i^r \tag{6.7}$$

$$M_i^{rW} = m_i^{AW} \cdot D_i^r \tag{6.8}$$

(5) The imbalance between supply and demand by sector in each municipality is defined as net export by the sector of each municipality $E_i^{rA} - M_i^{rA}$.

**Table 6.2** List of 106 sectors

| Number | Sector code | Description |
|---|---|---|
| 1 | 011 | Crop cultivation |
| 2 | 012 | Livestock |
| 3 | 013 | Agricultural services |
| 4 | 015 | Forestry |
| 5 | 017 | Fishery |
| 6 | 061 | Metallic ores |
| 7 | 062 | Coal mining, crude petroleum and natural gas |
| 8 | 063 | Non-metallic ores |
| 9 | 111 | Foods |
| 10 | 112 | Beverage |
| 11 | 113 | Feeds and organic fertilizer, n.e.c |
| 12 | 114 | Tobacco |
| 13 | 151 | Textile products |
| 14 | 152 | Wearing apparel and miscellaneous ready-made textile products |
| 15 | 161 | Lumber and wood products |
| 16 | 162 | Furniture and fixtures |
| 17 | 163 | Pulp, paper, paperboard and building paper |
| 18 | 164 | Paper products |
| 19 | 191 | Printing, plate making and book binding |
| 20 | 201 | Chemical fertilizer |
| 21 | 202 | Industrial inorganic chemicals |
| 22 | 203 | Petrochemical basic products |
| 23 | 204 | Organic chemical products (except petrochemical basic products) |
| 24 | 205 | Synthetic resins |
| 25 | 206 | Synthetic fibers |
| 26 | 207 | Medicaments |
| 27 | 208 | Final chemical products (except medicaments) |
| 28 | 211 | Petroleum refinery products |
| 29 | 212 | Coal products |
| 30 | 221 | Plastic products |
| 31 | 222 | Rubber products |
| 32 | 231 | Leather, fur skins and miscellaneous leather products |
| 33 | 251 | Glass and glass products |
| 34 | 252 | Cement and cement products |
| 35 | 253 | Pottery, china and earthenware |
| 36 | 259 | Miscellaneous ceramic, stone and clay products |

(continued)

**Table 6.2** (continued)

| Number | Sector code | Description |
|---|---|---|
| 37 | 261 | Pig iron and crude steel |
| 38 | 262 | Steel products |
| 39 | 263 | Cast and forged steel products |
| 40 | 269 | Miscellaneous iron or steel products |
| 41 | 271 | Non-ferrous metals |
| 42 | 272 | Non-ferrous metal products |
| 43 | 281 | Metal products for construction and architecture |
| 44 | 289 | Miscellaneous metal products |
| 45 | 291 | General-purpose machinery |
| 46 | 301 | Production machinery |
| 47 | 311 | Business oriented machinery |
| 48 | 321 | Electronic devices |
| 49 | 329 | Miscellaneous electronic components |
| 50 | 331 | Electrical devices and parts |
| 51 | 332 | Household electric appliances |
| 52 | 333 | Applied electronic equipment and electric measuring instruments |
| 53 | 339 | Miscellaneous electrical machinery |
| 54 | 341 | Household electronics equipment |
| 55 | 342 | Electronic computing equipment and accessory equipment of electronic computing equipment |
| 56 | 351/352 | Automobiles |
| 57 | 353 | Motor vehicle parts and accessories |
| 58 | 354 | Ships and repair of ships |
| 59 | 359 | Miscellaneous transportation equipment and repair of transportation equipment |
| 60 | 391 | Miscellaneous manufacturing products |
| 61 | 392 | Reuse and recycling |
| 62 | 411 | Building construction |
| 63 | 412 | Repair of construction |
| 64 | 413 | Public construction |
| 65 | 419 | Miscellaneous civil engineering and construction |
| 66 | 461 | Electricity |
| 67 | 462 | Gas and heat supply |
| 68 | 471 | Water supply |
| 69 | 481 | Waste management service |
| 70 | 511 | Commerce |
| 71 | 531 | Finance and insurance |

(continued)

**Table 6.2** (continued)

| Number | Sector code | Description |
|---|---|---|
| 72 | 551 | Real estate agencies and rental services |
| 73 | 552 | House rent |
| 74 | 553 | House rent (imputed house rent) |
| 75 | 571 | Railway transport |
| 76 | 572 | Road transport (except self-transport) |
| 77 | 574 | Water transport |
| 78 | 575 | Air transport |
| 79 | 576 | Freight forwarding |
| 80 | 577 | Storage facility service |
| 81 | 578 | Services relating to transport |
| 82 | 579 | Postal services and mail delivery |
| 83 | 591 | Communications |
| 84 | 592 | Broadcasting |
| 85 | 593 | Information services |
| 86 | 594 | Internet based services |
| 87 | 595 | Image information, sound information and character information |
| 88 | 611 | Public administration |
| 89 | 631 | Education |
| 90 | 632 | Research |
| 91 | 641 | Medical service |
| 92 | 642 | Health and hygiene |
| 93 | 643 | Social insurance and social welfare |
| 94 | 644 | Nursing care |
| 95 | 659 | Miscellaneous non-profit services |
| 96 | 661 | Goods rental and leasing services |
| 97 | 662 | Advertising services |
| 98 | 663 | Motor vehicle maintenance and machine repair services |
| 99 | 669 | Miscellaneous business services |
| 100 | 671 | Hotels |
| 101 | 672 | Eating and drinking services |
| 102 | 673 | Cleaning, barber shops, beauty shops and public baths |
| 103 | 674 | Amusement and recreational services |
| 104 | 679 | Miscellaneous personal services |
| 105 | 681 | Office supplies |
| 106 | 691 | Activities not elsewhere classified |
| 107 | 700 | Total of intermediate sectors |

*Source* Prepared by the author

**Table 6.3** Trade flow among 54 municipalities of the ith sector

| | Region 1 | Region 2 | ... | Region 54 | Supply, total |
|---|---|---|---|---|---|
| Region 1 | $T_i^{11}$ | $T_i^{12}$ | ... | $T_i^{1,54}$ | $T_i^{1\cdot}$ |
| Region 2 | $T_i^{21}$ | $T_i^{22}$ | ... | $T_i^{2,54}$ | $T_i^{2\cdot}$ |
| ⋮ | ⋮ | ⋮ | | ⋮ | ⋮ |
| Region54 | $T_i^{54,1}$ | $T_i^{54,2}$ | ... | $T_i^{54,54}$ | $T_i^{54\cdot}$ |
| Demand, total | $T_i^{\cdot 1}$ | $T_i^{\cdot 2}$ | ... | $T_i^{\cdot 54}$ | $T_i^{\cdot\cdot}$ |

*Source* Prepared by the author

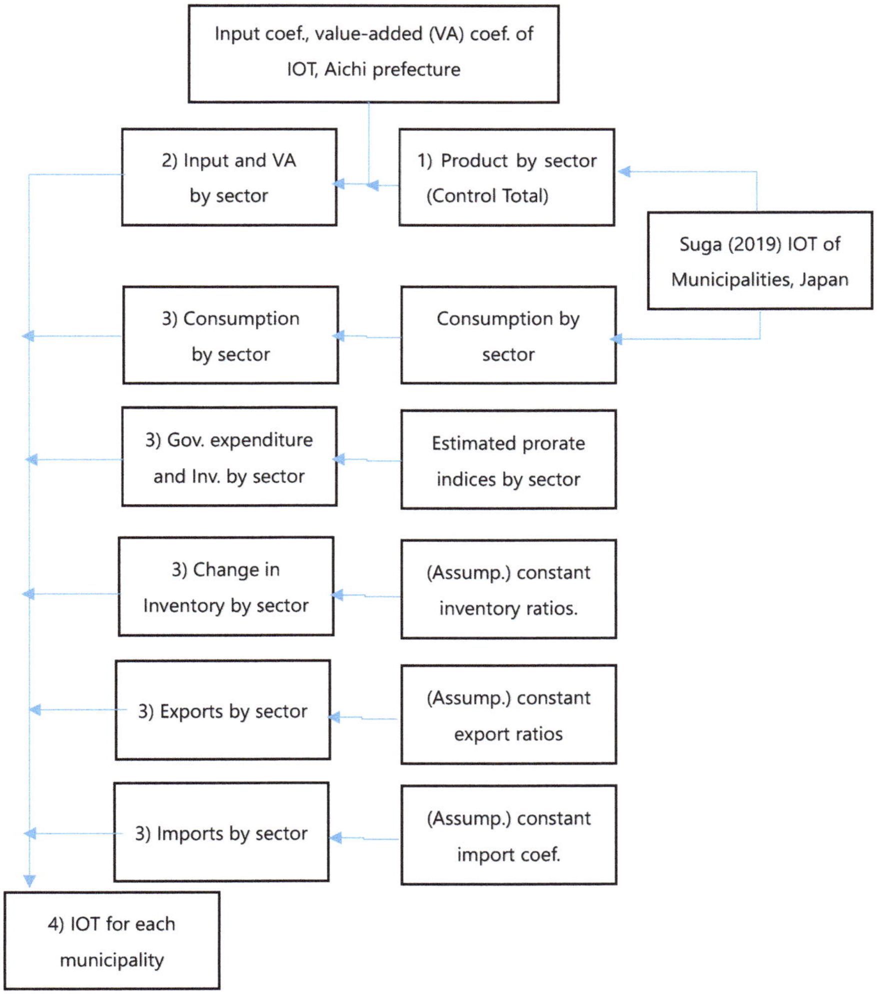


**Fig. 6.1** Estimation flow of each municipal input–output table. *Source* Prepared by the author

$$E_i^{rA} - M_i^{rA} = X_{ij}^r + M_i^{rJ} + M_i^{rW} - \left( \sum_j X_{ij}^r + \sum_j F_{ij}^r + E_i^{rJ} + E_i^{rW} \right) \quad (6.9)$$

As for the division index of products by sector to municipalities, we used the product by sector estimated in the all-municipal IOTs. However, the division index was estimated from other sources for the automobile, electric power, water transport, and air transport sectors.

The estimation of input and added value is based on the corresponding coefficients in the Aichi prefectural IOT in principle. However, in the power sector, municipalities differ significantly in input structure depending on whether power plants are present. Thus, we divided the "electricity" sector into two sectors: the "power generation" and the "distribution and sales" sectors. The input structure of the "distribution and sales" sectors is estimated from that of the "head office" sector obtained from the 2011 Tokyo IOT, with some adjustments. The input structure of the "power generation" sector is obtained by subtracting that of the "distribution and sale" sector from the total. We estimated two input structures for each municipality, and then the sum was used as the input and added value of the "electricity" sector for each municipality.[2]

Next, we estimate the volume of trade among the 54 municipalities by sector. Table 6.3 depicts the diagram of an i-sector's trade flow among the municipalities. Goods and services flow in the horizontal direction. The rightmost column shows the total number of goods and services supplied from r region to each municipality in the prefecture. This can be obtained from sector i's "Supply to municipalities in the prefecture," which refers to the total volume of products minus exports to the ROJ and the ROW in the r municipal IOT. The vertical direction represents purchases (demands) from municipalities in the prefecture for the s municipality, and the bottom line shows the total demand. This is obtained from sector i's "Demand from municipalities within the prefecture," which is equal to the demand within a prefecture minus imports from the ROJ and from the ROW in the s municipality's IOT. Here, the value of "supply to municipalities in the prefecture" minus "demand from municipalities within the prefecture" is equal to the net exports of each municipality.

Here, the amount of trade between r and s municipalities ($T_i^{rs}$) is estimated by a gravity model,[3]and the estimated values are used as the initial value of the RAS method to adjust the constraint to ensure the sum of the trade values between each

---

[2] IN the municipal IOT of Suga (2019), the automobile sector has products even in municipalities that do not have an automobile assembly plant. We estimated the product only for municipalities in which automobile assembly plants exist. For the same reason, for water transport and air transport, product estimates are used by limiting the municipalities to those in which ports are located.

[3] The gravity model describes interregional trade volume using the total demand, supply, and distance in the region. Here, the distance is the road distance between municipalities measured using Google Maps. We used the parameters for each variable estimated in Yamada (2013). This was measured from the interregional flow in the 2005 interregional IOT of the Ministry of Economy, Trade, and Industry, Japan. The target year is different, and the parameters obtained from relatively long-distance trade data are applied to the description of trade between municipalities, where the trade distance is relatively short. These are issues to be considered.

municipality, in the vertical and horizontal directions, is equal to the total value. This two-stepwise method is called the gravity-RAS method.

Gravity parameters for each sector are basically estimated by using the regional trade database from the 2005 interregional input–output table, which is compiled by the Ministry of Economy, Trade and Industry (METI), Japan.[4] Here, it is assumed that the trade amount within the region can also be approximately estimated by a gravity model. The distance in such a case uses an average distance within the region.[5]

In some sectors, there is no trade among municipalities because there is no production in Aichi of the "metal ores," "coal mining, crude petroleum, and natural gas," and "tobacco" sectors. In addition, for each sector of "building construction," "public construction," "miscellaneous civil engineering and construction," "house rent," "house rent (imputed house rent)," "public administration," "social insurance and social welfare," "nursing care," "office supplies," and "activities not elsewhere classified," it is assumed that the product in each municipality is not traded among municipalities. As for "medical services" and "health and hygiene," appropriate parameters could not be estimated; hence, the "total supply" and "total demand" parameters were set to 1 and the "distance" parameter was set to -2.

## 6.3 Comparison of Municipalities from the Interregional Input–Output Table

### *6.3.1 Production*

Table 6.4 presents the comparative advantage index obtained by summarizing the product of 54 municipalities and 106 sectors into six areas (see Table 6.1) and 40 sectors from the compiled inter-municipal IOT. The cell of the value greater than one is highlighted in italic.

According to the table, Nagoya City has an advantage in each of the tertiary industries, and Owari area has competitiveness in manufacturing, especially "textile products," "pulp, paper, and wood products," "metal products," "general machinery," "electronic components," "electric machinery," and "information and communication electronics equipment." The Ama area has an advantage in the "transport" sector. The Chita area excels in "chemicals," "petroleum and coal products," "ceramic, stone, and clay products," "iron and steel," "electricity, gas, heat supply," and "air transport." Nishimikawa area has strength in "transportation equipment," and Higashimikawa area has competitiveness in "agriculture, forestry, and fisheries."

[4] 2005 interregional IOT of METI is the latest version because METI does not compile the next table for 2011.

[5] The average distance within the region was measured as an average distance from the center, assuming that the area is circular.

**Table 6.4** Comparative advantages of products in Aichi Prefecture

| | | 01 Nagoya city | 02 Owaro area | 03 Ama area | 04 Chita area | 05 Nishi-Mikawa area | 06 Higishi-Mikawa area |
|---|---|---|---|---|---|---|---|
| 1 | Agriculture, forestry and fishery | 0.040 | 0.466 | *1.490* | *1.350* | 0.725 | *5.726* |
| 2 | Mining | 0.094 | 0.978 | 0.894 | *2.405* | *1.177* | *1.970* |
| 3 | Beverages and Foods | 0.694 | *1.727* | *1.225* | *1.302* | 0.702 | *1.390* |
| 4 | Textile products | 0.408 | *2.080* | *1.152* | 0.158 | *1.079* | *2.076* |
| 5 | Pulp, paper and wooden products | 0.427 | *3.150* | *2.619* | 0.613 | 0.415 | *1.338* |
| 6 | Chemical products | 0.505 | *1.186* | 0.581 | *3.574* | 0.531 | 0.823 |
| 7 | Petroleum and coal products | 0.077 | 0.123 | 0.252 | *7.812* | 0.123 | 0.171 |
| 8 | Ceramic, stone and clay products | 0.667 | *1.409* | 0.422 | *2.930* | 0.544 | 0.683 |
| 9 | Iron and steel | 0.446 | 0.135 | *1.938* | *4.890* | 0.547 | 0.699 |
| 10 | Non-ferrous metals | *1.446* | *1.126* | 0.924 | 0.410 | 0.712 | 0.891 |
| 11 | Metal products | 0.552 | *2.239* | *2.133* | 0.820 | 0.929 | 0.632 |
| 12 | General machinery | 0.704 | *2.167* | 0.758 | 0.460 | 0.961 | 0.964 |
| 13 | Electronic components | 0.196 | *2.158* | 0.133 | 0.653 | *1.742* | 0.191 |
| 14 | Electrical machinery | 0.711 | *2.127* | 0.649 | 0.378 | *1.031* | 0.917 |
| 15 | Information and communication electronics equipment | 0.175 | *2.447* | 0.724 | 0.293 | *1.654* | 0.353 |
| 16 | Transportation equipment | 0.091 | 0.165 | 0.294 | 0.375 | *2.640* | *1.362* |
| 17 | Miscellaneous manufacturing products | 0.430 | *1.895* | *1.477* | 0.748 | 0.955 | *1.867* |
| 18 | Construction | *1.738* | 0.896 | *1.026* | 0.476 | 0.504 | 0.797 |
| 19 | Electricity, gas and heat supply | 0.675 | 0.069 | *1.987* | *3.831* | 0.644 | *1.010* |
| 20 | Water supply and waste management service | 0.937 | *1.644* | 2.429 | 0.764 | 0.685 | *1.046* |

(continued)

**Table 6.4** (continued)

| | | 01 Nagoya city | 02 Owaro area | 03 Ama area | 04 Chita area | 05 Nishi-Mikawa area | 06 Higishi-Mikawa area |
|---|---|---|---|---|---|---|---|
| 21 | Commerce | *1.841* | 0.958 | 0.770 | 0.305 | 0.481 | 0.686 |
| 22 | Finance and insurance | *1.997* | 0.735 | 0.529 | 0.320 | 0.427 | 0.727 |
| 23 | Real estate | *1.408* | *1.399* | *1.240* | 0.567 | 0.524 | 0.883 |
| 24 | Railway transport | *1.779* | 0.921 | *2.672* | 0.189 | 0.319 | *1.099* |
| 25 | Road transport (except self-transport) | 0.890 | *1.804* | *2.942* | 0.637 | 0.702 | 0.903 |
| 26 | Water transport | *2.265* | 0.001 | *2.133* | 0.564 | 0.143 | *1.170* |
| 27 | Air transport | 0.003 | 0.241 | 0.000 | *8.354* | 0.006 | 0.001 |
| 28 | Other transport and postal services | *1.496* | 0.909 | *3.053* | *1.188* | 0.379 | 0.557 |
| 29 | Information and communications | *2.611* | 0.242 | 0.146 | 0.096 | 0.296 | 0.173 |
| 30 | Public administration | *1.089* | *1.492* | *1.571* | 0.702 | 0.669 | *1.137* |
| 31 | Education and research | *1.464* | *1.015* | *1.045* | 0.604 | 0.642 | 0.963 |
| 32 | Medical, health care and welfare | 0.933 | *1.642* | *1.501* | 0.894 | 0.618 | *1.387* |
| 33 | Miscellaneous non-profit services | *1.484* | 0.962 | 0.540 | 0.655 | 0.506 | *1.509* |
| 34 | Business services | *1.835* | 0.860 | 0.686 | 0.329 | 0.580 | 0.541 |
| 35 | Hotels | *1.843* | 0.465 | 0.169 | 0.597 | 0.396 | *1.604* |
| 36 | Eating and drinking services | *1.477* | *1.178* | *1.162* | 0.535 | 0.573 | 0.918 |
| 37 | Amusement and recreational services | *1.341* | *1.340* | 0.618 | 0.361 | 0.645 | *1.279* |
| 38 | Personal services | *1.419* | *1.452* | 0.869 | 0.443 | 0.533 | 0.990 |
| 39 | Office supplies | *1.460* | *1.075* | *1.009* | 0.574 | 0.658 | 0.869 |
| 40 | Activities not elsewhere classified | *1.342* | *1.087* | *1.134* | 0.796 | 0.679 | 0.888 |
| 41 | Total of intermediate sectors | 1.000 | 1.000 | 1.000 | 1.000 | 1.000 | 1.000 |

*Source* Prepared by the author

### 6.3.2 *Comparison of Procurement and Supply Rates by Region*

Table 6.5 presents the regional procurement rate and supply rate for each municipality. On the demand side, it shows the domestic demand, the self-sufficiency rate, and the import coefficient from the ROA Prefecture and the ROJ. However, the supply information considers the product, supply rate in the municipality, and export rates to the ROA and ROJ. In addition to the 54 municipalities, the table depicts the values for six areas: Nagoya City, Owari area, Ama area, Chita area, Nishimikawa area, and Higashimikawa area. We calculated the average values, the maximum, the minimum, and the standard deviation for 54 municipalities.

Figure 6.2 shows the relationship between regional demand (logarithmic value) and self-sufficiency rates. In general, a downwardly convex relationship is observed. The municipalities with larger domestic demands have higher self-sufficiency rates, while the smaller ones have higher rates of imports from other regions.

However, the municipalities with the smallest demand increase their self-sufficiency rates. This is thought to be because they have an industrial structure centered on the tertiary industry and not so much on the manufacturing industry, which requires increased trade with the other regions.

The white circles in the figure indicate the relationship based on the aggregated values in the six regions. They are excluded to derive the approximate curve except Nagoya City, which is a common region in both definitions, but as a result, they are close to the approximate curve.

Figure 6.3 depicts the relationship between the product (logarithmic value) of each municipality and its supply rates; the export rate to the municipality, the ROA, and the ROJ. This figure indicates that municipalities with larger products have a higher export rate to the ROJ and, conversely, lower supply rates to the municipality and to the ROA. The larger the municipalities, the greater the proportion of supplies outside the prefecture. This means that smaller municipalities tend to concentrate on the market in the prefecture.

## 6.4 Interdependence Among the Municipalities in Aichi Prefecture

Here, we calculated the amount of value-added induced by the final demand based on the compiled 2011 inter-municipal IOT and examined the interdependency among municipalities. This IOT has 106 sectors in 55 regions, including the ROJ, with 5,830 endogenous sectors. To examine the interdependence among municipalities, the 5,830 values of the value-added induced by the final demand of 54 municipalities were totaled for 54 municipalities. This information has a 54 by 54 matrix size, which is still too large. The data were then aggregated to ensure the values of the 54 municipalities that provide the final demand were also counted for the six areas

**Table 6.5** Procurement and supply by region for each municipality (unit: billion yen, %)

| | | Domestic demand | Procurement from own region | Imports from the ROA | Imports from the ROJ | Imports from the ROW | Production | Supply to own region | Exports to the ROA | Exports to the ROJ | Exports to the ROW |
|---|---|---|---|---|---|---|---|---|---|---|---|
| 1 | Nagoya city | 20,603.0 | 0.562 | 0.136 | 0.233 | 0.069 | 22,125.5 | 0.524 | 0.249 | 0.168 | 0.060 |
| 2 | Owari area | 11,644.9 | 0.391 | 0.264 | 0.271 | 0.075 | 10,785.2 | 0.422 | 0.193 | 0.292 | 0.092 |
| 3 | Ama area | 2,014.1 | 0.338 | 0.322 | 0.253 | 0.088 | 1,836.4 | 0.370 | 0.296 | 0.261 | 0.073 |
| 4 | Chita area | 7,711.1 | 0.351 | 0.215 | 0.241 | 0.193 | 8,087.1 | 0.335 | 0.281 | 0.300 | 0.083 |
| 5 | Nishi-Mikawa area | 19,029.2 | 0.402 | 0.215 | 0.305 | 0.078 | 20,563.0 | 0.372 | 0.108 | 0.300 | 0.215 |
| 6 | Higashi-Mikawa area | 62,54.1 | 0.429 | 0.211 | 0.276 | 0.084 | 6,240.0 | 0.430 | 0.154 | 0.277 | 0.136 |
| 1 | Nagoya city | 20,603.0 | 0.562 | 0.136 | 0.233 | 0.069 | 22,125.5 | 0.524 | 0.249 | 0.168 | 0.060 |
| 2 | Toyohashi city | 2,606.0 | 0.402 | 0.261 | 0.261 | 0.075 | 2,489.7 | 0.421 | 0.259 | 0.242 | 0.076 |
| 3 | Okazaki city | 2,832.9 | 0.275 | 0.387 | 0.273 | 0.065 | 2,739.7 | 0.284 | 0.303 | 0.246 | 0.164 |
| 4 | Ichinomiya city | 1,908.2 | 0.395 | 0.305 | 0.236 | 0.064 | 1,586.7 | 0.475 | 0.282 | 0.198 | 0.046 |
| 5 | Seto city | 805.3 | 0.227 | 0.402 | 0.291 | 0.080 | 755.1 | 0.242 | 0.337 | 0.337 | 0.083 |
| 6 | Handa city | 1,058.3 | 0.327 | 0.330 | 0.258 | 0.084 | 1,059.1 | 0.327 | 0.316 | 0.271 | 0.085 |
| 7 | Kasugai city | 1,839.1 | 0.315 | 0.358 | 0.258 | 0.069 | 1,604.7 | 0.361 | 0.306 | 0.257 | 0.075 |
| 8 | Toyokawa city | 1,314.2 | 0.270 | 0.375 | 0.280 | 0.075 | 1,271.2 | 0.279 | 0.270 | 0.319 | 0.130 |
| 9 | Tsushima city | 322.6 | 0.324 | 0.368 | 0.243 | 0.064 | 264.6 | 0.395 | 0.385 | 0.175 | 0.045 |
| 10 | Hekikai city | 1,156.1 | 0.261 | 0.300 | 0.251 | 0.188 | 1,273.2 | 0.237 | 0.428 | 0.248 | 0.085 |
| 11 | Kariya city | 1,688.1 | 0.247 | 0.378 | 0.307 | 0.068 | 1,865.3 | 0.224 | 0.276 | 0.298 | 0.198 |
| 12 | toyohashi city | 8,080.5 | 0.258 | 0.351 | 0.323 | 0.068 | 9,011.5 | 0.231 | 0.156 | 0.315 | 0.291 |
| 13 | Aoji city | 1,723.5 | 0.233 | 0.379 | 0.315 | 0.074 | 1,812.3 | 0.221 | 0.322 | 0.309 | 0.144 |

(continued)

**Table 6.5** (continued)

| | | Domestic demand | Procurement from own region | Imports from the ROA | Imports from the ROJ | Imports from the ROW | Production | Supply to own region | Exports to the ROA | Exports to the ROJ | Exports to the ROW |
|---|---|---|---|---|---|---|---|---|---|---|---|
| 14 | Bisai city | 1,282.0 | 0.266 | 0.380 | 0.285 | 0.068 | 1,401.4 | 0.244 | 0.376 | 0.251 | 0.126 |
| 15 | Gamagori city | 526.3 | 0.296 | 0.349 | 0.271 | 0.083 | 506.1 | 0.308 | 0.314 | 0.277 | 0.099 |
| 16 | Inuyama city | 530.1 | 0.271 | 0.357 | 0.296 | 0.076 | 508.3 | 0.283 | 0.271 | 0.332 | 0.112 |
| 17 | Tokoname city | 469.0 | 0.297 | 0.369 | 0.257 | 0.076 | 489.3 | 0.285 | 0.395 | 0.210 | 0.111 |
| 18 | Konan city | 442.7 | 0.314 | 0.390 | 0.234 | 0.062 | 311.0 | 0.447 | 0.296 | 0.213 | 0.044 |
| 19 | komaki city | 1,527.1 | 0.254 | 0.343 | 0.311 | 0.092 | 1,757.6 | 0.221 | 0.303 | 0.367 | 0.107 |
| 20 | Inazawa city | 980.3 | 0.255 | 0.356 | 0.296 | 0.093 | 1,001.9 | 0.250 | 0.288 | 0.345 | 0.116 |
| 21 | Shinshiro city | 375.1 | 0.214 | 0.391 | 0.300 | 0.095 | 385.5 | 0.208 | 0.324 | 0.345 | 0.121 |
| 22 | Tokai city | 2,433.3 | 0.406 | 0.219 | 0.250 | 0.124 | 2697.4 | 0.366 | 0.241 | 0.310 | 0.082 |
| 23 | Obu city | 827.9 | 0.213 | 0.406 | 0.307 | 0.073 | 859.7 | 0.205 | 0.357 | 0.289 | 0.145 |
| 24 | Chita city | 1,807.7 | 0.154 | 0.198 | 0.165 | 0.484 | 1,912.3 | 0.145 | 0.523 | 0.291 | 0.040 |
| 25 | Chiryu city | 350.3 | 0.258 | 0.428 | 0.245 | 0.069 | 269.6 | 0.336 | 0.358 | 0.225 | 0.080 |
| 26 | Owariasahi city | 471.5 | 0.258 | 0.396 | 0.263 | 0.084 | 385.8 | 0.315 | 0.246 | 0.196 | 0.236 |
| 27 | Takahama city | 420.1 | 0.187 | 0.418 | 0.308 | 0.087 | 458.3 | 0.172 | 0.218 | 0.388 | 0.218 |
| 28 | Iwakura city | 229.5 | 0.270 | 0.424 | 0.237 | 0.068 | 176.7 | 0.351 | 0.343 | 0.238 | 0.068 |
| 29 | Toyoake city | 365.5 | 0.252 | 0.419 | 0.260 | 0.070 | 299.8 | 0.307 | 0.333 | 0.287 | 0.072 |
| 30 | Nisshin city | 426.0 | 0.275 | 0.433 | 0.230 | 0.061 | 320.7 | 0.365 | 0.381 | 0.177 | 0.076 |
| 31 | Tahara city | 1,372.0 | 0.264 | 0.327 | 0.301 | 0.109 | 1,546.5 | 0.234 | 0.217 | 0.286 | 0.257 |
| 32 | Aisai city | 270.0 | 0.257 | 0.451 | 0.228 | 0.064 | 192.8 | 0.359 | 0.373 | 0.218 | 0.050 |
| 33 | Kiyosu city | 467.9 | 0.231 | 0.410 | 0.286 | 0.072 | 484.8 | 0.223 | 0.291 | 0.402 | 0.083 |

(continued)

**Table 6.5** (continued)

| | | Domestic demand | Procurement from own region | Imports from the ROA | Imports from the ROJ | Imports from the ROW | Production | Supply to own region | Exports to the ROA | Exports to the ROJ | Exports to the ROW |
|---|---|---|---|---|---|---|---|---|---|---|---|
| 34 | Kitanagoya city | 464.0 | 0.296 | 0.383 | 0.254 | 0.067 | 412.8 | 0.332 | 0.315 | 0.296 | 0.056 |
| 35 | Yatomi city | 287.4 | 0.242 | 0.403 | 0.273 | 0.082 | 295.8 | 0.235 | 0.340 | 0.312 | 0.112 |
| 36 | Miyoshi city | 796.6 | 0.143 | 0.473 | 0.314 | 0.071 | 870.9 | 0.130 | 0.383 | 0.325 | 0.157 |
| 37 | Ama city | 428.0 | 0.268 | 0.425 | 0.244 | 0.064 | 314.1 | 0.365 | 0.316 | 0.249 | 0.070 |
| 38 | Nagakute city | 288.8 | 0.275 | 0.426 | 0.235 | 0.064 | 203.7 | 0.391 | 0.431 | 0.125 | 0.053 |
| 39 | Togo town | 243.3 | 0.202 | 0.452 | 0.279 | 0.067 | 203.8 | 0.242 | 0.367 | 0.322 | 0.068 |
| 40 | Toyoyama town | 167.8 | 0.179 | 0.445 | 0.297 | 0.079 | 232.1 | 0.129 | 0.366 | 0.347 | 0.155 |
| 41 | Oguchi town | 342.8 | 0.183 | 0.365 | 0.368 | 0.084 | 436.0 | 0.144 | 0.273 | 0.383 | 0.196 |
| 42 | Fuso town | 144.9 | 0.262 | 0.429 | 0.242 | 0.066 | 103.8 | 0.367 | 0.319 | 0.238 | 0.076 |
| 43 | Oharu town | 153.7 | 0.226 | 0.427 | 0.274 | 0.073 | 116.2 | 0.299 | 0.310 | 0.309 | 0.080 |
| 44 | Kanie town | 203.2 | 0.321 | 0.373 | 0.243 | 0.062 | 159.7 | 0.408 | 0.325 | 0.227 | 0.039 |
| 45 | Tobishima village | 349.2 | 0.240 | 0.304 | 0.270 | 0.186 | 493.2 | 0.170 | 0.445 | 0.301 | 0.084 |
| 46 | Agui town | 127.7 | 0.228 | 0.445 | 0.254 | 0.072 | 104.2 | 0.280 | 0.331 | 0.218 | 0.167 |
| 47 | Higashiura town | 326.0 | 0.169 | 0.480 | 0.267 | 0.084 | 282.0 | 0.195 | 0.337 | 0.269 | 0.195 |
| 48 | Minamichita town | 97.9 | 0.262 | 0.407 | 0.259 | 0.072 | 80.7 | 0.317 | 0.408 | 0.249 | 0.027 |
| 49 | Mihama town | 130.5 | 0.288 | 0.384 | 0.253 | 0.075 | 104.3 | 0.361 | 0.310 | 0.314 | 0.017 |
| 50 | Taketoyo town | 432.7 | 0.209 | 0.353 | 0.279 | 0.159 | 498.1 | 0.181 | 0.272 | 0.482 | 0.063 |
| 51 | Koda town | 698.9 | 0.151 | 0.373 | 0.352 | 0.124 | 860.8 | 0.123 | 0.249 | 0.419 | 0.203 |
| 52 | Shidara town | 32.2 | 0.302 | 0.436 | 0.202 | 0.061 | 22.3 | 0.435 | 0.367 | 0.175 | 0.024 |

(continued)

**Table 6.5** (continued)

| | | Domestic demand | Procurement from own region | Imports from the ROA | Imports from the ROJ | Imports from the ROW | Production | Supply to own region | Exports to the ROA | Exports to the ROJ | Exports to the ROW |
|---|---|---|---|---|---|---|---|---|---|---|---|
| 53 | Toei town | 17.2 | 0.318 | 0.422 | 0.205 | 0.056 | 10.6 | 0.517 | 0.308 | 0.141 | 0.034 |
| 54 | Toyone village | 11.2 | 0.339 | 0.420 | 0.194 | 0.047 | 8.0 | 0.474 | 0.455 | 0.059 | 0.013 |
| | Average | 1245.5 | 0.266 | 0.378 | 0.267 | 0.088 | 1,289.6 | 0.295 | 0.325 | 0.274 | 0.104 |
| | Maximal value | 20,603.0 | 0.562 | 0.480 | 0.368 | 0.484 | 22,125.5 | 0.524 | 0.523 | 0.482 | 0.291 |
| | Minimal Value | 11.2 | 0.143 | 0.136 | 0.165 | 0.047 | 8.0 | 0.123 | 0.156 | 0.059 | 0.013 |
| | Standard deviation | 2,946.2 | 0.071 | 0.066 | 0.038 | 0.062 | 3,181.3 | 0.101 | 0.066 | 0.078 | 0.064 |

*Source* Prepared by the author

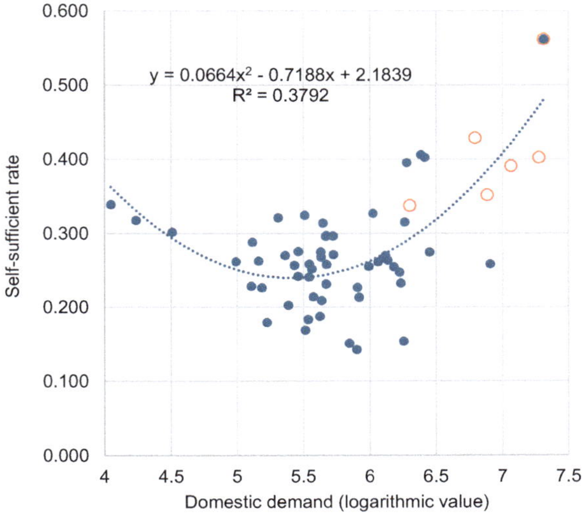


**Fig. 6.2** Domestic demand and the self-sufficient rate. *Source* Prepared by the author

mentioned above. Consequently, observing 54 municipalities' value-added-induced amounts for the final demand generated in the municipalities of each area became possible.

## 6.4.1 Induced Value-Added by the Domestic Final Demand of Each Municipality

Table 6.6 depicts municipalities' value-added induced by the domestic final demand within each municipality. This is summarized in the form of the total value-added-induced value of 54 municipalities and the composition ratio of six areas. The cell with the largest share is denoted as itatic modification. The total value refers to the amount of value-added induction for the domestic final demand in Aichi Prefecture. Nagoya City has the largest at 8,232.1 billion yen, followed by Toyohashi City at 743.2 billion yen, Toyota City at 730.8 billion yen, Okazaki City at 696.3 billion yen, Ichinomiya City at 655.8 billion yen, and Kasugai City at 539.4 billion yen. As the value-added is induced by regional domestic final demand, the order is roughly proportional to the population size.

For regional composition, the ratio is obviously the largest in its own region. It is approximately 80% in large areas and 60% in small areas. Municipalities with smaller ratios are more dependent on the final demand in other regions.

The value-added induced in Nagoya City depends on its own area at 66.49%, which is relatively low. It also depends on regional final demand in other areas, such as the Owari area, (13.50%), and the Nishimikawa area, (9.65%). Conversely, Ichinomiya City obtains the value-added inducement at 82.11% from its own area,

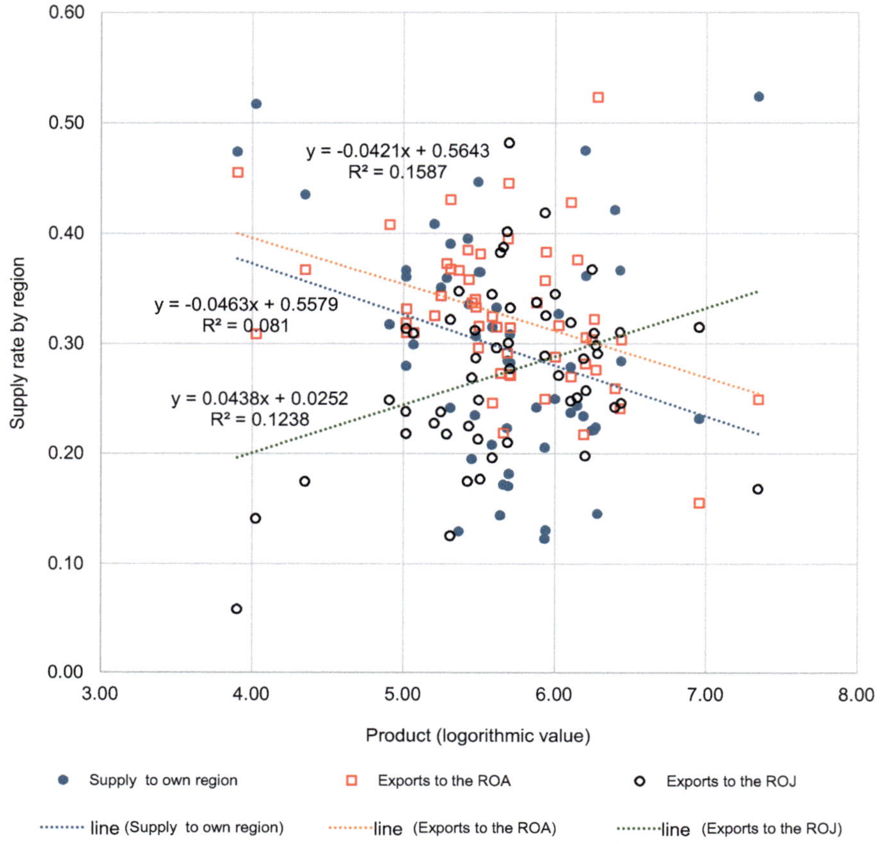


**Fig. 6.3** Product and supply rates by region. *Source* Prepared by the author

with 9.72% from Nagoya City, which indicates that the dependency on the other area is low. Konan City also has a large share in its own area at 87.53%, and Nagoya City at 6.70%. Both cities have a certain relationship with Nagoya City, but they have a low connection with other areas.

In addition, in all municipalities, the percentage of value-added induced by the final demand originating from Nagoya is larger than that in other regions, apart from their own area, and accounts for 10–20% in most cases. In that sense, all municipalities depend on the final demand in Nagoya.

Using 10% as one criterion, we measured the interregional dependency by the regional ripple effect of the value-added induced by the final demand in each area. Mutual dependency between Nagoya City and Owari Area was observed, although one-sided dependency was observed from Nagoya City to Chita Area, to Ama Area, and from Owari Area to Ama Area. By contrast, the relationship between the Nishimikawa area and the Higashimikawa area is relatively weak.

**Table 6.6** Value-added induced from the domestic final demand by region, and the regional composition rates (unit: billion yen, %)

| Area code | Municipality name | Total | Nagoya city | Owari area | Ama area | Chita area | Nishi-mikawa area | Higashi-mikawa area |
|---|---|---|---|---|---|---|---|---|
| R01 | 01 Nagoya city | 8,232.1 | *66.49* | 13.50 | 2.56 | 4.69 | 9.65 | 3.11 |
| R06 | 02 Toyohashi city | 743.2 | 4.55 | 2.96 | 0.53 | 1.63 | 7.81 | *82.51* |
| R05 | 12 Toyota city | 730.8 | 13.63 | 10.37 | 1.28 | 4.42 | *65.09* | 5.21 |
| R05 | 03 Okazaki city | 696.3 | 7.18 | 4.37 | 0.74 | 3.26 | *78.08* | 6.36 |
| R02 | 04 Ichinomiya city | 655.8 | 9.72 | *82.11* | 1.82 | 1.57 | 3.49 | 1.28 |
| R02 | 07 Kasugai city | 539.4 | 16.27 | *74.22* | 1.19 | 1.94 | 4.96 | 1.43 |
| R02 | 19 Komaki city | 364.3 | 16.45 | *71.52* | 1.54 | 2.57 | 5.89 | 2.04 |
| R05 | 11 Kariya city | 331.8 | 8.72 | 5.44 | 0.87 | 10.61 | *70.98* | 3.40 |
| R05 | 13 Anjo city | 311.2 | 8.41 | 5.07 | 0.86 | 5.18 | *76.62* | 3.85 |
| R06 | 08 Toyokawa city | 309.2 | 4.98 | 3.03 | 0.56 | 1.74 | 9.18 | *80.52* |
| R05 | 14 Nishio city | 263.4 | 7.59 | 4.68 | 0.81 | 5.56 | ***75.33*** | 6.04 |
| R04 | 24 Chita city | 247.1 | 22.45 | 14.48 | 2.36 | 43.68 | 12.66 | 4.36 |
| R02 | 20 Inazawa city | 241.9 | 13.96 | *73.26* | 4.32 | 2.12 | 4.69 | 1.64 |
| R04 | 06 Handa city | 235.7 | 8.26 | 4.26 | 0.81 | *71.29* | 13.17 | 2.22 |
| R04 | 22 Tokai city | 225.7 | 16.40 | 6.84 | 1.36 | *63.23* | 9.68 | 2.49 |
| R02 | 05 Seto city | 212.5 | 18.42 | *65.62* | 1.22 | 2.18 | 10.77 | 1.80 |
| R04 | 23 Obu city | 158.5 | 14.73 | 6.80 | 1.08 | *59.19* | 16.21 | 1.99 |
| R05 | 10 Hekinan city | 155.0 | 9.36 | 6.40 | 0.97 | 7.85 | *71.32* | 4.09 |
| R06 | 15 Gomagori city | 149.1 | 6.40 | 4.30 | 0.73 | 2.96 | 19.98 | *65.62* |
| R02 | 34 Kitanagoya city | 140.2 | 14.12 | *76.20* | 1.92 | 2.07 | 4.23 | 1.47 |
| R02 | 18 Konan city | 126.4 | 6.70 | *87.53* | 0.90 | 1.17 | 2.71 | 0.99 |
| R02 | 16 Inuyama city | 126.1 | 11.29 | *78.82* | 1.17 | 2.13 | 4.90 | 1.69 |
| R06 | 31 Tahara city | 124.3 | 11.96 | 9.00 | 1.33 | 3.33 | 10.82 | *63.56* |
| R04 | 17 Tokoname city | 122.8 | 15.11 | 8.82 | 1.61 | *57.73* | 12.69 | 4.04 |
| R02 | 30 Nisshin city | 121.2 | 12.36 | *69.82* | 0.89 | 2.49 | 12.40 | 2.04 |
| R02 | 33 Kiyosu city | 120.0 | 23.78 | *61.67* | 2.76 | 3.07 | 6.53 | 2.18 |
| R03 | 09 Tsushima city | 110.6 | 13.65 | 9.66 | *69.74* | 1.78 | 3.86 | 1.31 |
| R03 | 37 Ama city | 109.6 | 14.78 | 7.74 | *71.06* | 1.68 | 3.60 | 1.15 |
| R02 | 26 Owariasahi city | 109.1 | 11.13 | *79.30* | 0.75 | 1.68 | 5.71 | 1.42 |

(continued)

**Table 6.6** (continued)

| Area code | Municipality name | Total | Nagoya city | Owari area | Ama area | Chita area | Nishi-mikawa area | Higashi-mikawa area |
|---|---|---|---|---|---|---|---|---|
| R05 | 36 Miyoshi city | 99.7 | 11.77 | 13.02 | 0.96 | 3.04 | *68.76* | 2.45 |
| R02 | 29 Toyoake city | 97.8 | 12.42 | *64.03* | 1.03 | 5.80 | 14.68 | 2.04 |
| R02 | 38 Nagakute city | 94.4 | 17.49 | *69.51* | 0.99 | 1.91 | 8.62 | 1.49 |
| R05 | 25 Chiryu city | 89.0 | 6.95 | 4.60 | 0.67 | 4.71 | *80.55* | 2.52 |
| R06 | 21 Shinshiro city | 80.8 | 8.69 | 5.16 | 0.98 | 2.79 | 12.17 | *70.21* |
| R03 | 35 Yatomi city | 76.9 | 19.28 | 9.95 | *57.46* | 3.46 | 7.38 | 2.48 |
| R03 | 32 Aisai city | 76.7 | 12.92 | 8.90 | *69.53* | 2.31 | 4.78 | 1.57 |
| R03 | 45 Tobishima village | 69.6 | 33.76 | 19.18 | 20.01 | 7.43 | 14.66 | 4.95 |
| R02 | 28 Iwakura city | 63.1 | 10.57 | *81.46* | 1.31 | 1.61 | 3.72 | 1.33 |
| R05 | 51 Koda town | 62.2 | 13.51 | 8.36 | 1.39 | 4.65 | *62.40* | 9.68 |
| R04 | 50 Taketiyi town | 59.5 | 11.51 | 7.35 | 1.24 | *66.35* | 10.66 | 2.89 |
| R02 | 41 Oguchi town | 58.4 | 16.09 | *68.54* | 1.61 | 3.38 | 7.63 | 2.74 |
| R03 | 44 Kanie town | 58.4 | 12.34 | 6.94 | *72.20* | 2.32 | 4.66 | 1.53 |
| R04 | 47 Higashiura town | 58.3 | 8.26 | 4.20 | 0.72 | *68.90* | 16.21 | 1.71 |
| R05 | 27 Takahama city | 53.9 | 6.78 | 3.93 | 0.64 | 8.13 | *78.12* | 2.40 |
| R02 | 39 Togo town | 53.0 | 11.09 | *64.10* | 0.78 | 2.64 | 19.58 | 1.82 |
| R02 | 40 Toyoyama town | 48.5 | 25.08 | *54.99* | 2.65 | 4.22 | 9.55 | 3.50 |
| R02 | 42 Fusu town | 39.4 | 6.67 | *87.31* | 0.80 | 1.24 | 2.90 | 1.07 |
| R04 | 49 Mihama town | 34.1 | 8.80 | 5.27 | 1.00 | *73.30* | 9.30 | 2.34 |
| R03 | 43 Oharu town | 32.4 | 14.25 | 7.46 | *71.30* | 1.82 | 3.87 | 1.30 |
| R04 | 46 Agui town | 32.1 | 9.47 | 4.65 | 0.91 | *72.22* | 10.70 | 2.05 |
| R04 | 48 Minimichita town | 27.3 | 12.87 | 8.98 | 1.72 | *60.81* | 12.50 | 3.13 |
| R06 | 52 Shidara town | 9.5 | 9.03 | 6.84 | 1.03 | 2.35 | 10.34 | *70.42* |
| R06 | 53 Toei town | 4.9 | 6.56 | 4.87 | 0.76 | 2.00 | 7.55 | *78.26* |
| R06 | 54 Toyone village | 3.8 | 10.96 | 8.04 | 1.28 | 3.01 | 11.14 | *65.57* |
| 1 | Nagoya city | 8,232.1 | *66.49* | 13.50 | 2.56 | 4.69 | 9.65 | 3.11 |
| 2 | Owari area | 3,211.5 | 13.95 | *74.50* | 1.66 | 2.18 | 6.08 | 1.63 |
| 5 | Nishi-Mikawa area | 2,793.2 | 9.64 | 6.68 | 0.95 | 5.28 | *72.44* | 5.01 |

(continued)

**Table 6.6** (continued)

| Area code | Municipality name | Total | Nagoya city | Owari area | Ama area | Chita area | Nishi-mikawa area | Higashi-mikawa area |
|---|---|---|---|---|---|---|---|---|
| 6 | Higishi-Mikawa area | 1,424.9 | 5.77 | 3.81 | 0.66 | 2.02 | 9.91 | *77.82* |
| 4 | Chita area | 1,201.1 | 14.58 | 7.95 | 1.39 | *60.59* | 12.59 | 2.90 |
| 3 | Ama area | 534.3 | 17.10 | 10.01 | *62.10* | 2.87 | 5.94 | 1.98 |
| | Total | 17,397.0 | 37.59 | 22.38 | 3.73 | 7.90 | 19.19 | 9.21 |

*Source* Prepared by the author

Figure 6.4 depicts the value-added induced in each municipality due to the final demand in Nagoya City. Naturally, the value-added of Nagoya City, which is in its own area, is large, and the value-added in other municipalities is relatively low. Not only municipalities around Nagoya City (each of the Owari, Ama, and Chita areas) but also municipalities in the Nishimikawa and Higashimikawa regions have a certain amount of induced value-added.

Figure 6.5 also depicts the value-added induced in each municipality due to the final demand in the Nishimikawa area. Not only is the added value in the Nishimikawa area, its own area, large, but the value added in Nagoya City is also large. The procurement of intermediate goods from Nagoya City is important for satisfying domestic demand in the Nishimikawa area.

## 6.4.2 *Value Added Induced by Exports from Each Municipality*

Table 6.7 presents each municipality's value-added induced by exports in each region, the total value, and the composition ratios by area. The cell with the largest share is showm in italic. The value-added composition ratio of its own area is the largest, as in Table 6.6, ranging from 50 to 95%. In particular, the values of municipalities in the Nishi-mikawa area are higher.

Nagoya City has the largest total value-added inducement of 1,386.3 billion yen, but its composition ratio in its area is low at 56.87% compared to the other municipalities. The proportion of added value derived from exports in other regions is correspondingly large, with the Nishi-mikawa area accounting for 27.52%, which stands out from other regions. Looking at the regional composition of each municipality, unlike the case of domestic final demand, the proportion of the Nishimikawa area is larger than that of Nagoya. This means that municipalities depend on the Nishi-mikawa area for export goods.

Figure 6.6 depicts the value-added of each municipality induced by the exports of Nagoya City, and Fig. 6.7 shows the value-added of each municipality induced by the exports of the Nishi-mikawa area. According to Fig. 6.6, the spillover effect

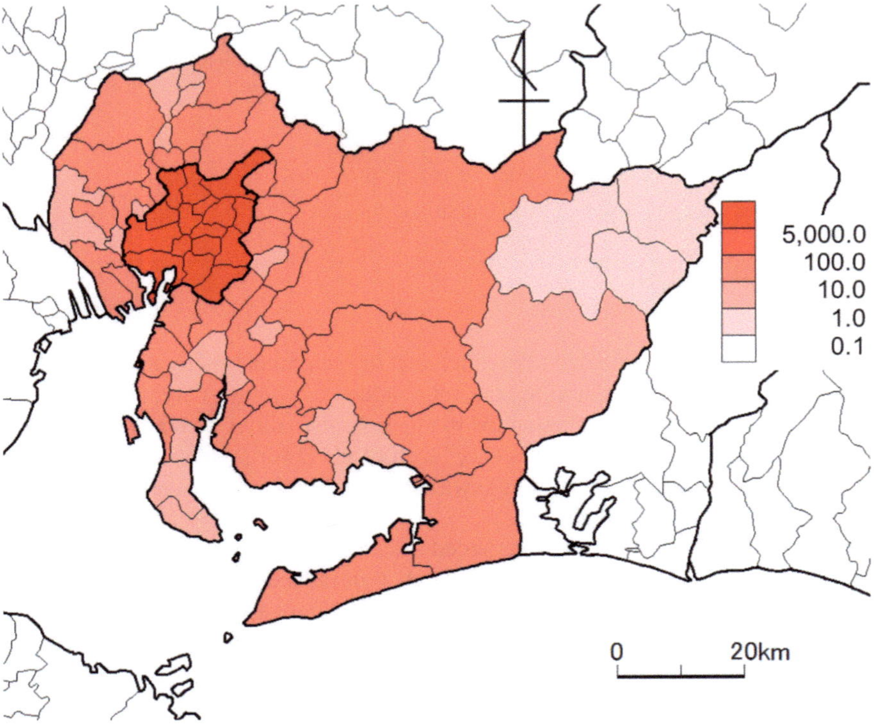


**Fig. 6.4** Value-added induced from the domestic final demand in Nagoya City. *Source* Created by the author using the MANDARA support system for geographic information analysis (http://ktgis.net/mandara/)

on the regional value-added due to the exports of Nagoya City widely spreads to the Owari area (Ichinomiya City, Inazawa City, Kiyosu City, Komaki City, and Kasugai City), the Chita area (Tokai City, Chita City, Tokoname City, Obu City, and Handa City), and the Nishi-mikawa area (Toyota City, Okazaki City, Kariya City, Chiryu City, Nishio City, Takahama City, and Hekinan City).

However, Fig. 6.7 reveals that in the case of exports in the Nishi-mikawa area, the value-added inducement brought to Toyota City is the largest, followed by Okazaki City, Anjo City, and Kariya City. Outside the Nishi-mikawa area, the value-added inducement of Nagoya is large, followed by Ichinomiya City, Komaki City, and Kasugai City in the Owaria area, and Tokai City, Chiryu City, and Obu City in the Chita Area. The ripple effect through automobile-related industries is observed in municipalities such as Toyokawa City, Toyohashi City, and Tahara City in the Higashi-mikawa area.

Comparing Figs. 6.4 and 6.6, cases of the final demand originating from Nagoya City, the value-added induced spreads to more municipalities in the case of domestic

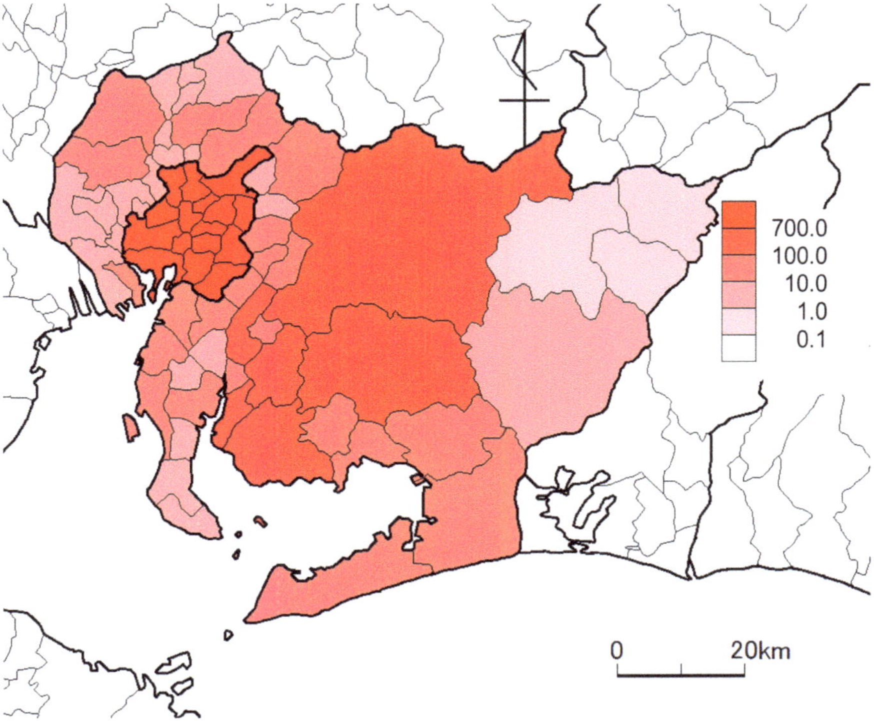


**Fig. 6.5** Value-added induced by the domestic final demand in the Nishi-mikawa area. *Source* Created by the author using the MANDARA support system for geographic information analysis (http://ktgis.net/mandara/)

final demand, like consumption in Nagoya City, than in the case of exports. This can also be observed in the comparison of Figs. 6.5 and 6.7 for the Nishi-mikawa area.

Exports mainly consist of goods, and Aichi Prefecture has significant exports of transportation equipment; the sectors related to such intermediate inputs are relatively concentrated in municipalities in the Nishi-mikawa area. By contrast, domestic final demand in the region, such as consumption, includes not only goods but also services in a wide range of sectors, and the spread between municipalities is expected to be spatially wider. This leads to differences in municipal impact.

**Table 6.7** Value-added induced from the export by region, and the regional composition rates (unit: billion yen, %)

| Area code | Municipality name | Total | Nagoya city | Owari area | Ama area | Chita area | Nishi-mikawa area | Higashi-mikawa area |
|---|---|---|---|---|---|---|---|---|
| R01 | 01 nagoya city | 1,386.3 | *56.87* | 6.81 | 0.91 | 3.66 | 27.52 | 4.23 |
| R05 | 12 Toyota city | 764.6 | 0.94 | 0.98 | 0.12 | 0.91 | *94.48* | 2.56 |
| R05 | 03 Okazaki city | 194.6 | 1.18 | 1.25 | 0.16 | 1.39 | *91.56* | 4.45 |
| R05 | 13 Anji city | 158.2 | 1.18 | 1.31 | 0.17 | 1.97 | *91.29* | 4.08 |
| R05 | 11 kariya city | 149.7 | 1.34 | 1.21 | 0.17 | 3.20 | *91.68* | 2.39 |
| R06 | 02 Toyohashi city | 135.0 | 1.48 | 1.45 | 0.24 | 1.28 | 20.89 | *74.66* |
| R04 | 22 Tokai city | 130.8 | 9.00 | 3.54 | 1.51 | *59.40* | 23.23 | 3.32 |
| R06 | 31 Takara city | 113.2 | 0.68 | 0.77 | 0.12 | 0.59 | 12.36 | *85.49* |
| R02 | 19 Komaki city | 107.4 | 3.85 | *76.17* | 0.37 | 1.75 | 15.44 | 2.42 |
| R05 | 14 Nishio city | 102.3 | 1.37 | 1.43 | 0.21 | 2.16 | *88.68* | 6.15 |
| R02 | 07 Kasugai city | 76.5 | 5.74 | *71.56* | 0.45 | 1.98 | 17.71 | 2.56 |
| R05 | 10 Hakikai city | 71.7 | 2.31 | 1.92 | 0.37 | 3.73 | *86.73* | 4.94 |
| R05 | 51 Koda city | 69.5 | 1.90 | 3.67 | 0.17 | 1.59 | *89.63* | 3.04 |
| R06 | 08 Toyakawa city | 68.6 | 1.10 | 1.19 | 0.17 | 0.97 | 16.89 | 79.69 |
| R05 | 36 Miyoshi city | 67.8 | 1.36 | 1.57 | 0.16 | 1.18 | *93.24* | 2.48 |
| R04 | 23 Obu city | 66.0 | 1.89 | 1.60 | 0.25 | *61.49* | 31.63 | 3.15 |
| R04 | 06 Handa city | 63.7 | 3.33 | 2.43 | 0.56 | *56.78* | 32.60 | 4.31 |
| R02 | 04 Ichinomiya city | 60.3 | 4.18 | *71.76* | 0.71 | 2.16 | 17.89 | 3.30 |
| R02 | 20 Inazawa city | 56.3 | 3.29 | *80.58* | 0.76 | 1.30 | 12.01 | 2.06 |
| R04 | 24 Chita city | 50.6 | 11.45 | 6.60 | 1.10 | 47.32 | 28.65 | 4.88 |
| R05 | 27 Takahama city | 45.2 | 1.22 | 0.74 | 0.21 | 2.13 | *93.96* | 1.73 |
| R02 | 41 Oguchi town | 41.9 | 2.19 | *85.57* | 0.23 | 0.83 | 9.59 | 1.59 |
| R02 | 05 Seto city | 36.1 | 3.45 | *69.35* | 0.30 | 1.42 | 22.78 | 2.71 |
| R02 | 26 Owariasahi city | 33.5 | 1.67 | *88.16* | 0.14 | 0.64 | 8.30 | 1.09 |
| R04 | 17 Tokoname city | 32.5 | 3.67 | 2.82 | 0.35 | *71.57* | 18.41 | 3.19 |
| R02 | 16 Inuyama city | 31.2 | 2.79 | *82.20* | 0.31 | 1.18 | 11.58 | 1.94 |
| R03 | 45 Tobishima village | 29.9 | 8.69 | 5.61 | *58.46* | 3.91 | 19.97 | 3.36 |
| R06 | 15 Gamagori city | 28.0 | 1.58 | 1.48 | 0.20 | 1.37 | 22.55 | *72.82* |
| R06 | 21 Shinshiyo city | 27.0 | 1.68 | 1.85 | 0.23 | 1.30 | 22.56 | *72.39* |

(continued)

**Table 6.7** (continued)

| Area code | Municipality name | Total | Nagoya city | Owari area | Ama area | Chita area | Nishi-mikawa area | Higashi-mikawa area |
|---|---|---|---|---|---|---|---|---|
| R02 | 33 Kiyosu city | 25.1 | 5.92 | *75.17* | 0.60 | 1.78 | 14.28 | 2.25 |
| R04 | 47 Higashiura town | 22.8 | 1.70 | 2.07 | 0.19 | *72.01* | 21.81 | 2.22 |
| R04 | 50 Takatoyo town | 21.3 | 2.24 | 2.46 | 0.34 | *65.35* | 25.75 | 3.86 |
| R02 | 40 Toyoyama town | 21.1 | 3.66 | *82.88* | 0.41 | 1.32 | 10.07 | 1.66 |
| R03 | 35 Yatomi city | 19.8 | 4.98 | 3.25 | *71.81* | 2.30 | 15.02 | 2.64 |
| R02 | 30 Nisshin city | 17.8 | 4.37 | *53.59* | 0.37 | 2.44 | 35.76 | 3.46 |
| R05 | 25 Chiryu city | 17.8 | 1.99 | 2.01 | 0.25 | 3.27 | *88.48* | 4.00 |
| R02 | 34 Kitanagoya city | 17.2 | 5.79 | *71.68* | 0.71 | 2.19 | 16.88 | 2.75 |
| R02 | 29 Toyoake city | 13.8 | 3.27 | *63.42* | 0.32 | 3.27 | 26.68 | 3.04 |
| R02 | 38 nagakute city | 12.7 | 4.00 | 48.08 | 0.36 | 2.19 | 40.93 | 4.43 |
| R03 | 37 Ama city | 12.0 | 6.17 | 5.53 | *63.39* | 2.15 | 19.62 | 3.14 |
| R02 | 39 Togo town | 11.0 | 3.74 | *50.24* | 0.31 | 2.01 | 40.67 | 3.02 |
| R02 | 18 Konan city | 10.4 | 3.45 | *74.94* | 0.45 | 1.78 | 16.55 | 2.83 |
| R03 | 09 Tsushima city | 9.3 | 5.25 | 6.20 | *62.63* | 2.42 | 19.99 | 3.52 |
| R02 | 28 Iwakura city | 9.0 | 4.13 | *74.25* | 0.55 | 1.67 | 16.73 | 2.67 |
| R04 | 46 Agui town | 8.0 | 1.55 | 1.43 | 0.20 | *82.90* | 12.25 | 1.67 |
| R03 | 32 Aisai city | 7.4 | 5.70 | 5.87 | *60.04* | 2.79 | 21.79 | 3.81 |
| R03 | 44 Anie town | 5.8 | 7.10 | 6.18 | *55.75* | 3.14 | 23.96 | 3.86 |
| R03 | 43 Oharu town | 5.6 | 5.18 | 5.05 | *66.15* | 1.78 | 18.98 | 2.86 |
| R02 | 42 Fuso town | 4.4 | 2.88 | *80.12* | 0.35 | 1.42 | 12.92 | 2.32 |
| R04 | 48 Minamichita town | 2.3 | 3.44 | 3.89 | 0.47 | *51.31* | 34.27 | 6.63 |
| R04 | 49 Mihama town | 1.9 | 3.60 | 3.56 | 0.45 | *55.73* | 31.10 | 5.57 |
| R06 | 52 Shidara town | 0.6 | 3.40 | 4.33 | 0.51 | 2.65 | 31.44 | *57.67* |
| R06 | 53 Toei town | 0.3 | 2.55 | 3.15 | 0.41 | 2.14 | 25.04 | *66.72* |
| R06 | 54 Toyone village | 0.1 | 5.32 | 6.11 | 0.89 | 4.66 | 30.92 | *52.11* |
| 5 | Nishi-Mikawa area | 1,641.4 | 1.19 | 1.28 | 0.16 | 1.58 | *92.54* | 3.25 |
| 1 | Nagoya city | 1,386.3 | *56.87* | 6.81 | 0.91 | 3.66 | 27.52 | 4.23 |
| 2 | Owari area | 585.8 | 3.88 | *74.75* | 0.45 | 1.67 | 16.81 | 2.44 |
| 4 | Chita area | 399.9 | 5.82 | 3.19 | 0.83 | *60.23* | 26.34 | 3.60 |

(continued)

**Table 6.7** (continued)

| Area code | Municipality name | Total | Nagoya city | Owari area | Ama area | Chita area | Nishi-mikawa area | Higashi-mikawa area |
|---|---|---|---|---|---|---|---|---|
| 6 | Higashi-Mikawa area | 372.8 | 1.19 | 1.23 | 0.19 | 1.02 | 17.83 | *78.53* |
| 3 | Ama area | 90.0 | 6.61 | 5.17 | *62.93* | 2.89 | 19.18 | 3.23 |
| | Total | 17,397.0 | 37.59 | 22.38 | 3.73 | 7.90 | 19.19 | 9.21 |

*Source* Prepared by the author

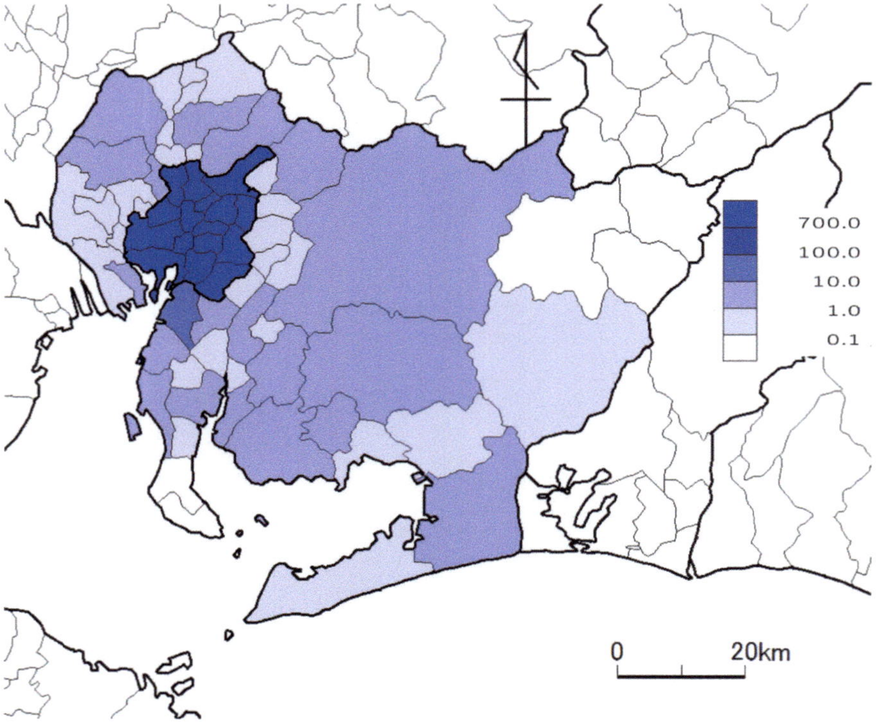


**Fig. 6.6** Value-added induced from the export in Nagoya City. *Source* Created by the author using the MANDARA support system for geographic information analysis (http://ktgis.net/mandara/)

## 6.5 Concluding Remarks

In recent years, there has been increasing interest in constructing and applying municipal-based IOT. Here, an inter-municipal IOT is compiled for Aichi Prefecture. There are 106 sectors for each of the 55 regions, including the ROJ, and the endogenous sector size is 5,830, forming a huge IOT.

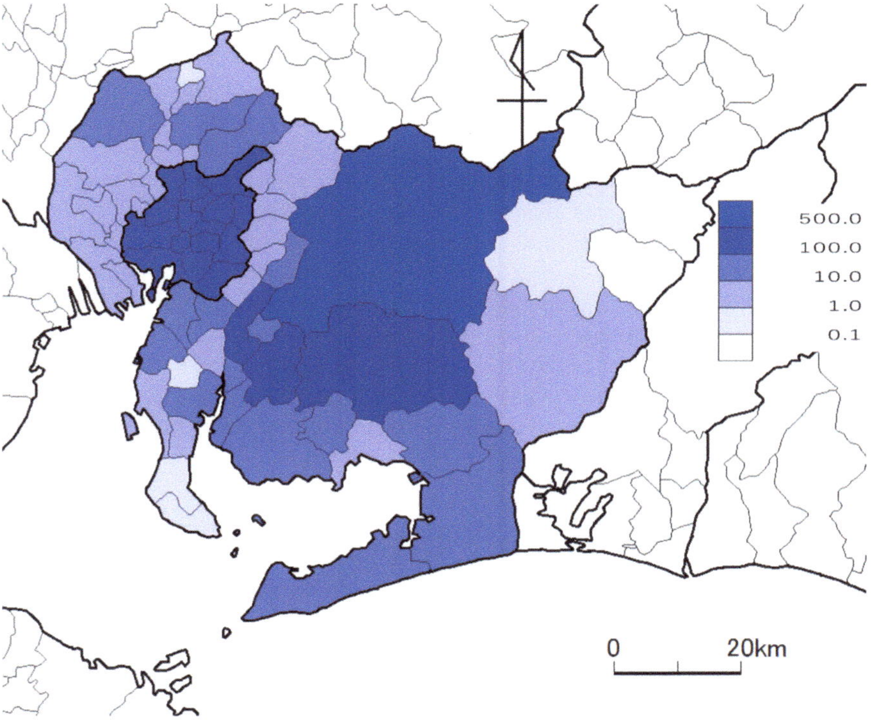


**Fig. 6.7** Value-added induced from the export in Nishi-mikawa area. *Source* Created by the author using the MANDARA support system for geographic information analysis (http://ktgis.net/mandara/)

The estimated product values in the inter-municipal IOT were aggregated for 40 sectors in six areas, and their advantage indices were compared. Nagoya City has an advantage in the tertiary industry, Owari Area in the manufacturing industry, Ama Area in transport, and Chita Area in "chemical products," "petroleum and coal products," "ceramics and stone products," "iron and steel," "electricity, gas, and heat supply," and "air transport." Nishi-mikawa area has competitiveness in "transportation equipment," and Higashi-mikawa area in "agriculture, forestry, and fisheries."

The municipal demand and the self-sufficiency rate have a downwardly convex relationship overall. The municipalities with higher demand have higher self-sufficiency rates. Furthermore, the municipalities with higher production had a higher export rate to the ROJ, and conversely, they had lower supply rates to their own region and the ROA.

Next, using the 54 inter-municipal IOTs constructed, we examined the inter-dependency among the municipalities by the value-added induced for the final demand. Nagoya City gained added value through trade with other municipalities, and conversely, the final demand in Nagoya City is greatly related to the formation of added value in other municipalities. A strong relationship is observed with municipalities in the Owari, Ama, and Chita areas, which are adjacent to Nagoya City. However, the Nishi-mikawa area, centered on Toyota City, contributes to the value-added of nearby municipalities, in which the manufacturing industry is thriving by exporting transportation equipment. The extent of the impact will be more intensive than that brought by domestic demand, such as consumption.

The difficulty in estimating municipal-level IOTs lies in the estimation of trade flow among regions within the prefecture. No survey statistics are available for this, and conducting new regional shipping and sales surveys is necessary. If this is not possible, estimating it using non-survey methods is necessary. The gravity-RAS method adopted here is one of the most powerful. Its usefulness has not been verified in situations in which primary statistics are not available. However, past studies reinforce that, although there are issues that can be improved, the results of this method are valuable.

## References

Suga, M. 2019. Estimation of input-output tables for all Japanese municipalities (Year 2011). *Bulletin of Japan Statistics Research Institute (Hosei University)* 51:1–24 (in Japanese).

Tsukamoto, T., N. Komiyama, and J. Nemoto. 2018. Construction of inter-regional input-output table among all municipalities in Aichi Prefecture and analysis on spatial interdependence between municipalities. *Sango Renkan (Business Journal of PAPAIOS)* 26 (1): 1–20 (in Japanese).

Yamada, M. 1995. Estimation of Mie Prefecture inter-regional input-output table. *Sango Renkan (Business Journal of PAPAIOS)* 5 (4): 52–67 (in Japanese).

Yamada, Mitsuo. 2013. Estimation of inter-regional trade using gravity–RAS methods: A case study of the inter-regional input-output table within Aichi Prefecture. Chukyo University, *Institute of Economics Discussion Paper* No.1301 (in Japanese).

Yamada, M. 2015. Construction of a multi-regional input-output table for Nagoya Metropolitan Area, Japan. *Journal of Economic Structures* 4 (11): 1–18.

Yamada, Mitsuo, and Yuichi Owaki. 2012. Estimation of 2005 inter-regional input-output table of four-regions within Aichi Prefecture. Chukyo University, *Institute of economics discussion paper* No. 1205 (in Japanese).

Yamada, M., and Y. Horiuchi. 2015. Comparison of inter-regional input-output tables for Mie Prefecture from 1985 to 2010. *Sango Renkan (Business Journal of PAPAIOS)* 23 (1–2): 15–28 (in Japanese).

# Chapter 7
# Linking Adjacent Prefectures' Multi-Regional Input–Output Tables

## 7.1 Introduction

In previous chapters, we discussed two types of MRIOTs. The first type is an MRIOT linking several prefectural IOTs, and we focused on the Chubu Region's nine prefectures as an example (see Table 7.1). The second is an MRIOT dividing one prefecture into several small areas within it, and we applied it to the 54 municipalities in Aichi Prefecture.

In this chapter, using the IOTs for the three prefectures of Aichi, Gifu, and Mie, respectively, we recompile them into another type of MRIOT for the Tokai Region covering those prefectures (see Fig. 7.1). For this purpose, we first break down each prefecture's table into the tables for several small areas. Then the commodity flows among the areas for each sector are estimated with the gravity-RAS method, in which the initial values for the RAS iterative calculation are reduced from the estimated gravity model. Finally, we integrated all the small area tables into an MRIOT, using the estimated transaction shares of the commodity flows. This MRIOT for the Tokai Region comprises 186 sectors for each of the 14 areas. The characteristics of each area in the Tokai Region are depicted in Table 7.2. More than 11 million people live in this region. The population of Nagoya City is 2.2 million, and it has the highest population density—about 6900 people per km$^2$ in this region. Owari surrounding Nagoya City has the second highest density—about 2000 people per km$^2$. In Gifu Prefecture, the Gifu City area has the highest density—814 people per km$^2$, and the Hokusei area has 759 people per km$^2$ in Mie Prefecture.

Why do we break down the prefecture IOTs into those of several small areas and integrate the small area IOTs into one multi-regional IOT? Because, we think that such a type of IOT makes it possible to solve the analytical problem that a region identified in terms of economic activity is not necessarily the same as the administrative region.

Nagoya is the third-largest metropolitan area in Japan, following Tokyo and Osaka. Nagoya City, the capital city of Aichi Prefecture, is the economic center of the Tokai


M. Yamada, *Multi-Regional Input–Output Analysis of the Japanese Economy*,
https://doi.org/10.1007/978-981-97-9041-8_7

**Table 7.1** Regional relations of Chubu and Tokai

| Region | | Prefecture | Area | | | | |
|---|---|---|---|---|---|---|---|
| Chubu | Tokai | Aichi | Nagoya | Owari | Nishimikawa | Higashimikawa | |
| | | Gifu | Gifu | Seino | Chuno | Tono | Hida |
| | | Mie | Hokusei | Chusei | Nansei | Iga | Higashikishu |
| | Hokuriku | Toyama | – | | | | |
| | | Ishikawa | – | | | | |
| | | Fukui | – | | | | |
| | Others | Nagano | – | | | | |
| | | Shizuoka | – | | | | |
| | | Shiga | – | | | | |

*Source* Prepared by the author

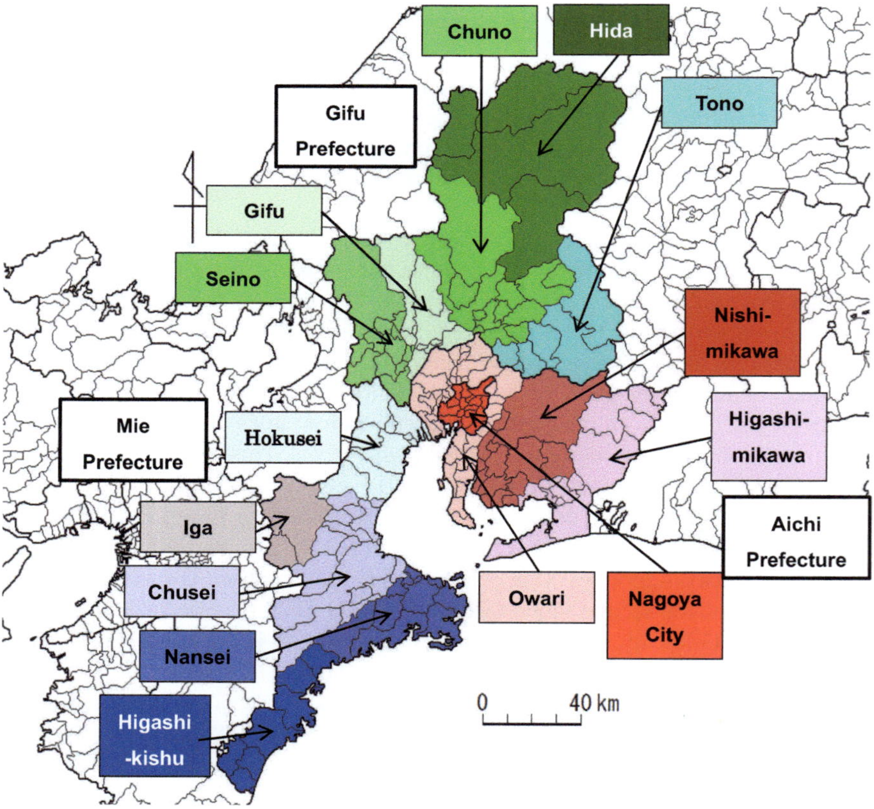


**Fig. 7.1** Fourteen areas of the three prefectures in the Tokai region. *Source* Created by the author using the MANDARA support system for geographic information analysis (http://ktgis.net/mandara/)

**Table 7.2** Statistics of each area in the Tokai region

| | | Area | Population in 2005 | Population in 2010 | Population density in 2010 |
|---|---|---|---|---|---|
| | | Km$^2$ | Thousand | Thousand | People/Km$^2$ |
| Aichi Prefecture | | 5,163.9 | 7,254.7 | 7,410.7 | 1,435.1 |
| 1 | Nagoya | 326.4 | 2,215.1 | 2,263.9 | 6,935.3 |
| 2 | Owari | 1,393.0 | 2,806.9 | 2,875.2 | 2,064.0 |
| 3 | Nishimikawa | 1,724.5 | 1,466.0 | 1,506.0 | 873.3 |
| 4 | Higashimikawa | 1,720.0 | 766.8 | 765.7 | 445.2 |
| Gifu Prefecture | | 10,621.2 | 2,107.2 | 2,080.8 | 195.9 |
| 5 | Gifu | 992.5 | 802.2 | 807.6 | 813.6 |
| 6 | Seno | 1,433.4 | 391.6 | 385.0 | 268.6 |
| 7 | Chuno | 2,454.9 | 388.9 | 382.6 | 155.8 |
| 8 | Tono | 1,562.8 | 358.9 | 348.1 | 222.7 |
| 9 | Hida | 4,177.6 | 165.6 | 157.5 | 37.7 |
| Mie Prefecture | | 5,777.3 | 1,867.0 | 1,854.7 | 321.0 |
| 10 | Hokusei | 1,107.3 | 823.6 | 840.2 | 758.7 |
| 11 | Chusei | 1,841.6 | 507.0 | 502.5 | 272.8 |
| 12 | Nansei | 1,148.7 | 267.7 | 255.0 | 222.0 |
| 13 | Iga | 687.9 | 182.8 | 177.5 | 258.0 |
| 14 | Higashikishu | 991.7 | 85.8 | 79.6 | 80.2 |
| Tokai Region | | 21,562.3 | 11,228.9 | 11,346.2 | 526.2 |

*Source* Census of Population, Japan

Region. However, each surrounding area is not equally connected to Nagoya City. The closer the distance between areas, the stronger their economic connection. Thus, we can investigate such relations by using the MRIOT for the Tokai Region.

In Sect. 7.2, we introduce a method to recompile our MRIOT of the Tokai Region. Section 7.3 discusses the structural characteristics of the Tokai Region, and Sect. 7.4 provides concluding remarks.

## 7.2 Construction of a Multi-regional Input–Output Table

In this section, we explain the outline for constructing an MRIOT of the Tokai Region, which consists of three prefectures: Aichi, Gifu, and Mie. First, each prefecture's table is divided into several areas' IOT of 186 sectors. These tables are imperfect in the sense that they include intra-prefectural transactions as net values. Second, we estimated the transaction values of commodity flows among the areas in two steps: the transactions within each prefecture and the transactions among areas of different prefectures. The two-stepwise estimations were adopted for consistency with the domestic trade of each prefecture's table.

### 7.2.1 Regional Decomposition of Each Prefecture's IOT

Here we explain the method to divide a prefecture's IOT into several IOTs of the smaller areas. This decomposition of the prefectural IOT is essentially the same as that explained in the previous chapter.

(1) **Output Values**

The output values of each smaller area were estimated by multiplying the appropriate ratio to the prefecture's value by sector as follows:

$$X_i^s = r_i^s X_i, \tag{7.1}$$

where $X_i^s$ is the output value of the ith sector in the sth area, $r_i^s$ denotes the dividing index of the ith sector in the sth area, and $X_i$ means the output value of the ith sector in a given prefecture. In the manufacturing sectors for example, the product values of each municipal area were added to those of each area, the area's share of which is used as the dividing index.

(2) **Intermediate Input and Value-Added**

Assuming that the input coefficient and value-added ratios to the outputs are the same for each area within the prefecture, the intermediate input values and value-added of each sector are estimated as follows:

$$X_{ij}^s = a_{ij} X_i^s, \tag{7.2}$$

$$V_{ij}^s = v_{ij} X_i^s, \tag{7.3}$$

where $X_{ij}^s$ is the intermediate input of the ith commodity for the jth sector in the sth area, $a_{ij}$ denotes the input coefficient of the ith commodity for the jth sector in the prefecture, $V_{ij}^s$ means the ith value-added of the jth sector in the sth area, and $v_{ij}$ is the ith value-added ratio of the jth sector in the prefecture.

(3) **Domestic Final Demand**

The domestic final demand comprises private consumption,[1] government consumption, private investment, public investment, and changes in inventory.

[1] Japanese IOTs, national and regional, include "consumption expenditure outside households" as the exogenous sector in both value-added parts and final demand parts. We estimate them in the value-added part if the ratio to output for each sector is the same as that of the prefecture. We can acquire the total value in the final demand part by summing the sectoral values in the value-added

The private consumption of each area is estimated by multiplying the appropriate ratio to the prefecture's value by sector as follows:

$$C_i^s = \gamma_i^s C_i, \tag{7.4}$$

where $C_i^s$ is the consumption of the ith commodity in the sth area, and $\gamma_i^s$ denotes the dividing index of the ith sector in the sth area, and $C_i$ means the consumption of the ith commodity in the prefecture. The dividing factor is estimated as follows:

$$\gamma_{ij}^s = c_{i1} n_{j1}^s + c_{i2} n_{j2}^s, \tag{7.5}$$

where $c_{i1}$ and $c_{i2}$ are the consumptions for each household of the ith commodity in the prefecture, for two-or-more-person households and one-person households, respectively, which are obtained from the NSFIE, MIC. $n_{j1}^s$ and $n_{j2}^s$ means the number of households; two-or-more-person and one-person, respectively.

The estimation of government consumption, private investment, and public investment is conducted in almost the same way to divide them into those areas by using the appropriate dividing shares.

The change in inventory is estimated assuming that the inventory change's ratio to the output in an area is the same in the prefecture.

$$J_i^s = (J_i / X_i) X_i^s \tag{7.6}$$

where $J_i^s$ is the inventory change of the ith sector in the sth area, and $J_i$ is the corresponding value of the prefecture.

(4) **International Trade**

Here we must estimate the export and import values for each small area. We assume that the export ratio to the output for each sector is the same within the prefecture. Then the export for each area is reduced as follows:

$$E_i^s = e_i X_i^s, \tag{7.7}$$

where $E_i^s$ means the export of the ith commodity in the sth area, and $e_i$ denotes the export ratio to output by sector in the prefecture, that is $e_i = E_i / X_i$. Here $E_i$ is the export of the ith sector in the prefecture.

Assuming that the import coefficient for each area is the same within the prefecture, the import of the area is reduced as follows:

$$M_i^s = m_i D_i^s, \tag{7.8}$$

part. Then each value of the item in the final demand part is estimated by multiplying the total value by the corresponding share value, assuming the share values are the same for all areas in the prefecture.

where $M_i^s$ means the import of the ith commodity in the sth area, $m_i$ denotes the import coefficient by sector in the prefecture, and $D_i^s$ shows the domestic demand for the ith commodity in the sth area. The import coefficient of the prefecture is defined as $m_i = M_i/D_i$, where $M_i$ is the import of the ith sector and $D_i$ is the domestic demand of the ith sector in the prefecture.

(5) **Internal Trade Outside the Prefecture**

We estimate the export and import values with the ROJ for each area. Assuming that the export ratio to the output for each sector is the same for the internal trade with the ROJ, the export for each area is reduced as follows:

$$E_i^{*s} = e_i^* X_i^s, \tag{7.9}$$

where $E_i^{*s}$ means the ith commodity's export to the ROJ in the sth area, and $e_i^*$ denotes the corresponding export ratio to output by sector in the prefecture, $e_i^* = E_i^*/X_i$. Here $E_i^*$ is the export of the ith sector in the prefecture.

For the import, we assume that the import coefficient from the ROJ is the same for each area within the prefecture. Then the import of the area is reduced as follows:

$$M_i^{*s} = m_i^* D_i^s, \tag{7.10}$$

where $M_i^{*s}$ means the ith commodity's import in the sth area, and $m_i^*$ denotes the import coefficient by sector in the prefecture. The import coefficient of the prefecture is defined as $m_i^* = M_i^*/D_i$, where $M_i^*$ is the ith commodity's import from the ROJ.

(6) **Balancing Equation**

After estimating each item by sector, the total demand must equal the total supply. Then the following equation holds for each sector in each area:

$$D_i^s + E_i^s + E_i^{*s} - M_i^s - M_i^{*s} + \Delta N_i^s = X_i^s, \tag{7.11}$$

where $D_i^s = \sum X_{ij}^s + F_i^s$.

Here $D_i^s$ denotes the total domestic demand of the ith commodity in the sth area, which consists of the intermediate demands $\sum X_{ij}^s$ and the final demand, $F_i^s$. The variable $\Delta N_i^R$ means the net export to the other areas within the prefecture, which works as the balancing factor after estimating all the other items independently.

### *7.2.2 Estimation of Commodity Flows Between Areas*

Here we use the gravity-RAS method, in which the estimates from the gravity model are used as the initial values for the RAS iterations to obtain the commodity flow among areas.

**Table 7.3** Interregional flows of the ith commodity

| Origin\Destination | | Prefecture-1 | | Prefecture-2 | | ROJ | ROW | Total |
|---|---|---|---|---|---|---|---|---|
| | | Area-1 | Area-2 | Area-3 | Area-4 | | | |
| Prefecture-1 | Area-1 | $T_i^{11}$ | $T_i^{12}$ | $T_i^{13}$ | $T_i^{14}$ | $E_i^{1o}$ | $E_i^{1}$ | $T_i^{1\cdot}$ |
| | Area-2 | $T_i^{21}$ | $T_i^{22}$ | $T_i^{23}$ | $T_i^{24}$ | $E_i^{2o}$ | $E_i^{2}$ | $T_i^{2\cdot}$ |
| Prefecture-2 | Area-3 | $T_i^{31}$ | $T_i^{32}$ | $T_i^{33}$ | $T_i^{34}$ | $E_i^{3o}$ | $E_i^{3}$ | $T_i^{3\cdot}$ |
| | Area-4 | $T_i^{41}$ | $T_i^{42}$ | $T_i^{43}$ | $T_i^{44}$ | $E_i^{4o}$ | $E_i^{4}$ | $T_i^{4\cdot}$ |
| ROJ | | $M_i^{o1}$ | $M_i^{o2}$ | $M_i^{o3}$ | $M_i^{o4}$ | – | – | $M_i^{o\cdot}$ |
| ROW | | $M_i^{1}$ | $M_i^{2}$ | $M_i^{3}$ | $M_i^{4}$ | – | – | $M_i^{\cdot}$ |
| Total | | $T_i^{\cdot 1}$ | $T_i^{\cdot 2}$ | $T_i^{\cdot 3}$ | $T_i^{\cdot 4}$ | $E_i^{\cdot o}$ | $E_i^{\cdot}$ | $T_i^{\cdot\cdot}$ |

*Source* Prepared by the author

Table 7.3 presents the illustrative flows of the ith commodity among four areas, two of which are included in each of the two prefectures, respectively.[2] Two regions, the ROJ and the ROW, appear in the table to capture the domestic and international transactions.$T_i^{rs}$ depicts the transaction of the ith commodity from the rth area to the sth area; $T_i^{r\cdot}$ denotes the total values of the transaction of the ith commodity from the rth area; and $T_i^{\cdot s}$ means the total values of the transaction of the ith commodity to the sth area. $E_i^s$ and $M_i^s$ are respective exports and imports to and from the world, and $E_i^{so}$ and $M_i^{os}$ are exports and imports to and from the ROJ, which is defined as the region excluding the two prefectures in Japan in this case.

The following equations must be considered:

$$\sum_s T_i^{rs} + E_i^{ro} + E_i^r = T_i^{r\cdot} \text{ for r } = 1, 2, 3, \text{ and } 4, \tag{7.12}$$

$$\sum_r T_i^{rs} + M_i^{os} + M_i^s = T_i^{\cdot s} \text{ for s } = 1, 2, 3, \text{ and } 4. \tag{7.13}$$

In this table, the values of the following variables are determined in each of the decomposed IOTs.

(1) The total value supplied from the rth area to all areas and regions $T_i^{r\cdot}$ is equal to the output of the area $X_i^r$, and the total value received from all areas and regions to the rth area $T_i^{\cdot s}$ is the same as the total demand of the sth area, $D_i^s$, that is,

$$T_i^{r\cdot} = X_i^r, \tag{7.14}$$

$$T_i^{\cdot s} = D_i^s. \tag{7.15}$$

Here, $X_i^r$ and $D_i^s$ are obviously obtained from the divided IOT.

[2] The two prefectures comprise not two areas but fourteen areas for three prefectures in all.

(2) Export $E_i^s$ and import $M_i^s$ are obtained with the Eqs. (7.7) and (7.8) for s = 1, 2, 3, and 4.
(3) Domestic transactions $E_i^{*r}$ and $M_i^{*s}$ of each area with the outside of the prefecture that are determined with the Eqs. (7.9) and (7.10) have the following relations:

$$\text{Prefecture-1}: \sum_{s=3,4} T_i^{rs} + E_i^{ro} = E_i^{*r} \text{for r} = 1, 2 \tag{7.16}$$

$$\sum_{r=3,4} T_i^{rs} + M_i^{os} = M_i^{*s} \text{for s} = 1, 2 \tag{7.17}$$

$$\text{Prefecture-2}: \sum_{s=1,2} T_i^{rs} + E_i^{*ro} = E_i^{*r} \text{for r} = 3, 4 \tag{7.18}$$

$$\sum_{r=1,2} T_i^{rs} + M_i^{os} = M_i^{*s} \text{for s} = 3, 4. \tag{7.19}$$

Considering the above restrictions, we must determine the transaction values $T_i^{rs}$ in an appropriate manner. To solve this model, we use a two-step estimation strategy that distinguishes the intra-prefectural transaction from the transactions between prefectures in the estimation.

#### 7.2.2.1 Estimation of Intra-prefectural Flows

Table 7.4 presents the intra-prefectural flows of the ith commodity, and the row sum values and column sum values are obtained from each decomposed IOT. Holding the following equations, we can determine the values of intra-prefectural transaction $T_i^{rs}$.

$$\sum_{s=1,2/3,4} T_i^{rs} = X_i^r - E_i^{*r} - E_i^r \tag{7.20}$$

$$\sum_{r=1,2/3,4} T_i^{rs} = D_i^s - M_i^{*s} - M_i^s \tag{7.21}$$

Then we apply the RAS method with appropriate initial values. In Table 7.4, we apply the gravity model, which is to be explained in Sect. 3.3.3, to obtain the initial values.

#### 7.2.2.2 Estimation of Inter-prefectural Flows

After estimating the intra-regional commodity flows, we must determine the values of inter-prefectural commodity flows, as depicted in Table 7.5.

**Table 7.4** Intra-prefectural flows of the ith commodity

| Origin\Destination | | Prefecture-1 | | Prefecture-2 | | Total |
|---|---|---|---|---|---|---|
| | | Area-1 | Area-2 | Area-3 | Area-4 | |
| Prefecture-1 | Area-1 | $T_i^{11}$ | $T_i^{12}$ | – | – | $X_i^1 - E_i^{*1} - E_i^1$ |
| | Area-2 | $T_i^{21}$ | $T_i^{22}$ | – | – | $X_i^2 - E_i^{*2} - E_i^2$ |
| Prefecture-2 | Area-3 | – | – | $T_i^{33}$ | $T_i^{34}$ | $X_i^3 - E_i^{*3} - E_i^3$ |
| | Area-4 | – | – | $T_i^{43}$ | $T_i^{44}$ | $X_i^4 - E_i^{*4} - E_i^4$ |
| Total | | $D_i^1 - M_i^{*1} - M_i^1$ | $D_i^2 - M_i^{*2} - M_i^2$ | $D_i^3 - M_i^{*3} - M_i^3$ | $D_i^4 - M_i^{*4} - M_i^4$ | |

*Source* Prepared by the author

**Table 7.5** Inter-prefectural flows of the ith commodity

| Origin Destination | | Prefecture-1 | | Prefecture-2 | | Total |
|---|---|---|---|---|---|---|
| | | Area-1 | Area-2 | Area-3 | Area-4 | |
| Prefecture-1 | Area-1 | – | – | $T_i^{13}$ | $T_i^{14}$ | $E_i^{*1} - E_i^{1o}$ |
| | Area-2 | – | – | $T_i^{23}$ | $T_i^{24}$ | $E_i^{*2} - E_i^{2o}$ |
| Prefecture-2 | Area-3 | $T_i^{31}$ | $T_i^{32}$ | – | – | $E_i^{*3} - E_i^{3o}$ |
| | Area-4 | $T_i^{41}$ | $T_i^{42}$ | – | – | $E_i^{*4} - E_i^{4o}$ |
| Total | | $M_i^{*1} - M_i^{o1}$ | $M_i^{*2} - M_i^{o2}$ | $M_i^{*3} - M_i^{o3}$ | $M_i^{*4} - M_i^{o4}$ | |

*Source* Prepared by the author

In the following equations, both exports and imports to and from the region outside of both prefectures $E_i^{ro}$ and $M_i^{os}$ are not known, though exports and imports with the ROJ, $E_i^{*r}$ and $M_i^{*s}$, are obtained from the IOT.

$$\sum_{s=1,2/3,4} T_i^{rs} = E_i^{*r} - E_i^{ro} \tag{7.22}$$

$$\sum_{r=1,2/3,4} T_i^{rs} = M_i^{*s} - M_i^{os} \tag{7.23}$$

To obtain their values, we multiply the predicted share by the gravity model to the total values as follows:

$$\hat{E}_i^{ro} = \frac{\hat{E}_i^{ro}}{\sum_s \hat{T}_i^{rs} + \hat{E}_i^{ro}} E_i^{*r}, \tag{7.24}$$

$$\hat{M}_i^{os} = \frac{\hat{M}_i^{os}}{\sum_r \hat{T}_i^{rs} + \hat{M}_i^{os}} M_i^{*s}, \tag{7.25}$$

where the variables with hats denote the predicted ones by the gravity model with some modification to fulfill the condition that the sum of the "total" column is equal to that of the "total" row.[3] This condition means that the sum of the exports within the prefectures concerned is equal to the sum of the imports within the same prefectures. Here we apply the gravity-RAS method to obtain the transaction values $T_i^{rs}$, that keep the condition expressed by the Eqs. (7.9) and (7.10), within the concerned prefectures.

#### 7.2.2.3 The Modified Gravity Model

The gravity model indicates that the volume of transactions from region r to region s $T_i^{rs}$ is proportionally related to the total volumes of both the origin $T_i^{r\cdot}$ and the destination $T_i^{\cdot s}$ and disproportionally to the distance between the regions[4] $\overline{L}^{rs}$ as follows:

$$T_i^{rs} = k_i^{rs} \frac{\left(T_i^{r\cdot}\right)^{\alpha}\left(T_i^{\cdot s}\right)^{\beta}}{\left(\overline{L}^{rs}\right)^{\gamma}}, \tag{7.26}$$

where $\alpha$, $\beta$, and $\gamma$ are parameters of the two volume variables and distance variables, respectively. Taking the logarithm on both sides of the Eq. (7.13), the parameters are estimated from the transaction data among nine regions of the 2005 METI MRIOT for each of 186 sectors. Because some sectors have no transactions with the other regions, 153 sectors are estimated. The transactions within each region are not included in the gravity model. However, we estimated the model with the transaction data not only between regions but also within each region, because we needed some estimates for the transactions within regions.

Table 7.6 describes the characteristics of the estimated parameters. Almost all the parameters are estimated to be statistically significant. The average values of

---

[3] Here we adopted the adjusting rule that the larger sum is adjusted to the smaller sum by decreasing each item proportionally. As a result, either export shares or import shares are modified from the estimated values.

[4] There are variations to show the distance between regions: geographical distance, time distance, and cost distance. Yamada and Owaki (2012) adopted the geographical distance. They measured the distance $L^{rs}$ between two points, each of which belongs to the different regions to be measured, by the root searching on the Google website. Then they calculated the average distance $\overline{L}^{RS}$ with the weight of the employment number as follows:

$$\overline{L}^{RS} = \frac{\sum_{r\in R}\sum_{s\in S} L^{rs}E^{r}E^{s}}{\sum_{r\in R}\sum_{s\in S} E^{r}E^{s}}$$

**Table 7.6** Characteristics of the estimated parameters

| | Total volume of the origin | Total volume of the destination | Distance |
|---|---|---|---|
| Maximum value | 1.92 | 1.27 | 3.08 |
| Minimum value | −0.02 | −0.08 | 0.20 |
| Average | 0.99 | 0.74 | 1.29 |
| Of commodity sectors | 0.96 | 0.75 | 1.12 |
| Of service sectors | 1.06 | 0.70 | 1.77 |
| Standard deviation | 0.28 | 0.23 | 0.57 |
| No. of equations | 153 | 153 | 153 |
| No. of significant values | 150 | 149 | 149 |

*Source* Prepared by the author

the volume parameters for the origin and the destination are 0.99 and 0.74, respectively. The average of the distance parameters is 1.29. The distance average of the commodity sectors is 1.12, which is lower than that of the service sectors, 1.77, as expected. Figure 7.2 presents the distribution of each estimated parameter. We can confirm that the distance parameters are scattered wider than the two-volume parameters and that the distance parameters of the service sectors are more widely dispersed than those of the commodity sectors.

For our purpose, we applied the gravity model asymptotically to induce the transaction coefficients $\hat{t}_i^{rs}$ between areas of our IOT, and the estimates were used as initial values for the RAS iterative method to estimate the transaction values $T_i^{rs}$.

$$\hat{t}_i^{rs} = \frac{\hat{T}_i^{rs}}{\sum_r \hat{T}_i^{rs}}, \tag{7.27}$$

$$\hat{T}_i^{rs} = \hat{k}_i^{rs} \frac{\left(\hat{T}_i^{r\cdot}\right)^{\hat{\alpha}} \left(\hat{T}_i^{\cdot s}\right)^{\hat{\beta}}}{\left(\hat{L}^{rs}\right)^{\hat{\gamma}}} \tag{7.28}$$

where $\hat{\alpha}$, $\hat{\beta}$, $\hat{\gamma}$, and $\hat{k}_i^{rs}$ are the estimated parameters. The variables $\hat{T}_i^{r\cdot}$, $\hat{T}_i^{\cdot s}$, and $\hat{L}^{rs}$[5] are values corresponding to the MRIOT compiled here.

Table 7.7 presents the estimated transaction matrix among areas for all commodities. In this table, there are exports and imports, international and domestic, of the Tokai region. The export and import shares are also calculated. The cells in italics represent the areas whose transaction share amounts to 5% or more in Tokai region.The cells in bold show the transaction with the outside of Tokai region and the total. Looking at these shares, we note that four areas in Aichi Prefecture have

[5] The average distances were calculated from the distance between municipals region that belonged to each area with employment weights.

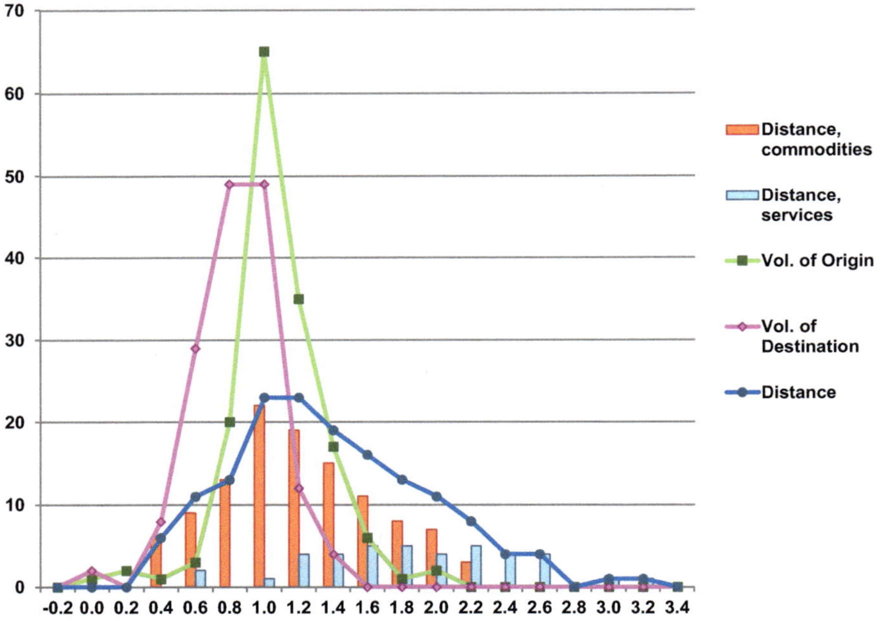


**Fig. 7.2** Distribution of the estimated parameters. *Source* Created by the author

strong relations among them. Furthermore, there appears to be strong interdependence among the Gifu, Seino, Chuno, and Tono areas in Gifu Prefecture, though the Hida area seems to have a slightly weak relationship with them. In Mie Prefecture, the Hokusei and Chusei areas have relatively strong links.

There are relatively strong relations between the Owari area in Aichi Prefecture and three areas in Gifu Prefecture: Gifu, Seino, and Chuno. The Hokusei area in Mie Prefecture and the Nishimikawa area in Aichi Prefecture are also linked.

### *7.2.3 The Compiled Multi-regional Input–Output Table*

We divided the three prefectures' IOTs with 186 sectors into fourteen areas' IOTs and estimated the transaction flows among areas and the outside regions, domestic and international for each sector. Here we can combine the fourteen tables into one multi-regional IOT using the sectoral transaction flow matrices. Table 7.8 depicts the MRIOT compiled for the Tokai Region with fourteen areas, in which 186 sectors are integrated into one sector. Unlike a typical regional input-output table, this table separates imports as independent sectors for the convenience of calculation in the analysis.

**Table 7.7** Estimated transaction matrix (unit: billion yen, %)

| Transaction flows (->) | | 1 | 2 | 3 | 4 | 5 | 6 | 7 | 8 | 9 | 10 | 11 | 12 | 13 | 14 | 15 | 16 | 17 |
|---|---|---|---|---|---|---|---|---|---|---|---|---|---|---|---|---|---|---|
| | | Nagoya | Owari | Nishi-mikawa | Higa shi-mi kawa | Gifu | Seno | Chuno | Tono | Hida | Hoku sei | Chusei | Nansei | Iga | Higa shi-ki shu | Export to the ROJ | Export, inter-national | Total |
| 1 | Nagoya | 10,949 | 4,091 | 2,129 | 586 | 129 | 74 | 87 | 49 | 12 | 324 | 105 | 38 | 51 | 6 | **2,876** | **1,932** | *23,438* |
| 2 | Owari | 2,516 | 8,891 | 2,517 | 667 | 245 | 128 | 161 | 80 | 18 | 435 | 155 | 41 | 62 | 8 | **4,767** | **2,235** | *22,925* |
| 3 | Nishi-mikawa | 768 | 1,493 | 8,824 | 1,223 | 154 | 78 | 134 | 58 | 15 | 578 | 1 | 43 | 59 | 8 | **4,819** | **5,356** | *23,608* |
| 4 | Higashi-mikawa | 249 | 409 | 831 | 2,653 | 35 | 21 | 27 | 16 | 5 | 99 | 52 | 20 | 16 | 4 | **1,744** | **1,628** | *7,809* |
| 5 | Gifu | 129 | 166 | 164 | 34 | 2,896 | 315 | 257 | 140 | 46 | 28 | 16 | 2 | 3 | 0 | **737** | **140** | *5,074* |
| 6 | Seno | 81 | 115 | 133 | 28 | 187 | 1,100 | 136 | 85 | 24 | 31 | 8 | 2 | 3 | 0 | **486** | **210** | *2,629* |
| 7 | Chuno | 118 | 185 | 161 | 78 | 164 | 96 | 1,127 | 113 | 29 | 29 | 10 | 3 | 5 | 1 | **538** | **261** | *2,920* |
| 8 | Tono | 48 | 70 | 96 | 19 | 63 | 58 | 104 | 968 | 21 | 10 | 6 | 2 | 2 | 0 | **377** | **110** | *1,953* |
| 9 | Hida | 13 | 16 | 21 | 6 | 56 | 41 | 60 | 42 | 552 | 10 | 5 | 2 | 2 | 0 | **152** | **25** | *,1003* |
| 10 | Hokusei | 444 | 544 | 635 | 143 | 26 | 30 | 18 | 11 | 3 | 3,764 | 333 | 139 | 116 | 51 | **2,544** | **1,163** | *9,966* |
| 11 | Chusei | 85 | 104 | 135 | 39 | 11 | 9 | 8 | 5 | 2 | 297 | 1,640 | 99 | 62 | 22 | **1,047** | **421** | *3,988* |
| 12 | Nansei | 37 | 43 | 46 | 21 | 4 | 2 | 3 | 2 | 0 | 82 | 106 | 748 | 20 | 13 | **424** | **125** | *1,677* |
| 13 | Iga | 58 | 67 | 79 | 20 | 4 | 2 | 3 | 2 | 0 | 85 | 49 | 18 | 526 | 7 | **485** | **138** | *1,544* |
| 14 | Higashi-kishu | 7 | 10 | 7 | 3 | 1 | 0 | 0 | 0 | 0 | 54 | 35 | 12 | 28 | 272 | **71** | **10** | *511* |
| 15 | **The Rest of Japan** | **3,848** | **4,510** | **4,615** | **1,626** | **718** | **412** | **472** | **324** | **183** | **2,734** | **1,138** | **470** | **434** | **169** | **0** | **0** | *21,652* |
| 16 | **Import** | **1,308** | **2,075** | **1,389** | **499** | **249** | **155** | **169** | **110** | **49** | **948** | **453** | **192** | **156** | **50** | **0** | **0** | *7,800* |
| *17* | ***Total*** | *20,658* | *22,792* | *21,781* | *7,646* | *4,941* | *2,521* | *2,767* | *2,004* | *959* | *9,508* | *4,110* | *1,831* | *1,545* | *612* | *21,066* | *13,755* | *138,497* |

(continued)

**Table 7.7** (continued)

| Share of origins | | 1 | 2 | 3 | 4 | 5 | 6 | 7 | 8 | 9 | 10 | 11 | 12 | 13 | 14 | 15 | 16 | 17 |
|---|---|---|---|---|---|---|---|---|---|---|---|---|---|---|---|---|---|---|
| | | Nagoya | Owari | Nishi-mikawa | Higa shi-mi kawa | Gifu | Seno | Chuno | Tono | Hida | Hoku sei | Chusei | Nansei | Iga | Higa shi-ki shu | Export to the ROJ | Export, inter-national | Total |
| 1 | Nagoya | *53.0* | *17.9* | *9.8* | *7.7* | 2.6 | 2.9 | 3.1 | 2.4 | 1.3 | 3.4 | 2.6 | 2.1 | 3.3 | 1.1 | **13.7** | **14.0** | ***16.9*** |
| 2 | Owari | *12.2* | *39.0* | *11.6* | *8.7* | *5.0* | *5.1* | *5.8* | 4.0 | 1.9 | 4.6 | 3.8 | 2.3 | 4.0 | 1.3 | **22.6** | **16.2** | ***16.6*** |
| 3 | Nishi-mikawa | 3.7 | *6.5* | *40.5* | *16.0* | 3.1 | 3.1 | 4.8 | 2.9 | 1.5 | *6.1* | 0.0 | 2.3 | 3.8 | 1.2 | **22.9** | **38.9** | ***17.0*** |
| 4 | Higashi-mikawa | 1.2 | 1.8 | 3.8 | *34.7* | 0.7 | 0.8 | 1.0 | 0.8 | 0.5 | 1.0 | 1.3 | 1.1 | 1.1 | 0.6 | **8.3** | **11.8** | ***5.6*** |
| 5 | Gifu | 0.6 | 0.7 | 0.8 | 0.4 | *58.6* | *12.5* | *9.3* | *7.0* | 4.8 | 0.3 | 0.4 | 0.1 | 0.2 | 0.1 | **3.5** | **1.0** | ***3.7*** |
| 6 | Seno | 0.4 | 0.5 | 0.6 | 0.4 | 3.8 | *43.6* | 4.9 | 4.3 | 2.5 | 0.3 | 0.2 | 0.1 | 0.2 | 0.1 | **2.3** | **1.5** | ***1.9*** |
| 7 | Chuno | 0.6 | 0.8 | 0.7 | 1.0 | 3.3 | 3.8 | *40.7* | *5.7* | 3.0 | 0.3 | 0.2 | 0.2 | 0.3 | 0.1 | **2.6** | **1.9** | ***2.1*** |
| 8 | Tono | 0.2 | 0.3 | 0.4 | 0.3 | 1.3 | 2.3 | 3.8 | *48.3* | 2.1 | 0.1 | 0.1 | 0.1 | 0.1 | 0.1 | **1.8** | **0.8** | ***1.4*** |
| 9 | Hida | 0.1 | 0.1 | 0.1 | 0.1 | 1.1 | 1.6 | 2.2 | 2.1 | *57.5* | 0.1 | 0.1 | 0.1 | 0.1 | 0.1 | **0.7** | **0.2** | ***0.7*** |
| 10 | Hokusei | 2.1 | 2.4 | 2.9 | 1.9 | 0.5 | 1.2 | 0.7 | 0.5 | 0.3 | *39.6* | *8.1* | *7.6* | *7.5* | *8.4* | **12.1** | **8.5** | ***7.2*** |
| 11 | Chusei | 0.4 | 0.5 | 0.6 | 0.5 | 0.2 | 0.3 | 0.3 | 0.2 | 0.2 | 3.1 | *39.9* | *5.4* | 4.0 | 3.7 | **5.0** | **3.1** | ***2.9*** |
| 12 | Nansei | 0.2 | 0.2 | 0.2 | 0.3 | 0.1 | 0.1 | 0.1 | 0.1 | 0.0 | 0.9 | 2.6 | *40.9* | 1.3 | 2.2 | **2.0** | **0.9** | ***1.2*** |
| 13 | Iga | 0.3 | 0.3 | 0.4 | 0.3 | 0.1 | 0.1 | 0.1 | 0.1 | 0.0 | 0.9 | 1.2 | 1.0 | *34.1* | 1.1 | **2.3** | **1.0** | ***1.1*** |
| 14 | Higashi-kishu | 0.0 | 0.0 | 0.0 | 0.0 | 0.0 | 0.0 | 0.0 | 0.0 | 0.0 | 0.6 | 0.8 | 0.6 | 1.8 | *44.4* | **0.3** | **0.1** | ***0.4*** |
| 15 | **The Rest of Japan** | **18.6** | **19.8** | **21.2** | **21.3** | **14.5** | **16.4** | **17.1** | **16.1** | **19.1** | **28.8** | **27.7** | **25.7** | **28.1** | **27.6** | **0.0** | **0.0** | *15.6* |
| 16 | **Import** | **6.3** | **9.1** | **6.4** | **6.5** | **5.0** | **6.1** | **6.1** | **5.5** | **5.1** | **10.0** | **11.0** | **10.5** | **10.1** | **8.1** | **0.0** | **0.0** | *5.6* |
| *17* | ***Total*** | ***100.0*** | ***100.0*** | ***100.0*** | ***100.0*** | ***100.0*** | ***100.0*** | ***100.0*** | ***100.0*** | ***100.0*** | ***100.0*** | ***100.0*** | ***100.0*** | ***100.0*** | ***100.0*** | ***100.0*** | ***100.0*** | ***100.0*** |

(continued)

**Table 7.7** (continued)

| Share of the destinations | | 1 | 2 | 3 | 4 | 5 | 6 | 7 | 8 | 9 | 10 | 11 | 12 | 13 | 14 | 15 | 16 | 17 |
|---|---|---|---|---|---|---|---|---|---|---|---|---|---|---|---|---|---|---|
| | | Nagoya | Owari | Nishi-mikawa | Higa shi-mi kawa | Gifu | Seno | Chuno | Tono | Hida | Hoku sei | Chusei | Nansei | Iga | Higa shi-ki shu | Export to the ROJ | Export, inter-national | Total |
| 1 | Nagoya | 46.7 | 17.5 | 9.1 | 2.5 | 0.6 | 0.3 | 0.4 | 0.2 | 0.1 | 1.4 | 0.4 | 0.2 | 0.2 | 0.0 | 12.3 | 8.2 | 100.0 |
| 2 | Owari | 11.0 | 38.8 | 11.0 | 2.9 | 1.1 | 0.6 | 0.7 | 0.3 | 0.1 | 1.9 | 0.7 | 0.2 | 0.3 | 0.0 | 20.8 | 9.7 | 100.0 |
| 3 | Nishi-mikawa | 3.3 | 6.3 | 37.4 | 5.2 | 0.7 | 0.3 | 0.6 | 0.2 | 0.1 | 2.4 | 0.0 | 0.2 | 0.3 | 0.0 | 20.4 | 22.7 | 100.0 |
| 4 | Higashi-mikawa | 3.2 | 5.2 | 10.6 | 34.0 | 0.4 | 0.3 | 0.4 | 0.2 | 0.1 | 1.3 | 0.7 | 0.3 | 0.2 | 0.0 | 22.3 | 20.8 | 100.0 |
| 5 | Gifu | 2.5 | 3.3 | 3.2 | 0.7 | 57.1 | 6.2 | 5.1 | 2.8 | 0.9 | 0.5 | 0.3 | 0.0 | 0.1 | 0.0 | 14.5 | 2.8 | 100.0 |
| 6 | Seno | 3.1 | 4.4 | 5.1 | 1.1 | 7.1 | 41.8 | 5.2 | 3.2 | 0.9 | 1.2 | 0.3 | 0.1 | 0.1 | 0.0 | 18.5 | 8.0 | 100.0 |
| 7 | Chuno | 4.1 | 6.3 | 5.5 | 2.7 | 5.6 | 3.3 | 38.6 | 3.9 | 1.0 | 1.0 | 0.3 | 0.1 | 0.2 | 0.0 | 18.4 | 8.9 | 100.0 |
| 8 | Tono | 2.5 | 3.6 | 4.9 | 1.0 | 3.2 | 3.0 | 5.3 | 49.5 | 1.1 | 0.5 | 0.3 | 0.1 | 0.1 | 0.0 | 19.3 | 5.6 | 100.0 |
| 9 | Hida | 1.3 | 1.6 | 2.1 | 0.6 | 5.6 | 4.1 | 6.0 | 4.2 | 55.0 | 1.0 | 0.5 | 0.2 | 0.2 | 0.0 | 15.1 | 2.5 | 100.0 |
| 10 | Hokusei | 4.5 | 5.5 | 6.4 | 1.4 | 0.3 | 0.3 | 0.2 | 0.1 | 0.0 | 37.8 | 3.3 | 1.4 | 1.2 | 0.5 | 25.5 | 11.7 | 100.0 |
| 11 | Chusei | 2.1 | 2.6 | 3.4 | 1.0 | 0.3 | 0.2 | 0.2 | 0.1 | 0.0 | 7.4 | 41.1 | 2.5 | 1.5 | 0.6 | 26.2 | 10.6 | 100.0 |
| 12 | Nansei | 2.2 | 2.6 | 2.7 | 1.3 | 0.2 | 0.1 | 0.2 | 0.1 | 0.0 | 4.9 | 6.3 | 44.6 | 1.2 | 0.8 | 25.3 | 7.4 | 100.0 |
| 13 | Iga | 3.7 | 4.4 | 5.1 | 1.3 | 0.2 | 0.1 | 0.2 | 0.1 | 0.0 | 5.5 | 3.2 | 1.2 | 34.1 | 0.5 | 31.4 | 8.9 | 100.0 |
| 14 | Higashi-kishu | 1.4 | 1.9 | 1.4 | 0.7 | 0.2 | 0.1 | 0.1 | 0.1 | 0.1 | 10.6 | 6.8 | 2.3 | 5.4 | 53.1 | 14.0 | 2.0 | 100.0 |
| 15 | **The Rest of Japan** | 17.8 | 20.8 | 21.3 | 7.5 | 3.3 | 1.9 | 2.2 | 1.5 | 0.8 | 12.6 | 5.3 | 2.2 | 2.0 | 0.8 | 0.0 | 0.0 | 100.0 |
| 16 | **Import** | 16.8 | 26.6 | 17.8 | 6.4 | 3.2 | 2.0 | 2.2 | 1.4 | 0.6 | 12.2 | 5.8 | 2.5 | 2.0 | 0.6 | 0.0 | 0.0 | 100.0 |
| *17* | ***Total*** | 14.9 | 16.5 | 15.7 | 5.5 | 3.6 | 1.8 | 2.0 | 1.4 | 0.7 | 6.9 | 3.0 | 1.3 | 1.1 | 0.4 | 15.2 | 9.9 | 100.0 |

*Source* Created by the author

**Table 7.8** Estimated IOT for the Tokai Region 14 areas and one sector (unit: billion yen)

| | | Intermediate demand | | | | | | | | | | | | | | |
|---|---|---|---|---|---|---|---|---|---|---|---|---|---|---|---|---|
| | | 1 | 2 | 3 | 4 | 5 | 6 | 7 | 8 | 9 | 10 | 11 | 12 | 13 | 14 | 15 |
| | | Nagoya | Owari | Nishi-mikawa | Higashi-mikawa | Gifu | Seno | Chuno | Tono | Hida | Hokusei | Chusei | Nansei | Iga | Higashi-kishu | Inter-mediate Demand, Total |
| 1 | Nagoya | 3,994 | 2,304 | 1,405 | 349 | 78 | 51 | 64 | 31 | 7 | 248 | 72 | 24 | 39 | 3 | *8,670* |
| 2 | Owari | 1,509 | 3,280 | 1,996 | 501 | 188 | 104 | 137 | 62 | 13 | 342 | 113 | 28 | 49 | 5 | *8,328* |
| 3 | Nishi-mikawa | 466 | 1,100 | 5,484 | 1,022 | 125 | 65 | 119 | 45 | 10 | 480 | 1 | 24 | 45 | 3 | *8,988* |
| 4 | Higashi-mikawa | 127 | 256 | 665 | 1,039 | 26 | 17 | 23 | 12 | 4 | 74 | 33 | 12 | 12 | 2 | *2,300* |
| 5 | Gifu | 73 | 112 | 143 | 28 | 848 | 162 | 151 | 59 | 23 | 13 | 5 | 1 | 2 | 0 | *1,621* |
| 6 | Seno | 49 | 87 | 119 | 24 | 113 | 384 | 83 | 44 | 13 | 21 | 6 | 1 | 3 | 0 | *948* |
| 7 | Chuno | 67 | 142 | 135 | 71 | 99 | 50 | 350 | 71 | 16 | 20 | 7 | 2 | 4 | 0 | *1,034* |
| 8 | Tono | 25 | 50 | 82 | 15 | 29 | 33 | 68 | 260 | 11 | 8 | 4 | 1 | 1 | 0 | *589* |
| 9 | Hida | 7 | 10 | 18 | 4 | 28 | 21 | 34 | 26 | 167 | 8 | 3 | 1 | 1 | 0 | *329* |
| 10 | Hokusei | 260 | 401 | 542 | 118 | 16 | 24 | 15 | 8 | 2 | 1,768 | 132 | 55 | 57 | 18 | *3,415* |
| 11 | Chusei | 52 | 75 | 116 | 32 | 7 | 8 | 7 | 4 | 1 | 197 | 489 | 47 | 37 | 9 | *1,081* |
| 12 | Nansei | 16 | 23 | 31 | 13 | 2 | 2 | 2 | 1 | 0 | 50 | 55 | 189 | 12 | 6 | *403* |
| 13 | Iga | 28 | 44 | 60 | 14 | 3 | 2 | 2 | 1 | 0 | 60 | 30 | 10 | 166 | 3 | *424* |
| 14 | Higashi-kishu | 5 | 7 | 5 | 2 | 1 | 0 | 0 | 0 | 0 | 40 | 24 | 7 | 19 | 62 | *173* |
| 15 | The Rest of Japan | 2,157 | 2,980 | 3,541 | 1,176 | 476 | 300 | 353 | 218 | 121 | 2,206 | 784 | 300 | 315 | 104 | *15,032* |
| 16 | Import | 782 | 1,602 | 1,087 | 373 | 154 | 114 | 128 | 75 | 31 | 577 | 253 | 94 | 85 | 15 | *5,371* |
| *17* | *Interme-diate Input* | *9,617* | *12,472* | *15,428* | *4,784* | *2,194* | *1,337* | *1,536* | *918* | *421* | *6,110* | *2,012* | *799* | *848* | *230* | *58,705* |
| 18 | Value Added | 13,821 | 10,453 | 8,180 | 3,025 | 2,880 | 1,293 | 1,384 | 1,035 | 582 | 3,855 | 1,977 | 878 | 696 | 281 | *50,339* |
| *19* | *Total Input* | *23,438* | *22,925* | *23,608* | *7,809* | *5,074* | *2,629* | *2,920* | *1,953* | *1,003* | *9,966* | *3,988* | *1,677* | *1,544* | *511* | *109,044* |

(continued)

**Table 7.8** (continued)

| | | Final demand | | | | | | | | | | | | | | | | | |
|---|---|---|---|---|---|---|---|---|---|---|---|---|---|---|---|---|---|---|---|
| | | 16 | 17 | 18 | 19 | 20 | 21 | 22 | 23 | 24 | 25 | 26 | 27 | 28 | 29 | 30 | 31 | 32 | 33 |
| | | Nagoya | Owari | Nishi-mikawa | Higashi-mikawa | Gifu | Seno | Chuno | Tono | Hida | Hokusei | Chusei | Nansei | Iga | Higashi-kishu | Export to the ROJ | Export, inter-national | Import, domestic and Inter-national | Output |
| 1 | Nagoya | 6,955 | 1,788 | 723 | 237 | 51 | 23 | 23 | 18 | 5 | 76 | 33 | 13 | 12 | 3 | 2,876 | 1,932 | 0 | *23,438* |
| 2 | Owari | 1,007 | 5,611 | 521 | 165 | 57 | 23 | 25 | 18 | 5 | 93 | 41 | 13 | 12 | 4 | 4,767 | 2,235 | 0 | *22,925* |
| 3 | Nishi-mikawa | 302 | 393 | 3,339 | 201 | 29 | 13 | 15 | 13 | 4 | 98 | 1 | 18 | 14 | 5 | 4,819 | 5,356 | 0 | *23,608* |
| 4 | Higashi-mikawa | 122 | 153 | 165 | 1,614 | 9 | 4 | 5 | 4 | 2 | 25 | 19 | 8 | 4 | 2 | 1,744 | 1,628 | 0 | *7,809* |
| 5 | Gifu | 56 | 54 | 21 | 6 | 2,048 | 153 | 106 | 80 | 23 | 15 | 11 | 1 | 1 | 0 | 737 | 140 | 0 | *5,074* |
| 6 | Seno | 32 | 28 | 14 | 4 | 74 | 715 | 53 | 41 | 11 | 10 | 1 | 1 | 1 | 0 | 486 | 210 | 0 | *2,629* |
| 7 | Chuno | 51 | 44 | 27 | 7 | 65 | 46 | 777 | 42 | 13 | 10 | 2 | 1 | 1 | 0 | 538 | 261 | 0 | *2,920* |
| 8 | Tono | 23 | 21 | 14 | 4 | 34 | 25 | 36 | 708 | 9 | 2 | 1 | 1 | 0 | 0 | 377 | 110 | 0 | *1,953* |
| 9 | Hida | 6 | 6 | 4 | 1 | 28 | 20 | 26 | 16 | 385 | 2 | 1 | 1 | 1 | 0 | 152 | 25 | 0 | *1,003* |
| 10 | Hokusei | 184 | 144 | 93 | 25 | 9 | 6 | 4 | 3 | 1 | 1,996 | 202 | 85 | 58 | 34 | 2,544 | 1,163 | 0 | *9,966* |
| 11 | Chusei | 34 | 30 | 19 | 7 | 4 | 1 | 2 | 1 | 1 | 100 | 1,151 | 52 | 25 | 13 | 1,047 | 421 | 0 | *3,988* |
| 12 | Nansei | 21 | 20 | 15 | 8 | 2 | 0 | 1 | 1 | 0 | 31 | 51 | 559 | 8 | 8 | 424 | 125 | 0 | *1,677* |
| 13 | Iga | 30 | 23 | 19 | 6 | 1 | 0 | 1 | 1 | 0 | 25 | 19 | 8 | 361 | 4 | 485 | 138 | 0 | *1,544* |
| 14 | Higashi-kishu | 3 | 3 | 2 | 1 | 0 | 0 | 0 | 0 | 0 | 15 | 11 | 4 | 8 | 210 | 71 | 10 | 0 | *511* |
| 15 | The Rest of Japan | 1,690 | 1,530 | 1,074 | 449 | 241 | 113 | 119 | 106 | 62 | 529 | 353 | 170 | 119 | 65 | 0 | 0 | −21,652 | *0* |
| 16 | Import | 526 | 473 | 302 | 126 | 95 | 41 | 41 | 35 | 18 | 371 | 199 | 98 | 71 | 34 | 0 | 0 | −7,800 | *0* |
| *17* | *Total* | *11,041* | *10,320* | *6,353* | *2,862* | *2,748* | *1,184* | *1,232* | *1,086* | *538* | *3,398* | *2,098* | *1,032* | *697* | *382* | *21,066* | *13,755* | *−29,453* | *109,044* |

*Source* Created by the author

## 7.3 Comparison of Output Structures

In this section, we integrate the MRIOT with 14 areas and 186 sectors for each area with the 14 areas and 40 sectors and discuss the characteristics of the output structures in Tables 7.9, 7.10, and 7.11. Those tables contain sectoral outputs and the Revealed Comparative Advantage (RCA) indices of output in the Tokai Region.

Table 7.9 shows that Nagoya City has relative advantages in "Information and communications," "Commerce," "Finance and insurance," "Real estate," and "Business services." Those sectors are strongly related to the core industries in the metropolitan area. However, the Owari area has advantages in "Petroleum and coal products," "Pottery, china, and earthenware," "Aircraft and repair of aircraft," and "Miscellaneous manufactured products." The Nishimikawa area, where Toyota Motor Co. is headquartered, along with its factories and group companies, has advantages in "Information and communication electronics equipment," "Electronic components," and "Motor vehicles." The Higashimikawa area has advantages in "Agriculture," "Motor Vehicles," "Other transportation equipment," and "Precision instruments."

Table 7.10 presents the output structures of five areas in Gifu Prefecture. The Gifu area, where the capital city of the prefecture is located, has strong industries in "Aircraft and repair of aircraft," and "Textile products." Historically, textile industries prospered in this area. The Seino area, located west of the Gifu area, has advantages in its manufacturing industries as "Other ceramic, stone, and clay products," "Metal products," "Electrical machinery," "Precision instruments," "Textile products," and "Plastic products" in addition to the "Mining." The Tono area, in eastern Gifu Prefecture, has advantages in manufacturing industries like "Pulp, paper and wood products," "Metal products," "General machinery," and "Information and communication electronics equipment," along with "Forestry." However, the Hida area, located in northern Gifu Prefecture, has many natural resources, with superiority in "Forestry," "Fishery," "Mining," "Pulp, paper, and wood products," and "Electricity, gas, and heat supply," that is generated by hydropower stations.

Table 7.11 shows the output structures of five areas in Mie Prefecture. The Hokusei area, the northern parts of Mie Prefecture and next to the Owari area, has advantages in its "Chemical products," "Petroleum and coal products," "Iron and steel," "Non-ferrous metals," "Information and communication electronics equipment," and "Motor vehicles." Contrarily, the Chusei area, located in the central part of Mie Prefecture, has advantages in not only manufacturing industries like "Electronic components," "Miscellaneous manufactured products," and "Other ceramic, stone and clay products," but also tertiary sectors such as "Information and communications" and "Public administration." In the Nansei area, the "Aircraft and repair of aircraft" sector is one of the competitive industries, though its production is not so large. "Fishery" also has a large sector in this area. The Iga area, deep in Mie Prefecture, is relatively close to the Kansai Region and boasts of "Pottery, china, and earthenware," "Plastic products," "Pulp, paper and wood products," and "General machinery." In the Higashikishu area, the "Forestry" and "Fishery" sectors have

**Table 7.9** Output structure of Aichi Prefecture

| | | Output (billion Yen) | | | | | Revealed comparative advantages | | | |
|---|---|---|---|---|---|---|---|---|---|---|
| | | Nagoya | Owari | Nishi-mikawa | Higashi-mikawa | Aichi Pref | Nagoya | Owari | Nishi-mikawa | Higashi-mikawa |
| 01 | Agriculture | 12.7 | 103.9 | 63.4 | 192.9 | 372.9 | 0.090 | 0.758 | 0.449 | 4.133 |
| 02 | Forestry | 0.0 | 0.5 | 2.5 | 3.0 | 6.1 | 0.004 | 0.045 | 0.221 | 0.801 |
| 03 | Fishery | 0.0 | 20.5 | 8.4 | 4.4 | 33.3 | 0.000 | 0.940 | 0.371 | 0.589 |
| 04 | Mining | 0.5 | 5.4 | 9.9 | 5.6 | 21.5 | 0.035 | 0.363 | 0.647 | 1.110 |
| 05 | Beverages and Foods | 388.4 | 936.9 | 426.9 | 217.8 | 1,970.0 | 0.609 | 1.503 | 0.665 | 1.026 |
| 06 | Textile products | 48.3 | 196.6 | 149.2 | 91.3 | 485.5 | 0.298 | 1.242 | 0.915 | 1.694 |
| 07 | Pulp, paper and wood products | 94.1 | 506.4 | 103.7 | 91.6 | 795.7 | 0.310 | 1.705 | 0.339 | 0.905 |
| 08 | Chemical products | 192.4 | 609.1 | 182.2 | 82.2 | 1,065.9 | 0.338 | 1.093 | 0.317 | 0.433 |
| 09 | Petroleum and coal products | 6.6 | 474.4 | 32.5 | 4.5 | 518.1 | 0.019 | 1.363 | 0.091 | 0.038 |
| 10 | Plastic products | 145.6 | 702.3 | 483.7 | 271.3 | 1,603.0 | 0.297 | 1.462 | 0.978 | 1.658 |
| 11 | Pottery, china and earthenware | 39.3 | 185.3 | 7.4 | 3.4 | 235.4 | 0.459 | 2.213 | 0.086 | 0.118 |
| 12 | Other ceramic, stone and clay products | 72.7 | 305.6 | 143.4 | 45.9 | 567.6 | 0.311 | 1.337 | 0.609 | 0.590 |
| 13 | Iron and steel | 282.1 | 1,653.6 | 555.1 | 179.5 | 2,670.2 | 0.455 | 2.724 | 0.888 | 0.868 |
| 14 | Non-ferrous metals | 200.3 | 121.7 | 93.7 | 117.8 | 533.5 | 0.923 | 0.574 | 0.429 | 1.630 |
| 15 | Metal products | 252.5 | 695.2 | 321.4 | 102.3 | 1,371.4 | 0.583 | 1.641 | 0.737 | 0.709 |
| 16 | General machinery | 802.1 | 1,744.3 | 956.0 | 204.5 | 3,707.0 | 0.698 | 1.553 | 0.826 | 0.535 |
| 17 | Electrical machinery | 262.8 | 693.1 | 417.2 | 154.3 | 1,527.4 | 0.501 | 1.352 | 0.790 | 0.884 |

(continued)

**Table 7.9** (continued)

| | | Output (billion Yen) | | | | | Revealed comparative advantages | | | |
|---|---|---|---|---|---|---|---|---|---|---|
| | | Nagoya | Owari | Nishi-mikawa | Higashi-mikawa | Aichi Pref | Nagoya | Owari | Nishi-mikawa | Higashi-mikawa |
| 18 | Information and communication electronics equipment | 24.9 | 282.1 | 629.4 | 46.3 | 982.7 | 0.077 | 0.894 | 1.937 | 0.431 |
| 19 | Electronic components | 13.6 | 283.2 | 706.0 | 25.7 | 1,028.5 | 0.025 | 0.538 | 1.303 | 0.143 |
| 20 | Motor vehicle | 415.6 | 1,631.1 | 11,175.1 | 2,681.3 | 15,903.0 | 0.104 | 0.416 | 2.768 | 2.008 |
| 21 | Aircraft and repair of aircraft | 121.2 | 188.6 | 0.1 | 0.1 | 309.9 | 1.170 | 1.860 | 0.001 | 0.002 |
| 22 | Other transportation equipment | 33.8 | 120.0 | 164.1 | 122.9 | 440.8 | 0.298 | 1.082 | 1.437 | 3.253 |
| 23 | Precision instruments | 13.1 | 47.5 | 86.9 | 70.6 | 218.1 | 0.241 | 0.895 | 1.592 | 3.910 |
| 24 | Miscellaneous manufactured products | 116.7 | 807.8 | 283.8 | 196.1 | 1,404.4 | 0.277 | 1.960 | 0.669 | 1.397 |
| 25 | Construction | 1,369.5 | 1,304.3 | 804.9 | 346.3 | 3,824.9 | 1.066 | 1.038 | 0.622 | 0.809 |
| 26 | Electricity, gas and heat supply | 479.0 | 491.6 | 251.2 | 84.8 | 1,306.6 | 1.133 | 1.189 | 0.590 | 0.603 |
| 27 | Water supply and waste disposal business | 101.7 | 223.0 | 110.6 | 44.7 | 480.0 | 0.658 | 1.475 | 0.711 | 0.868 |
| 28 | Commerce | 5,691.7 | 1,467.1 | 1,016.3 | 428.4 | 8,603.5 | 2.501 | 0.659 | 0.443 | 0.565 |

(continued)

**Table 7.9** (continued)

| | | Output (billion Yen) | | | | | Revealed comparative advantages | | | |
|---|---|---|---|---|---|---|---|---|---|---|
| | | Nagoya | Owari | Nishi-mikawa | Higashi-mikawa | Aichi Pref | Nagoya | Owari | Nishi-mikawa | Higashi-mikawa |
| 29 | Finance and insurance | 1,203.0 | 517.3 | 413.8 | 243.2 | 2,377.3 | 1.631 | 0.717 | 0.557 | 0.990 |
| 30 | Real estate | 1,975.1 | 1,276.4 | 726.1 | 345.8 | 4,323.4 | 1.495 | 0.988 | 0.546 | 0.786 |
| 31 | Transport | 1,239.3 | 1,116.4 | 342.2 | 167.2 | 2,865.0 | 1.475 | 1.358 | 0.404 | 0.597 |
| 32 | Information and communications | 1,918.1 | 160.6 | 115.5 | 71.3 | 2,265.5 | 3.046 | 0.261 | 0.182 | 0.340 |
| 33 | Public administration | 406.7 | 401.2 | 228.1 | 125.2 | 1,161.3 | 1.022 | 1.030 | 0.569 | 0.944 |
| 34 | Education and research | 679.0 | 814.1 | 764.7 | 219.2 | 2,477.0 | 0.971 | 1.190 | 1.085 | 0.941 |
| 35 | Medical service, health, social security and nursing care | 1,060.1 | 898.5 | 477.0 | 255.8 | 2,691.4 | 1.181 | 1.023 | 0.528 | 0.855 |
| 36 | Other public services | 92.9 | 58.5 | 34.8 | 23.2 | 209.3 | 1.069 | 0.689 | 0.397 | 0.801 |
| 37 | Business services | 2,263.8 | 848.6 | 679.4 | 222.9 | 4014.7 | 2.104 | 0.806 | 0.627 | 0.622 |
| 38 | Personal services | 1,303.9 | 932.8 | 547.1 | 283.1 | 3,067.0 | 1.354 | 0.990 | 0.564 | 0.882 |
| 39 | Office supplies | 44.1 | 30.9 | 24.2 | 8.8 | 108.0 | 1.282 | 0.918 | 0.700 | 0.769 |
| 40 | Activities not elsewhere classified | 70.5 | 68.4 | 70.5 | 23.4 | 232.7 | 0.849 | 0.842 | 0.844 | 0.846 |
| 41 | Sectors, total | 23,437.8 | 22,924.7 | 23,608.5 | 7,808.5 | 77,779.5 | 1.000 | 1.000 | 1.000 | 1.000 |

*Source* Computed by the author

**Table 7.10** Output structure of Gifu Prefecture

| | | Output (Billion Yen) | | | | | | Revealed comparative advantages | | | | |
|---|---|---|---|---|---|---|---|---|---|---|---|---|
| | | Gifu | Seino | Chuno | Tono | Hida | Gifu Pref | Gifu | Seino | Chuno | Tono | Hida |
| 01 | Agriculture | 30.6 | 29.6 | 25.7 | 26.6 | 25.3 | 137.7 | 1.008 | 1.881 | 1.474 | 2.275 | 4.221 |
| 02 | Forestry | 4.0 | 0.1 | 8.1 | 1.4 | 14.5 | 28.1 | 1.637 | 0.072 | 5.773 | 1.448 | 29.929 |
| 03 | Fishery | 0.6 | 1.6 | 0.8 | 0.2 | 2.1 | 5.3 | 0.121 | 0.642 | 0.289 | 0.105 | 2.182 |
| 04 | Mining | 4.7 | 13.0 | 1.0 | 8.2 | 2.2 | 29.2 | 1.435 | 7.645 | 0.532 | 6.454 | 3.418 |
| 05 | Beverages and Foods | 148.4 | 104.7 | 41.3 | 31.2 | 36.1 | 361.7 | 1.076 | 1.464 | 0.520 | 0.587 | 1.322 |
| 06 | Textile products | 107.6 | 69.7 | 22.3 | 2.8 | 3.7 | 206.1 | 3.069 | 3.839 | 1.104 | 0.209 | 0.536 |
| 07 | Pulp, paper and wood products | 82.5 | 47.5 | 173.7 | 88.7 | 45.8 | 438.2 | 1.255 | 1.393 | 4.593 | 3.503 | 3.528 |
| 08 | Chemical products | 192.9 | 55.7 | 22.6 | 17.2 | 11.4 | 300.0 | 1.565 | 0.872 | 0.318 | 0.363 | 0.470 |
| 09 | Petroleum and coal products | 2.3 | 1.5 | 2.4 | 1.1 | 1.0 | 8.4 | 0.030 | 0.038 | 0.055 | 0.036 | 0.067 |
| 10 | Plastic products | 71.7 | 144.9 | 92.0 | 62.3 | 4.2 | 375.1 | 0.675 | 2.629 | 1.503 | 1.523 | 0.199 |
| 11 | Pottery, china and earthenware | 0.8 | 10.2 | 14.2 | 114.3 | 2.1 | 141.7 | 0.044 | 1.065 | 1.332 | 16.020 | 0.584 |
| 12 | Other ceramic, stone and clay products | 52.2 | 102.5 | 28.1 | 39.1 | 9.4 | 231.4 | 1.032 | 3.910 | 0.967 | 2.011 | 0.944 |
| 13 | Iron and steel | 34.0 | 8.0 | 57.0 | 21.3 | 1.0 | 121.3 | 0.253 | 0.115 | 0.738 | 0.412 | 0.039 |
| 14 | Non-ferrous metals | 16.0 | 19.6 | 13.8 | 18.3 | 21.9 | 89.6 | 0.341 | 0.804 | 0.509 | 1.014 | 2.361 |
| 15 | Metal products | 67.7 | 108.0 | 165.4 | 31.6 | 8.9 | 381.6 | 0.722 | 2.222 | 3.065 | 0.875 | 0.480 |
| 16 | General machinery | 136.9 | 136.6 | 326.4 | 73.6 | 17.1 | 690.6 | 0.551 | 1.060 | 2.282 | 0.769 | 0.348 |
| 17 | Electrical machinery | 28.2 | 65.8 | 54.3 | 121.8 | 0.4 | 270.5 | 0.248 | 1.119 | 0.832 | 2.788 | 0.020 |

(continued)

**Table 7.10** (continued)

| | | Output (Billion Yen) | | | | | | Revealed comparative advantages | | | | |
|---|---|---|---|---|---|---|---|---|---|---|---|---|
| | | Gifu | Seino | Chuno | Tono | Hida | Gifu Pref | Gifu | Seino | Chuno | Tono | Hida |
| 18 | Information and communication electronics equipment | 2.2 | 5.0 | 205.1 | 49.3 | 8.0 | 269.5 | 0.031 | 0.137 | 5.105 | 1.833 | 0.577 |
| 19 | Electronic components | 1.6 | 228.7 | 30.7 | 18.0 | 8.5 | 287.5 | 0.014 | 3.788 | 0.458 | 0.401 | 0.369 |
| 20 | Motor vehicle | 295.1 | 120.9 | 297.8 | 67.3 | 20.6 | 801.7 | 0.340 | 0.269 | 0.597 | 0.201 | 0.120 |
| 21 | Aircraft and repair of aircraft | 142.9 | 6.9 | 5.0 | 0.8 | 0.0 | 155.5 | 6.370 | 0.595 | 0.384 | 0.088 | 0.000 |
| 22 | Other transportation equipment | 12.0 | 6.0 | 1.1 | 0.0 | 0.1 | 19.2 | 0.489 | 0.469 | 0.079 | 0.002 | 0.015 |
| 23 | Precision instruments | 3.7 | 0.9 | 7.6 | 15.8 | 0.0 | 27.9 | 0.312 | 0.148 | 1.128 | 3.490 | 0.000 |
| 24 | Miscellaneous manufactured products | 63.8 | 64.5 | 38.0 | 18.5 | 20.8 | 205.7 | 0.699 | 1.365 | 0.725 | 0.526 | 1.156 |
| 25 | Construction | 417.0 | 194.2 | 201.3 | 158.7 | 88.5 | 1059.6 | 1.499 | 1.347 | 1.257 | 1.482 | 1.609 |
| 26 | Electricity, gas and heat supply | 39.3 | 37.8 | 78.4 | 26.1 | 91.5 | 273.1 | 0.429 | 0.797 | 1.490 | 0.741 | 5.062 |
| 27 | Water supply and waste disposal business | 45.0 | 19.2 | 20.2 | 16.4 | 11.1 | 112.0 | 1.346 | 1.110 | 1.051 | 1.271 | 1.686 |
| 28 | Commerce | 599.5 | 166.5 | 135.5 | 159.9 | 79.4 | 1,140.8 | 1.217 | 0.652 | 0.478 | 0.843 | 0.816 |
| 29 | Finance and insurance | 245.3 | 98.6 | 75.2 | 73.8 | 58.6 | 551.6 | 1.536 | 1.191 | 0.819 | 1.201 | 1.855 |
| 30 | Real estate | 355.9 | 167.8 | 171.8 | 163.5 | 75.1 | 934.1 | 1.245 | 1.132 | 1.044 | 1.486 | 1.328 |
| 31 | Transport | 181.8 | 88.8 | 56.9 | 74.0 | 34.7 | 436.2 | 0.999 | 0.942 | 0.544 | 1.057 | 0.966 |

(continued)

**Table 7.10** (continued)

| | | Output (Billion Yen) | | | | | | Revealed comparative advantages | | | | |
|---|---|---|---|---|---|---|---|---|---|---|---|---|
| | | Gifu | Seino | Chuno | Tono | Hida | Gifu Pref | Gifu | Seino | Chuno | Tono | Hida |
| 32 | Information and communications | 251.9 | 38.6 | 12.4 | 16.9 | 10.5 | 330.3 | 1.848 | 0.547 | 0.158 | 0.321 | 0.392 |
| 33 | Public administration | 190.9 | 52.5 | 58.1 | 50.6 | 35.1 | 387.2 | 2.214 | 1.175 | 1.172 | 1.526 | 2.062 |
| 34 | Education and research | 219.0 | 71.2 | 89.4 | 68.4 | 29.1 | 477.2 | 1.446 | 0.908 | 1.027 | 1.174 | 0.973 |
| 35 | Medical service, health, social security and nursing care | 363.5 | 135.2 | 136.7 | 107.0 | 62.4 | 804.9 | 1.870 | 1.342 | 1.223 | 1.431 | 1.626 |
| 36 | Other public services | 39.6 | 21.4 | 16.8 | 10.1 | 9.7 | 97.6 | 2.109 | 2.197 | 1.553 | 1.394 | 2.608 |
| 37 | Business services | 295.0 | 72.2 | 73.4 | 68.1 | 48.4 | 557.0 | 1.267 | 0.598 | 0.547 | 0.760 | 1.051 |
| 38 | Personal services | 290.7 | 96.3 | 139.2 | 116.4 | 96.2 | 738.9 | 1.394 | 0.891 | 1.160 | 1.449 | 2.334 |
| 39 | Office supplies | 9.8 | 4.5 | 4.7 | 3.8 | 1.9 | 24.7 | 1.314 | 1.162 | 1.100 | 1.330 | 1.279 |
| 40 | Activities not elsewhere classified | 27.2 | 12.8 | 14.8 | 10.2 | 5.2 | 70.1 | 1.514 | 1.370 | 1.428 | 1.473 | 1.451 |
| 41 | Sectors, total | 5,073.8 | 2,629.5 | 2,919.5 | 1,953.0 | 1,002.9 | 13,578.7 | 1.000 | 1.000 | 1.000 | 1.000 | 1.000 |

*Source* Computed by the author

**Table 7.11** Output structure of Mie Prefecture

| | | Output (Billion Yen) | | | | | | Revealed comparative advantages | | | | |
|---|---|---|---|---|---|---|---|---|---|---|---|---|
| | | Hokusei | Chusei | Nansei | Iga | Higashi-kishu | Mie Pref | Hokusei | Chusei | Nansei | Iga | Higashi-kishu |
| 01 | Agriculture | 58.0 | 42.0 | 18.1 | 15.5 | 7.7 | 141.2 | 0.973 | 1.760 | 1.806 | 1.679 | 2.522 |
| 02 | Forestry | 4.5 | 6.2 | 2.4 | 0.8 | 4.6 | 18.5 | 0.935 | 3.235 | 2.901 | 1.106 | 18.525 |
| 03 | Fishery | 7.7 | 4.8 | 41.4 | 0.3 | 11.3 | 65.3 | 0.807 | 1.257 | 25.899 | 0.184 | 23.103 |
| 04 | Mining | 7.8 | 1.0 | 6.4 | 4.1 | 0.8 | 20.1 | 1.202 | 0.387 | 5.903 | 4.089 | 2.512 |
| 05 | Beverages and Foods | 294.8 | 170.4 | 73.1 | 77.4 | 18.2 | 633.9 | 1.088 | 1.571 | 1.602 | 1.843 | 1.310 |
| 06 | Textile products | 35.6 | 17.5 | 3.4 | 4.5 | 0.4 | 61.5 | 0.518 | 0.636 | 0.297 | 0.425 | 0.121 |
| 07 | Pulp, paper and wood products | 46.9 | 38.7 | 7.0 | 49.9 | 36.5 | 179.0 | 0.363 | 0.749 | 0.323 | 2.495 | 5.506 |
| 08 | Chemical products | 1,088.5 | 46.2 | 15.4 | 134.1 | 0.0 | 1,284.2 | 4.494 | 0.476 | 0.378 | 3.575 | 0.000 |
| 09 | Petroleum and coal products | 1,123.3 | 0.4 | 1.0 | 3.7 | 0.6 | 1,128.9 | 7.425 | 0.006 | 0.038 | 0.157 | 0.072 |
| 10 | Plastic products | 167.7 | 40.1 | 3.8 | 91.5 | 4.0 | 307.0 | 0.803 | 0.479 | 0.107 | 2.828 | 0.376 |
| 11 | Pottery, china and earthenware | 10.3 | 0.7 | 1.8 | 8.5 | 0.0 | 21.3 | 0.282 | 0.045 | 0.296 | 1.512 | 0.020 |
| 12 | Other ceramic, stone and clay products | 128.4 | 128.1 | 3.5 | 24.9 | 3.0 | 288.0 | 1.293 | 3.221 | 0.212 | 1.618 | 0.592 |
| 13 | Iron and steel | 78.7 | 6.8 | 2.2 | 8.1 | 0.2 | 96.0 | 0.298 | 0.065 | 0.050 | 0.197 | 0.014 |
| 14 | Non-ferrous metals | 296.2 | 64.1 | 2.0 | 23.7 | 0.0 | 386.0 | 3.211 | 1.738 | 0.129 | 1.659 | 0.000 |
| 15 | Metal products | 110.5 | 68.3 | 39.0 | 43.3 | 1.2 | 262.4 | 0.600 | 0.927 | 1.258 | 1.517 | 0.126 |

(continued)

**Table 7.11** (continued)

| | | Output (Billion Yen) | | | | | | Revealed comparative advantages | | | | |
|---|---|---|---|---|---|---|---|---|---|---|---|---|
| | | Hokusei | Chusei | Nansei | Iga | Higashi-kishu | Mie Pref | Hokusei | Chusei | Nansei | Iga | Higashi-kishu |
| 16 | General machinery | 522.6 | 90.0 | 79.5 | 253.0 | 0.1 | 945.3 | 1.070 | 0.460 | 0.968 | 3.346 | 0.004 |
| 17 | Electrical machinery | 400.6 | 119.2 | 59.6 | 57.7 | 3.2 | 640.3 | 1.798 | 1.336 | 1.591 | 1.673 | 0.277 |
| 18 | Information and communication electronics equipment | 211.9 | 4.4 | 29.0 | 0.6 | 2.5 | 248.4 | 1.545 | 0.080 | 1.255 | 0.028 | 0.357 |
| 19 | Electronic components | 373.6 | 699.6 | 97.0 | 11.2 | 6.1 | 1,187.4 | 1.633 | 7.641 | 2.518 | 0.315 | 0.517 |
| 20 | Motor vehicle | 1,659.1 | 175.8 | 22.6 | 86.2 | 0.3 | 1,943.9 | 0.973 | 0.258 | 0.079 | 0.326 | 0.003 |
| 21 | Aircraft and repair of aircraft | 2.0 | 0.0 | 14.7 | 0.0 | 0.0 | 16.7 | 0.045 | 0.000 | 1.986 | 0.000 | 0.000 |
| 22 | Other transportation equipment | 10.5 | 36.7 | 19.6 | 0.5 | 0.1 | 67.5 | 0.219 | 1.901 | 2.417 | 0.069 | 0.058 |
| 23 | Precision instruments | 2.8 | 1.6 | 1.0 | 0.7 | 0.0 | 6.2 | 0.123 | 0.178 | 0.260 | 0.198 | 0.000 |
| 24 | Miscellaneous manufactured products | 103.1 | 97.9 | 83.6 | 61.8 | 4.0 | 350.4 | 0.575 | 1.366 | 2.772 | 2.228 | 0.434 |
| 25 | Construction | 503.5 | 295.4 | 138.7 | 93.0 | 64.4 | 1,094.9 | 0.921 | 1.351 | 1.508 | 1.098 | 2.296 |

(continued)

**Table 7.11** (continued)

| | | Output (Billion Yen) | | | | | | Revealed comparative advantages | | | | |
|---|---|---|---|---|---|---|---|---|---|---|---|---|
| | | Hokusei | Chusei | Nansei | Iga | Higashi-kishu | Mie Pref | Hokusei | Chusei | Nansei | Iga | Higashi-kishu |
| 26 | Electricity, gas and heat supply | 156.4 | 53.9 | 85.0 | 7.7 | 83.6 | 386.6 | 0.870 | 0.749 | 2.810 | 0.276 | 9.073 |
| 27 | Water supply and waste disposal business | 60.1 | 32.5 | 16.7 | 12.5 | 5.3 | 127.1 | 0.915 | 1.234 | 1.506 | 1.224 | 1.582 |
| 28 | Commerce | 393.3 | 258.4 | 103.2 | 62.7 | 26.6 | 844.0 | 0.406 | 0.667 | 0.634 | 0.418 | 0.535 |
| 29 | Finance and insurance | 185.8 | 185.5 | 69.1 | 35.4 | 27.6 | 503.4 | 0.592 | 1.478 | 1.309 | 0.729 | 1.713 |
| 30 | Real estate | 373.9 | 244.8 | 134.9 | 83.3 | 51.7 | 888.7 | 0.666 | 1.089 | 1.427 | 0.958 | 1.794 |
| 31 | Transport | 350.2 | 125.8 | 76.2 | 43.2 | 12.2 | 607.7 | 0.980 | 0.880 | 1.268 | 0.781 | 0.668 |
| 32 | Information and communications | 93.4 | 164.7 | 33.5 | 16.5 | 25.5 | 333.6 | 0.349 | 1.537 | 0.744 | 0.397 | 1.855 |
| 33 | Public administration | 87.2 | 128.9 | 45.4 | 25.0 | 17.4 | 303.9 | 0.515 | 1.903 | 1.592 | 0.954 | 2.003 |
| 34 | Education and research | 143.9 | 86.2 | 38.2 | 24.1 | 7.2 | 299.6 | 0.484 | 0.724 | 0.763 | 0.523 | S0.472 |
| 35 | Medical service, health, social security and nursing care | 291.7 | 189.4 | 99.4 | 66.0 | 33.8 | 680.3 | 0.764 | 1.240 | 1.548 | 1.116 | 1.726 |
| 36 | Other public services | 29.4 | 38.8 | 14.3 | 8.7 | 5.8 | 97.1 | 0.796 | 2.625 | 2.307 | 1.528 | 3.068 |

(continued)

**Table 7.11** (continued)

| | | Output (Billion Yen) | | | | | | Revealed comparative advantages | | | | |
|---|---|---|---|---|---|---|---|---|---|---|---|---|
| | | Hokusei | Chusei | Nansei | Iga | Higashi-kishu | Mie Pref | Hokusei | Chusei | Nansei | Iga | Higashi-kishu |
| 37 | Business services | 204.0 | 128.4 | 50.7 | 33.7 | 16.2 | 433.1 | 0.446 | 0.701 | 0.659 | 0.476 | 0.691 |
| 38 | Personal services | 294.3 | 166.0 | 132.2 | 58.6 | 24.9 | 676.0 | 0.718 | 1.013 | 1.918 | 0.924 | 1.183 |
| 39 | Office supplies | 12.7 | 7.7 | 3.3 | 2.6 | 0.9 | 27.3 | 0.870 | 1.315 | 1.343 | 1.160 | 1.249 |
| 40 | Activities not elsewhere classified | 40.6 | 21.6 | 9.2 | 8.6 | 3.4 | 83.3 | 1.150 | 1.527 | 1.543 | 1.576 | 1.862 |
| 41 | Sectors, total | 9,965.6 | 3,988.2 | 1,677.0 | 1,543.7 | 511.3 | 17,685.8 | 1.000 | 1.000 | 1.000 | 1.000 | 1.000 |

*Source* Computed by the author

relative advantages, and the "Pulp, paper and wood products" sector also has relatively larger production. In this area there are thermal power plants; therefore, the production of the "Electricity, gas, and heat supply" sector is also extensive.

## 7.4 Concluding Remarks

In this chapter, we recompiled three adjacent prefectures' IOTs into an MRIOT to discuss the regional structure of the Nagoya metropolitan area. For this purpose, we first broke down each prefecture's IOT into tables for several small areas. Then the commodity flows among the areas for each sector were estimated by the gravity-RAS method, in which the initial values for the RAS iterative calculation are reduced from the estimated gravity model. Finally, we integrated all the small area tables into an MRIOT, using the estimated transaction shares of the commodity flows. This MRIOT consists of 186 sectors for each of the 14 areas.

We adopted a two-step method for estimating the transaction among areas, first estimating the internal transaction among areas in each prefecture and then estimating the inter-prefectural transaction among areas, to utilize the information about inter-prefectural transactions that are included in the prefectural IOTs.

Such kinds of MRIOTs could resolve the analytical problem that a region identified in terms of economic activity is not necessarily the same as the administrative region. For example, Nagoya is the third-largest metropolitan area in Japan, following Tokyo and Osaka. Nagoya City, the capital city of Aichi Prefecture, is the economic center of the Tokai Region. However, each surrounding area is not equally connected to Nagoya City. The closer the distance between areas, the stronger their economic connection. Thus, we can investigate such relations by using the MRIOT for the Tokai Region.

Using the estimated MRIOT of the Tokai Region, we compared the output structures of each area with an RCA index. Nagoya City has the edge in tertiary industries as the core city of the region. Owari and Nishimikawa in Aichi Prefecture are well-known for their machinery industries, especially the motor vehicle and electric industries.

We were able to demonstrate how subdividing the prefecture's IOT into several small areas and integrating them into an MRIOT yields an analytical tool to solve how the region may be identified in terms of economic activities, which is not necessarily the same as for an administrative region.

## Reference

Yamada, Mitsuo, and Yuichi Owaki. 2012. Estimation of 2005 inter-regional input-output table of four-regions within Aichi Prefecture. Chukyo University, *Institute of economics discussion paper* No. 1205 (in Japanese).

# Part II
# Some Applications of the Multi-Regional Input–Output Tables

# Chapter 8
# Multiplier Decomposition and Regional Interdependence in the Chubu Region

## 8.1 Introduction

It is a critical issue to investigate the spatial structure of regional economic studies. Relationships among economic activities in regions are obtained as the economic linkage factors from the economic ripple analysis of an interregional IOT.

Chubu Region consists of nine prefectures centered in Aichi Prefecture and is located between Osaka and Tokyo. Chen et al. (2016) focused on the spatial structure of the Chubu region and attempted to quantitatively understand its temporal and spatial transformation processes using the framework of the Chubu Region interregional IOTs for 2005 and 2010. They explicitly and quantitatively discussed the interdependence between Aichi Prefecture and the eight surrounding prefectures.

They conducted an analysis that focused only on the intermediate input structure through the multiplier decomposition analysis. However, it is necessary to explicitly consider differences in the economic size and final demand structure of each prefecture. There are differences in the economic scale between prefectures, and even if the spillover effect is relatively small for Aichi Prefecture, it might be evaluated as a relatively large effect for the other prefectures. Therefore, here we conduct an analysis that considers actual changes in interdependence according to differences in final demands and its dynamic changes through factor analysis.

In Chap. 1, we use the Chubu Region interregional IOTs for 2011 and 2015, which are conducted in Chap. 4, to examine the mutual relationships between each prefecture in the region by decomposing induced productions of final demands by region. In Chap. 2, we decompose the secular changes in the induced productions in both periods into technological change factors and market change factors. Furthermore, in relation to the technological change factors, in Chap. 3, we apply the multiplier decomposition method that was used by Chen et al. (2016) to measure the spillover multiplier and feedback multiplier among the nine prefectures in the Chubu region.



M. Yamada, *Multi-Regional Input–Output Analysis of the Japanese Economy*,
https://doi.org/10.1007/978-981-97-9041-8_8

This will reveal changes in the interdependent relationship among the Aichi Prefecture as its core, its eight surrounding prefectures, and the rest of the country for the updated years.

This chapter is structured as follows: Sect. 8.2 provides an overview of the analytical model, followed by Sect. 8.3, which describes the analysis results. Section 8.4 summarizes the findings obtained from the analytical results and discusses the remaining issues.

## 8.2 Decomposition of Multiplier

### 8.2.1 *Decomposition of Induced Production by Final-Demand-Generating Region*

In the two-region interregional IOT as expressed in Eq. (8.1),

$$\begin{bmatrix} \mathbf{X}^1 \\ \mathbf{X}^2 \end{bmatrix} = \begin{bmatrix} \mathbf{A}^{11} & \mathbf{A}^{12} \\ \mathbf{A}^{21} & \mathbf{A}^{22} \end{bmatrix} \begin{bmatrix} \mathbf{X}^1 \\ \mathbf{X}^2 \end{bmatrix} + \begin{bmatrix} \mathbf{F}^1 \\ \mathbf{F}^2 \end{bmatrix} \tag{8.1}$$

the production value induced by final demand is expressed as Eq. (8.2).

$$\begin{bmatrix} \mathbf{X}^1 \\ \mathbf{X}^2 \end{bmatrix} = \begin{bmatrix} \mathbf{I} - \mathbf{A}^{11} & -\mathbf{A}^{12} \\ -\mathbf{A}^{21} & \mathbf{I} - \mathbf{A}^{22} \end{bmatrix}^{-1} \begin{bmatrix} \mathbf{F}^1 \\ \mathbf{F}^2 \end{bmatrix} = \begin{bmatrix} \mathbf{B}^{11} & \mathbf{B}^{12} \\ \mathbf{B}^{21} & \mathbf{B}^{22} \end{bmatrix} \begin{bmatrix} \mathbf{F}^1 \\ \mathbf{F}^2 \end{bmatrix} \tag{8.2}$$

To find out how much production of each region is induced by a certain region's final demand, we multiply the Leontief inverse matrix by the matrix $\hat{\mathbf{F}}^r$, which is the diagonalization of the final demand vector $\mathbf{F}^r$, as shown in Eq. (8.3).

$$\begin{bmatrix} \mathbf{X}^{11} & \mathbf{X}^{12} \\ \mathbf{X}^{21} & \mathbf{X}^{22} \end{bmatrix} = \begin{bmatrix} \mathbf{B}^{11} & \mathbf{B}^{12} \\ \mathbf{B}^{21} & \mathbf{B}^{22} \end{bmatrix} \begin{bmatrix} \hat{\mathbf{F}}^1 & \mathbf{0} \\ \mathbf{0} & \hat{\mathbf{F}}^2 \end{bmatrix} = \begin{bmatrix} \mathbf{B}^{11}\hat{\mathbf{F}}^1 & \mathbf{B}^{12}\hat{\mathbf{F}}^2 \\ \mathbf{B}^{21}\hat{\mathbf{F}}^1 & \mathbf{B}^{22}\hat{\mathbf{F}}^2 \end{bmatrix} \tag{8.3}$$

Here, $\mathbf{X}^{rs}$ represents the production value of region r induced by the final demand of region s. The relationship $\mathbf{X}^1 = \mathbf{X}^{11}\mathbf{e} + \mathbf{X}^{12}\mathbf{e}$ shows how much production in Region 1 is induced by final demand in each region, where $\mathbf{e}$ is a vector with each element being 1.

$$\begin{aligned} \begin{bmatrix} \mathbf{X}^1 \\ \mathbf{X}^2 \end{bmatrix} &= \begin{bmatrix} \mathbf{X}^{11} & \mathbf{X}^{12} \\ \mathbf{X}^{21} & \mathbf{X}^{22} \end{bmatrix} \begin{bmatrix} \mathbf{e} \\ \mathbf{e} \end{bmatrix} = \begin{bmatrix} \mathbf{B}^{11}\hat{\mathbf{F}}^1 & \mathbf{B}^{12}\hat{\mathbf{F}}^2 \\ \mathbf{B}^{21}\hat{\mathbf{F}}^1 & \mathbf{B}^{22}\hat{\mathbf{F}}^2 \end{bmatrix} \begin{bmatrix} \mathbf{e} \\ \mathbf{e} \end{bmatrix} \\ &= \begin{bmatrix} \mathbf{B}^{11}\hat{\mathbf{F}}^1\mathbf{e} + \mathbf{B}^{12}\hat{\mathbf{F}}^2\mathbf{e} \\ \mathbf{B}^{21}\hat{\mathbf{F}}^1\mathbf{e} + \mathbf{B}^{22}\hat{\mathbf{F}}^2\mathbf{e} \end{bmatrix} = \begin{bmatrix} \mathbf{B}^{11}\mathbf{F}^1 + \mathbf{B}^{12}\mathbf{F}^2 \\ \mathbf{B}^{21}\mathbf{F}^1 + \mathbf{B}^{22}\mathbf{F}^2 \end{bmatrix} \end{aligned} \tag{8.4}$$

Similarly, we can find out which region's production is affected by the final demand of each region by aggregating the matrix in (8.3) in the column direction.

$$\left[\tilde{\mathbf{X}}^{1\prime}\ \tilde{\mathbf{X}}^{2\prime}\right]=\left[\mathbf{e}'\ \mathbf{e}'\right]\begin{bmatrix}\mathbf{X}^{11} & \mathbf{X}^{12}\\ \mathbf{X}^{21} & \mathbf{X}^{22}\end{bmatrix}=\left[\mathbf{e}'\ \mathbf{e}'\right]\begin{bmatrix}\mathbf{B}^{11}\hat{\mathbf{F}}^{1} & \mathbf{B}^{12}\hat{\mathbf{F}}^{2}\\ \mathbf{B}^{21}\hat{\mathbf{F}}^{1} & \mathbf{B}^{22}\hat{\mathbf{F}}^{2}\end{bmatrix} \tag{8.5}$$

Next, we will consider the factor decomposition of production changes. Changes in induced productions (8.6) and (8.7) by the final demands at two points in time, 0 and 1, can be decomposed into technological change factors based on changes in input coefficients and market change factors based on changes in final demand.

$$\begin{bmatrix}\mathbf{X}_0^1\\ \mathbf{X}_0^2\end{bmatrix}=\begin{bmatrix}\mathbf{B}_0^{11} & \mathbf{B}_0^{12}\\ \mathbf{B}_0^{21} & \mathbf{B}_0^{22}\end{bmatrix}\begin{bmatrix}\mathbf{F}_0^1\\ \mathbf{F}_0^2\end{bmatrix} \tag{8.6}$$

$$\begin{bmatrix}\mathbf{X}_1^1\\ \mathbf{X}_1^2\end{bmatrix}=\begin{bmatrix}\mathbf{B}_1^{11} & \mathbf{B}_1^{12}\\ \mathbf{B}_1^{21} & \mathbf{B}_1^{22}\end{bmatrix}\begin{bmatrix}\mathbf{F}_1^1\\ \mathbf{F}_1^2\end{bmatrix} \tag{8.7}$$

The difference between the two Eqs. (8.6) and (8.7) is expressed as

$$\begin{aligned}\begin{bmatrix}\mathbf{X}_1^1\\ \mathbf{X}_1^2\end{bmatrix}-\begin{bmatrix}\mathbf{X}_0^1\\ \mathbf{X}_0^2\end{bmatrix}&=\begin{bmatrix}\mathbf{B}_1^{11} & \mathbf{B}_1^{12}\\ \mathbf{B}_1^{21} & \mathbf{B}_1^{22}\end{bmatrix}\begin{bmatrix}\mathbf{F}_1^1\\ \mathbf{F}_1^2\end{bmatrix}-\begin{bmatrix}\mathbf{B}_0^{11} & \mathbf{B}_0^{12}\\ \mathbf{B}_0^{21} & \mathbf{B}_0^{22}\end{bmatrix}\begin{bmatrix}\mathbf{F}_0^1\\ \mathbf{F}_0^2\end{bmatrix}\\
&=\left[\begin{bmatrix}\mathbf{B}_1^{11} & \mathbf{B}_1^{12}\\ \mathbf{B}_1^{21} & \mathbf{B}_1^{22}\end{bmatrix}-\begin{bmatrix}\mathbf{B}_0^{11} & \mathbf{B}_0^{12}\\ \mathbf{B}_0^{21} & \mathbf{B}_0^{22}\end{bmatrix}\right]\cdot\frac{1}{2}\left[\begin{bmatrix}\mathbf{F}_1^1\\ \mathbf{F}_1^2\end{bmatrix}+\begin{bmatrix}\mathbf{F}_0^1\\ \mathbf{F}_0^2\end{bmatrix}\right]\\
&\quad+\frac{1}{2}\left[\begin{bmatrix}\mathbf{B}_1^{11} & \mathbf{B}_1^{12}\\ \mathbf{B}_1^{21} & \mathbf{B}_1^{22}\end{bmatrix}+\begin{bmatrix}\mathbf{B}_0^{11} & \mathbf{B}_0^{12}\\ \mathbf{B}_0^{21} & \mathbf{B}_0^{22}\end{bmatrix}\right]\left[\begin{bmatrix}\mathbf{F}_1^1\\ \mathbf{F}_1^2\end{bmatrix}-\begin{bmatrix}\mathbf{F}_0^1\\ \mathbf{F}_0^2\end{bmatrix}\right]\end{aligned} \tag{8.8}$$

The first term on the right is the technological change factor, and the second term is the market change factor.

### 8.2.2 *Multiplier Decomposition*

Using an IOT with two sectors, a goods sector and a service sector, Miyazawa (1963) decomposed the Leontief inverse matrix into two compositions, an external multiplier and an internal multiplier, to analyze the interdependence between the two. Miyazawa (1966), Yamada and Ihara (1966), and Ihara (1968) expanded the model to three groups and applied it to regional input–output models.

Arranging the Asia International IOT of ten regions to a two-region table of Japan and others, Okamoto (2012) decomposed the total multiplier into three factors: a domestic multiplier, a spillover multiplier, and a feedback multiplier. In addition, Kuwamori (2014) extended the multiplier decomposition to the case of the international input–output model with more than two countries.

Below, we discuss the multiplier decomposition of the interregional Leontief inverse matrix according to Okamoto (2012) and Kuwamori (2014). The interregional Leontief inverse matrix of the two-regional input–output model is

$$\begin{bmatrix} \mathbf{I}-\mathbf{A}^{11} & -\mathbf{A}^{12} \\ -\mathbf{A}^{21} & \mathbf{I}-\mathbf{A}^{22} \end{bmatrix}^{-1} = \begin{bmatrix} \tilde{\mathbf{B}}^{11} & \tilde{\mathbf{B}}^{12} \\ \tilde{\mathbf{B}}^{21} & \tilde{\mathbf{B}}^{22} \end{bmatrix} \tag{8.9}$$

Here, $\mathbf{A}^{\mathrm{rs}}$ means a region-$s'$ input–output coefficient matrix from region-$r$, $\mathbf{I}$ is a unit matrix, and $\tilde{\mathbf{B}}^{\mathrm{rs}}$ denotes a sub-matrix of the Leontief inverse matrix that measures region-$s'$ induced production induced by the final demand of region-$r$. Expanding this interregional Leontief inverse matrix using the matrix partitioning method, we get

$$\begin{bmatrix} \tilde{\mathbf{B}}^{11} & \tilde{\mathbf{B}}^{12} \\ \tilde{\mathbf{B}}^{21} & \tilde{\mathbf{B}}^{22} \end{bmatrix} = \begin{bmatrix} \mathbf{B}^{11}+\mathbf{B}^{11}\mathbf{A}^{12}\mathbf{T}^{2}\mathbf{B}^{22}\mathbf{A}^{21}\mathbf{B}^{11} & \mathbf{B}^{11}\mathbf{A}^{12}\mathbf{T}^{2}\mathbf{B}^{22} \\ \mathbf{B}^{22}\mathbf{A}^{21}\mathbf{T}^{1}\mathbf{B}^{11} & \mathbf{B}^{22}+\mathbf{B}^{22}\mathbf{A}^{21}\mathbf{T}^{1}\mathbf{B}^{11}\mathbf{A}^{12}\mathbf{B}^{22} \end{bmatrix} \tag{8.10}$$

where each element of the matrix is

$$\textbf{Inner multiplier}: \mathbf{B}^{11} = \left(\mathbf{I}-\mathbf{A}^{11}\right)^{-1}, \mathbf{B}^{22} = \left(\mathbf{I}-\mathbf{A}^{22}\right)^{-1} \tag{8.11}$$

$$\textbf{External multiplier}: \mathbf{T}^{1} = \left(\mathbf{I}-\mathbf{B}^{11}\mathbf{A}^{12}\mathbf{B}^{22}\mathbf{A}^{21}\right)^{-1} \tag{8.12}$$

$$\mathbf{T}^{2} = \left(\mathbf{I}-\mathbf{B}^{22}\mathbf{A}^{21}\mathbf{B}^{11}\mathbf{A}^{12}\right)^{-1} \tag{8.13}$$

In addition, there is a **feedback multiplier** that returns to the own region via other regions, a **spillover multiplier** that induces production in other regions, and an **internal multiplier** that shows the induced production within the own region (intra-region multiplier). We disassemble the Leontief inverse matrix for those three factors as follows[1]:

$$\begin{aligned} \begin{bmatrix} \tilde{\mathbf{B}}^{11} & \tilde{\mathbf{B}}^{12} \\ \tilde{\mathbf{B}}^{21} & \tilde{\mathbf{B}}^{22} \end{bmatrix} &= \begin{bmatrix} \mathbf{B}^{11}\mathbf{A}^{12}\mathbf{T}^{2}\mathbf{B}^{22}\mathbf{A}^{21}\mathbf{B}^{11} & \mathbf{0} \\ \mathbf{0} & \mathbf{B}^{22}\mathbf{A}^{21}\mathbf{T}^{1}\mathbf{B}^{11}\mathbf{A}^{12}\mathbf{B}^{22} \end{bmatrix} \\ &+ \begin{bmatrix} \mathbf{0} & \mathbf{B}^{11}\mathbf{A}^{12}\mathbf{T}^{2}\mathbf{B}^{22} \\ \mathbf{B}^{22}\mathbf{A}^{21}\mathbf{T}^{1}\mathbf{B}^{11} & \mathbf{0} \end{bmatrix} \\ &+ \begin{bmatrix} \mathbf{B}^{11} & \mathbf{0} \\ \mathbf{0} & \mathbf{B}^{22} \end{bmatrix} \end{aligned}$$

[1] Refer to Okamoto (2012), pp. 42–44. In the application to ten regions, the spillover multiplier is defined as the off-diagonal element remaining after calculating the intra-regional multiplier (third term on the right-hand side of Eq. 8.13) and the feedback multiplier (first term on the right-hand side of Eq. 8.13). According to Kuwamori (2014), although this simple method leaves ambiguity in its meaning as an interregional spillover effect, as the number of regions increases, it becomes difficult to strictly decompose the multiplier; therefore, the simple method is the most effective. He points out that this is considered a realistic method.

$$= \begin{bmatrix} \tilde{\mathbf{B}}^{11} - \mathbf{B}^{11} & \mathbf{0} \\ \mathbf{0} & \tilde{\mathbf{B}}^{22} - \mathbf{B}^{22} \end{bmatrix} + \begin{bmatrix} \mathbf{0} & \tilde{\mathbf{B}}^{12} \\ \tilde{\mathbf{B}}^{21} & \mathbf{0} \end{bmatrix} + \begin{bmatrix} \mathbf{B}^{11} & \mathbf{0} \\ \mathbf{0} & \mathbf{B}^{22} \end{bmatrix} \tag{8.14}$$

## 8.3 Analytical Results

### *8.3.1 Results of the Decomposition of the Induced Production by the Final Demand-Generating Region*

Table 8.1 depicts the regional production value induced by the final demand for each region expressed by Eq. (8.3) in the previous section. Table 8.1 is divided into three parts, with the top rows depicting the production-induced amount by each regional final demand. The middle rows present the share of each regional production-induced value brought about by the final demand in a certain region (in the vertical direction). Conversely, the bottom rows show the share (horizontal direction) of a certain region's production value induced by each region's final demand. The cells with a share greater than 2 percent are in itallics.

In the top rows, which indicate the amount of production induced, we can see the difference in the regional scale. Looking at the production value of the nine prefectures that make up the Chubu region, excluding other regions, Aichi Prefecture has the highest at 79.6 trillion yen, followed by Shizuoka Prefecture at 34.1 trillion yen and Mie Prefecture at 18.1 trillion yen.

Looking at the share of each region's production induced by a certain final demand in the middle rows, each prefecture has the largest impact on its own prefecture, with the range from Mie Prefecture at 69.72% to Toyama Prefecture at 78.34%. Furthermore, in terms of the impact on other prefectures, all prefectures have a significant impact on the ROJ, ranging from 11.09% in Gifu Prefecture to 20.33% in Shiga Prefecture. Within the Chubu region, the influence on Aichi Prefecture is relatively large, with three prefectures relying on Aichi Prefecture's production: Gifu Prefecture 7.58%, Shizuoka Prefecture 6.09%, and Mie Prefecture 7.74%. In other prefectures, excluding Toyama Prefecture, the rate is around 3%.

The bottom rows show the share of a certain region's production induced by each region's final demand. The share of the own prefecture is from 69.19 to 79.35%, the relationship with the ROJ is from 12.89 to 21.55%, and within the Chubu area, the ratio of dependence on final demand from Aichi Prefecture is from 2.90 to 9.20%. Among them, Gifu Prefecture has the largest share at 9.20%, Shizuoka Prefecture at 6.07%, and Mie Prefecture at 8.02%.

Thus, the Chubu Region has Aichi Prefecture at its core, which trades closely with neighboring prefectures Gifu, Shizuoka, and Mie, though all prefectures are trading with Aichi Prefecture as the largest market except the ROJ. However, Toyama, Ishikawa, and Fukui Prefectures also interact with each other to form the Hokuriku region.

**Table 8.1** Decomposition of the regionally induced production by final demand-generating region, 2015 input–output table (unit: billion yen, %)

| 2015 | | Region generating final demand | | | | | | | | | | |
|---|---|---|---|---|---|---|---|---|---|---|---|---|
| | | Toyama | Ishikawa | Fukui | Nagano | Gifu | Shizuoka | Aichi | Mie | Shiga | Rest of Japan | Japan, total |
| Induced production (unit: bil. Yen) | Toyama | 6,256.41 | 127.63 | 54.70 | 116.10 | 53.17 | 89.54 | 344.83 | 63.33 | 54.46 | 1,882.51 | 9,042.69 |
| | Ishikawa | 207.80 | 6,247.82 | 161.78 | 51.40 | 32.59 | 121.34 | 309.75 | 88.52 | 45.15 | 1,164.19 | 8,430.32 |
| | Fukui | 42.02 | 83.40 | 4,127.74 | 64.64 | 27.69 | 76.56 | 165.96 | 51.78 | 166.45 | 912.94 | 5,719.19 |
| | Nagano | 39.44 | 56.46 | 31.27 | 11,686.27 | 69.02 | 192.08 | 522.61 | 105.81 | 54.55 | 2,093.62 | 14,851.13 |
| | Gifu | 31.87 | 48.96 | 38.24 | 78.38 | 10,199.96 | 208.25 | 1,285.27 | 138.00 | 126.83 | 1,811.14 | 13,966.90 |
| | Shizuoka | 92.58 | 81.01 | 44.01 | 224.21 | 138.85 | 23,936.52 | 1,974.27 | 288.05 | 102.29 | 5,662.27 | 32,544.05 |
| | Aichi | 145.06 | 329.39 | 196.45 | 447.33 | 1,003.05 | 2,081.79 | 61,656.87 | 1,405.08 | 415.51 | 10,019.37 | 77,699.91 |
| | Mie | 55.08 | 86.81 | 44.81 | 191.36 | 178.75 | 407.60 | 1,526.66 | 12,649.62 | 240.59 | 3,665.51 | 19,046.79 |
| | Shiga | 30.83 | 56.32 | 38.45 | 60.82 | 60.19 | 185.16 | 374.65 | 229.37 | 8,486.95 | 2,615.36 | 12,138.11 |
| | Rest of Japan | 1,084.94 | 1,611.36 | 975.85 | 2,851.42 | 1,467.97 | 6,868.79 | 11,486.97 | 3,124.62 | 2,473.33 | 764,535.50 | 796,480.74 |
| | Japan, total | 7,986.04 | 8,729.15 | 5,713.29 | 15,771.95 | 13,231.24 | 34,167.62 | 79,647.83 | 18,144.20 | 12,166.11 | 794,362.40 | 989,919.82 |
| Share of induced production by the region receiving the effect (unit: %) | Toyama | *78.34* | 1.46 | 0.96 | 0.74 | 0.40 | 0.26 | 0.43 | 0.35 | 0.45 | 0.24 | 0.91 |
| | Ishikawa | *2.60* | *71.57* | *2.83* | 0.33 | 0.25 | 0.36 | 0.39 | 0.49 | 0.37 | 0.15 | 0.85 |
| | Fukui | 0.53 | 0.96 | *72.25* | 0.41 | 0.21 | 0.22 | 0.21 | 0.29 | 1.37 | 0.11 | 0.58 |
| | Nagano | 0.49 | 0.65 | 0.55 | *74.10* | 0.52 | 0.56 | 0.66 | 0.58 | 0.45 | 0.26 | 1.50 |
| | Gifu | 0.40 | 0.56 | 0.67 | 0.50 | *77.09* | 0.61 | 1.61 | 0.76 | 1.04 | 0.23 | 1.41 |
| | Shizuoka | 1.16 | 0.93 | 0.77 | 1.42 | 1.05 | *70.06* | *2.48* | 1.59 | 0.84 | 0.71 | *3.29* |
| | Aichi | 1.82 | *3.77* | *3.44* | *2.84* | *7.58* | *6.09* | *77.41* | *7.74* | *3.42* | 1.26 | *7.85* |

(continued)

**Table 8.1** (continued)

| 2015 | | Region generating final demand | | | | | | | | | | |
|---|---|---|---|---|---|---|---|---|---|---|---|---|
| | | Toyama | Ishikawa | Fukui | Nagano | Gifu | Shizuoka | Aichi | Mie | Shiga | Rest of Japan | Japan, total |
| | Mie | 0.69 | 0.99 | 0.78 | 1.21 | 1.35 | 1.19 | 1.92 | *69.72* | 1.98 | 0.46 | 1.92 |
| | Shiga | 0.39 | 0.65 | 0.67 | 0.39 | 0.45 | 0.54 | 0.47 | 1.26 | *69.76* | 0.33 | 1.23 |
| | Rest of Japan | *13.59* | *18.46* | *17.08* | *18.08* | *11.09* | *20.10* | *14.42* | *17.22* | *20.33* | *96.25* | *80.46* |
| | Japan, total | 100.00 | 100.00 | 100.00 | 100.00 | 100.00 | 100.00 | 100.00 | 100.00 | 100.00 | 100.00 | 100.00 |
| Share of induced production by the region generating final demand (unit: %) | Toyama | *69.19* | 1.41 | 0.60 | 1.28 | 0.59 | 0.99 | *3.81* | 0.70 | 0.60 | *20.82* | 100.00 |
| | Ishikawa | *2.46* | *74.11* | 1.92 | 0.61 | 0.39 | 1.44 | *3.67* | 1.05 | 0.54 | *13.81* | 100.00 |
| | Fukui | 0.73 | 1.46 | *72.17* | 1.13 | 0.48 | 1.34 | *2.90* | 0.91 | *2.91* | *15.96* | 100.00 |
| | Nagano | 0.27 | 0.38 | 0.21 | *78.69* | 0.46 | 1.29 | *3.52* | 0.71 | 0.37 | *14.10* | 100.00 |
| | Gifu | 0.23 | 0.35 | 0.27 | 0.56 | *73.03* | 1.49 | *9.20* | 0.99 | 0.91 | *12.97* | 100.00 |
| | Shizuoka | 0.28 | 0.25 | 0.14 | 0.69 | 0.43 | *73.55* | *6.07* | 0.89 | 0.31 | *17.40* | 100.00 |
| | Aichi | 0.19 | 0.42 | 0.25 | 0.58 | 1.29 | *2.68* | *79.35* | 1.81 | 0.53 | *12.89* | 100.00 |
| | Mie | 0.29 | 0.46 | 0.24 | 1.00 | 0.94 | *2.14* | *8.02* | *66.41* | 1.26 | *19.24* | 100.00 |
| | Shiga | 0.25 | 0.46 | 0.32 | 0.50 | 0.50 | 1.53 | *3.09* | 1.89 | *69.92* | *21.55* | 100.00 |
| | Rest of Japan | 0.14 | 0.20 | 0.12 | 0.36 | 0.18 | 0.86 | 1.44 | 0.39 | 0.31 | *95.99* | 100.00 |
| | Japan, total | 0.81 | 0.88 | 0.58 | 1.59 | 1.34 | *3.45* | *8.05* | 1.83 | 1.23 | *80.25* | 100.00 |

*Source* The author's calculation

Next, based on Eq. (8.7) in the previous section, we calculated a factor decomposition of the intertemporal regional induced production value, resulting in Table 8.2, by using the 2011 and the 2015 Chubu Region interregional IOTs.

Referring to Table 8.2, all the prefectures' changes in production-induced amounts caused by final demand in 2011 and 2015 have increased except for Fukui Prefecture. In the Chubu region, Aichi Prefecture has the largest amount with 7005.1 billion yen, followed by Shizuoka Prefecture with 2455.6 billion yen, and Mie Prefecture with 1609.4 billion yen. In addition, the ROJ has 59,916.6 billion yen, and the national total amounts to 73,195.7 billion yen.

Changes in production-induced amounts can be broken down into technological change factors based on changes in input coefficients and market change factors based on changes in final demand. Comparing the values for each factor, in all prefectures except for Ishikawa Prefecture, technological change factors have decreased while market change factors have increased. In Aichi Prefecture, market change factors increase by 12,152.7 billion yen and technological change factors decrease by 5147.6 billion yen, resulting in a production-induced amount of 7005.1 billion yen.

In Ishikawa Prefecture, an exception, both factors are positive and contribute to the increase in production-induced amounts, though these values are relatively low. In addition, in Fukui Prefecture, like other prefectures, there are positive market change factors and negative technological change factors, but the market change factor is smaller than the absolute value of the technological change factor; hence, the number of induced production changes has decreased.

**Table 8.2** Factor decomposition of Production change between 2011 and 2015

| | | Change of Production | Change in Technology | Change in the market Scale | Change of Production | Change in Technology | Change in the market Scale |
|---|---|---|---|---|---|---|---|
| Unit | | Billion yen | | | % | | |
| 1 | Toyama | 179.4 | −527.7 | 707.1 | 100.0 | −294.1 | 394.1 |
| 2 | Ishikawa | 658.2 | 65.4 | 592.8 | 100.0 | 9.9 | 90.1 |
| 3 | Fukui | −198.4 | −387.3 | 188.9 | 100.0 | 195.2 | −95.2 |
| 4 | Nagano | 71.6 | −1,622.5 | 1,694.1 | 100.0 | −2,266.6 | 2,366.6 |
| 5 | Gifu | 634.6 | −935.0 | 1,569.5 | 100.0 | −147.3 | 247.3 |
| 6 | Shizuoka | 2466.5 | −1,481.8 | 3,948.3 | 100.0 | −60.1 | 160.1 |
| 7 | Aichi | 7005.1 | −5,147.6 | 12,152.7 | 100.0 | −73.5 | 173.5 |
| 8 | Mie | 1609.4 | −285.8 | 1,895.2 | 100.0 | −17.8 | 117.8 |
| 9 | Shiga | 852.8 | −587.8 | 1,440.5 | 100.0 | −68.9 | 168.9 |
| 10 | ROJ | 59,916.6 | −51,761.9 | 111,678.4 | 100.0 | −86.4 | 186.4 |
| Japan, Total | | 73,195.7 | −62,671.8 | 135,867.5 | 100.0 | −85.6 | 185.6 |

*Source* The author's calculation

### 8.3.2 Results of Multiplier Decomposition

Table 8.3 applies the multiplier decomposition method of Eq. (8.6) in the previous section to the Chubu Region interregional IOTs (104 sector tables) for 2011 and 2015 and calculates the sectoral multiplier values for each prefecture as weighted average values of each sector using final demand weights. The total multiplier,[2] which is the Leontief inverse matrix multiplier indicating the economic ripple effect per unit of final demand in each prefecture, was decomposed into an internal, spillover, and feedback multipliers. Here, the spillover multiplier is displayed separately for within and outside the Chubu region.

Table 8.3 is divided into three parts: top, middle, and bottom. The top rows present the multiplier value for 2011, the middle rows show the multiplier value for 2015, and the bottom rows indicate the increase/decrease value for both years. In addition, the table is divided into two parts: the left side depicts the multiplier value, and the right side presents the composition ratio of the decomposed multiplier value for each prefecture.

Looking at the total multiplier in 2011, Shizuoka Prefecture had the highest value at 1.95, followed by Aichi Prefecture with 1.94 and Mie Prefecture with 1.88. In 2015, Aichi Prefecture had the highest rate of 1.84, followed by Shizuoka Prefecture with 1.80 and Mie Prefecture with 1.80. The multiplier in 2015 decreased, albeit slightly, in all prefectures compared to 2011.

Looking at the composition ratio of the decomposed multipliers, in 2011, the ratio of internal multipliers to the total multipliers for each of the nine prefectures in the Chubu Region was in the range of 65.3–75.6%, the spillover multiplier accounted for 24.0–34.5%, and the feedback multiplier was 0.2–1.7%. In 2015, the internal multiplier ratio was 69.3–78.2%, the spillover multiplier was 21.7–30.3%, and the feedback multiplier was 0.1–1.4%. In both years, internal multipliers are dominant, followed by spillover multipliers, and feedback multipliers are negligible.

Figure 8.1 displays the multiplier decomposition for each prefecture in the Chubu region, the ROJ, and Japan's average in 2015. The multiplier for each prefecture in the Chubu Region except Toyama Prefecture is larger than the multiplier for the ROJ, and the largest multiplier is in Aichi Prefecture, which is also the largest in the Chubu Region when comparing multipliers within the region. Furthermore, except for Gifu Prefecture, the spillover effect outside the Chubu area is larger than the effect within the Chubu area.

Focusing on Aichi Prefecture, which has the largest production scale in the Chubu region, although the total multiplier has been decreasing over the years, it continues to be large compared to other prefectures. The intra-prefecture multiplier of Aichi Prefecture is also the largest compared to other prefectures; conversely, its spillover multiplier is not the largest compared to other prefectures, and the feedback multiplier is the highest among them.

[2] As the Chubu region interregional IOT is not a real table that considers the factors of price changes, the calculated multipliers include not only the effect of quantity changes but also that of price changes when making intertemporal comparisons.

**Table 8.3** Decomposition of multiplier effect

| 2011 | | Multiplier within prefecture | Spillover effect | | | Feed back effect | Multiplier, Total | Multiplier within prefecture | Spillover effect | | | Feed back effect | Multiplier, total |
|---|---|---|---|---|---|---|---|---|---|---|---|---|---|
| | | | Within Chubu region | Without Chubu region | Total | | | | Within Chubu region | Without Chubu region | Total | | |
| 1 | Toyama | 1.28 | 0.18 | 0.23 | 0.41 | 0.00 | 1.69 | 75.6 | 10.4 | 13.9 | 24.2 | 0.2 | 100.0 |
| 2 | Ishikawa | 1.25 | 0.20 | 0.27 | 0.48 | 0.00 | 1.74 | 72.3 | 11.8 | 15.7 | 27.5 | 0.2 | 100.0 |
| 3 | Fukui | 1.25 | 0.21 | 0.32 | 0.53 | 0.00 | 1.78 | 70.0 | 12.0 | 17.8 | 29.8 | 0.2 | 100.0 |
| 4 | Nagano | 1.30 | 0.18 | 0.29 | 0.46 | 0.00 | 1.77 | 73.7 | 10.1 | 16.1 | 26.2 | 0.2 | 100.0 |
| 5 | Gifu | 1.29 | 0.23 | 0.21 | 0.43 | 0.00 | 1.72 | 74.7 | 13.2 | 11.9 | 25.1 | 0.2 | 100.0 |
| 6 | Shizuoka | 1.27 | 0.30 | 0.36 | 0.66 | 0.01 | 1.95 | 65.4 | 15.6 | 18.4 | 34.0 | 0.6 | 100.0 |
| 7 | Aichi | 1.44 | 0.18 | 0.29 | 0.46 | 0.03 | 1.94 | 74.3 | 9.2 | 14.7 | 24.0 | 1.7 | 100.0 |
| 8 | Mie | 1.23 | 0.28 | 0.36 | 0.64 | 0.01 | 1.88 | 65.5 | 14.9 | 19.1 | 34.0 | 0.5 | 100.0 |
| 9 | Shiga | 1.20 | 0.25 | 0.38 | 0.63 | 0.00 | 1.84 | 65.3 | 13.6 | 20.9 | 34.5 | 0.2 | 100.0 |
| 10 | Rest of Japan | 1.65 | 0.06 | 0.00 | 0.06 | 0.02 | 1.73 | 95.4 | 3.6 | 0.0 | 3.6 | 1.1 | 100.0 |
| Japan, average | | 1.59 | 0.09 | 0.06 | 0.15 | 0.02 | 1.76 | 90.5 | 5.2 | 3.3 | 8.5 | 1.0 | 100.0 |
| 2015 | | Multiplier within prefecture | Spillover effect | | | Feed back effect | Multiplier, Total | Multiplier within prefecture | Spillover effect | | | Feed back effect | Multiplier, total |
| | | | Within Chubu region | Without Chubu region | Total | | | | Within Chubu region | Without Chubu region | Total | | |
| 1 | Toyama | 1.27 | 0.13 | 0.22 | 0.35 | 0.00 | 1.63 | 78.2 | 8.1 | 13.6 | 21.7 | 0.2 | 100.0 |
| 2 | Ishikawa | 1.21 | 0.17 | 0.31 | 0.48 | 0.00 | 1.69 | 71.4 | 10.0 | 18.5 | 28.4 | 0.2 | 100.0 |
| 3 | Fukui | 1.25 | 0.19 | 0.30 | 0.48 | 0.00 | 1.74 | 72.1 | 10.7 | 17.1 | 27.8 | 0.2 | 100.0 |
| 4 | Nagano | 1.23 | 0.13 | 0.30 | 0.43 | 0.00 | 1.67 | 74.0 | 7.8 | 18.1 | 25.9 | 0.1 | 100.0 |

(continued)

**Table 8.3** (continued)

| 2015 | | Multiplier within prefecture | Spillover effect | | | Feed back effect | Multiplier, Total | Multiplier within prefecture | Spillover effect | | | Feed back effect | Multiplier, total |
|---|---|---|---|---|---|---|---|---|---|---|---|---|---|
| | | | Within Chubu region | Without Chubu region | Total | | | | Within Chubu region | Without Chubu region | Total | | |
| 5 | Gifu | 1.26 | 0.19 | 0.18 | 0.37 | 0.00 | 1.64 | 76.9 | 11.8 | 11.1 | 22.9 | 0.2 | 100.0 |
| 6 | Shizuoka | 1.25 | 0.18 | 0.36 | 0.54 | 0.01 | 1.80 | 69.6 | 9.8 | 20.1 | 29.9 | 0.4 | 100.0 |
| 7 | Aichi | 1.40 | 0.15 | 0.27 | 0.42 | 0.02 | 1.84 | 76.1 | 8.2 | 14.4 | 22.6 | 1.4 | 100.0 |
| 8 | Mie | 1.25 | 0.24 | 0.31 | 0.55 | 0.01 | 1.80 | 69.3 | 13.1 | 17.2 | 30.3 | 0.5 | 100.0 |
| 9 | Shiga | 1.21 | 0.17 | 0.35 | 0.53 | 0.01 | 1.74 | 69.4 | 9.9 | 20.3 | 30.2 | 0.4 | 100.0 |
| 10 | Rest of Japan | 1.55 | 0.06 | 0.00 | 0.06 | 0.02 | 1.63 | 95.2 | 3.8 | 0.0 | 3.8 | 1.1 | 100.0 |
| Japan, average | | 1.51 | 0.08 | 0.05 | 0.13 | 0.02 | 1.66 | 90.9 | 4.9 | 3.2 | 8.1 | 1.0 | 100.0 |
| Difference | | Multiplier within prefecture | Spillover effect | | | Feed back effect | Multiplier, total | Multiplier within prefecture | Spillover effect | | | Feed back effect | Multiplier, total |
| | | | Within Chubu region | Without Chubu region | Total | | | | Within Chubu region | Without Chubu region | Total | | |
| 1 | Toyama | 0.00 | −0.04 | −0.01 | −0.06 | 0.00 | −0.06 | −0.2 | −2.6 | −0.8 | −3.4 | −0.1 | −3.6 |
| 2 | Ishikawa | −0.05 | −0.04 | 0.04 | 0.00 | 0.00 | −0.05 | −2.8 | −2.1 | 2.2 | 0.2 | −0.1 | −2.7 |
| 3 | Fukui | 0.00 | −0.03 | −0.02 | −0.05 | 0.00 | −0.04 | 0.2 | −1.6 | −1.1 | −2.8 | 0.0 | −2.5 |
| 4 | Nagano | −0.07 | −0.05 | 0.02 | −0.03 | 0.00 | −0.10 | −4.0 | −2.7 | 0.9 | −1.8 | 0.0 | −5.8 |
| 5 | Gifu | −0.03 | −0.03 | −0.02 | −0.06 | 0.00 | −0.09 | −1.6 | −1.9 | −1.4 | −3.3 | −0.1 | −5.0 |
| 6 | Shizuoka | −0.02 | −0.13 | 0.00 | −0.12 | 0.00 | −0.15 | −1.2 | −6.5 | 0.1 | −6.4 | −0.3 | −7.8 |
| 7 | Aichi | −0.04 | −0.03 | −0.02 | −0.05 | −0.01 | −0.10 | −2.0 | −1.5 | −1.0 | −2.5 | −0.5 | −5.0 |

(continued)

**Table 8.3** (continued)

| Difference | | Multiplier within prefecture | Spillover effect | | | Feed back effect | Multiplier, total | Multiplier within prefecture | Spillover effect | | | Feed back effect | Multiplier, total |
|---|---|---|---|---|---|---|---|---|---|---|---|---|---|
| | | | Within Chubu region | Without Chubu region | Total | | | | Within Chubu region | Without Chubu region | Total | | |
| 8 | Mie | 0.02 | −0.04 | −0.05 | −0.09 | 0.00 | −0.08 | 0.9 | −2.3 | −2.6 | −5.0 | −0.1 | −4.2 |
| 9 | Shiga | 0.01 | −0.08 | −0.03 | −0.11 | 0.00 | −0.09 | 0.6 | −4.2 | −1.6 | −5.8 | 0.1 | −5.1 |
| 10 | Rest of Japan | −0.10 | 0.00 | 0.00 | 0.00 | 0.00 | −0.10 | −5.8 | 0.0 | 0.0 | 0.0 | −0.1 | −5.9 |
| Japan, average | | −0.09 | −0.01 | 0.00 | −0.01 | 0.00 | −0.10 | −4.8 | −0.6 | −0.2 | −0.8 | −0.1 | −5.8 |

*Source* Calculated by the author

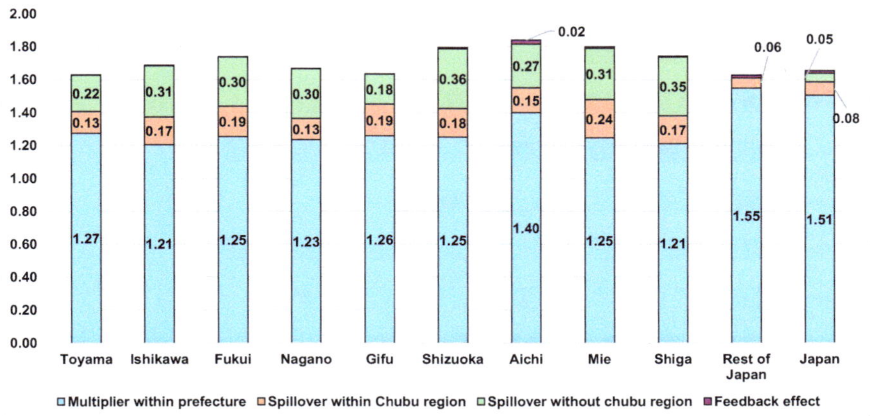


**Fig. 8.1** Multiplier decomposition of Chubu Region in 2015. *Source* Calculated by the author

Figure 8.2 presents the spillover effects for each prefecture in the Chubu Region. The figure compares the extent to which one unit of final demand in each prefecture leaks as induced production to other prefectures within the Chubu region. The prefecture with the largest leakage is Mie Prefecture, followed by Gifu, Fukui, Shizuoka, Shiga, and Ishikawa Prefectures. Aichi Prefecture obtains the largest leakage of their demand, which indicates that Aichi Prefecture's production supports their production in the Chubu region. In particular, the values are large for Mie Prefecture at 0.14, Gifu Prefecture at 0.12, and Shizuoka Prefecture at 0.11. Those prefectures are close to Aichi Prefecture. However, it can be observed that within the three Hokuriku Prefectures of Toyama, Ishikawa, and Fukui, the mutual spillover effects are greater than those in other prefectures. Conversely, if we focus on the spillover effect from Aichi Prefecture, there is a large leakage to Shizuoka Prefecture at 0.05, Mie Prefecture at 0.04, and Gifu Prefecture at 0.03, indicating that the relationship between these prefectures is strong with Aichi Prefecture at the center.

Figure 8.3 illustrates the changes in each prefecture's internal multiplier, spillover multiplier (within and outside the Chubu area), and feedback multiplier from 2011 to 2015. Overall, the multiplier is on the decline, and the internal multiplier is decreasing except for Fukui, Mie, and Shiga Prefectures. Among them, Nagano and Ishikawa Prefectures present the largest decreases.

Changes in spillover effects within the Chubu Region are decreasing without exception. Among them, the decrease in spillover effects to the Chubu area in Shizuoka Prefecture was the largest, followed by the decrease in Shiga Prefecture. However, spillover effects to areas outside the Chubu Region (the ROJ) are generally on the decline, with the exception of Ishikawa, Nagano, and Shizuoka Prefectures. The decline was large in Mie and Shiga Prefectures.

Compared to these changes, changes in feedback effects are small. Decreases in Shizuoka, Aichi, and Mie Prefectures and slight increases in Fukui and Shiga Prefectures were observed.

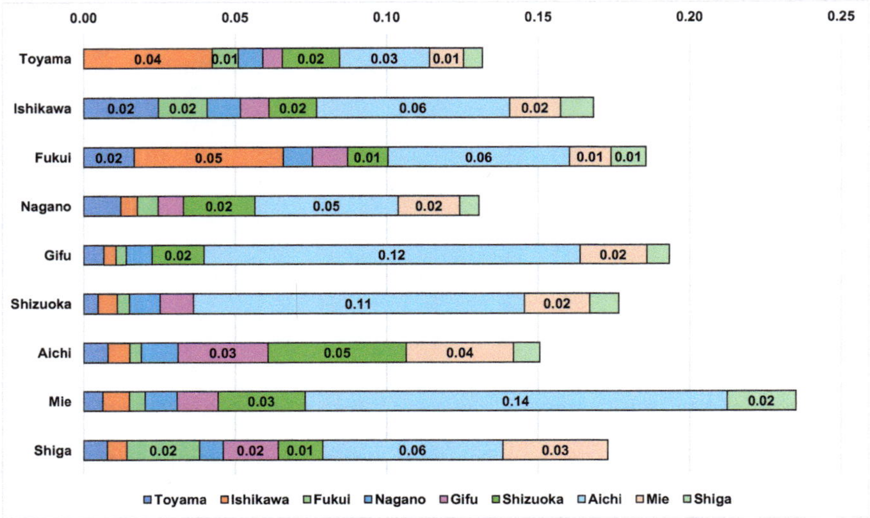


Fig. 8.2 Spillover effect within the Chubu Region in 2015. *Source* Calculated by the author

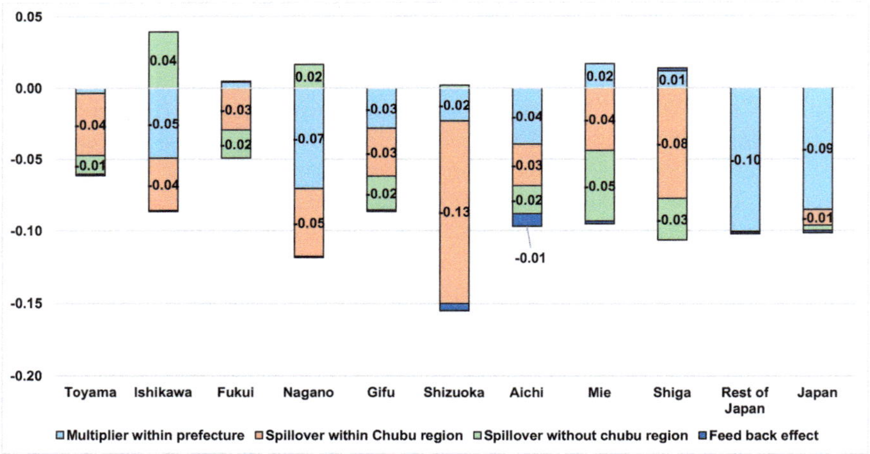


**Fig. 8.3** Change in multiplier decomposition of the Chubu Region in 2011 and 2015. *Source* Calculated by the author

Figure 8.4 depicts the spillover effect within the Chubu Region in Fig. 8.3 in detail as a relationship between prefectures. Large decreases in spillover effects can be observed in Shizuoka, Shiga, Mie, Nagano, and Toyama Prefectures; however, in all these prefectures, spillover effects to Aichi Prefecture, the core of the Chubu Region, have decreased. This seems to indicate a slight decline in the centripetal force of Aichi Prefecture as the core; however, as illustrated in Fig. 8.2, Aichi Prefecture

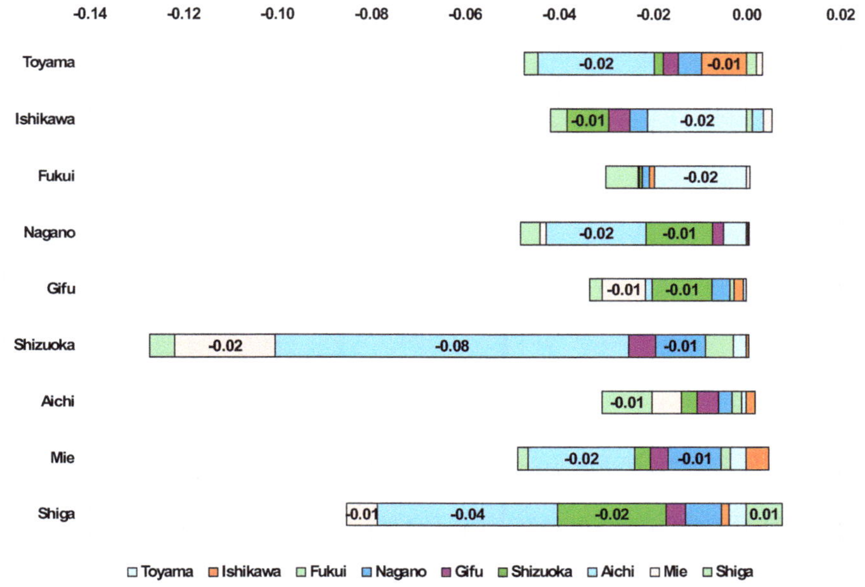


**Fig. 8.4** Changes in the spillover effect within the Chubu Region between 2011 and 2015. *Source* Calculated by the author

remained the core of the Chubu Region in 2015. Furthermore, although the changes were small, looking at the increased effect, it appears that the relationships between Fukui and Shiga Prefectures, as well as those between Ishikawa, Aichi, and Mie Prefectures, have strengthened.

Examining the spillover effects, the Chubu Region displays an interdependent relationship between the Aichi Prefecture, which serves as the regional core, and eight surrounding prefectures. The spillover effects of Aichi Prefecture have a stronger relationship with neighboring prefectures, Gifu, Shizuoka, and Mie. Aichi Prefecture's economic scale is large compared to other prefectures; hence, even if the spillover effect from Aichi Prefecture is not large, it will have a considerable influence on the prefecture. Therefore, the feedback effect for Aichi Prefecture is greater than that of other prefectures.

In the Chubu Region, Aichi Prefecture and the three neighboring prefectures of Gifu, Shizuoka, and Mie form one economic zone. Large spillover effects were also observed among Toyama, Ishikawa, and Fukui Prefectures, which are referred to as the three prefectures in Hokuriku. As such, they form another small economic zone. The change in spillover effects from 2011 to 2015 has decreased overall, especially in the relationship with Aichi Prefecture. However, this is not enough to change the role of Aichi Prefecture as the core.

### 8.3.3 Multiplier Decomposition by Sector

The results regarding the multiplier decomposition in the previous section have been viewed as interdependent relationships between prefectures. However, this is a result based on the average value of the industries that are components of the region (actually, a weighted average using final demand as the weight). Trends in some industrial sectors may possibly differ from average trends. Next, we will examine trends in representative industrial sectors.

As we do not have the space to cover all 104 industrial sectors, we will focus on Aichi Prefecture, the core of the Chubu Region, and limit ourselves to the top ten sectors in terms of production value,[3] and organize their intra-regional, spillover, and feedback multipliers. Table 8.4 presents the results.

The industries selected in Table 8.4 are "Iron, steel, and steel materials," which is a material-based manufacturing industry; "Passenger car," "Auto parts and accessories," and "Production machinery," which are the centers of the manufacturing industry. In addition, among the service industries, "Finance/Insurance," "Research," and "Other office services," which are considered to become the core of the agglomeration economy, are included, and together with "Food products," "Commercial," and "Medical care," there will be a total of ten sectors. The results for the industry average are also included.

Table 8.4 comprises three parts, with the top rows displaying the values of each type of multiplier by sector in 2011. The left side is the numerical value, and the right side is the ratio to the total multiplier. The middle rows show the corresponding value for 2015, and the bottom rows present the amount of change from 2011 to 2015.

Looking at the total multiplier values by sector, the five manufacturing sectors are higher than the prefectural average each year, and the remaining five sectors belonging to the tertiary industry are lower than the prefectural average. The internal multipliers, spillover multipliers, and feedback multipliers also display similar trends.

Comparing the composition ratio of multipliers with the prefectural average value, the five manufacturing sectors have low internal multipliers and correspondingly large spillover and feedback multipliers. However, the five sectors belonging to the tertiary industry have large internal multipliers and small proportions of spillover and feedback multipliers. This reflects the fact that parts and raw materials for the manufacturing industry are procured over a wider area than for the tertiary industry.

Examining the spillover multipliers for both the prefecture average and the sectoral values, the spillover multiplier within the Chubu area is smaller than the spillover outside the area. In general, the five manufacturing sectors have higher multiplier values than the five tertiary industry sectors, both within and outside the Chubu area. Production is spreading from Aichi Prefecture to the Chubu Region, mainly through the procurement of parts and raw materials for the manufacturing sector.

---

[3] The "housing rent (imputed rent)" sector is located fourth in the top ten of Aichi sectoral productions. However, this sector is a hypothetical one and is not an actual industrial activity. Hence, it has been excluded.

**Table 8.4** Decomposition of the multiplier effect by sector in Aichi Prefecture

| 2011 | | Multiplier within prefecture | Spillover effect | | | Feed back effect | Multiplier, Total | Multiplier within prefecture | Spillover effect | | | Feed back effect | Multiplier, total |
|---|---|---|---|---|---|---|---|---|---|---|---|---|---|
| | | | Within Chubu region | Without Chubu region | Total | | | | Within Chubu region | Without Chubu region | Total | | |
| 52 | Passenger car | 1.91 | 0.46 | 0.55 | 1.01 | 0.12 | 3.04 | 62.8 | 15.1 | 18.0 | 33.1 | 4.1 | 100.0 |
| 34 | Iron, steel, and steel materials | 1.69 | 0.05 | 1.04 | 1.09 | 0.04 | 2.81 | 59.9 | 1.8 | 36.8 | 38.6 | 1.4 | 100.0 |
| 54 | Auto parts and accessories | 1.80 | 0.41 | 0.48 | 0.89 | 0.10 | 2.79 | 64.6 | 14.6 | 17.2 | 31.8 | 3.7 | 100.0 |
| 8 | Food products | 1.45 | 0.21 | 0.45 | 0.66 | 0.03 | 2.14 | 68.1 | 9.7 | 21.1 | 30.7 | 1.2 | 100.0 |
| 42 | Production machinery | 1.42 | 0.27 | 0.38 | 0.65 | 0.04 | 2.11 | 67.2 | 12.9 | 17.9 | 30.8 | 2.1 | 100.0 |
| 88 | Research | 1.35 | 0.08 | 0.17 | 0.25 | 0.01 | 1.61 | 83.9 | 4.9 | 10.7 | 15.6 | 0.5 | 100.0 |
| 89 | Medical care | 1.29 | 0.11 | 0.31 | 0.42 | 0.01 | 1.72 | 75.1 | 6.2 | 18.1 | 24.4 | 0.6 | 100.0 |
| 69 | Finance/ Insurance | 1.36 | 0.05 | 0.15 | 0.20 | 0.00 | 1.56 | 87.0 | 2.9 | 9.9 | 12.8 | 0.3 | 100.0 |
| 68 | Commercial | 1.32 | 0.04 | 0.13 | 0.18 | 0.00 | 1.50 | 88.0 | 2.9 | 8.9 | 11.7 | 0.3 | 100.0 |
| 97 | Other office services | 1.23 | 0.03 | 0.11 | 0.14 | 0.00 | 1.38 | 89.5 | 2.2 | 8.0 | 10.2 | 0.2 | 100.0 |
| | Aichi, average | 1.44 | 0.18 | 0.29 | 0.46 | 0.03 | 1.94 | 74.3 | 9.2 | 14.7 | 24.0 | 1.7 | 100.0 |

(continued)

**Table 8.4** (continued)

| 2015 | | Multiplier within prefecture | Spillover effect | | | Feed back effect | Multiplier, Total | Multiplier within prefecture | Spillover effect | | | Feed back effect | Multiplier, total |
|---|---|---|---|---|---|---|---|---|---|---|---|---|---|
| | | | Within Chubu region | Without Chubu region | Total | | | | Within Chubu region | Without Chubu region | Total | | |
| 52 | Passenger car | 1.79 | 0.37 | 0.52 | 0.89 | 0.09 | 2.77 | 64.6 | 13.3 | 18.9 | 32.2 | 3.2 | 100.0 |
| 34 | Iron, steel, and steel materials | 1.79 | 0.06 | 0.69 | 0.75 | 0.01 | 2.56 | 70.2 | 2.2 | 27.1 | 29.3 | 0.5 | 100.0 |
| 54 | Auto parts and accessories | 1.66 | 0.32 | 0.45 | 0.76 | 0.07 | 2.49 | 66.6 | 12.7 | 17.9 | 30.7 | 2.7 | 100.0 |
| 8 | Food products | 1.39 | 0.24 | 0.40 | 0.63 | 0.03 | 2.05 | 67.8 | 11.6 | 19.3 | 30.9 | 1.3 | 100.0 |
| 42 | Production machinery | 1.33 | 0.18 | 0.36 | 0.54 | 0.03 | 1.90 | 70.1 | 9.7 | 18.9 | 28.6 | 1.3 | 100.0 |
| 88 | Research | 1.38 | 0.09 | 0.17 | 0.26 | 0.01 | 1.65 | 83.8 | 5.3 | 10.4 | 15.7 | 0.5 | 100.0 |
| 89 | Medical care | 1.25 | 0.10 | 0.21 | 0.31 | 0.01 | 1.57 | 79.7 | 6.3 | 13.6 | 19.8 | 0.5 | 100.0 |
| 69 | Finance/ Insurance | 1.33 | 0.04 | 0.12 | 0.16 | 0.00 | 1.50 | 88.8 | 2.9 | 8.0 | 10.9 | 0.2 | 100.0 |
| 68 | Commercial | 1.29 | 0.04 | 0.11 | 0.15 | 0.00 | 1.44 | 89.7 | 2.8 | 7.3 | 10.1 | 0.2 | 100.0 |
| 97 | Other office services | 1.24 | 0.03 | 0.10 | 0.12 | 0.00 | 1.37 | 90.9 | 1.9 | 7.0 | 8.9 | 0.2 | 100.0 |

(continued)

**Table 8.4** (continued)

| 2015 | | Multiplier within prefecture | Spillover effect | | | Feed back effect | Multiplier, Total | Multiplier within prefecture | Spillover effect | | | Feed back effect | Multiplier, total |
|---|---|---|---|---|---|---|---|---|---|---|---|---|---|
| | | | Within Chubu region | Without Chubu region | Total | | | | Within Chubu region | Without Chubu region | Total | | |
| | Aichi, average | 1.40 | 0.15 | 0.27 | 0.42 | 0.02 | 1.84 | 76.1 | 8.2 | 14.4 | 22.6 | 1.4 | 100.0 |
| Difference | | Multiplier within prefecture | Spillover effect | | | Feed back effect | Multiplier, Total | Multiplier within prefecture | Spillover effect | | | Feed back effect | Multiplier, total |
| | | | Within Chubu region | Without Chubu region | Total | | | | Within Chubu region | Without Chubu region | Total | | |
| 54 | Passenger car | −0.12 | −0.09 | −0.03 | −0.12 | −0.04 | −0.28 | −4.1 | −3.0 | −0.8 | −3.8 | −1.2 | −9.1 |
| 68 | Iron, steel, and steel materials | 0.11 | 0.01 | −0.34 | −0.34 | −0.03 | −0.26 | 3.8 | 0.2 | −12.2 | −12.0 | −1.0 | −9.2 |
| 52 | Auto parts and accessories | −0.14 | −0.09 | −0.03 | −0.12 | −0.04 | −0.30 | −5.2 | −3.2 | −1.2 | −4.4 | −1.3 | −10.8 |
| 97 | Food products | −0.06 | 0.03 | −0.05 | −0.02 | 0.00 | −0.08 | −2.9 | 1.5 | −2.5 | −1.0 | 0.0 | −3.9 |
| 34 | Production machinery | −0.09 | −0.09 | −0.02 | −0.11 | −0.02 | −0.21 | −4.2 | −4.2 | −0.9 | −5.1 | −0.9 | −10.1 |
| 89 | Research | 0.03 | 0.01 | 0.00 | 0.01 | 0.00 | 0.04 | 2.0 | 0.6 | −0.1 | 0.5 | 0.0 | 2.5 |
| 42 | Medical care | −0.04 | −0.01 | −0.10 | −0.11 | 0.00 | −0.15 | −2.4 | −0.5 | −5.8 | −6.3 | −0.2 | −8.9 |
| 69 | Finance/ Insurance | −0.03 | 0.00 | −0.03 | −0.04 | 0.00 | −0.06 | −1.8 | −0.1 | −2.2 | −2.3 | 0.0 | −4.1 |

(continued)

**Table 8.4** (continued)

| Difference | | Multiplier within prefecture | Spillover effect | | | Feed back effect | Multiplier, Total | Multiplier within prefecture | Spillover effect | | | Feed back effect | Multiplier, total |
|---|---|---|---|---|---|---|---|---|---|---|---|---|---|
| | | | Within Chubu region | Without Chubu region | Total | | | | Within Chubu region | Without Chubu region | Total | | |
| 88 | Commercial | −0.02 | 0.00 | −0.03 | −0.03 | 0.00 | −0.06 | −1.6 | −0.2 | −1.8 | −2.0 | −0.1 | −3.7 |
| 8 | Other office services | 0.01 | 0.00 | −0.01 | −0.02 | 0.00 | −0.01 | 0.7 | −0.3 | −1.1 | −1.4 | −0.1 | −0.7 |
| | Aichi, average | −0.04 | −0.03 | −0.02 | −0.05 | −0.01 | −0.10 | −2.0 | −1.5 | −1.0 | −2.5 | −0.5 | −5.0 |

*Source* Calculated by the author

A look at the changes over time in the bottom rows reveals that the multiplier values for both the Aichi Prefecture average value and the sectoral value are on a decreasing trend. The exceptions are the internal multiplier and spillover multiplier within the Chubu Region for "Iron, steel, and steel materials," the spillover multiplier within the Chubu Region for "Food products," the internal multiplier and spillover multiplier within the Chubu Region for "Research," and the internal multiplier for "business office services." They are on the rise.

Figure 8.5 breaks down the spillover multiplier within the Chubu Region by prefecture, which was brought about by each sector of Aichi Prefecture in 2015. The "Passenger cars," "Auto parts and accessories," "Food products," and "Production machinery" sectors have a high rate of leakage to Nagano, Gifu, Shizuoka, and Mie Prefectures, like the prefectural average trend.

Additionally, a considerable number of leakages were observed in Ishikawa Prefecture for "production machinery." Furthermore, in the field of "Medical care," there is a dependence on Toyama Prefecture, which produces a large number of pharmaceuticals.

Figure 8.6 shows the change from 2011 to 2015 in the spillover multiplier within the Chubu Region brought about by each sector of Aichi Prefecture. For "passenger cars," "Auto parts and accessories," and "production machinery," dependence has increased in some prefectures, but in many prefectures, it has decreased. Dependence on prefectures that previously had strong ties with Aichi Prefecture, such as Nagano, Gifu, Shizuoka, Mie, and Shiga, has decreased.

In other sectors, dependence on some prefectures is decreasing, and that on others is increasing. For "Food products," dependence on Ishikawa, Nagano, and Shizuoka

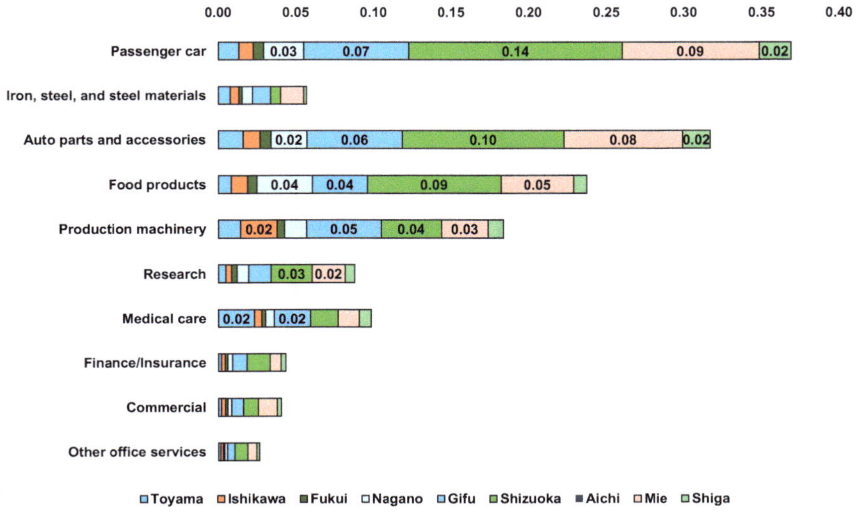


**Fig. 8.5** Spillover effect by sector, from Aichi Prefecture, 2015. *Source* Calculated by the author

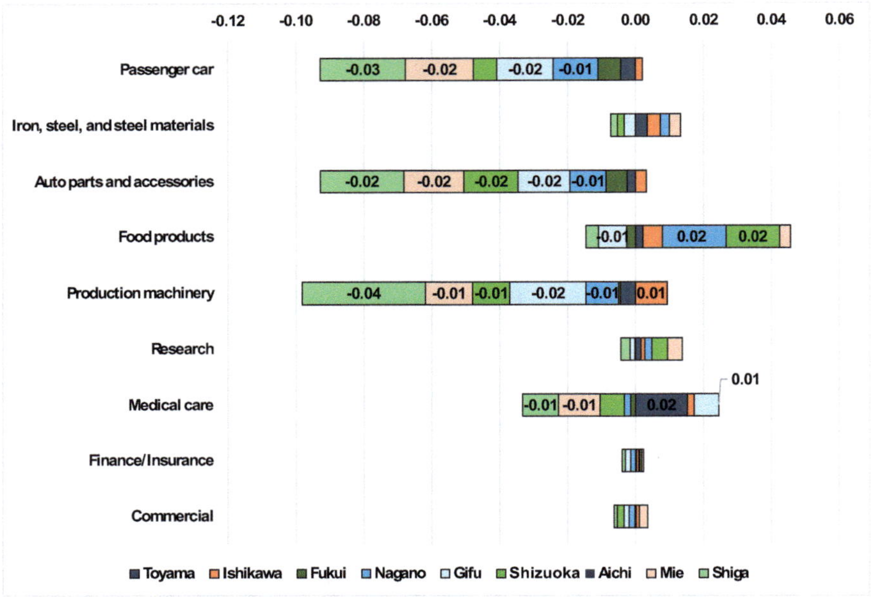


**Fig. 8.6** Changes of spillover effect by sector, from Aichi Prefecture, between 2011 and 2015. *Source* Calculated by the author

Prefectures has increased, and dependence on Gifu Prefectures has decreased. In "Medical care," that of Shiga, Shizuoka, and Mie Prefectures has decreased, whereas in Toyama and Gifu Prefectures they have increased.

## 8.4 Concluding Remarks

In this chapter, we used the Chubu Region interregional IOT for 2011, 2015 described in Chap. 4, which covers the nine prefectures in the region, and calculated (1) production-induced amount by prefecture based on final demand by prefecture and (2) the multiplier decomposition method based on the Leontief inverse matrix to investigate the interdependence between prefectures in the Chubu Region.

The Chubu Region has a structure with Aichi Prefecture as the core and eight other prefectures as peripheral regions, which can be confirmed from the regional decomposition of production-induced amounts based on final demand and the interdependence seen from the spillover effect. Furthermore, Aichi Prefecture forms a close economic zone with neighboring Gifu, Shizuoka, and Mie Prefectures, and there are also mutual dependencies among Toyama, Ishikawa, and Fukui Prefectures, which form a multiple structure.

The production-induced amount by prefecture increased between 2011 and 2015. If we divide this fluctuation into technological change factors based on changes in input coefficients and market change factors based on changes in final demand, the amount of induced production will increase because, although the technological change factors decreased, the market change factors increased.

Next, we decomposed the multiplier expressed by the Leontief inverse matrix into an internal multiplier, a spillover multiplier, and a feedback multiplier. The spillover multiplier indicates interregional dependence based on the input structure, and from the feedback multiplier, we can observe the effects of economic agglomeration.

These dependencies are mainly formed through the procurement of parts and raw materials necessary for production in the manufacturing industry. Focusing on Aichi Prefecture's main industries—the automobile industry ("Passenger cars" and "Auto parts and accessories") and the production machinery—demand for these is expanding, whereas the procurement of parts necessary for production is becoming wider and more international. This tends to reduce the domestic multiplier because of the spillover of domestic production. The decreasing trend in each multiplier observed here from 2011 to 2015 is thought to reflect such a phenomenon.

In the automobile sector, supplies from Shizuoka Prefecture are increasing in response to the increased demand for electric mechanical products such as motors and batteries owing to the spread of EVs, including hybrid cars. Additionally, production at Toyota's Kyushu and Tohoku plants involves a mutual supply of parts to Aichi Prefecture. These dynamic changes, including the international procurement of parts and raw materials, are bringing about changes in the relationship between the Chubu Region and regions outside the region and even among the prefectures within the region.

Finally, we will summarize the remaining issues.

First, although we used regional IOTs to examine the economic structure of the Chubu region, is it possible to examine regional structures in other regions using a similar method? For example, in the Kanto and Kansai regions, regional IOTs targeting those regions[4] have been developed over several years.It remains to be seen whether common analysis results can be obtained using these methods.

Second, although we investigated the four-year change after 2011, tracking changes over a longer period is necessary. In fact, according to the results obtained by using the same interregional IOTs but for different years, 2005 and 2010,[5] although there were similarities in the regional structure at a time, they found a tendency for an expansive spillover effect in terms of changes over time. This is different from the reductive spillover effect in our analysis. As the direction of change differs depending on the year in question, it is necessary to interpret the changes that have remained.

---

[4] For the Kanto region, there are Ishiro (2012, 2014), and for the Kansai region, there are the Kansai Socioeconomic Research Institute (2008) and the Asia–Pacific Institute of Research (2012).

[5] Chen et al. (2016).

## References

Asia Pacific Institute of Research. 2012. *Compilation and use of the 2005 Kansai interregional input-output table* (in Japanese).

Asia Pacific Institute of Research (former Kansai Institute of Social and Economic Research). 2008. *Compilation of 2000 Kansai interregional input-output table* (in Japanese).

Chen, Yantian, Mitsuo Yamada, and Takeo Ihara. 2016. Research on spatial interdependence of the Chubu region economy—based on the Chubu region inter-regional input-output table. *Sango Renkan (Business Journal of PAPAIOS)* 23(3), 88–101 (in Japanese).

Ihara, T. 1968. Structural analysis of regional economies. *Economic Review (Kyoto University)* 101 (1): 111–130 (in Japanese).

Ishiro, Taku. 2012. The analysis of interregional specialization in Kanto region: The compilation of Kanto interregional input-output table and the verification of inducement effect in Tokyo to Kanto or other region. *Ryutsu Keizai University Review* 47(3), 95–114 (in Japanese).

Ishiro, Taku. 2014. The analysis of interregional specialization of Kanto region in 2005: The compilation of Kanto interregional input-output table in 2005 and the comparative analysis of 2005 and 2000. *Ryutsu Keizai University Review* 48(4), 19–39 (in Japanese).

Kuwamori, Hiroshi. 2014. Decomposition and measurement of international production spillovers. In *International input-output analysis: Theory and applications*, vol 609, ed. Chiharu Tamamura, and Hiroshi Kuwamori, 105–144. Institute of Developing Economies Research Series (in Japanese).

Miyazawa, Ken-ichi. 1963. *Multiplier analysis of economic structure.* Tokyo: Toyo Keizai Inc. (in Japanese).

Miyazawa, Ken-ichi. 1966. Internal and external matrix multipliers in the input-output model. *Hitotsubashi Journal of Economics* 7(1), 38–55 (in Japanese).

Okamoto, Nobuhiro. 2012. *Regional economies of China: Spatial structure and interdependence.* Tokyo: Nippon Hyoron Sha Co., Ltd. (in Japanese).

Yamada, H., and T. Ihara. 1966. A three-sector division of input-output model. *Economic Review (Kyoto University)* 98 (5): 36–53 (in Japanese).

# Chapter 9
# Average Propagation Length and the Economic Zone of Nagoya Metropolitan Area

## 9.1 Introduction

In Japan, all 47 prefectures have released their IOTs for every five years beginning, with 1990. The prefectures' IOTs have been effectively used for the evaluation of many events, the policy evaluation of local governments, and the economic planning of the regions. Recently, the prefectures' tables have been applied to compile them into a multi-regional IOT. This tendency stems from the recognition that the multi-regional input–output analysis becomes more important because the regional economies are strongly connected domestically and internationally.

It is well known that there are two types in the MRIOT—Isard-type and Chenery-Moses-type (Millor and Blair 2009). They differ in the assumption of an interregional trade coefficient. The former requires a complete set of intra-regional and interregional data, though it is difficult to obtain such interregional trade coefficients for each sector in each region, especially within a country. However, the latter has advantages in compiling the table because of the simplification in applying the common interregional trade coefficient for each sector in each region. For this reason, MRIOTs within a country are usually compiled as Chenery-Moses types. Nevertheless, the interregional trade data within a country are still difficult to obtain completely, which forces one to shift from adopting the survey method to some kind of non-survey method in the estimation of the interregional trade coefficients. LQ techniques, gravity models, the RAS method, and others have been developed or applied for such estimation. Lahr (1993) reviewed typical regional input–output models from 1963 to 1992 and pointed out the importance of the hybrid approach, both survey-based and non-survey-based, to construct an accurate IOT with reasonable costs.

Cross-hauling (the simultaneous exporting and importing of the same type of product) is important in interregional trade because ignoring it induces an underestimation of trade and an overestimation of the regional output multiplier (see Kronenberg 2009). LQ techniques are easy to manipulate, at least for two regions, though the

 
M. Yamada, *Multi-Regional Input–Output Analysis of the Japanese Economy*,
https://doi.org/10.1007/978-981-97-9041-8_9

techniques are disadvantageous as cross-hauling is inevitably eliminated in interregional trade. The gravity model, which originally stems from the theory of physics, is applied to explain commodity flows among regions, allowing cross-hauling in interregional trade. The RAS method was originally developed for the estimation of the input–output coefficients, for which only the peripheral information of the column sums and the row sums is known, in an iterative way. This method requires initial values, on which the solution depends. Sargento et al. (2012) compared and assessed the performance of some gravity models for explaining interregional trade among regions. Nakano and Nishimura (2013) estimated one type of gravity model with cross-hauling using a survey on interregional transactions and constructed three regional IOTs for Japan.

In Chap. 7, we compile the IOTs for the three prefectures of Aichi, Gifu, and Mie, respectively, into one type of MRIOT for the Tokai Region covering those prefectures. For this purpose, we first break down each prefecture's table into the tables for several small areas. Then the commodity flows among the areas for each sector are estimated using the gravity-RAS method, in which the initial values for the RAS iterative calculation are reduced from the estimated gravity model. Finally, we integrated all the small area tables into an MRIOT, using the estimated transaction shares of the commodity flows. This MRIOT for the Tokai Region consists of 186 sectors for each of the 14 areas.

Breaking down the prefectural IOTs into several small areas and integrating the small area IOTs into one MRIOT may make it possible to solve the analytical issue that a region identified in terms of economic activity is not necessarily the same as the administrative region. In this chapter, using the MRIOT for the Tokai Region, we investigated such relations with the APL index proposed by Dietzenbacher et al. (2005). Nagoya is the third-largest metropolitan area in Japan, following Tokyo and Osaka. Nagoya City, the capital city of Aichi Prefecture, is the economic center of the Tokai Region.

APL reveals the economic distance between two sectors through their economic linkage. Inomata (2008) used the Institute of Developing Economies' Asia International IOT to analyze the international input–output structure of the Asia–Pacific region. They considered that the APL presents the length of the supply chain between industries through international trade and attempted to capture the characteristics of the trade structure between Asian countries and its changes.

Nozaki et al. (2014) also used the Chubu Region Interregional IOT to calculate the APL between industries in prefectures and considered it an indicator of the proximity between industries based on the economic distance between the industries that make up the supply chain, and attempted to capture the existence of regional industrial clusters from them.

In contrast, this chapter examines whether the economic proximity of the Nagoya metropolitan area to the surrounding areas of Nagoya can be expressed as an average ripple length. Each surrounding area is not equally connected to Nagoya City. The closer the distance between areas, the stronger their economic connection. The economic distance of APL is based on the relationship between industries. However, rather than the proximity between industries as in Nozaki et al. (2014), we focus on the indicator that aggregates it by region and attempt to capture the characteristics of the relationship between regions. In that sense, it is close to the perspective of Inomata (2008) through international trade.

In Sect. 9.2, we present a summary of the APL index proposed by Dietzenbacher et al. (2005). In Sect. 9.3, the characteristics of the Nagoya Metropolitan Area are examined in terms of the APL index. Finally, Sect. 9.4 provides concluding remarks.

## 9.2 Definition of a Metropolitan Area

According to the Statistics Bureau of the MIC, "metropolitan areas" are statistical regional divisions established beyond administrative districts to define broad urban areas and are composed of central cities and the surrounding cities, towns, and villages that are socially and economically connected to them. Since the 1960 census, metropolitan areas have been established based on the results of each census regarding work and school places.

Each metropolitan area consists of a central city and surrounding municipalities. The "central cities" of metropolitan areas are the special wards of Tokyo and cities designated by government ordinance. However, when central cities are close to each other, such as in the Kanto metropolitan area, metropolitan areas are not created for each city, but rather the areas are combined to form a single metropolitan area.

"Surrounding municipalities" are those where the ratio of people aged 15 or older commuting to the central city of a metropolitan area is 1.5% or more of the total permanent population of the municipality and where the municipality is adjacent to the central city. However, even if a municipality has less than 1.5% of its total permanent population commuting to the central city, it is considered a surrounding municipality if it is surrounded by municipalities that meet the criteria for surrounding municipalities.

In the 2020 census, 11 metropolitan areas and their "central cities" were defined as indicated in Table 9.1.

In the 1960 definition, there were four major metropolitan areas: the Keihin metropolitan area (included in the current Kanto metropolitan area), the Chukyo metropolitan area, the Keihanshin metropolitan area (included in the current Kinki metropolitan area), and the Kitakyushu-Fukuoka metropolitan area. However, because of subsequent population changes and changes in the definition of a metropolitan area, there are currently ten major metropolitan areas.

However, the MLIT has defined the Tokyo, Osaka, and Nagoya areas as the "three major metropolitan areas" for planned regional development. The "Tokyo Area" is defined as the area of cities, wards, and towns including existing urban areas and suburban development zones under the Capital Region Development Act; the "Osaka Area" is defined as the area of municipalities including existing urban areas and suburban development zones under the Kinki Region Development Act; the "Nagoya Area" is defined as the area of municipalities including urban development zones under the Chubu Region Development and Improvement Act (see Table. 9.2).

**Table. 9.1** Metropolitan areas and their central cities based on the 2020 census

| Metropolitan area | Central city | Metropolitan area | Central city |
|---|---|---|---|
| Sapporo metropolitan area | Sapporo City | Kinki metropolitan area | Kyoto City, Osaka City, Sakai City, and Kobe City |
| Sendai metropolitan area | Sendai City | Okayama metropolitan area | Okayama City |
| Kanto metropolitan area | Saitama City, Chiba City, Special wards of Tokyo, Yokohama City, Kawasaki City, and Sagamihara City | Hiroshima metropolitan area | Hiroshima City |
| Niigata metropolitan area | Niigata City | Kitakyushu-Fukuoka metropolitan area | Kitakyushu City, and Fukuoka City |
| Shizuoka-Hamamatsu metropolitan area | Shizuoka City and Hamamatsu City | Kumamoto metropolitan area | Kumamoto City |
| Chukyo metropolitan area | Nagoya City | | |

*Source* Compiled by the author based on the 2020 Population Census data from the Statistics Bureau of the MIC

"Nagoya Area" does not include the municipalities in Gifu Prefecture compared to the "Chukyo Metropolitan Area," defined by the connection of population.

Furthermore, the Chubu Region Institute for Social and Economic Research (2018) defined the area of approximately 40 km around Nagoya City as the "Nagoya Metropolitan Area" and examined the positioning and role of the Nagoya Metropolitan Area in Japan and among the three major metropolitan areas, as well as its comprehensive development strategy.

According to this definition, the Nagoya Metropolitan Area has a population of 9.18 million people and an economic scale GDP of 42 trillion yen. It is in the center of the three major metropolitan areas and serves as a hub for the trunk transportation network. The Nagoya Metropolitan Area has been functionally developed because of post-war reconstruction and has become a center of global manufacturing industries such as automobiles, aerospace, and advanced materials.

Furthermore, they pointed out that it is the only area that has the most spatial and economic flexibility among the three major metropolitan areas. It is expected to become the center of the largest two-hour travel population in Japan among the super mega-regions that will connect three major metropolitan areas with the introduction of maglev trains from 2027 onwards.[1]

The range of municipalities included in the Nagoya metropolitan area also differs slightly depending on the criteria used to define it (see Fig. 9.1). Below, we will examine how the scope of these areas corresponds to economic distance.

[1] According to the Central Japan Railway Company, the construction of the maglev trains is delayed, and the opening date for the Linear Shinkansen has been changed to 2034.

**Table. 9.2** Municipalities included in the Nagoya metropolitan area

| Metropolitan area | Prefecture | Municipality | Source |
|---|---|---|---|
| Chukyo metropolitan area | Aichi Prefecture | Nagoya City, Okazaki City, Ichinomiya City, Seto City, Handa City, Kasugai City, Toyokawa City, Tsushima City, Hekinan City, Kariya City, Toyota City, Anjo City, Nishio City, Gamagori City, Inuyama City, Tokoname City, Konan City, Komaki City, Inazawa City, Tokai City, Obu City, Chita City, Chiryu City, Owariasahi City, Takahama City, Iwakura City, Toyoake City, Nisshin City, Aisai City, Kiyosu City, Kitanagoya City, Yatomi City, Miyoshi City, Ama City, Nagakute City, Togo Town, Toyoyama Town, Oguchi Town, Fuso Town, Oharu Town, Kanie Town, Tobishima Village, Agui Town, Higashiura Town, Minamichita Town, Mihama Town, Taketoyo Town, Koda Town | 2020 Census |
| | Gifu Prefecture | Gifu City, Ogaki City, Tajimi City, Mizunami City, Hashima City, Ena City, Minokamo City, Toki City, Kakamigahara City, Kani City, Mizuho City, Motosu City, Kaizu City, Ginan Town, Kasamatsu Town, Yoro Town, Tarui Town, Sekigahara Town, Godo Town, Wanouchi Town, Anpachi Town, Ono Town, Ikeda Town, Kitagata Town, Sakahogi Town, Kawabe Town, Mitake Town | |
| | Mie Prefecture | Yokkaichi City, Kuwana City, Inabe City, Kisosaki Town, Toin Town, Komono Town, Asahi Town, Kawagoe Town | |

(continued)

**Table. 9.2** (continued)

| Metropolitan area | Prefecture | Municipality | Source |
|---|---|---|---|
| Nagoya Area | Aichi Prefecture | Nagoya City, Okazaki City, Ichinomiya City, Seto City, Handa City, Kasugai City, Tsushima City, Hekinan City, Kariya City, Toyota City, Anjo City, Nishio City, Inuyama City, Tokoname City, Konan City, Komaki City, Inazawa City, Tokai City, Obu City, Chita City, Chiryu City, Owariasahi City, Takahama City, Iwakura City, Toyoake City, Nisshin City, Aisai City, Kiyosu City, Kitanagoya City, Yatomi City, Miyoshi City, Ama City, Nagakute City, Togo Town, Toyoyama Town, Oguchi Town, Fuso Town, Oharu Town, Kanie Town, Tobishima Village, Agui Town, Higashiura Town, Minamichita Town, Mihama Town, Taketoyo Town, Koda Town | Municipalities including existing urban areas and suburban development zones based on the Chubu Region Development Law |
| | Mie Prefecture | Yokkaichi City, Kuwana City, Inabe City, Kisosaki Town, Toin Town, Asahi Town, Kawagoe Town | |
| 40 km's region of Nagoya | Aichi Prefecture | Nagoya City, Okazaki City, Ichinomiya City, Seto City, Handa City, Kasugai City, Tsushima City, Hekinan City, Kariya City, Toyota City, Anjo City, Nishio City, Inuyama City, Tokoname City, Konan City, Komaki City, Inazawa City, Tokai City, Obu City, Chita City, Chiryu City, Owariasahi City, Takahama City, Iwakura City, Toyoake City, Nisshin City, Aisai City, Kiyosu City, Kitanagoya City, Yatomi City, Miyoshi City, Ama City, Nagakute City, Togo Town, Toyoyama Town, Oguchi Town, Fuso Town, Oharu Town, Kanie Town, Tobishima Village, Agui Town, Higashiura Town, Taketoyo Town, Koda Town | 2020 Census: cities. municipalities within a 40 km zones from Nagoya City Hall |

(continued)

**Table. 9.2** (continued)

| Metropolitan area | Prefecture | Municipality | Source |
|---|---|---|---|
| | Gifu Prefecture | Gifu City, Ogaki City, Tajimi City, Seki City, Mino City, Mizunami City, Hashima City, Minokamo City, Toki City, Kakamigahara City, Kani City, Yamagata City, Mizuho City, Motosu City, Kaizu City, Ginan Town, Kasamatsu Town, Yoro Town, Tarui Town, Godo Town, Wanouchi Town, Anpachi Town, Ono Town, Ikeda Town, Kitagata Town, Sakahogi Town, Tomika Town, Kawabe Town, Yaotsu Town, Mitake Town | |
| | Mie Prefecture | Yokkaichi City, Kuwana City, Suzuka City, Inabe City, Kisosaki Town, Toin Town, Komono Town, Asahi Town, Kawagoe Town | |

*Source* Compiled by the author based on 2020 Population Census data from the Statistics Bureau of the MIC and the website of MLIT

## 9.3 Average Propagation Lengths

The Average Propagation Lengths (APL) index, proposed by Dietzenbacher et al. (2005), is used to measure the economic distances between industries. This index is defined as follows:

The Leontief inverse matrix **L** for the standard Leontief quantity model is denoted as follows:

$$\mathbf{L} = (\mathbf{I} - \mathbf{A})^{-1} = \mathbf{I} + \mathbf{A} + \mathbf{A}^2 + \mathbf{A}^3 + \cdots \tag{9.1}$$

where **A** means the input coefficient matrix of the model, the overall indirect effects are expressed as

$$\mathbf{L} - \mathbf{I} = \mathbf{A} + \mathbf{A}^2 + \mathbf{A}^3 + \mathbf{A}^4 + \cdots \tag{9.2}$$

On the other hand, we can define the weighted sum of the intermediate input, with the number of each diffusion stage as the weight, as follows:

$$\mathbf{\Phi} = \mathbf{A} + \mathbf{2A}^2 + \mathbf{3A}^3 + \mathbf{4A}^4 + \cdots = \mathbf{L}(\mathbf{L} - \mathbf{1}) \tag{9.3}$$

Then the APL $APL_{ij}$ between the j-th sector and the i-th sector in the model is defined as

$$\mathbf{APL_{ij}} = [\mathbf{L}(\mathbf{L} - \mathbf{I})]_{\mathbf{ij}}/[\mathbf{L} - \mathbf{I}]_{\mathbf{ij}} \tag{9.4}$$

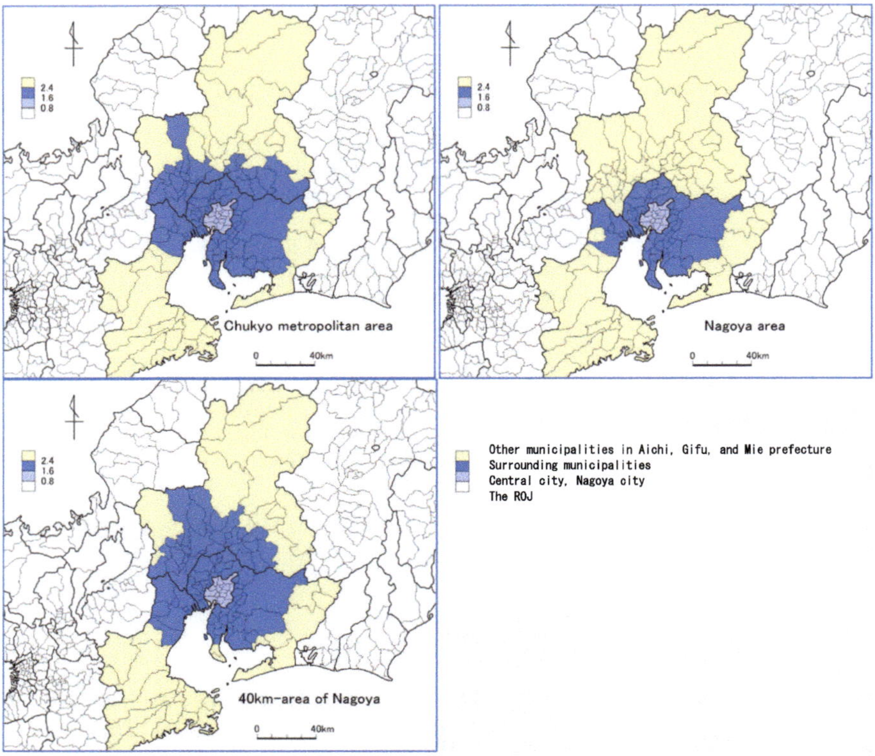


**Fig. 9.1** Ranges of the Nagoya metropolitan area in different definitions. *Source* Created by the author, using the MANDARA supporting system for geographic information analysis. (http://ktgis.net/mandara/)

where $[\mathbf{L} - \mathbf{I}]_{mathbf\,ij}$denotes the $i - j$ element of the matrix $\mathbf{L} - \mathbf{I}$.

In this chapter, we calculated APL using an interregional IOT, which is based on the IOTs for Aichi, Gifu, and Mie Prefectures discussed in Chap. 7. We break each prefecture down into multiple sub-regions, integrating all 14 regions into a single interregional table. Each of the calculated APL shows the distance between one sector in a sub-region and the other sector in the other sub-region. Here, we focus on the Nagoya metropolitan area, with Nagoya City at its core, and use the APL index to capture the proximity of regions adjacent to Nagoya City. Therefore, it is necessary to aggregate the APL index by industry, to show regional distance. Here, we calculate regional aggregation as follows

Calculating the APL between the $j$ and $i$ for the model with 40 sectors for each of the 14 areas, we have integrated them as the index between the r-th area and the s-th area, $\mathbf{APL^{rs}}$,

$$\mathbf{APL^{rs}} = \sum_{\mathbf{i}\in\mathbf{r}} \sum_{\mathbf{j}\in\mathbf{s}} \mathbf{v_i^r APL_{ij} f_j^s} \tag{9.5}$$

where $\mathbf{v_i^r}$ is the share vector of the value-added in region r and $\mathbf{f_j^s}$ is the share vector of the final demand in region s. The APL index is usually interpreted as the distance between industries, as Dietzenbacher et al. (2005) originally applied to a regional IOT. Here we can obtain the APL for the regions and examine it as the index to measure the spatial distance. The regional comparison of the APL index appears in the analysis using the international input–output model (Dietzenbacher et al. 2007). However, we compare the APL with respect to the areas and the geographical distance to measure the relationship between the core city and the surrounding areas in the MRIOT.

## 9.4 Analytical Results

Figure 9.2 depicts the relationship between the APL and the logarithm of the geographical distance. The positive relationship is observed with a correlation coefficient of 0.681. The triangle points in Fig. 9.1 denote the APL distance of Nagoya City to the other areas in the forward direction, and the square points show them in the backward direction. Both indicate that the APL distance of Nagoya City becomes larger as the geographical distance becomes longer. The area closer to Nagoya city has deeper connections with the city, and the transactions between them become larger, which makes the APL distance lower.

We estimated the regression of the APL on the logarithm of the distance with some prefectural dummies from 196 samples. The estimated equation is

$$\begin{aligned} APL^{rs} &= \alpha + \beta \ln(D^{rs}) + \gamma_G^F D_G^F + \gamma_G^B D_G^B \\ &\quad + \gamma_M^F D_M^F + \gamma_G^B D_G^B + \gamma_N^F D_N^F + \gamma_N^B D_N^B, \end{aligned}$$

where $D^{rs}$ is the geographical distance between r and s. $D_G^F$ and $D_G^B$ denote dummy variables of Gifu Prefecture in the forward and backward directions, respectively. $D_M^F$ and $D_M^B$ are also dummy variables for Mie Prefecture, and $D_N^F$ and $D_N^B$ are for Nagoya City. The estimated results are shown in Table 9.3. The relation is significant in the sense of a relatively high determinant coefficient of 0.5706. The APL index is positively correlated to the logarithm of the geographical distance. Among the prefectural dummy variables, the dummy of Gifu Prefecture in the forward direction is not significant, though the others are. The prefectural dummies are negative, which means that the industries of Aichi Prefecture are more closely concentrated than in the other two prefectures. The Nagoya dummy is also not significant, which means there is no difference from Aichi Prefecture.

Figure 9.3 indicates the APL distance from Nagoya City, which is defined as the average of two variations: the forward and backward direction:

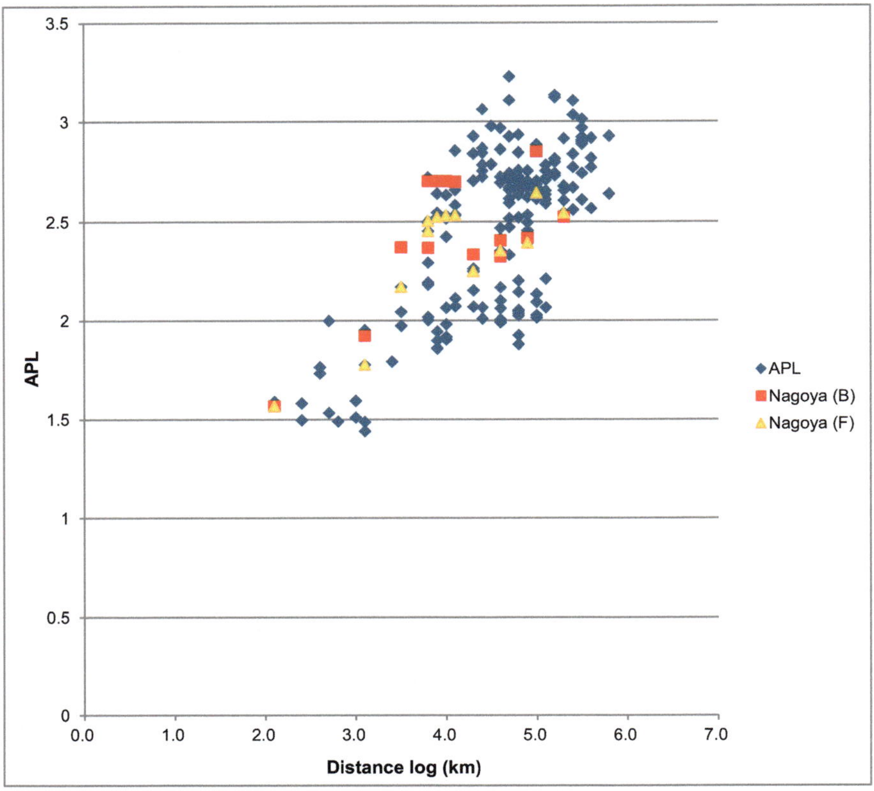


**Fig. 9.2** Average propagation length and physical distance. *Source* Computed and created by the author

**Table. 9.3** Regression results of the APL on the logarithm of the distance

| Variable | Coefficient | Std. Error | *t*-Statistic | Prob. |
|---|---|---|---|---|
| C | 0.907905 | 0.124932 | 7.267164 | 0.0000 |
| LOG (DISTANCE) | 0.403806 | 0.026481 | 15.24903 | 0.0000 |
| GIFUF | – 0.078902 | 0.052282 | – 1.509181 | 0.1329 |
| GIFUB | – 0.170883 | 0.052282 | – 3.268515 | 0.0013 |
| MIEF | – 0.202266 | 0.052698 | – 3.838196 | 0.0002 |
| MIEB | – 0.280918 | 0.052698 | – 5.330704 | 0.0000 |
| NAGOYAF | – 0.063877 | 0.082821 | – 0.771270 | 0.4415 |
| NAGOYAB | – 0.029044 | 0.082821 | – 0.350683 | 0.7262 |
| R-squared | 0.570567 | Adjusted R-squared | 0.554577 | |
| S.E. of regression | 0.267254 | Sum squared residuals | 13.42782 | |
| F-statistic | 35.68379 | Probability (F-statistic) | 0.000000 | |

*Source* Calculated by the author

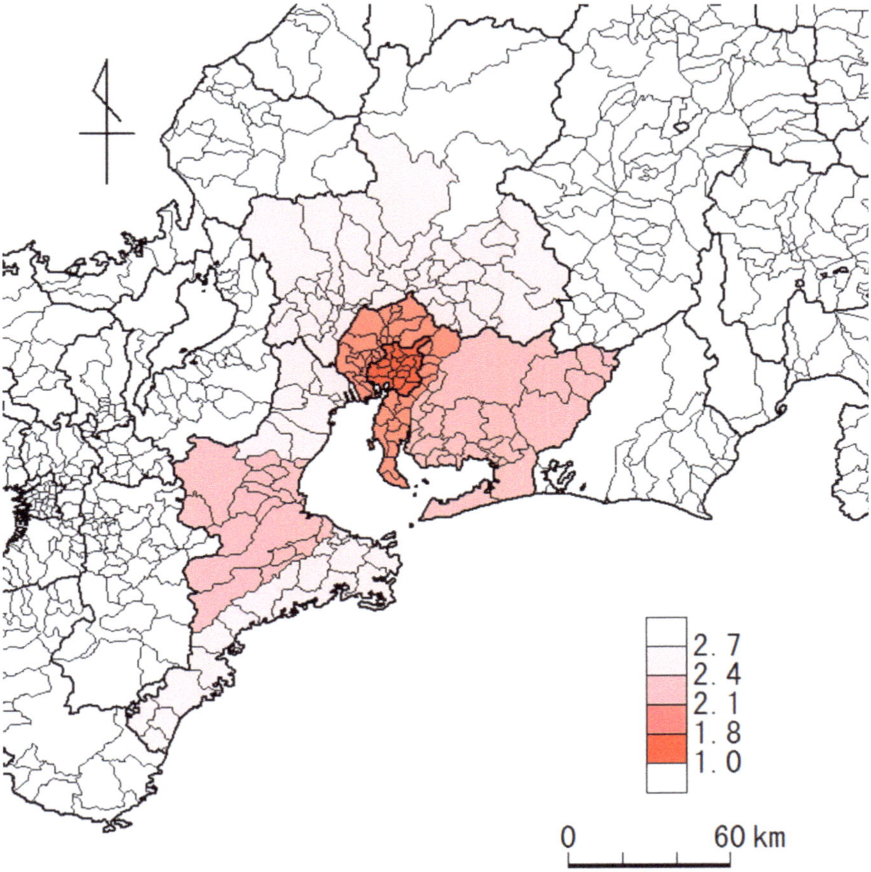


**Fig. 9.3** APL distance from Nagoya City. *Source* Created by the author, using the MANDARA supporting system for geographic information analysis. (http://ktgis.net/mandara/)

$$\mathbf{APL}^{*\mathbf{rs}} = \frac{1}{2}\left(\mathbf{APL}^{\mathbf{rs}} + \mathbf{APL}^{\mathbf{sr}}\right)$$

In this figure, relatively wide areas surrounding Nagoya City are linked to Nagoya City. Among them, the Hida area in Gifu Prefecture has little connection to Nagoya City. The Owari area is strongly connected to Nagoya City, whereas Nishimikawa and Higashimikawa in Aichi Prefecture also have connections. Chusei and Iga in Mie Prefecture also have a relatively stronger linkage to Nagoya City than Hokusei, although the geographical distances are in reverse order.[2] The APL index is useful to measure the degree of linkage among areas.

[2] Area names are listed in Fig. 7.1.

## 9.5 Concluding Remarks

In this chapter, we used the MRIOT discussed in Chap. 7, which integrates three prefectures' IOTs by breaking them down into 14 subregions, and discussed the regional structure of the Nagoya metropolitan area.

Using the estimated MRIOT of the Tokai Region, we investigated the characteristics of economic linkage among areas in terms of the APL index to measure the regional linkage strength. A simple regression of the APL index on the geographical distance indicates a good positive correlation. We found that relatively wide areas surrounding Nagoya City have some linkage to Nagoya City, though the Hida area in Gifu Prefecture has little connection to it. The APL index revealed its usefulness in measuring the degree of spatial linkage among areas.

We were able to demonstrate that subdividing the prefecture's IOT into several small areas and integrating them into an MRIOT yields an analytical tool to solve how the region may be identified in terms of economic activities, which is not necessarily the same for an administrative region. However, our MRIOT discussed here consists of 14 subregions, and ideally, it ought to be broken down by the municipalities of each prefecture. Such extensions remain in future work.

## References


Dietzenbacher, E., I. Remero Luna, and, N.S. Bosma. 2005. Using average propagation lengths to identify production chains in the Andalusian economy. *Estudios de Economia Aplicada* 23 (2): 405–422.

Inomata, T. 2008. Measuring the distance between industries: Measuring the average propagation lengths using the Asian international input-output table. *Sango Renkan (Business Journal of PAPAIOS)* 16 (1): 46–55 (in Japanese).

Kronenberg, T. 2009. Construction of regional input-output tables using nonsurvey methods, the role of cross-hauling. *International Regional Science Review* 32 (1): 40–64.

Lahr, M. L. 1993. A review of the literature supporting the hybrid approach to constructing regional input-output models. *Economic Systems Research* 5 (3): 277–293.

Nakano, S., and K. Nishimura. 2013. A nonsurvey multiregional input-output estimation allowing cross-hauling: Partitioning two regions into three or more parts. *Annals of Regional Science* 50:935–951.

Nozaki, M., T. Okuda, and S. Kimura. 2014. Tourism-related clusters in the Chubu region: An input-output analysis based on average propagation lengths. *Studies in Regional Science* 44 (2): 205–221 (in Japanese).

Sargento, A. L. M., P. N. Ramos, and G. J. D. Hewings. 2012. Inter-regional trade flow estimation through non-survey models: An empirical assessment. *Economic Systems Research* 24 (2): 173–193.

# Chapter 10
# Impact of Consumption Fluctuations by a Declining Population on the Regional Economy

## 10.1 Introduction

The revitalization of declining local economies (owing to declining populations) is a critical issue. Population decline leads to a labor shortage, which is a limiting factor for economic growth. Population decline is one of the major factors that cause regional economies to stagnate owing to reduced demand and, therefore, consumption.

At the municipality level, there are some cities where the population is declining rapidly, while in other cities, populations are expected to increase. In areas where population growth is expected, consumption will increase, and so will production and value-added. However, because municipal economies are interdependent, the impact of a declining population in one municipality can spill over to its neighbors, even if the neighbors are experiencing population increases.

Here, based on the population and consumption data of 54 municipalities in Aichi Prefecture, we estimate future fluctuations in consumption by sector and measure the ripple effect of production and value-added within municipalities.

In Sect. 10.2, we discuss the background of the research. In Sect. 10.3, we summarize the estimation method for future fluctuations in consumption by sector and the input–output model. In Sect. 10.4, we describe the results of the input–output analysis. In Sect. 10.5, we summarize the analysis results and implications.

## 10.2 Background

The effects of a declining national population in Japan on the economy are wide-ranging. The Japan Federation of Economic Organizations (2008) elucidates two effects of a declining national population in Japan: a decline in economic growth (due to a decrease in the labor force) and the unsustainability of the financial and

 
M. Yamada, *Multi-Regional Input–Output Analysis of the Japanese Economy*,
https://doi.org/10.1007/978-981-97-9041-8_10

pension systems (due to an imbalance between generations). To maintain the vitality of the economy and society, it is recommended that measures such as human resource development, research and development, innovation, measures against the declining birthrate, promotion of women's social advancement, and acceptance and retention of foreign human resources be considered. Adachi (2004) discussed the impact of a declining birthrate and an aging population on the household sector in many aspects.

Population decline appeared early and prominently in rural areas, reducing the competitiveness of the local economy. Therefore, the revitalization of the local economy has become an urgent issue. To correct this situation, the Promotion Office of "Regional Revitalization," Cabinet Office, which started in 2014, is promoting measures to solve various issues for regional revitalization, such as correcting the excessive concentration of population in the Tokyo metropolitan area and securing comfortable environments for living in each area.

Population decline will result in a decrease in consumption if there is no change in per capita consumption. However, if consumption is activated, it may contribute to economic growth in terms of demand. The decline in the number of children will cause a decrease in children's clothing and education-related expenditures, and the aging population will increase not only nursing care costs and medical expenses but also tourism expenses.

Mo and Ida (2013a) analyzed the effects of demographic changes, such as total population, age structure, and household size, on the consumption structure. From 2005 to 2010 and from 2010 to 2020, they estimated consumption expenditures nationwide and in Osaka Prefecture based on the census population data and "consumption expenditure by item for householder-age group" in the 2004 and 2009 National Survey of Family Income and Expenditure (hereafter denoted as NSFIE) and analyzed the decomposition by factor. The estimation of the first half of the period is based on census data, and it is based on the "Future Estimated Population of Japan" estimated by the National Institute of Population and Social Security Research (hereafter denoted as NIPSSR) for the second half.

From their research, household consumption is expected to shrink as the population declines; however, a decrease in household members may increase per capita consumption. By item, it was pointed out that housing-related items, insurance and medical-related items, travel-related items, etc. increased, while items such as education-related items and children's clothing decreased, reflecting the declining birthrate.

Additionally, Mo and Ida (2013b, 2014) further analyzed the economic spillover effect using the 2005 interregional IOT of the METI and the Osaka Prefecture interregional IOT.

Regarding the analysis of economic spillover, Wada (2018) estimated the decrease in consumption expenditure from 2015 to 2030 due to population decline and analyzed the spillover effect using the 2013 Fukushima IOT. He also used the data from the forecasted population database by the NIPSSR and the consumption expenditure per household by the householder-age group in the 2014 NSFIE. However, he obtained the change in total consumption expenditure by summing the total consumption per household multiplied by the changing number of households for each householder-age group in 2030 compared to 2015.

Furthermore, he multiplied the total consumption amount by the composition ratio of private consumption expenditure by sector in the 2013 Fukushima IOT to obtain the consumption amount by sector and estimated the ripple effect. It was revealed that the decrease in consumption due to the population decline in Fukushima Prefecture in 2030 would hurt the prefecture's production, value-added, and employment. By sector, he pointed out that the negative spillover effect is large in real estate, personal services, commerce, finance and insurance, medical and health care, and welfare.

In this study, the estimation method for future consumption changes due to depopulation, described in the next section, is the same as in the preceding studies. However, our research target years are 2015 to 2040, and the region is Aichi Prefecture, especially the municipalities, which is our characteristic.

## 10.3 Model and Data

In this section, we describe the estimation method for future consumption expenditure by the municipality, the data to be used, and explain the analytical model.

### 10.3.1 Population and Number of Households

In NIPSSR's "Future Estimated Population by Region (Prefectures/Municipalities) in Japan," released in 2018, the future population of prefectures and municipalities up to the year 2045, by gender and age (with 5-year intervals), is estimated for every five years based on the 2015 census data.

The year $t$'s population of gender $s$ in municipality $r$ is expressed as follows:

$$P^{r}_{t,s} = \sum_{a} P^{r,a}_{t,s} \tag{10.1}$$

Here, $P^{r,a}_{t,s}$ denotes year $t$'s population of age class $a$ and gender $s$ in municipality $r$.

Then, year $t$'s population of gender $s$ in Aichi Prefecture, $A$, is

$$P^{A}_{t,s} = \sum_{r} P^{r}_{t,s} \tag{10.2}$$

Figure 10.1 depicts the changing rates of population growth in each municipality in Aichi Prefecture as estimated by NIPSSR. Although the population growth of Nagakute City and Takahama Town exceeds 10%, the population of many municipalities is declining. Among them, Toyone Village, Toei Town, Shitara Town, and Shinshiro City in the Higashimikawa area, Minamichita Town, and Mihama Town in the Chita area have a decrease rate of over 30%. In addition, the population of

Okazaki City, Anjo City, Kota Town, Kariya City, Chiryu City in the Nishimikawa area, Obu City, Tokai City, Tokoname City, Agui Town, and Nisshin City in the eastern part of the Owari area increased slightly during this period.

In the same estimates, the number of households by gender, householder age (with 5-year intervals), and family type in each prefecture can be obtained every five years until 2040. However, the number of households is estimated only for prefectures and not for each municipality.

The number of households in Aichi Prefecture $A$, householder's gender $s$, householder age class $a$, and family type $h$ are denoted as

$$H_{t,s}^{A,a,h} = \varphi_{t,s}^{A,a,h} \cdot P_{t,s}^{A,a} \tag{10.3}$$

Here, the householder rate of year $t$, gender $s$, age group $a$, and family type $h$ is $\varphi_{t,s}^{A,a,h}$.

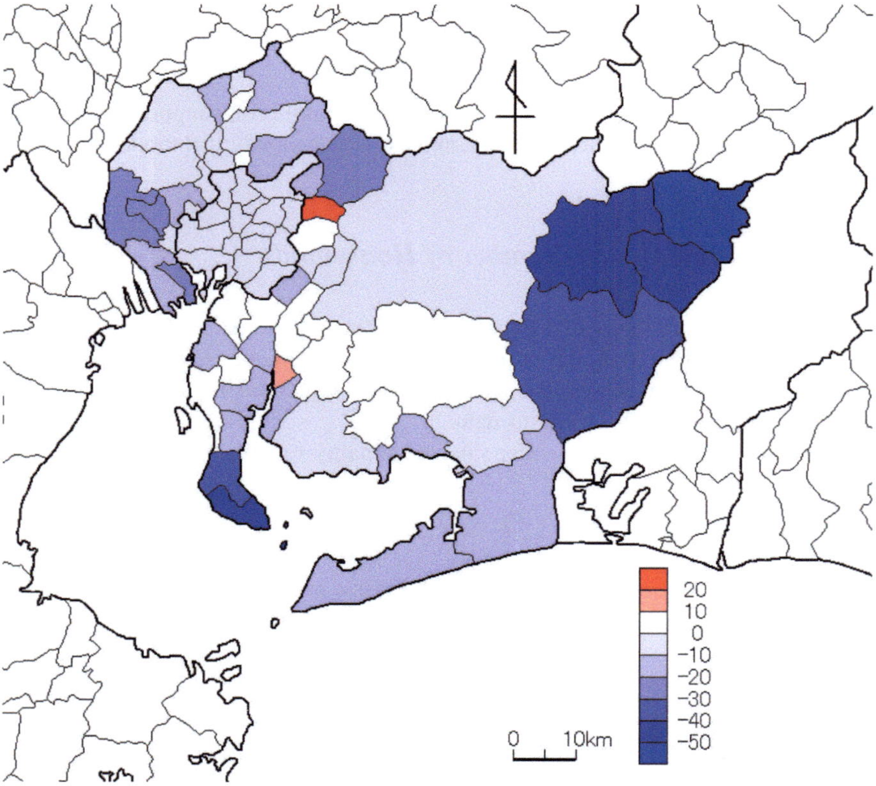


**Fig. 10.1** Changing rate of municipal population in Aichi Prefecture (Rate in 2040 compared to 2015). *Source* Created by the author, using the MANDARA supporting system for geographic information analysis. (http://ktgis.net/mandara/)

The number of households in municipality $r$ is estimated using the householder rate in Aichi Prefecture $\varphi_{t,s}^{A,a,h}$. That is,

$$H_{t,s}^{r,a,h} = \varphi_{t,s}^{A,a,h} \cdot P_{t,s}^{r,a} \tag{10.4}$$

Figure 10.2 illustrates the future changes in the householder rate by age group and family type in Aichi Prefecture, as estimated by NIPSSR. Here, three graphs depict the cases of single-person households (male), single-person households (female), and households with two or more members.

For single-person households (males), the householder rate tends to decrease gradually as they get older in 2015, but the rate of those aged 50 and over will increase to 2040. In contrast, in 2015, the rate in single-person households (female) declined until the age of 40 as the age increased and then tended to increase afterward. Although this tendency does not change significantly, the value of the householder rate after the age of 40 seems to be on the rise.

For households with two or more members in 2015, the higher the age group, the higher the value of the householder rate due to marriage. However, for the year 2020 and after, it is predicted that the rate will tend to decrease slightly in the age group after around 60 years old, as it is thought to be related to various factors such as a decrease in the number of marriages, a reduction in the number of births, and a diminishing multi-generational cohabitation.

Figure 10.3 presents the estimated changing rate in the number of households by municipality in 2040 compared to 2015. Unlike the changes in population, the number of households is relatively increasing in many municipalities. In particular, the number of households increased, and the population has increased by more than 10% like the eastern parts of the Owari and Nishimikawa areas, such as Nagakute City, Okazaki City, Anjo City, and Takahama City. However, the number of households will decrease significantly in the mountainous areas of the Higashimikawa area, where the population is expected to decline extraordinarily; these include Toyone Village, Toei Town, Shitara Town, Shinshiro City, as well as Minamichita Town and Mihama Town in the southern part of the Chita area.

Figure 10.4 shows the gender ratio by municipality in Aichi Prefecture in 2040. The ratio of males to females is higher than that in the Nishimikawa area and lower than that in the Owari area. Nishimikawa Area is an area where the manufacturing industry, especially transportation machinery, is concentrated, and there is a relatively enormous number of younger employees in this area. By 2040, many municipalities in the eastern Owari and Nishimikawa areas will have an increasing population and number of households. The rate of increase in the number of households was relatively high. This is because the manufacturing industry is well developed in these areas, and the proportion of male workers is high, which is thought to contribute to an increase in the number of single-male households.

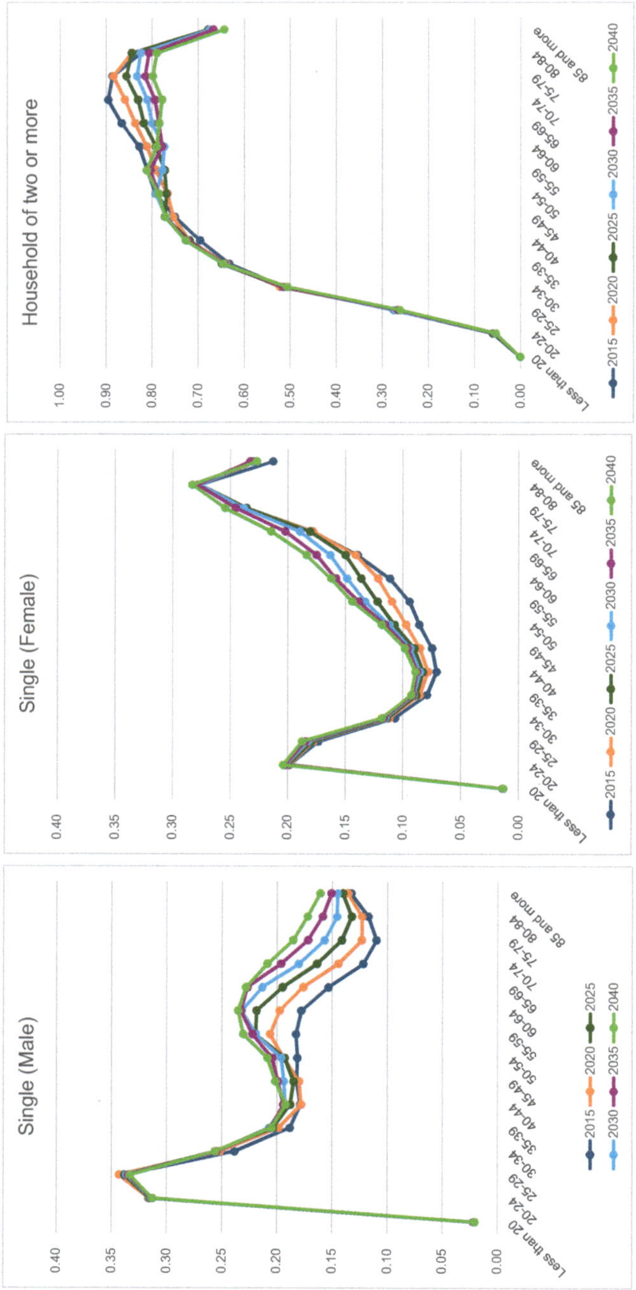


**Fig. 10.2** Changes in the rate of household head by age group and family type in Aichi Prefecture. *Source* Created by the author

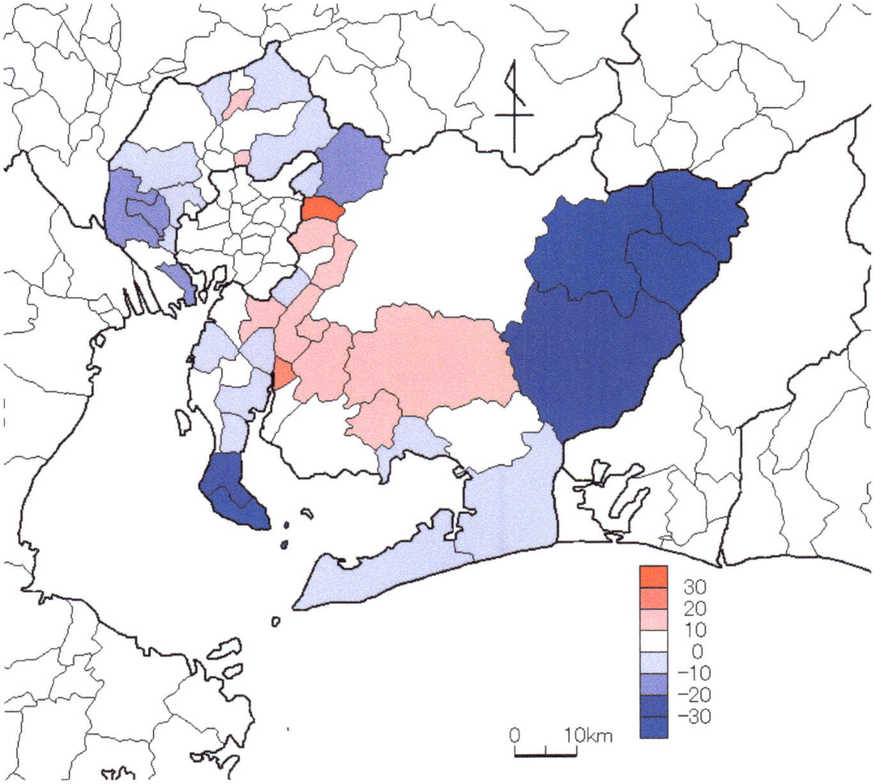


**Fig. 10.3** Changing rate of municipal households in Aichi Prefecture (Rate in 2040 compared to 2015). *Source* Created by the author, using the MANDARA supporting system for geographic information analysis. (http://ktgis.net/mandara/)

## 10.3.2 Estimate of Municipal Consumption by Sector

Here, we discuss a method to estimate the consumption amount by municipality from 2015 to 2040 for input–output analysis.

First, we obtain the product of monthly average consumption expenditure per household and the number of households by householder age group, expenditure item, and family type for each municipality, based on the 2014 NSFIE. We then sum them with respect to the householder-age group and family type to obtain estimates of the consumption expenditure by municipality and item for every five years from 2010 to 2040.

Municipality $r$'s consumption expenditure of the $i$-th item, family type $h$, and householder's gender $s$ in year $t$ is

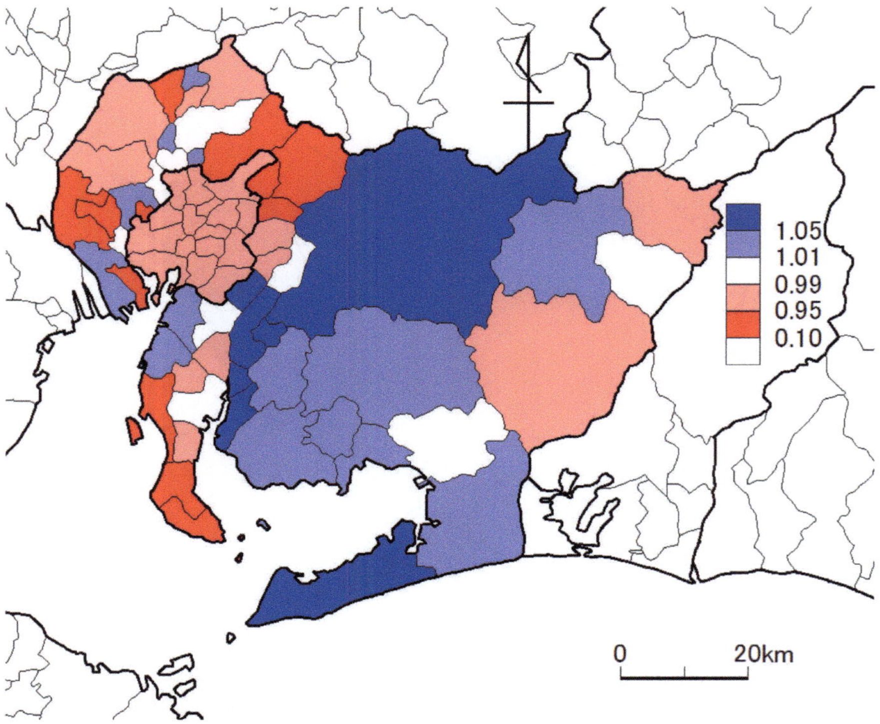


**Fig. 10.4** Gender ratio in 2040. *Source* Created by the author, using the MANDARA supporting system for geographic information analysis. (http://ktgis.net/mandara/)

$$C_{i,t}^{r} = \sum_{h,s,a} 12 \cdot \left(\frac{n_t^r}{n_t^J}\right) \cdot \gamma_{i,o,s}^{J,a,h} \cdot H_{t,s}^{r,a,h} \tag{10.5}$$

Here, $\gamma_{i,o,s}^{J,a,h}$ shows the average monthly consumption expenditures for base year 0, family type $h$, householder's age group $a$, gender $s$, and item $i$. $J$ denotes Japan.

Additionally, $H_{t,s}^{r,a,h}$ represents the number of households at time $t$ in municipality $r$, householder-age class $a$, family type $h$, and gender $s$. Since the national consumption amount by item in the base year is commonly applied to municipality $r$ here, the ratio of the average number of household members in the region to the national value $(\frac{n_t^r}{n_t^J})$ is added to adjust it in consideration of the influence on the consumption amount due to the difference in the number of household members in the municipalities.

As the municipal consumption amounts by item obtained in this way are based on the classification defined in the NSFIE, we convert them into the sector classification of the input–output table, that is, 106 sectors. Furthermore, they are converted from the purchaser's price evaluation to the producer's price evaluation using the commercial margin rate and the transportation margin rate of the 2011 input–output table.

In the next step, the input–output table-based consumption expenditure by municipality and sector for 2010–2040 (producer price evaluation) is indexed. Then, we use private consumption by 106 sectors in the 2011 Aichi Prefecture 54 municipalities IOT of Chap. 6 as base year values, and the amount of consumption for each year is estimated by multiplying the index for each item by municipality and by the base-year value.[1]

Figure 10.5 shows the changing rate of consumption expenditure by municipality in 2040 to the 2015 value. From this figure, the total consumption increases in municipalities where the population and number of households are increasing but decreases when they decrease. In particular, the consumption of all municipalities in the Higashimikawa area and the southern part of the Chita area has also declined significantly. Looking at the Owari area, consumption increases in Nagoya City and some of the surrounding municipalities, but in many municipalities it decreases. In the southern municipalities of the Nishimikawa area, where the manufacturing industry is thriving, consumption will increase as the population and number of households increase.

### 10.3.3 Model for Municipal Input–Output Analysis

The spillover effect on the production value can be examined with an interregional IOT. To simplify the explanation, we use the non-competitive IOT of the two regions and two sectors, as shown in Table 10.1.

The following equations hold for the equilibrium of the demand and supply of products in this interregional IOT:

$$\begin{bmatrix} a_{11}^{11} & a_{12}^{11} & a_{11}^{12} & a_{12}^{12} \\ a_{21}^{11} & a_{22}^{11} & a_{21}^{12} & a_{22}^{12} \\ a_{11}^{21} & a_{12}^{21} & a_{11}^{22} & a_{12}^{22} \\ a_{21}^{21} & a_{22}^{21} & a_{21}^{22} & a_{22}^{22} \end{bmatrix} \begin{bmatrix} X_1^1 \\ X_2^1 \\ X_1^2 \\ X_2^2 \end{bmatrix} + \begin{bmatrix} C_1^{11} \\ C_2^{11} \\ C_1^{21} \\ C_2^{21} \end{bmatrix} + \begin{bmatrix} F_1^{11} \\ F_2^{11} \\ F_1^{21} \\ F_2^{21} \end{bmatrix} + \begin{bmatrix} C_1^{12} \\ C_2^{12} \\ C_1^{22} \\ C_2^{22} \end{bmatrix} + \begin{bmatrix} F_1^{12} \\ F_2^{12} \\ F_1^{22} \\ F_2^{22} \end{bmatrix} + \begin{bmatrix} E_1^1 \\ E_2^1 \\ E_1^2 \\ E_2^2 \end{bmatrix} = \begin{bmatrix} X_1^1 \\ X_2^1 \\ X_1^2 \\ X_2^2 \end{bmatrix} \tag{10.6}$$

Here, $a_{ij}^{rs}$ denotes the i-products' input coefficient in region $r$ of j-sector's production in s-region, $X_j^s$ is j-sector's production in s-region, $C_i^{rs}$ is i-sector's product in region $r$ consumed in region $s$, $F_i^{rs}$ is i-sector's final product (except consumption) in region $r$ consumed in region $s$, and $E_i^r$ is i sector's final products in region $r$ exported to the ROW.

[1] The base year is 2011 for the IOT. We calculated the index to have its base year the same by the linear interpolation of 2010 and 2015 values, which are estimated.

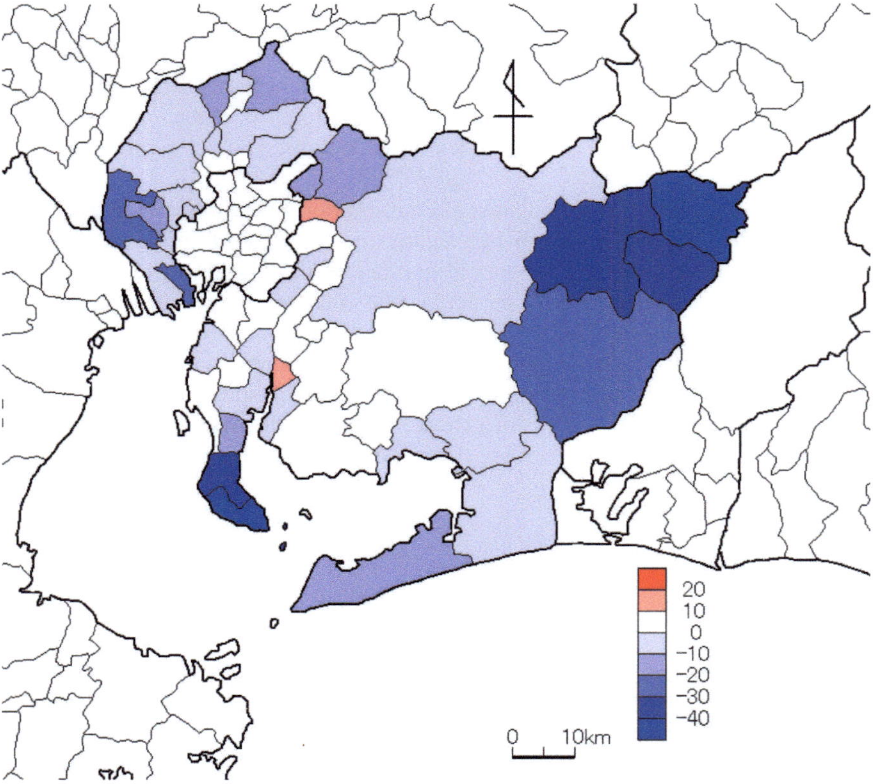


**Fig. 10.5** Changing rate of municipal consumption expenditure in Aichi Prefecture (Rate in 2040 compared to 2015). *Source* Created by the author, using the MANDARA supporting system for geographic information analysis. (http://ktgis.net/mandara/)

Additionally, regarding the compensation of employees,

$$Y^1 = W_1^{11} + W_2^{11} + W_1^{12} + W_2^{12} = \left[ w_1^{11} \; w_2^{11} \; w_1^{12} \; w_2^{12} \right] \begin{bmatrix} X_1^1 \\ X_2^1 \\ X_1^1 \\ X_2^1 \end{bmatrix} \tag{10.7}$$

$$Y^2 = W_1^{21} + W_2^{21} + W_1^{22} + W_2^{22} = \left[ w_1^{21} \; w_2^{21} \; w_2^{22} \; w_2^{22} \right] \begin{bmatrix} X_1^1 \\ X_2^1 \\ X_1^2 \\ X_2^2 \end{bmatrix} \tag{10.8}$$

holds for each region. Here, $Y^r$ denotes the compensation of employees in region $r$, $W_j^{rs}$ is the j-sector's compensation of employees paid in region $s$ to the person who

**Table 10.1** Interregional input–output table: non-competitive import type (Case of two regions and two sectors)

| | | Region 1 | | Region 2 | | Region 1 | | Region 2 | | Export and import | Output, Total |
|---|---|---|---|---|---|---|---|---|---|---|---|
| | | Sector 1 | Sector 2 | Sector 1 | Sector 2 | Consumptions | Other Final Demands | Consumptions | Other final Demands | | |
| Region 1 | Sector 1 | $X_{11}^{11}$ | $X_{12}^{11}$ | $X_{11}^{12}$ | $X_{12}^{12}$ | $C_1^{11}$ | $F_1^{11}$ | $C_1^{12}$ | $F_1^{12}$ | $E_1^1$ | $X_1^1$ |
| | Sector 2 | $X_{21}^{11}$ | $X_{22}^{11}$ | $X_{21}^{12}$ | $X_{22}^{12}$ | $C_2^{11}$ | $F_2^{11}$ | $C_2^{12}$ | $F_2^{12}$ | $E_2^1$ | $X_2^1$ |
| Region 2 | Sector 1 | $X_{11}^{21}$ | $X_{12}^{21}$ | $X_{11}^{22}$ | $X_{12}^{22}$ | $C_1^{21}$ | $F_1^{21}$ | $C_1^{22}$ | $F_1^{22}$ | $E_1^2$ | $X_1^2$ |
| | Sector 2 | $X_{21}^{21}$ | $X_{22}^{21}$ | $X_{21}^{22}$ | $X_{22}^{22}$ | $C_2^{21}$ | $F_2^{21}$ | $C_2^{22}$ | $F_2^{22}$ | $E_2^2$ | $X_2^2$ |
| ROW | Sector 1 | $X_{11}^{w1}$ | $X_{12}^{w1}$ | $X_{11}^{w2}$ | $X_{12}^{w2}$ | $C_1^{w1}$ | $F_1^{w1}$ | $C_1^{w2}$ | $F_1^{w2}$ | $-M_1$ | 0 |
| | Sector 2 | $X_{21}^{w1}$ | $X_{22}^{w1}$ | $X_{21}^{w2}$ | $X_{22}^{w2}$ | $C_1^{w1}$ | $F_2^{w1}$ | $C_1^{w2}$ | $F_2^{w2}$ | $-M_2$ | 0 |
| Compensation of Employees | | $W_1^1$ | $W_2^1$ | $W_1^2$ | $W_2^2$ | | | | | | |
| Other Value-added | | $V_1^1$ | $V_2^1$ | $V_1^2$ | $V_2^2$ | | | | | | |
| Input, Total | | $X_1^1$ | $X_2^1$ | $X_1^2$ | $X_2^2$ | | | | | | |

*Source* Created by the author

lives in region $r$, and $w_j^{rs}$ shows the ratio of the j-sector's r-regional compensation of employees to the j-sector's production in region s.

Income increases in each region create new consumption demand, which is expressed with the following equations:

$$\begin{bmatrix} C_1^{11} \\ C_2^{11} \\ C_1^{21} \\ C_2^{21} \end{bmatrix} = c^1 \begin{bmatrix} c_1^{11} \\ c_2^{11} \\ c_1^{21} \\ c_2^{21} \end{bmatrix} Y^1, \begin{bmatrix} C_1^{12} \\ C_2^{12} \\ C_1^{22} \\ C_2^{22} \end{bmatrix} = c^2 \begin{bmatrix} c_1^{12} \\ c_2^{12} \\ c_1^{22} \\ c_2^{22} \end{bmatrix} Y^2 \tag{10.9}$$

Here, $c_i^{rs}$ denotes the $i$ sector's consumption share of region $r$'s products in region $s$, and $c^r$ shows the average propensity to consume in region $r$.

Equations (10.6)–(10.9) can be collectively expressed with the following matrix:

$$\begin{bmatrix} \mathbf{A}^{11} & \mathbf{A}^{12} & c^1\mathbf{c}^{11} & c^2\mathbf{c}^{12} \\ \mathbf{A}^{21} & \mathbf{A}^{22} & c^1\mathbf{c}^{21} & c^2\mathbf{c}^{22} \\ \mathbf{w}^{11} & \mathbf{w}^{12} & \mathbf{0} & \mathbf{0} \\ \mathbf{w}^{21} & \mathbf{w}^{22} & \mathbf{0} & \mathbf{0} \end{bmatrix} \begin{bmatrix} \mathbf{X}^1 \\ \mathbf{X}^2 \\ \mathbf{Y}^1 \\ \mathbf{Y}^2 \end{bmatrix} + \begin{bmatrix} \mathbf{F}^{11} \\ \mathbf{F}^{21} \\ \mathbf{0} \\ \mathbf{0} \end{bmatrix} + \begin{bmatrix} \mathbf{F}^{12} \\ \mathbf{F}^{22} \\ \mathbf{0} \\ \mathbf{0} \end{bmatrix} + \begin{bmatrix} \mathbf{E}^1 \\ \mathbf{E}^2 \\ \mathbf{0} \\ \mathbf{0} \end{bmatrix} = \begin{bmatrix} \mathbf{X}^1 \\ \mathbf{X}^2 \\ \mathbf{Y}^1 \\ \mathbf{Y}^2 \end{bmatrix} \tag{10.10}$$

Solving Eq. (10.10) with respect to the production and income vector,

$$\begin{bmatrix} \mathbf{X}^1 \\ \mathbf{X}^2 \\ \mathbf{Y}^1 \\ \mathbf{Y}^2 \end{bmatrix} = \begin{bmatrix} \mathbf{I}-\mathbf{A}^{11} & -\mathbf{A}^{12} & -c^1\mathbf{c}^{11} & -c^2\mathbf{c}^{12} \\ -\mathbf{A}^{21} & \mathbf{I}-\mathbf{A}^{22} & -c^1\mathbf{c}^{21} & -c^2\mathbf{c}^{22} \\ -\mathbf{w}^{11} & -\mathbf{w}^{12} & \mathbf{1} & \mathbf{0} \\ -\mathbf{w}^{21} & -\mathbf{w}^{22} & \mathbf{0} & \mathbf{1} \end{bmatrix}^{-1} \left[ \begin{bmatrix} \mathbf{F}^{11} \\ \mathbf{F}^{21} \\ \mathbf{0} \\ \mathbf{0} \end{bmatrix} + \begin{bmatrix} \mathbf{F}^{12} \\ \mathbf{F}^{22} \\ \mathbf{0} \\ \mathbf{0} \end{bmatrix} + \begin{bmatrix} \mathbf{E}^1 \\ \mathbf{E}^2 \\ \mathbf{0} \\ \mathbf{0} \end{bmatrix} \right] \tag{10.11}$$

is obtained.

Here, the impact on production of the exogenous consumption change, due to the future population change in 2015–2040 obtained in Sect. 3.2, is calculated with the following equation:

$$\begin{bmatrix} \Delta\mathbf{X}^1 \\ \Delta\mathbf{X}^2 \\ \Delta\mathbf{Y}^1 \\ \Delta\mathbf{Y}^2 \end{bmatrix} = \begin{bmatrix} \mathbf{I}-\mathbf{A}^{11} & -\mathbf{A}^{12} & -c^1\mathbf{c}^{11} & -c^2\mathbf{c}^{12} \\ -\mathbf{A}^{21} & \mathbf{I}-\mathbf{A}^{22} & -c^1\mathbf{c}^{21} & -c^2\mathbf{c}^{22} \\ -\mathbf{w}^{11} & -\mathbf{w}^{12} & \mathbf{1} & \mathbf{0} \\ -\mathbf{w}^{21} & -\mathbf{w}^{22} & \mathbf{0} & \mathbf{1} \end{bmatrix}^{-1} \left[ \begin{bmatrix} \Delta\mathbf{C}^{1s} \\ \Delta\mathbf{C}^{2s} \\ \mathbf{0} \\ \mathbf{0} \end{bmatrix} \right] \tag{10.12}$$

where $\Delta\mathbf{C}^{1s}$ is the consumption change of Region 1's products in the region $s$, and $\Delta\mathbf{X}^1$ is the corresponding production change.

The consumption changes in Eq. (10.12) are exogenously brought about by the changes in demographic factors. Assuming that consumption $C$ is a function of income $Y$ and demographic factors such as the number of households $H$,

$$C = C(Y, H), \tag{10.13}$$

the exogenous change in consumption due to the change in the number of households is expressed as:

$$\Delta C = C(\overline{Y}, \Delta H), \tag{10.14}$$

given income, $Y$ invariant. The production inducement amount, obtained by the consumption endogenous model (10.12), can be considered to include the production value induced by the further change in consumer demand due to the income change, which is initially set as fixed in Eq. (10.14).

Using Model (10.12) to calculate the production inducement amount, input structure, consumption allocation structure, and employee's income coefficient are assumed to be unchanged in the base year, although we assume future changes in the population and number of households for the simulation.

## 10.4 Analytical Results and Discussion

### *10.4.1 Effect of Consumption Change by Municipality*

Table 10.2 presents the effects on the production and value-added of municipalities by changing consumption in the four regions of Aichi Prefecture, Nagoya City, Toyohashi City, and Nishio City. The consumption changes in 2040 due to depopulation are estimated by comparing the 2015 consumption.

We selected these for regions despite calculating each of the 54 municipalities. We can observe the sum-up effects in Aichi Prefecture's case. Nagoya is a central city. Toyohashi is a representative where the population is expected to decline significantly, and Nishio is a city in the Nishi-mikawa Area where population growth is expected to continue for some time.

Looking at the effects of consumption changes in Aichi Prefecture as a whole, because of the decrease in population and households in Aichi Prefecture, consumption will decrease by 578.89 billion yen, production by 1,399.75 billion yen, and value-added by 759.70 billion yen. Of this, the spillover to the prefecture area will be 818.48 billion yen for production and 489.60 billion yen for value-added, and the spillover to areas outside the prefecture will be 581.27 billion yen for production and 270.10 billion yen for value-added. As for the magnitude of the ripple effect on municipalities in terms of value-added, Nagoya City decreased by 213.21 billion yen, Toyohashi City by 30.54 billion yen, Ichinomiya City by 25.81 billion yen, Kasugai City by 20.20 billion yen, and Toyota City by 18.70 billion yen. The value added to all municipalities decreased.

Regarding the ripple effect on municipalities in response to the consumption change in Nagoya City, consumption will decrease by 84.85 billion yen, production

**Table 10.2** Consumption changes in four regions and the induced values of production and value-added by municipality (unit: billion yen)

| | | Aichi Pref. Total | | | Nagoya City | | | Toyohashi City | | | Nishio City | | |
|---|---|---|---|---|---|---|---|---|---|---|---|---|---|
| | | Consumption | Production | Value added | Consumption | Production | Value added | Consumption | Production | Value added | Consumption | Production | Value added |
| | Total | −578.89 | −1 ,399.75 | −759.70 | −84.85 | −193.47 | −113.91 | −53.61 | −129.78 | −69.23 | 3.08 | 7.17 | 3.64 |
| | Aichi prefecture total | −466.60 | −818.48 | −489.60 | −80.67 | −137.05 | −89.34 | −41.31 | −72.60 | −42.31 | 1.97 | 3.29 | 1.66 |
| 1 | Nagoya city | −177.37 | −342.43 | −213.21 | −71.75 | −108.22 | −73.33 | −5.63 | −15.29 | −9.09 | 0.55 | 1.14 | 0.69 |
| 2 | Toyohashi City | −32.55 | −49.40 | −30.54 | −0.15 | −0.82 | −0.49 | −24.12 | −32.14 | −20.35 | 0.07 | 0.12 | 0.07 |
| 3 | Okazaki City | −6.65 | −14.89 | −9.82 | −0.49 | −1.40 | −0.87 | −1.04 | −2.16 | −1.29 | 0.19 | 0.26 | 0.15 |
| 4 | Ichinomiya City | −27.14 | −40.06 | −25.81 | −0.61 | −1.79 | −1.20 | −0.20 | −0.57 | −0.35 | 0.02 | 0.04 | 0.03 |
| 5 | Seto City | −11.27 | −14.98 | −9.55 | 0.01 | −0.39 | −0.30 | −0.08 | −0.22 | −0.12 | 0.01 | 0.02 | 0.01 |
| 6 | Handa City | −11.98 | −16.72 | −10.63 | −0.20 | −0.58 | −0.38 | −0.10 | −0.31 | −0.17 | 0.04 | 0.06 | 0.03 |
| 7 | Kasugai City | −21.44 | −31.51 | −20.20 | −0.52 | −1.80 | −1.24 | −0.13 | −0.49 | −0.29 | 0.02 | 0.04 | 0.03 |
| 8 | Toyokawa City | −11.59 | −17.66 | −10.89 | −0.11 | −0.39 | −0.23 | −3.22 | −5.24 | −3.23 | 0.03 | 0.05 | 0.03 |
| 9 | Tsushima City | −8.27 | −10.76 | −6.58 | −0.11 | −0.33 | −0.23 | −0.03 | −0.09 | −0.06 | 0.00 | 0.01 | 0.00 |
| 10 | Hekinan City | −2.25 | −6.91 | −3.00 | −0.03 | −0.54 | −0.20 | −0.14 | −0.53 | −0.19 | 0.27 | 0.35 | 0.11 |
| 11 | Kariya city | −2.81 | −7.11 | −4.36 | −0.30 | −0.87 | −0.49 | −0.21 | −0.58 | −0.31 | 0.05 | 0.08 | 0.04 |
| 12 | Toyota City | −20.59 | −36.66 | −18.70 | −1.84 | −3.99 | −1.75 | −1.11 | −2.53 | −1.16 | 0.07 | 0.13 | 0.08 |
| 13 | Anjo City | −1.81 | −6.30 | −3.88 | −0.19 | −0.77 | −0.44 | −0.26 | −0.70 | −0.39 | 0.10 | 0.13 | 0.07 |

(continued)

**Table 10.2** (continued)

| | | Aichi Pref. Total | | | Nagoya City | | | Toyohashi City | | | Nishio City | | |
|---|---|---|---|---|---|---|---|---|---|---|---|---|---|
| | | Consumption | Production | Value added | Consumption | Production | Value added | Consumption | Production | Value added | Consumption | Production | Value added |
| 14 | Nishio City | −2.83 | −7.25 | −4.25 | −0.11 | −0.58 | −0.34 | −0.47 | −0.98 | −0.54 | 0.12 | 0.11 | −0.06 |
| 15 | Gamagori City | −5.07 | −7.39 | −4.55 | 0.02 | −0.13 | −0.08 | −0.36 | −0.72 | −0.42 | 0.10 | 0.12 | 0.07 |
| 16 | Inuyama City | −5.51 | −8.05 | −4.94 | −0.11 | −0.35 | −0.22 | −0.03 | −0.12 | −0.06 | 0.00 | 0.01 | 0.01 |
| 17 | Tokoname City | −3.52 | −6.82 | −2.88 | −0.51 | −0.96 | −0.36 | −0.28 | −0.54 | −0.21 | 0.02 | 0.03 | 0.02 |
| 18 | Kounan City | −7.14 | −9.56 | −5.77 | −0.03 | −0.22 | −0.14 | −0.03 | −0.09 | −0.05 | 0.00 | 0.01 | 0.00 |
| 19 | Komaki City | −11.43 | −19.09 | −11.40 | −0.23 | −1.06 | −0.60 | −0.14 | −0.45 | −0.25 | 0.02 | 0.04 | 0.02 |
| 20 | Inazawa City | −9.02 | −14.39 | −8.85 | −0.31 | −0.90 | −0.57 | −0.08 | −0.26 | −0.14 | 0.01 | 0.02 | 0.01 |
| 21 | Shinshiro City | −4.86 | −6.56 | −4.08 | −0.07 | −0.17 | −0.11 | −0.37 | −0.68 | −0.43 | 0.01 | 0.01 | 0.01 |
| 22 | Tokai City | −2.13 | −6.10 | −3.35 | −0.20 | −0.76 | −0.45 | −0.09 | −0.37 | −0.17 | 0.02 | 0.03 | 0.02 |
| 23 | Obu City | −1.04 | −3.11 | −1.97 | −0.21 | −0.53 | −0.35 | −0.06 | −0.20 | −0.10 | 0.01 | 0.02 | 0.01 |
| 24 | Chita City | −13.34 | −26.69 | −8.02 | −0.73 | −2.52 | −0.74 | −0.76 | −1.65 | −0.42 | 0.06 | 0.11 | 0.03 |
| 25 | Chiryu City | 0.21 | −0.68 | −0.57 | −0.06 | −0.19 | −0.13 | −0.05 | −0.13 | −0.08 | 0.01 | 0.02 | 0.01 |
| 26 | Owariasahi City | −5.77 | −7.82 | −4.82 | −0.12 | −0.37 | −0.25 | −0.04 | −0.10 | −0.06 | 0.00 | 0.01 | 0.00 |
| 27 | Takahama City | 0.61 | −0.08 | −0.02 | −0.05 | −0.15 | −0.08 | −0.03 | −0.09 | −0.04 | 0.01 | 0.01 | 0.01 |
| 28 | Iwakura City | −1.96 | −3.26 | −2.06 | −0.07 | −0.21 | −0.14 | −0.02 | −0.06 | −0.04 | 0.00 | 0.00 | 0.00 |

(continued)

**Table 10.2** (continued)

| | | Aichi Pref. Total | | | Nagoya City | | | Toyohashi City | | | Nishio City | | |
|---|---|---|---|---|---|---|---|---|---|---|---|---|---|
| | | Consumption | Production | Value added | Consumption | Production | Value added | Consumption | Production | Value added | Consumption | Production | Value added |
| 29 | Toyoake City | −2.37 | −3.75 | −2.38 | −0.05 | −0.25 | −0.17 | −0.04 | −0.13 | −0.08 | 0.01 | 0.02 | 0.01 |
| 30 | Nisshin City | −2.03 | −3.68 | −2.56 | −0.19 | −0.49 | −0.35 | −0.05 | −0.14 | −0.09 | 0.01 | 0.01 | 0.01 |
| 31 | Tahara City | −7.08 | −12.81 | −5.27 | 0.02 | −0.34 | −0.07 | −1.40 | −2.86 | −0.95 | 0.02 | 0.04 | 0.02 |
| 32 | Aisai City | −5.10 | −6.93 | −4.54 | −0.21 | −0.40 | −0.29 | −0.02 | −0.08 | −0.05 | 0.00 | 0.01 | 0.00 |
| 33 | Kiyosu City | −1.71 | −3.98 | −2.49 | −0.04 | −0.42 | −0.28 | −0.05 | −0.17 | −0.10 | 0.01 | 0.02 | 0.01 |
| 34 | Kitanagoya City | −2.56 | −5.03 | −3.26 | −0.11 | −0.46 | −0.31 | −0.04 | −0.14 | −0.08 | 0.01 | 0.01 | 0.01 |
| 35 | Yatomi City | −3.02 | −4.71 | −2.85 | −0.08 | −0.30 | −0.19 | −0.04 | −0.12 | −0.07 | 0.01 | 0.01 | 0.01 |
| 36 | Miyoshi City | −2.35 | −4.34 | −2.59 | −0.12 | −0.39 | −0.22 | −0.05 | −0.18 | −0.09 | 0.01 | 0.01 | 0.01 |
| 37 | Ama City | −4.17 | −6.09 | −3.86 | −0.21 | −0.49 | −0.33 | −0.03 | −0.09 | −0.05 | 0.00 | 0.01 | 0.00 |
| 38 | Nagakute City | −0.47 | −1.54 | −1.21 | −0.02 | −0.20 | −0.15 | −0.03 | −0.08 | −0.05 | 0.00 | 0.01 | 0.00 |
| 39 | Togo Town | −0.88 | −1.68 | −1.13 | −0.05 | −0.17 | −0.12 | −0.01 | −0.06 | −0.03 | 0.00 | 0.01 | 0.00 |
| 40 | Toyoyama Town | −1.11 | −2.14 | −1.29 | −0.04 | −0.17 | −0.10 | −0.04 | −0.10 | −0.06 | 0.01 | 0.01 | 0.01 |
| 41 | Oguchi Town | −1.02 | −2.14 | −1.31 | 0.01 | −0.10 | −0.06 | −0.02 | −0.07 | −0.04 | 0.00 | 0.01 | 0.00 |
| 42 | Fuso Town | −1.80 | −2.51 | −1.64 | −0.03 | −0.09 | −0.07 | −0.01 | −0.03 | −0.02 | 0.00 | 0.00 | 0.00 |
| 43 | Oharu Town | −1.15 | −1.78 | −1.13 | −0.06 | −0.16 | −0.11 | −0.01 | −0.03 | −0.02 | 0.00 | 0.00 | 0.00 |
| 44 | Kanie Town | −2.05 | −3.25 | −1.99 | −0.06 | −0.22 | −0.15 | −0.02 | −0.06 | −0.04 | 0.00 | 0.01 | 0.00 |

(continued)

**Table 10.2** (continued)

| | | Aichi Pref. Total | | | Nagoya City | | | Toyohashi City | | | Nishio City | | |
|---|---|---|---|---|---|---|---|---|---|---|---|---|---|
| | | Consumption | Production | Value added | Consumption | Production | Value added | Consumption | Production | Value added | Consumption | Production | Value added |
| 45 | Tobishima Village | −3.52 | −6.75 | −2.99 | −0.04 | −0.42 | −0.19 | −0.07 | −0.22 | −0.12 | 0.01 | 0.02 | 0.01 |
| 46 | Agui Town | −0.81 | −1.30 | −0.85 | −0.05 | −0.11 | −0.08 | −0.02 | −0.04 | −0.02 | 0.00 | 0.01 | 0.00 |
| 47 | Higashiura Town | −1.87 | −2.68 | −1.81 | −0.07 | −0.17 | −0.12 | −0.02 | −0.07 | −0.04 | 0.01 | 0.01 | 0.00 |
| 48 | Minamichita Town | −3.45 | −4.42 | −2.55 | 0.07 | 0.02 | 0.00 | −0.02 | −0.05 | −0.03 | 0.02 | 0.02 | 0.01 |
| 49 | Mihama Town | −3.56 | −4.65 | −2.69 | −0.01 | −0.07 | −0.04 | −0.02 | −0.06 | −0.03 | 0.01 | 0.01 | 0.01 |
| 50 | Taketoyo Town | −3.27 | −5.56 | −2.36 | −0.02 | −0.20 | −0.09 | −0.03 | −0.13 | −0.05 | 0.01 | 0.02 | 0.01 |
| 51 | Kota Town | −1.45 | −2.91 | −1.14 | −0.20 | −0.37 | −0.13 | −0.19 | −0.36 | −0.14 | 0.02 | 0.03 | 0.01 |
| 52 | Shitara Town | −0.63 | −0.82 | −0.51 | −0.01 | −0.02 | −0.02 | −0.02 | −0.04 | −0.03 | 0.00 | 0.00 | 0.00 |
| 53 | Toei Town | −0.45 | −0.55 | −0.35 | −0.01 | −0.01 | −0.01 | −0.01 | −0.02 | −0.01 | 0.00 | 0.00 | 0.00 |
| 54 | Toyone Village | −0.20 | −0.26 | −0.16 | −0.01 | −0.01 | −0.01 | −0.01 | −0.02 | −0.01 | 0.00 | 0.00 | 0.00 |
| 55 | The Rest of Japan | −112.28 | −581.27 | −270.10 | −4.19 | −56.42 | −24.57 | −12.31 | −57.18 | −26.93 | 1.11 | 3.88 | 1.99 |

*Source* Created by the author

by 193.47 billion yen, and value-added by 113.91 billion yen. As for value-added, Nagoya City will decrease by 89.34 billion yen, outside the prefecture by 24.57 billion yen, Toyota City by 1.75 billion yen, and Ichinomiya City by 1.20 billion yen. The value-added in all other municipalities, except Minamichita Town, will decrease.

In the case of Toyohashi City, the total induced production will decrease by 129.78 billion yen and the value-added by 69.23 billion yen. In terms of value-added, it will decrease by 26.93 billion yen outside the prefecture, 20.35 billion yen in Toyohashi City, 9.09 billion yen in Nagoya City, 1.29 billion yen in Okazaki City, and 1.16 billion yen in Toyota City. The value-added in all other municipalities will also decrease owing to the changes in consumption in Toyohashi City.

However, consumption in Nishio City is increasing, and the total induced production is 7.17 billion yen and the value-added is 3.64 billion yen. Within Aichi Prefecture, the value-added increased by 1.66 billion yen and outside the prefecture by 1.99 billion yen. The value-added in most municipalities increased. The value-added in Nagoya City increased by 690 million yen and in Hekinan City by 110 million yen, although the effect of Nishio City has been reduced by about 60 million yen.

Table 10.2 depicts the extent to which the change in consumption demand of each municipality affects the production and value-added of other municipalities. Table 10.3 displays the amount of production inducement and value-added generated in each municipality. It is possible to determine the origin of each municipality's consumption change and how it is related to the induced amount.

Considering the total effect of Aichi Prefecture, consumption will decrease by 466.60 billion yen, production by 818.48 billion yen, and value-added by 489.60 billion yen. The value-added will increase in municipalities in the eastern Owari and Nishi-mikawa areas, where the population and number of households are increasing, such as Nagakute City (7.79 billion yen), Takahama City (6.89 billion yen), Okazaki City (6.83 billion yen), and Obu City (3.80 billion yen). However, value-added will decrease in the municipalities where the population and the number of households are decreasing, such as Nagoya City (89.34 billion yen), Kasugai City (47.43 billion yen), Toyohashi City (42.31 billion yen), and Seto City (36.11 billion yen). Consequently, the total effects become negative for all municipalities.

In the case of Nagoya City, owing to the decline in consumption demand within the prefecture, consumption will decline by 177.37 billion yen, production by 342.43 billion yen, and value-added by 213.21 billion yen. In Toyohashi City's case, consumption will decrease by 32.55 billion yen, production by 49.40 billion yen, and value-added by 30.54 billion yen. In the case of Nishio City, consumption will decrease by 2.83 billion yen, production by 7.25 billion yen, and value-added by 4.25 billion yen, although consumption demand in this city is increasing.

**Table 10.3** Consumption changes, induced production, and value-added in four regions by municipality (unit: billion yen)

| | | Aichi Pref. Total | | | Nagoya City | | | Toyohashi City | | | Nishio City | | |
|---|---|---|---|---|---|---|---|---|---|---|---|---|---|
| | | Consumption | Production | Value added | Consumption | Production | Value added | Consumption | Production | Value added | Consumption | Production | Value added |
| | Aichi prefecture total | −466.60 | −818.48 | −489.60 | −177.37 | −342.43 | −213.21 | −32.55 | −49.40 | −30.54 | −2.83 | −7.25 | −4.25 |
| 1 | Nagoya city | −80.67 | −137.05 | −89.34 | −71.75 | −108.22 | −73.33 | −0.15 | −0.82 | −0.49 | −0.11 | −0.58 | −0.34 |
| 2 | Toyohashi City | −41.31 | −72.60 | −42.31 | −5.63 | −15.29 | −9.09 | −24.12 | −32.14 | −20.35 | −0.47 | −0.98 | −0.54 |
| 3 | Okazaki City | 8.56 | 14.41 | 6.83 | 2.72 | 5.47 | 3.34 | 0.47 | 0.75 | 0.41 | 0.33 | 0.45 | 0.22 |
| 4 | Ichinomiya City | −34.04 | −59.37 | −35.02 | −7.76 | −18.51 | −10.97 | −0.14 | −0.48 | −0.26 | −0.07 | −0.28 | −0.14 |
| 5 | Seto City | −36.10 | −63.41 | −36.11 | −14.31 | −28.26 | −16.81 | −0.32 | −0.83 | −0.46 | −0.14 | −0.42 | −0.22 |
| 6 | Handa City | −20.25 | −35.35 | −20.62 | −4.15 | −10.22 | −6.14 | −0.17 | −0.45 | −0.26 | −0.43 | −0.78 | −0.45 |
| 7 | Kasugai City | −46.82 | −81.97 | −47.43 | −18.06 | −36.03 | −21.43 | −0.23 | −0.73 | −0.39 | −0.12 | −0.42 | −0.21 |
| 8 | Toyokawa City | −14.93 | −26.50 | −15.38 | −2.40 | −6.15 | −3.66 | −3.06 | −5.05 | −3.07 | −0.20 | −0.41 | −0.23 |
| 9 | Tsushima City | −16.15 | −28.34 | −16.17 | −5.51 | −11.43 | −6.86 | −0.09 | −0.27 | −0.15 | −0.04 | −0.15 | −0.08 |
| 10 | Hekinan City | −5.11 | −9.11 | −5.28 | −0.96 | −2.40 | −1.45 | −0.07 | −0.17 | −0.10 | −0.56 | −0.85 | −0.51 |
| 11 | Kariya city | 4.16 | 7.10 | 3.49 | 1.51 | 2.91 | 1.78 | 0.08 | 0.16 | 0.09 | 0.09 | 0.15 | 0.08 |
| 12 | Toyota City | −19.94 | −35.63 | −21.29 | −5.67 | −12.65 | −7.50 | −0.24 | −0.61 | −0.37 | −0.17 | −0.42 | −0.25 |
| 13 | Anjo City | 3.53 | 5.76 | 2.64 | 1.11 | 2.19 | 1.34 | 0.10 | 0.17 | 0.09 | 0.12 | 0.16 | 0.07 |
| 14 | Nishio City | 1.97 | 3.29 | 1.66 | 0.55 | 1.14 | 0.69 | 0.07 | 0.12 | 0.07 | 0.12 | 0.11 | −0.06 |

(continued)

**Table 10.3** (continued)

| | | Aichi Pref. Total | | | Nagoya City | | | Toyohashi City | | | Nishio City | | |
|---|---|---|---|---|---|---|---|---|---|---|---|---|---|
| | | Consumption | Production | Value added | Consumption | Production | Value added | Consumption | Production | Value added | Consumption | Production | Value added |
| 15 | Gamagori City | −11.42 | −20.08 | −11.50 | −1.95 | −4.99 | −3.00 | −0.61 | −1.21 | −0.72 | −0.44 | −0.76 | −0.43 |
| 16 | Inuyama City | −11.60 | −20.13 | −11.51 | −3.65 | −7.60 | −4.53 | −0.08 | −0.21 | −0.12 | −0.04 | −0.12 | −0.06 |
| 17 | Tokoname City | 1.06 | 1.79 | 0.93 | 0.39 | 0.75 | 0.45 | 0.02 | 0.03 | 0.02 | 0.02 | 0.03 | 0.02 |
| 18 | Kounan City | −18.76 | −32.87 | −18.75 | −5.07 | −11.32 | −6.73 | −0.10 | −0.31 | −0.17 | −0.05 | −0.17 | −0.09 |
| 19 | Komaki City | −8.90 | −15.45 | −9.40 | −2.09 | −5.08 | −3.03 | −0.03 | −0.11 | −0.06 | −0.01 | −0.07 | −0.03 |
| 20 | Inazawa City | −13.58 | −23.89 | −13.76 | −4.13 | −8.87 | −5.27 | −0.07 | −0.21 | −0.12 | −0.03 | −0.12 | −0.06 |
| 21 | Shinshiro City | −13.97 | −24.61 | −13.87 | −3.33 | −7.42 | −4.43 | −1.65 | −2.78 | −1.63 | −0.22 | −0.40 | −0.22 |
| 22 | Tokai City | 0.96 | 1.48 | 0.61 | 0.68 | 1.03 | 0.61 | 0.01 | 0.03 | 0.01 | 0.01 | 0.01 | 0.01 |
| 23 | Obu City | 4.21 | 7.19 | 3.80 | 1.83 | 3.34 | 2.01 | 0.05 | 0.12 | 0.06 | 0.05 | 0.09 | 0.05 |
| 24 | Chita City | −9.02 | −15.93 | −9.20 | −3.26 | −6.62 | −3.98 | −0.07 | −0.20 | −0.11 | −0.06 | −0.15 | −0.08 |
| 25 | Chiryu City | 4.01 | 6.89 | 3.68 | 1.16 | 2.44 | 1.48 | 0.07 | 0.14 | 0.08 | 0.07 | 0.13 | 0.07 |
| 26 | Owariasahi City | −14.31 | −25.30 | −14.64 | −5.29 | −10.89 | −6.54 | −0.10 | −0.28 | −0.15 | −0.05 | −0.15 | −0.08 |
| 27 | Takahama City | 7.16 | 12.47 | 6.89 | 1.61 | 3.74 | 2.27 | 0.09 | 0.22 | 0.13 | 0.37 | 0.56 | 0.32 |
| 28 | Iwakura City | −1.86 | −3.31 | −2.01 | −0.42 | −1.05 | −0.63 | −0.01 | −0.02 | −0.01 | 0.00 | −0.01 | −0.01 |

(continued)

**Table 10.3** (continued)

| | | Aichi Pref. Total | | | Nagoya City | | | Toyohashi City | | | Nishio City | | |
|---|---|---|---|---|---|---|---|---|---|---|---|---|---|
| | | Consumption | Production | Value added | Consumption | Production | Value added | Consumption | Production | Value added | Consumption | Production | Value added |
| 29 | Toyoake City | −6.73 | −11.91 | −6.89 | −2.34 | −4.86 | −2.92 | −0.06 | −0.16 | −0.09 | −0.06 | −0.14 | −0.08 |
| 30 | Nisshin City | 1.24 | 1.94 | 0.73 | 1.14 | 1.60 | 0.93 | 0.02 | 0.04 | 0.02 | 0.01 | 0.02 | 0.01 |
| 31 | Tahara City | −8.99 | −15.89 | −9.03 | −1.80 | −4.26 | −2.54 | −1.39 | −2.36 | −1.40 | −0.13 | −0.25 | −0.14 |
| 32 | Aisai City | −17.09 | −29.93 | −16.93 | −6.32 | −12.64 | −7.59 | −0.12 | −0.33 | −0.18 | −0.07 | −0.18 | −0.10 |
| 33 | Kiyosu City | −0.06 | −0.21 | −0.26 | 0.25 | 0.21 | 0.10 | 0.00 | 0.00 | 0.00 | 0.00 | 0.00 | 0.00 |
| 34 | Kitanagoya City | −0.58 | −1.11 | −0.84 | 0.07 | −0.13 | −0.10 | 0.00 | 0.00 | 0.00 | 0.00 | 0.00 | 0.00 |
| 35 | Yatomi City | −3.42 | −5.98 | −3.48 | −1.18 | −2.46 | −1.49 | −0.02 | −0.06 | −0.04 | −0.01 | −0.04 | −0.02 |
| 36 | Miyoshi City | −1.61 | −2.97 | −1.98 | −0.28 | −0.84 | −0.49 | 0.00 | −0.02 | −0.01 | 0.00 | −0.02 | −0.01 |
| 37 | Ama City | −10.09 | −17.79 | −10.24 | −4.34 | −8.36 | −5.03 | −0.06 | −0.17 | −0.09 | −0.03 | −0.09 | −0.05 |
| 38 | Nagakute City | 8.51 | 14.57 | 7.79 | 4.20 | 7.51 | 4.41 | 0.07 | 0.18 | 0.09 | 0.04 | 0.10 | 0.05 |
| 39 | Togo Town | −2.70 | −4.84 | −2.85 | −0.92 | −1.95 | −1.17 | −0.02 | −0.06 | −0.03 | −0.02 | −0.04 | −0.02 |
| 40 | Toyoyama Town | 0.93 | 1.60 | 0.87 | 0.41 | 0.77 | 0.45 | 0.00 | 0.02 | 0.01 | 0.00 | 0.01 | 0.00 |
| 41 | Oguchi Town | 0.50 | 0.84 | 0.41 | 0.20 | 0.38 | 0.22 | 0.00 | 0.01 | 0.01 | 0.00 | 0.00 | 0.00 |
| 42 | Fuso Town | −2.61 | −4.59 | −2.67 | −0.66 | −1.52 | −0.90 | −0.01 | −0.04 | −0.02 | −0.01 | −0.02 | −0.01 |
| 43 | Oharu Town | −1.79 | −3.20 | −1.93 | −0.65 | −1.38 | −0.84 | −0.01 | −0.03 | −0.01 | 0.00 | −0.02 | −0.01 |

(continued)

**Table 10.3** (continued)

| | | Aichi Pref. Total | | | Nagoya City | | | Toyohashi City | | | Nishio City | | |
|---|---|---|---|---|---|---|---|---|---|---|---|---|---|
| | | Consumption | Production | Value added | Consumption | Production | Value added | Consumption | Production | Value added | Consumption | Production | Value added |
| 44 | Kanie Town | −2.84 | −5.04 | −2.93 | −0.94 | −2.01 | −1.22 | −0.02 | −0.05 | −0.03 | −0.01 | −0.03 | −0.02 |
| 45 | Tobishima Village | −1.71 | −2.85 | −1.71 | −0.54 | −1.16 | −0.70 | −0.01 | −0.03 | −0.01 | −0.01 | −0.02 | −0.01 |
| 46 | Agui Town | 0.23 | 0.36 | 0.14 | 0.16 | 0.24 | 0.15 | 0.01 | 0.01 | 0.01 | 0.01 | 0.01 | 0.01 |
| 47 | Higashiura Town | −6.43 | −11.29 | −6.57 | −1.73 | −3.84 | −2.30 | −0.05 | −0.15 | −0.08 | −0.10 | −0.19 | −0.11 |
| 48 | Minamichita Town | −9.43 | −16.52 | −9.30 | −2.70 | −5.84 | −3.56 | −0.14 | −0.30 | −0.17 | −0.15 | −0.28 | −0.16 |
| 49 | Mihama Town | −10.28 | −18.04 | −10.21 | −2.93 | −6.32 | −3.82 | −0.15 | −0.32 | −0.19 | −0.21 | −0.37 | −0.21 |
| 50 | Taketoyo Town | −6.36 | −11.24 | −6.41 | −1.79 | −3.88 | −2.34 | −0.07 | −0.17 | −0.10 | −0.14 | −0.24 | −0.14 |
| 51 | Kota Town | 2.74 | 4.72 | 2.54 | 0.61 | 1.40 | 0.85 | 0.13 | 0.23 | 0.13 | 0.14 | 0.20 | 0.11 |
| 52 | Shitara Town | −2.49 | −4.38 | −2.45 | −0.77 | −1.58 | −0.95 | −0.16 | −0.28 | −0.16 | −0.03 | −0.06 | −0.03 |
| 53 | Toei Town | −1.74 | −3.05 | −1.71 | −0.50 | −1.06 | −0.64 | −0.11 | −0.19 | −0.11 | −0.02 | −0.04 | −0.02 |
| 54 | Toyone Village | −0.67 | −1.18 | −0.66 | −0.23 | −0.46 | −0.27 | −0.04 | −0.06 | −0.04 | −0.01 | −0.02 | −0.01 |
| 55 | The Rest of Japan | – | – | – | – | – | – | – | – | – | – | – | – |

*Source* Created by the author

### 10.4.2 *Sectoral Effects of Consumption Changes*

Table 10.4 depicts the impact of the consumption changes of each municipality on sectoral production and value-added. Here, we examine the effects of Aichi Prefecture and the three cities of Nagoya, Toyohashi, and Nishio.

In the case of Aichi Prefecture, total consumption will decrease by 578.89 billion yen, production by 1,399.75 billion yen, and value-added by 759.70 billion yen, as seen in Table 10.4. The value-added has seen a large decrease in the following sectors: commerce (116.61 billion yen), real estate (113.55 billion yen), education and research (83.59 billion yen), business services (59.23 billion yen), finance and insurance (46.17 billion yen), and beverages and food (33.93 billion yen). Almost all sectors decrease in value-added. Only miscellaneous non-profit services of 15.98 billion yen have positive value-added. Medical and health care and welfare, which are expected to increase consumption expenditure because of an aging population, are thought to be offset by the effects of the decrease in the total number of households.

In the case of Nagoya City, consumption will decrease by 87.85 billion yen, production by 193.47 billion yen, and value-added by 113.91 billion yen. In addition to the value-added increases in miscellaneous non-profit services, by 6.93 billion yen, amusement and recreational services will increase by 2.46 billion yen, hotels by 420 million yen, and road transportation by 170 million yen.

Consumption will decrease by 53.61 billion yen, production by 129.78 billion yen, and value-added by 69.23 billion yen in the case of Toyohashi City. On the contrary, in the case of Nishio City, consumption increased by 3.08 billion yen, production increased by 7.17 billion yen, and value-added increased by 3.64 billion yen. In this case, the value-added in some sectors will decrease, such as education and research by 300 million yen, and medical, health, and welfare by 210 million yen. However, value-added for many sectors has a positive impact, such as commerce by 930 million yen, business services by 340 million yen, beverages and food by 320 million yen, and miscellaneous non-profit services by 300 million yen.

## 10.5 Concluding Remarks

In this study, based on the forecast of the future population and number of households estimated by the NIPSSR, we estimated the amount of future consumption by sector and municipality in Aichi Prefecture. Then, using the 2011 inter-municipal IOTs for 54 municipalities in Aichi Prefecture, we evaluated the effect on production and value-added by the consumption change from 2015 to 2040. In our model, we treated household income and consumption endogenously, considering commuting between municipalities.

According to the estimated rate of change in consumption expenditure by municipality from 2015 to 2040, total consumption will increase in municipalities where the population and number of households are increasing. However, the total consumption

**Table 10.4** Consumption changes in four regions and the total induced production and value-added by sectors (unit: billion yen)

| | | Aichi Pref. Total | | | Nagoya City | | | Toyohashi City | | | Nishio City | | |
|---|---|---|---|---|---|---|---|---|---|---|---|---|---|
| | | Consumption | Production | Value added | Consumption | Production | Value added | Consumption | Production | Value added | Consumption | Production | Value added |
| | Total | −578.89 | −1,399.75 | −759.70 | −84.85 | −193.47 | −113.91 | −53.61 | −129.78 | −69.23 | 3.08 | 7.17 | 3.64 |
| 1 | Agriculture, forestry and fishery | 0.28 | −21.71 | −10.00 | 1.35 | −0.53 | −0.14 | −0.24 | −2.41 | −1.13 | 0.08 | 0.24 | 0.12 |
| 2 | Mining | 0.00 | −0.39 | −0.20 | 0.00 | −0.05 | −0.02 | 0.00 | −0.04 | −0.02 | 0.00 | 0.00 | 0.00 |
| 3 | Beverages and Foods | −39.90 | −93.38 | −33.93 | −0.78 | −6.73 | −2.32 | −4.40 | −9.48 | −3.50 | 0.48 | 0.81 | 0.32 |
| 4 | Textile products | −4.03 | −7.78 | −2.67 | −0.53 | −0.94 | −0.32 | −0.37 | −0.73 | −0.25 | 0.01 | 0.03 | 0.01 |
| 5 | Pulp, paper and wooden products | −1.85 | −17.59 | −5.43 | −0.36 | −2.14 | −0.67 | −0.14 | −1.63 | −0.50 | 0.00 | 0.09 | 0.03 |
| 6 | Chemical products | −3.13 | −24.22 | −5.63 | 0.15 | −1.79 | −0.29 | −0.40 | −2.49 | −0.60 | 0.04 | 0.17 | 0.05 |
| 7 | Petroleum and coal products | −16.80 | −39.45 | −9.10 | −1.93 | −4.42 | −1.02 | −1.57 | −3.76 | −0.87 | 0.07 | 0.21 | 0.05 |
| 8 | Ceramic, stone and clay products | −0.51 | −4.21 | −1.87 | −0.09 | −0.63 | −0.28 | −0.04 | −0.37 | −0.17 | 0.00 | 0.01 | 0.01 |
| 9 | Iron and steel | 0.00 | −14.03 | −2.68 | 0.00 | −1.76 | −0.34 | 0.00 | −1.33 | −0.25 | 0.00 | 0.06 | 0.01 |
| 10 | Non-ferrous metals | 0.61 | −4.17 | −0.95 | 0.24 | −0.33 | −0.07 | 0.02 | −0.44 | −0.10 | 0.01 | 0.03 | 0.01 |
| 11 | Metal products | 1.99 | −5.80 | −2.22 | 0.76 | −0.25 | −0.08 | 0.06 | −0.68 | −0.26 | 0.03 | 0.07 | 0.03 |
| 12 | General machinery | 0.35 | −4.60 | −1.71 | 0.21 | −0.25 | −0.10 | 0.00 | −0.49 | −0.18 | 0.01 | 0.04 | 0.02 |

(continued)

**Table 10.4** (continued)

| | | Aichi Pref. Total | | | Nagoya City | | | Toyohashi City | | | Nishio City | | |
|---|---|---|---|---|---|---|---|---|---|---|---|---|---|
| | | Consumption | Production | Value added | Consumption | Production | Value added | Consumption | Production | Value added | Consumption | Production | Value added |
| 13 | Electronic components | −0.71 | −7.35 | −2.00 | −0.14 | −0.94 | −0.25 | −0.05 | −0.67 | −0.18 | 0.00 | 0.03 | 0.01 |
| 14 | Electrical machinery | −0.80 | −8.10 | −2.45 | 0.97 | −0.02 | −0.02 | −0.29 | −0.95 | −0.28 | 0.08 | 0.10 | 0.03 |
| 15 | Information and communication electronics equipment | −9.58 | −12.85 | −3.48 | −1.60 | −2.08 | −0.56 | −0.80 | −1.09 | −0.30 | 0.01 | 0.02 | 0.01 |
| 16 | Motor vehicle | −25.38 | −31.14 | −3.74 | −4.69 | −5.52 | −0.66 | −2.06 | −2.57 | −0.31 | −0.06 | −0.04 | 0.00 |
| 17 | Motor vehicle parts and accessories | −4.15 | −57.32 | −16.17 | −0.83 | −8.15 | −2.15 | −0.31 | −5.13 | −1.48 | -0.01 | 0.14 | 0.05 |
| 18 | Miscellaneous Transportation equipment | −0.93 | −3.52 | −1.19 | −0.23 | −0.62 | −0.21 | −0.06 | −0.29 | −0.10 | 0.00 | 0.01 | 0.00 |
| 19 | Miscellaneous manufacturing products | −4.61 | −8.56 | −3.13 | −0.90 | −1.41 | −0.52 | −0.36 | −0.72 | −0.26 | 0.00 | 0.01 | 0.01 |
| 20 | Construction | 0.00 | −16.85 | −7.29 | 0.00 | −3.16 | −1.37 | 0.00 | −1.46 | −0.63 | 0.00 | 0.06 | 0.03 |
| 21 | Electricity, gas and heat supply | −10.39 | −40.81 | −8.09 | 0.32 | −3.45 | −0.71 | −1.21 | −4.06 | −0.78 | 0.16 | 0.32 | 0.06 |

(continued)

**Table 10.4** (continued)

| | | Aichi Pref. Total | | | Nagoya City | | | Toyohashi City | | | Nishio City | | |
|---|---|---|---|---|---|---|---|---|---|---|---|---|---|
| | | Consumption | Production | Value added | Consumption | Production | Value added | Consumption | Production | Value added | Consumption | Production | Value added |
| 22 | Water supply and Waste management service | −3.69 | −15.62 | −8.01 | −0.01 | −1.55 | −0.76 | −0.41 | −1.51 | −0.78 | 0.04 | 0.10 | 0.05 |
| 23 | Commerce | −79.49 | −169.95 | −116.61 | −1.23 | −12.16 | −8.34 | −9.00 | −17.50 | −12.01 | 0.87 | 1.35 | 0.93 |
| 24 | Finance and insurance | −33.36 | −70.21 | −46.17 | −2.12 | −8.24 | −5.42 | −3.30 | −6.82 | −4.48 | 0.21 | 0.42 | 0.27 |
| 25 | Real estate | −64.42 | −148.01 | −113.55 | −36.64 | −50.25 | −37.57 | −3.83 | −11.26 | −8.70 | −0.04 | 0.33 | 0.25 |
| 26 | Railway transport | −11.16 | −18.32 | −12.61 | −1.71 | −2.61 | −1.80 | −1.03 | −1.70 | −1.17 | 0.05 | 0.09 | 0.06 |
| 27 | Road transport (except self-transport) | −0.11 | −16.25 | −12.00 | 2.15 | 0.23 | 0.17 | −0.49 | −2.00 | −1.48 | 0.17 | 0.25 | 0.19 |
| 28 | Water transport | −0.23 | −1.50 | −0.46 | 0.01 | −0.13 | −0.04 | −0.03 | −0.15 | −0.05 | 0.01 | 0.01 | 0.00 |
| 29 | Air transport | −3.78 | −6.14 | −1.26 | −0.74 | −1.01 | −0.21 | −0.31 | −0.53 | −0.11 | 0.00 | 0.01 | 0.00 |
| 30 | Miscellanous Transport and postal services | −9.14 | −21.85 | −14.06 | −1.36 | −2.83 | −1.78 | −0.76 | −1.98 | −1.28 | 0.02 | 0.09 | 0.06 |
| 31 | Information and communications | −52.45 | −114.78 | −59.26 | −9.72 | −18.00 | −9.47 | −4.10 | −9.85 | −5.05 | 0.00 | 0.30 | 0.14 |
| 32 | Public administration | −4.14 | −7.50 | −4.13 | −0.85 | −1.45 | −0.80 | −0.39 | −0.68 | −0.37 | 0.00 | 0.01 | 0.00 |

(continued)

**Table 10.4** (continued)

| | | Aichi Pref. Total | | | Nagoya City | | | Toyohashi City | | | Nishio City | | |
|---|---|---|---|---|---|---|---|---|---|---|---|---|---|
| | | Consumption | Production | Value added | Consumption | Production | Value added | Consumption | Production | Value added | Consumption | Production | Value added |
| 33 | Education and research | −85.06 | −105.10 | −83.59 | −21.80 | −24.38 | −19.64 | −5.08 | −6.92 | −5.44 | −0.44 | −0.36 | −0.30 |
| 34 | Medical, health care and welfare | −64.77 | −78.56 | −52.31 | −13.95 | −15.74 | −11.07 | −4.40 | −5.67 | −3.65 | −0.32 | −0.26 | −0.21 |
| 35 | Miscellaneous non-profit services | 32.58 | 26.96 | 15.98 | 12.42 | 11.70 | 6.93 | 1.13 | 0.60 | 0.36 | 0.48 | 0.51 | 0.30 |
| 36 | Business services | −7.69 | −100.05 | −59.23 | 0.29 | −12.21 | −7.44 | −0.99 | −9.60 | −5.65 | 0.10 | 0.59 | 0.34 |
| 37 | Hotels | −0.53 | −3.34 | −1.60 | 1.27 | 0.88 | 0.42 | −0.37 | −0.62 | −0.30 | 0.11 | 0.13 | 0.06 |
| 38 | Eating and drinking services | −42.37 | −61.19 | −26.35 | −3.67 | −6.31 | −2.72 | −4.31 | −6.01 | −2.59 | 0.43 | 0.51 | 0.22 |
| 39 | Amusement and recreational services | 3.18 | −4.19 | −2.90 | 4.49 | 3.58 | 2.46 | −0.68 | −1.37 | −0.95 | 0.33 | 0.37 | 0.26 |
| 40 | Personal services | −33.69 | −48.64 | −33.82 | −3.61 | −5.69 | −3.97 | −3.04 | −4.39 | −3.05 | 0.19 | 0.25 | 0.17 |
| 41 | Office supplies | 0.00 | −2.07 | 0.00 | 0.00 | −0.25 | 0.00 | 0.00 | −0.19 | 0.00 | 0.00 | 0.01 | 0.00 |
| 42 | Activities not elsewhere classified | 0.00 | −9.60 | −3.83 | 0.00 | −1.92 | −0.76 | 0.00 | −0.81 | −0.32 | 0.00 | 0.03 | 0.01 |

*Source* Created by the author

in many municipalities will decrease because of a reduction in population and households. The total consumption of all municipalities in the Higashi-mikawa area has decreased. In the mountainous part of the Higashi-mikawa area and the southern part of the Chita area, it has decreased significantly. For the Owari area, it has increased in Nagoya City and some of the surrounding municipalities; however, in other municipalities, it has decreased. In many municipalities in the Nishi-mikawa area, where the manufacturing industry is thriving, consumption will increase as the population and households increase.

As for the ripple effect of the change in future consumption, we selected three representative cities from 54 municipalities and Aichi Prefecture as a whole. In the cases of Nagoya City and Toyohashi City, where consumption has decreased, the amount of induced value-added in other municipalities has also decreased. However, in the case of Nishio City, where the population is expected to increase, other municipalities will be affected by the increase in value-added.

Although, when the value-added of each region is divided according to the origin received from other regions, there is a positive impact from the population-increasing region and a negative impact from the population-declining region. Because of this interregional interdependence, the influence of the latter is stronger than that of the former, and the value-added of most municipalities will decrease.

Regarding the impact of each sector, the value-added will reduce in a wide range of sectors, such as commerce, real estate, education and research, information and communications, business services, medical, health care, and welfare, finance and insurance, beverages and food, personal services, as well as eating and dining services.

Although consumer expenditure in the Nishi-mikawa area is in a relatively advantageous position, it will not decrease, and for the time being, their production and value-added will decrease, considering the interdependence between municipalities. Therefore, it is necessary to consider and prepare measures to mitigate the impact of the decline in consumption demand on the local economy.

Here, we estimated the consumption amount by sector for 2015 and 2040 based on the consumption expenditure by item in the 2014 NSFIE and used the economic structure represented by the 2011 inter-municipal IOT of Aichi Prefecture. The spillover effect was calculated based on the assumption that the input structure and commuting patterns are invariant. We did not adjust the price changes for the data at different time points. The use of the latest IOT of 2015 and the adjustment of price valuation remain future issues.

## References

Adachi, Makiko. 2004. Impact of declining birthrate and aging population on household sector. *Mizuho Soken Ronshu* (Review of Mizuho Research Institute), pp. 1–35 (in Japanese).

Japan Federation of Economic Organizations. 2008. *How should the economy and society respond to population decline?* (in Japanese). https://www.keidanren.or.jp/japanese/policy/2008/073.pdf

Mo, Tetsuo, and Norikazu Ida. 2013a. Impact of changes in population structure on consumption expenditure structure -nationwide and Osaka. *SanKaiken Ronshu (The Economic and Business Review)* 25: 23–35 (in Japanese).

Mo, Tetsuo, and Norikazu Ida. 2013b. Economic impact of aging population and declining birthrate: Demand-side analysis using the inter-regional input-output table. *Momoyama Gakuin University Review of Economics and Business* 55 (1–2): 195–224 (in Japanese).

Mo, Tetsuo, and Norikazu Ida. 2014. Economic impact of aging population and declining birthrate: Demand-side analysis using the 'Osaka Prefectural Input-Output Table'. SanKaiken Ronshu (*The Economic and Business Review*) 26: 17–30 (in Japanese).

Wada, Kenichi. 2018. Economic forecast for 2030 based on Fukushima prefectural input-output analysis–From the perspective of decreasing consumption due to the aging population and declining birthrate. *Fukushima no Shinro (Perspective of Fukushima)*, 31–40. Toho Area Research Institute (in Japanese).

# Chapter 11
# The Impact of Automobile Electrification on the Regional Economy

## 11.1 Introduction

The automobile industry is one of the most important industries in both Japan and Aichi Prefecture. According to a 2019 report by the JAMA,[1] the automobile industry produced 9.96 million units (including exports of 4.71 million units) in 2017, had a shipping income of 60.7 trillion yen (including exports of 16.7 trillion yen), employed 5.46 million people, and invested capital of 1.3 trillion yen.

Aichi Prefecture has many automobile and automotive parts businesses, including Toyota Motor Corporation. Toyota is concentrated in the municipalities surrounding Toyota City. The future of regional production in those municipalities will be greatly affected by the future production of the automobile industry.

The current trend in the automobile industry is toward so-called "CASE" technologies (i.e., connected, autonomous, shared, and electrified capabilities), because of which the industrial structure may change significantly (METI, New Automobile Strategy Conference, 2018). Meanwhile, global environmental issues, especially efforts to reduce greenhouse gas emissions, have become one of the most critical issues for the industry in the long term. To address such environmental issues while maintaining economic growth and global competitiveness, it is important not only to use fossil fuels efficiently but also to reduce carbon usage by replacing such fuels with other energies. The electrification of automobiles is one of the solutions to this problem, and several types of next-generation vehicles have begun to spread.

Input–output analysis of next-generation vehicles includes Shibusawa and Sugawara (2011), Osawa and Nakano (2015), Chubu Region Institute for Social and Economic Research (2015), Kimura (2019), and Mase (2019).

Shibusawa and Sugawara (2011) focused on the spread of HEVs and EVs, considering the differences in their input structures. They analyzed the nationwide and

[1] The Japan Automobile Manufacturers Association.

 
M. Yamada, *Multi-Regional Input–Output Analysis of the Japanese Economy*,
https://doi.org/10.1007/978-981-97-9041-8_11

international impact using the IOTs, national and regional data of the METI, and international data of the Institute of Developing Economies.

The Chubu Region Institute for Social and Economic Research (2015) and Kimura (2019) also focused on four passenger cars, including PHVs and FCVs, and analyzed the impact on the nine prefectures of the Chubu region. They estimated the differences in the input structure of next-generation vehicles based on the unit price of each key component and conducted a comparative analysis of the interdependence between prefectures.

Mase (2019) used the national IOT of Japan to study the effects of differences in input structures on the induced production of each sector for HEVs, PHVs, and EVs. In particular, he compared the effects of Japanese and overseas procurement of batteries for EVs.

Osawa and Nakano (2015) estimated the input structure for 24 types of next-generation vehicles, focusing on passenger cars as well as trucks and buses, and estimated the economic ripple effect based on a national updated IOT.

In this chapter, referring to the research of the Chubu Region Institute for Social and Economic Research (2015) and Kimura (2019), we revised part of the input structure estimation of their research for four next-generation passenger cars. We also used the newly estimated 2011 inter-municipal IOT of Aichi Prefecture to focus on how the diffusion of next-generation vehicles will affect the production of municipal economies in Aichi Prefecture, based on a comparative analysis between 2017 and 2030.

In the next section, we discuss the features of next-generation vehicles. The third section presents the input–output models and data. The impact analysis on municipalities in Aichi Prefecture is described in the fourth section. Finally, in Sect. 11.5, we summarize the results.

## 11.2 Diffusion of Next-Generation Automobiles

Among the next-generation vehicles that should gradually replace conventional vehicles, those that share the common feature of "electrification" are HEVs, PHVs, EVs, and FCVs.

The core technologies for the electrification of vehicles (see Fig. 11.1) are a motor, a battery, and a power control unit. An HEV combines those technologies with an internal combustion engine. A PHV adds a charger to enable electric power driving. Conversely, an EV runs on electric power stored in a battery by charging and has no internal combustion engine, while an FCV includes a fuel cell stack and a hydrogen tank and runs on electric power generated from hydrogen and oxygen. Of course, several types of vehicles have their own technological challenges, and thus, a simple replacement of one type of part for another is not enough from an engineering perspective. However, by changing unique units with electrified technology as the core, electrification can be applied to various next-generation vehicles to evaluate the impact on the local economy.

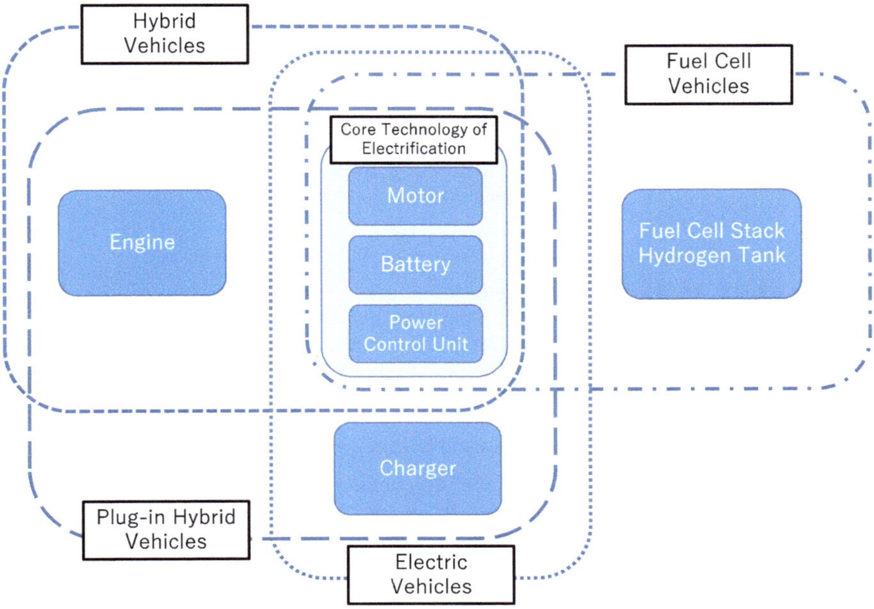


**Fig. 11.1** Core technologies for the electrification of automobiles. *Source* Created by the author, referring to the website of the Toyota Motor Corporation

As depicted in Table 11.1, next-generation vehicles (METI, Strategic Conference for the New Era of Automobiles, 2018) are the target of diffusion; their share should increase to 50–70% of all vehicles by 2030. Among them, HEVs account for 30–40%, EVs and PHVs together account for 20–30%, and hydrogen FCVs account for 3%. In this table, clean diesel vehicles are also included in next-generation vehicles, and their rate is assumed to be 5–10%.

Electrification of automobiles causes changes in components, as indicated in Table 11.2. Parts commonly required for electrification are motors, batteries, and

**Table 11.1** Diffusion targets of next-generation vehicles

| | 2017(million units) | (%) | 2030 (%) |
|---|---|---|---|
| Conventional vehicles | 280.6 | 63.97 | 30–50 |
| Next-generation vehicles | 158.0 | 36.02 | 50–70 |
| Hybrid vehicles | 137.0 | 31.2 | 30–40 |
| Electric vehicles | 1.8 | 0.41 | 20–30 |
| Plug-in hybrid vehicles | 3.6 | 0.82 | |
| Fuel cell vehicles | 0.0849 | 0.02 | 3 |
| Clean diesel vehicles | 15.4 | 3.52 | 5–10 |

*Sources* Compiled from METI, Strategic Conference on New Era of Vehicles (2018)

**Table 11.2** Automotive parts affected by electronic control and electrification

| | |
|---|---|
| Parts required for electrification | Motor and battery parts<br>Lithium-ion battery, Drive motor, Inverter, DC-DC converter |
| Unnecessary parts for EV or FCV | Engine parts<br>Engine parts, Valve train parts, Fuel parts, Intake and exhaust system components, Engine electrical components |
| | Transmission parts<br>Clutch cover, Clutch disc, Transmission unit |
| Parts that could be replaced | Body parts<br>Body outer plate (aluminum, CFRP), Backdoor sunroof<br>Headlamp (camera and sensor integrated)<br>Door mirror (electronic)<br>Bumper (millimeter wave radar compatible)<br>Front grille (for millimeter wave radar)<br>Windshield (for telematics) |

*Source* Quoted from Sumitomo Mitsui Banking Corporation (2017)

power control units, such as inverters. Compared to a conventional car that runs on only an engine, such core parts are added with the new intermediate demand for electrified vehicles.

Meanwhile, EVs are equipped with large-capacity batteries and high-powered motors, while FCVs are equipped with fuel cell stacks and hydrogen tanks. Additionally, because an internal combustion engine, engine parts, and transmission parts are not required, demand for automotive parts will decrease. This change in the input structure in automobile production is induced by the electrification of vehicles.

Even next-generation vehicles have different configurations of required core parts, and thus, depending on which type of vehicle becomes more widespread in the future, the required intermediate goods will differ and will increase or decrease.

## 11.3 Model and Data

### *11.3.1 Input–Output Model*

In this subsection, we discuss the framework of an input–output model to analyze what effect the diffusion of next-generation vehicles will have on automobile production in municipal economies. Therefore, we consider four types of next-generation vehicles: HEVs, PHVs, EVs, and FCVs, and we analyze the changes in their purchase share.

Table 11.3, top half, presents an IOT for a region. Imports and exports are ignored for simplicity. We divided the industry into two sectors—automotive and others—denoted as "automobile" and "industry," respectively. On the one hand, automobiles are represented as separate activities, as in Table 11.3, to consider the production of the four types of next-generation automobiles as well as conventional vehicles and to show that the input structure required for production of each type is different. On the other hand, various automobiles have the same uses and can be represented by one section. The supply–demand balance formula for goods and services in the IOT considering the next-generation vehicles in Table 3b is expressed as follows:

$$\begin{bmatrix} \mathbf{A_{11}} & \mathbf{a_{10}} & \mathbf{a_{11}} & \mathbf{a_{12}} & \mathbf{a_{13}} & \mathbf{a_{14}} \\ \mathbf{A_{21}} & \mathbf{a_{20}} & \mathbf{a_{21}} & \mathbf{a_{22}} & \mathbf{a_{23}} & \mathbf{a_{24}} \end{bmatrix} \begin{bmatrix} \mathbf{X_1} \\ \mathbf{x_0} \\ \mathbf{x_1} \\ \mathbf{x_2} \\ \mathbf{x_3} \\ \mathbf{x_4} \end{bmatrix} + \begin{bmatrix} \mathbf{F_1} \\ \mathbf{F_2} \end{bmatrix} = \begin{bmatrix} \mathbf{X_1} \\ \mathbf{X_2} \end{bmatrix} \tag{11.1}$$

However, as the total production of various vehicles is equal to the production of vehicles,

$$\mathbf{x_0}+\mathbf{x_1}+\mathbf{x_2}+\mathbf{x_3}+\mathbf{x_4} = \mathbf{X_2} \tag{11.2}$$

Then, expressing the production share of each vehicle as $z_i = \mathbf{x_i} \Big/ \sum_j \mathbf{x_j}$, we obtain

$$(z_0+z_1+z_2+z_3+z_4)\left(\sum_j \mathbf{x_j}\right) = \mathbf{X_2} \tag{11.3}$$

**Table 11.3** Treatment of next-generation vehicles in the regional input–output table

*(a) Ordinal input–output table*

| | Industry | Automobile | Final demand | Total output |
|---|---|---|---|---|
| Industry | $\mathbf{A_{11}X_1}$ | $\mathbf{A_{12}X_2}$ | $\mathbf{F_1}$ | $\mathbf{X_1}$ |
| Automobile | $\mathbf{A_{21}X_1}$ | $\mathbf{A_{22}X_2}$ | $\mathbf{F_2}$ | $\mathbf{X_2}$ |
| Value-added | $\mathbf{V_1}$ | $\mathbf{V_2}$ | | |
| Total input | $\mathbf{X_1}$ | $\mathbf{X_2}$ | | |

*(b) Input–output table considering next-generation vehicle*

| | Industry | Conventional vehicle | Hybrid vehicles | Plug-in hybrid vehicles | Electric vehicles | Fuel cell vehicles | Final demand | Total output |
|---|---|---|---|---|---|---|---|---|
| Industry | $\mathbf{A_{11}X_1}$ | $\mathbf{a_{10}x_0}$ | $\mathbf{a_{11}x_1}$ | $\mathbf{a_{12}x_2}$ | $\mathbf{a_{13}x_3}$ | $\mathbf{a_{14}x_4}$ | $\mathbf{F_1}$ | $\mathbf{X_1}$ |
| Automobile | $\mathbf{A_{21}X_1}$ | $\mathbf{a_{20}x_0}$ | $\mathbf{a_{21}x_1}$ | $\mathbf{a_{22}x_2}$ | $\mathbf{a_{23}x_3}$ | $\mathbf{a_{24}x_4}$ | $\mathbf{F_2}$ | $\mathbf{X_2}$ |
| Value added | $\mathbf{V_1}$ | $\mathbf{v_0}$ | $\mathbf{v_1}$ | $\mathbf{v_2}$ | $\mathbf{v_3}$ | $\mathbf{v_4}$ | | |
| Total input | $\mathbf{X_1}$ | $\mathbf{x_0}$ | $\mathbf{x_1}$ | $\mathbf{x_2}$ | $\mathbf{x_3}$ | $\mathbf{x_4}$ | | |

*Source* Prepared by the author

Equation (11.4) presents the input coefficient vector of the automobile sector as the weighted average of each vehicle's input coefficient vectors.

$$\begin{bmatrix} \mathbf{a}_{10} \\ \mathbf{a}_{20} \end{bmatrix} z_0 + \begin{bmatrix} \mathbf{a}_{11} \\ \mathbf{a}_{21} \end{bmatrix} z_1 + \begin{bmatrix} \mathbf{a}_{12} \\ \mathbf{a}_{22} \end{bmatrix} z_2 + \begin{bmatrix} \mathbf{a}_{13} \\ \mathbf{a}_{23} \end{bmatrix} z_3 + \begin{bmatrix} \mathbf{a}_{14} \\ \mathbf{a}_{24} \end{bmatrix} z_4 = \begin{bmatrix} \mathbf{A}_{12} \\ \mathbf{A}_{22} \end{bmatrix} \tag{11.4}$$

Then, we obtain the symmetric input-output model as the following Eq. (11.5) by substituting Eq. (11.4) with Eq. (11.1).[2]

$$\begin{bmatrix} \mathbf{A}_{11} & \mathbf{A}_{12} \\ \mathbf{A}_{21} & \mathbf{A}_{22} \end{bmatrix} \begin{bmatrix} \mathbf{X}_1 \\ \mathbf{X}_2 \end{bmatrix} + \begin{bmatrix} \mathbf{F}_1 \\ \mathbf{F}_2 \end{bmatrix} = \begin{bmatrix} \mathbf{X}_1 \\ \mathbf{X}_2 \end{bmatrix} \tag{11.5}$$

Then, the production induced by the final demand is obtained as follows:

$$\begin{bmatrix} \mathbf{X}_1 \\ \mathbf{X}_2 \end{bmatrix} = \begin{bmatrix} \mathbf{I} - \mathbf{A}_{11} & -\mathbf{A}_{12} \\ -\mathbf{A}_{21} & \mathbf{I} - \mathbf{A}_{22} \end{bmatrix}^{-1} \begin{bmatrix} \mathbf{F}_1 \\ \mathbf{F}_2 \end{bmatrix} = \begin{bmatrix} \mathbf{B}_{11} & \mathbf{B}_{12} \\ \mathbf{B}_{21} & \mathbf{B}_{22} \end{bmatrix} \begin{bmatrix} \mathbf{F}_1 \\ \mathbf{F}_2 \end{bmatrix} \tag{11.6}$$

Here, the production share of type-$i$ vehicle at time 0 (before diffusion) and time 1 (after diffusion) is expressed as $z_i^0$ and $z_i^1$, respectively. The input coefficient vector of the automobile sector at time 0 is expressed as Eq. (11.7).

$$\begin{bmatrix} \mathbf{a}_{10}^0 \\ \mathbf{a}_{20}^0 \end{bmatrix} z_0^0 + \begin{bmatrix} \mathbf{a}_{11}^0 \\ \mathbf{a}_{21}^0 \end{bmatrix} z_1^0 + \begin{bmatrix} \mathbf{a}_{12}^0 \\ \mathbf{a}_{22}^0 \end{bmatrix} z_2^0 + \begin{bmatrix} \mathbf{a}_{13}^0 \\ \mathbf{a}_{23}^0 \end{bmatrix} z_3^0 + \begin{bmatrix} \mathbf{a}_{14}^0 \\ \mathbf{a}_{24}^0 \end{bmatrix} z_4^0 = \begin{bmatrix} \mathbf{A}_{21}^0 \\ \mathbf{A}_{22}^0 \end{bmatrix} \tag{11.7}$$

Then, the production induced from the final demand of time 0, $\mathbf{F}_2^0$, which represents the purchases of various vehicle types, is obtained as follows:

$$\begin{bmatrix} \mathbf{X}_1^0 \\ \mathbf{X}_2^0 \end{bmatrix} = \begin{bmatrix} \mathbf{I} - \mathbf{A}_{11} & -\mathbf{A}_{21}^0 \\ -\mathbf{A}_{21} & \mathbf{I} - \mathbf{A}_{22}^0 \end{bmatrix}^{-1} \begin{bmatrix} \mathbf{0} \\ \mathbf{F}_2^0 \end{bmatrix} = \begin{bmatrix} \mathbf{B}_{11}^0 & \mathbf{B}_{12}^0 \\ \mathbf{B}_{21}^0 & \mathbf{B}_{22}^0 \end{bmatrix} \begin{bmatrix} \mathbf{0} \\ \mathbf{F}_2^0 \end{bmatrix} = \begin{bmatrix} \mathbf{B}_{12}^0 \\ \mathbf{B}_{22}^0 \end{bmatrix} \mathbf{F}_2^0 \tag{11.8}$$

In Eq. (11.7), $\mathbf{a}_{ji}^0$ shows the input coefficient of commodity $j$ in the production of type-$i$ vehicle at time 0.

The input coefficient vector of the automobile sector at time 1 is expressed as Eq. (11.9).

$$\begin{bmatrix} \mathbf{a}_{10}^1 \\ \mathbf{a}_{20}^1 \end{bmatrix} z_o^1 + \begin{bmatrix} \mathbf{a}_{11}^1 \\ \mathbf{a}_{21}^1 \end{bmatrix} z_1^1 + \begin{bmatrix} \mathbf{a}_{12}^1 \\ \mathbf{a}_{22}^1 \end{bmatrix} z_2^1 + \begin{bmatrix} \mathbf{a}_{13}^1 \\ \mathbf{a}_{23}^1 \end{bmatrix} z_3^1 + \begin{bmatrix} \mathbf{a}_{14}^1 \\ \mathbf{a}_{24}^1 \end{bmatrix} z_4^1 = \begin{bmatrix} \mathbf{A}_{21}^1 \\ \mathbf{A}_{22}^1 \end{bmatrix} \tag{11.9}$$

Then, the production induced from the final demand of time 1, $\mathbf{F}_2^1$, is obtained by Eq. (11.10).

---

[2] Input–output analysis with one product produced by multiple activities appears in Yoshioka and Suga (1997); Wan (2016); Fujikawa and Wan (2017); Yamada, Fujikawa, and Umeda (2019).

$$\begin{bmatrix} \mathbf{X}_1^1 \\ \mathbf{X}_2^1 \end{bmatrix} = \begin{bmatrix} \mathbf{I} - \mathbf{A}_{11} & -\mathbf{A}_{21}^1 \\ -\mathbf{A}_{21} & \mathbf{I} - \mathbf{A}_{22}^1 \end{bmatrix}^{-1} \begin{bmatrix} \mathbf{0} \\ \mathbf{F}_2^1 \end{bmatrix} = \begin{bmatrix} \mathbf{B}_{11}^1 & \mathbf{B}_{12}^1 \\ \mathbf{B}_{21}^1 & \mathbf{B}_{22}^1 \end{bmatrix} \begin{bmatrix} \mathbf{0} \\ \mathbf{F}_2^1 \end{bmatrix} = \begin{bmatrix} \mathbf{B}_{12}^1 \\ \mathbf{B}_{22}^1 \end{bmatrix} \mathbf{F}_2^1 \tag{11.10}$$

Here, $\mathbf{a}_{ji}^1$ shows the input coefficient of commodity $j$ in the production of type-$i$ vehicle at time 1.

Then the difference between the two induced production types, Eqs. (11.10) and (11.8), shows the effect of the diffusion of the next-generation vehicles on production, as the following Eq. (11.11):

$$\begin{bmatrix} \mathbf{X}_1^1 \\ \mathbf{X}_2^1 \end{bmatrix} - \begin{bmatrix} \mathbf{X}_1^0 \\ \mathbf{X}_2^0 \end{bmatrix} = \begin{bmatrix} \mathbf{B}_{12}^1 \\ \mathbf{B}_{22}^1 \end{bmatrix} \mathbf{F}_2^1 - \begin{bmatrix} \mathbf{B}_{12}^0 \\ \mathbf{B}_{22}^0 \end{bmatrix} \mathbf{F}_2^0 \tag{11.11}$$

Equation (11.12) shows that the effect on production is divided into two factors: the input coefficient changing effect (first term on the right-hand side of Eq. (11.12) and the final demand changing effect (second term).

$$\begin{bmatrix} \mathbf{X}_1^1 \\ \mathbf{X}_2^1 \end{bmatrix} - \begin{bmatrix} \mathbf{X}_1^0 \\ \mathbf{X}_2^0 \end{bmatrix} = \left[ \begin{bmatrix} \mathbf{B}_{12}^1 \\ \mathbf{B}_{22}^1 \end{bmatrix} - \begin{bmatrix} \mathbf{B}_{12}^0 \\ \mathbf{B}_{22}^0 \end{bmatrix} \right] \frac{\mathbf{F}_2^1 + \mathbf{F}_2^0}{2} + \frac{1}{2} \left[ \begin{bmatrix} \mathbf{B}_{12}^1 \\ \mathbf{B}_{22}^1 \end{bmatrix} + \begin{bmatrix} \mathbf{B}_{12}^0 \\ \mathbf{B}_{22}^0 \end{bmatrix} \right] \left[ \mathbf{F}_2^1 - \mathbf{F}_2^0 \right] \tag{11.12}$$

### *11.3.2 Inter-municipal Input–Output Table of Aichi Prefecture*

In this subsection, we discuss the 2001 inter-municipal IOT of Aichi Prefecture, which we have used for the analysis. In recent years, there has been interest in constructing IOTs for small regions within prefectures. Yamada (1995) and Yamada and Horiuchi (2015) constructed such an interregional IOT for Mie Prefecture, while Yamada and Owaki (2012) did so for Aichi Prefecture, and Yamada (2015) did so for Aichi, Mie, and Gifu Prefectures. Ishikawa (2004) estimated the regional IOT of Aichi Prefecture. Tsukamoto et al. (2018) estimated an inter-municipal IOT based on the 2005 Aichi prefectural IOT.

In this chapter, we use the inter-municipal IOT of 54 municipalities based on the 2011 Aichi Prefecture table in Chap. 6. This table has 55 regions, including the ROJ, 106 sectors for each region, and 5830 endogenous sectors.

Figure 11.2 geographically depicts the amount of production induced for each municipality when the final demand of the automobile sector in Toyota City increases by one unit. The value for Toyota City is 1.338 and that for the ROJ is 1.088, both of which exceed 1. In other municipalities, the impact on Nagoya City (0.173) is relatively large, followed by the adjacent Nishimikawa area (for the cities of Okazaki, it is 0.044, Anjo 0.044, Miyoshi 0.042, Nishio 0.035, Kariya 0.027, and Hekinan 0.026). There is a relatively large impact in the cities of Toyohashi (0.021) and Tahara

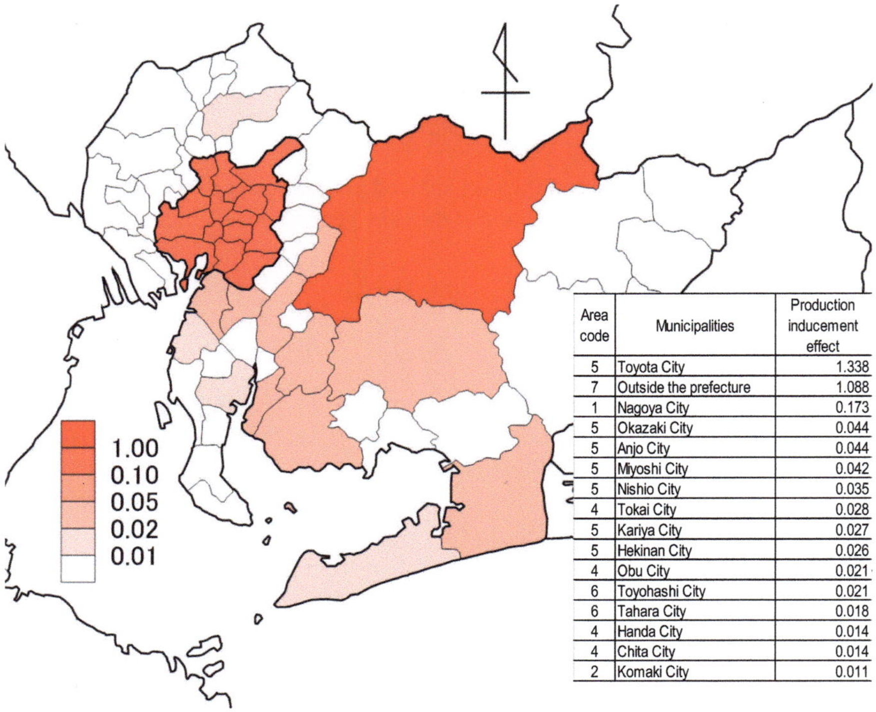


| Area code | Municipalities | Production inducement effect |
|---|---|---|
| 5 | Toyota City | 1.338 |
| 7 | Outside the prefecture | 1.088 |
| 1 | Nagoya City | 0.173 |
| 5 | Okazaki City | 0.044 |
| 5 | Anjo City | 0.044 |
| 5 | Miyoshi City | 0.042 |
| 5 | Nishio City | 0.035 |
| 4 | Tokai City | 0.028 |
| 5 | Kariya City | 0.027 |
| 5 | Hekinan City | 0.026 |
| 4 | Obu City | 0.021 |
| 6 | Toyohashi City | 0.021 |
| 6 | Tahara City | 0.018 |
| 4 | Handa City | 0.014 |
| 4 | Chita City | 0.014 |
| 2 | Komaki City | 0.011 |

**Fig. 11.2** Municipal production inducement from a one-unit increase of final demand in Toyota City's automotive sector. *Source* Created by the author, using the MANDARA supporting system for geographic information analysis (http://ktgis.net/mandara/)

(0.018) in the Higashimikawa area, while in the Chita area, there is a relatively large impact in the cities of Tokai (0.028), Obu (0.021), Handa (0.014), and Chita (0.014).[3] In the Owari area, only Komaki City (0.011) is affected.

### *11.3.3 Estimating the Input Coefficient and Final Demand of the Automobile Sector*

To measure the impact of the diffusion of next-generation vehicles on the regional economy, we calculated the difference between the amount of induced production before the diffusion (the latest data available is for 2017) and that after the diffusion (2030). We examined the diffusion of next-generation vehicles in both years and estimated the magnitude of the expected final demand for each year.

[3] See Table 6–1 for the definition of each area.

Table 11.4 presents the changes in Japanese domestic production and exports of passenger cars and their composition ratios. Until 2017, domestic sales of the four next-generation vehicles were obtained from the Next-Generation Vehicle Promotion Center website, and exports were obtained from the trade statistics of Japan's Ministry of Finance. The total number of passenger cars produced and exported was obtained from statistics published on the JAMA website, and the data for the number of conventional vehicles were obtained by subtracting the total number of next-generation vehicles from the total number of vehicles produced.

The values in 2030 were obtained from several sources. For domestic sales, Sogo Giken Co., Ltd. (2019) forecasts the number of vehicles to be sold in Japan in 2030; it projects that 4.488 million units of domestic and imported cars will be sold in 2030 compared to 4.626 million units in 2016. Based on this, we assumed that the domestic production of passenger cars in 2030 would be four million units after reducing the sale of imported cars.

As for next-generation vehicles, as indicated in Table 11.1, there is a certain range of diffusion (ratio) targets for 2030 (METI, Strategic Conference for the New Era of Automobiles, 2018). Here, the composition ratio of domestic production volume is set with reference to these values. By multiplying these composition ratios by 4 million units, the domestic production volume of each car in 2030 is obtained.

The total number of exports in 2030 is forecast to increase slightly to 4.5 million units from 2017, resulting in a total production of 8.5 million units. As automobiles will be exported to various regions of the world, from high-income regions to low-income ones, the share of next-generation vehicles in exports is likely to be lower than that in domestic ones. Here, we assume a mix of 60% of conventional vehicles and 40% of next-generation vehicles, mainly HEVs. This composition ratio is multiplied by the total number of vehicles exported in 2030 by 4.5 million units to determine the number of vehicles exported for each type.

Consequently, combined domestic production and exports are projected to yield passenger car production in Japan for 2030. The domestic electrification rate is assumed to be 70%, while the export electrification rate is 40%. The electrification rate of overall passenger car production is 54.1%.

Next, we discuss the differences in the input structure for several types of vehicles. Table 11.5 summarizes the input values for one-unit production of several types of vehicles in 2017 and 2030. In the 2011 IOT, the average purchaser price of a passenger car was 2.407 million yen. Thus, in this study, the unit price of a conventional car is set at 2.4 million yen. HEVs are assumed to cost 0.3 million yen more than conventional vehicles, and PHVs 0.6 million yen more. Meanwhile, the price of EVs is 3.25 million yen and that of FCVs is 7.26 million yen, based on their catalog prices.[4]

Next, for conventional automobiles, the producer price is obtained by considering the commercial margin and transportation cost of passenger cars in the 2011 IOT. Each input value to produce the passenger car is calculated by multiplying the input coefficient of the sector with the unit price. Although several types of next-generation

[4] The prices of EVs and FCVs are determined based on the selling price of Nissan Leaf and Toyota Mirai, respectively.

**Table 11.4** Changes in domestic production and export of passenger cars and their composition ratio

| Domestic use | Volume of production (thousand) | | | | Share (%) | | | |
|---|---|---|---|---|---|---|---|---|
| | 2011 | 2015 | 2017 | 2030 | 2011 | 2015 | 2017 | 2030 |
| EV | 3.2 | 13.8 | 24.1 | 600.0 | 0.4 | 0.4 | 0.6 | 15.0 |
| PHV | 3.8 | 15.0 | 34.1 | 600.0 | 0.1 | 0.1 | 0.8 | 15.0 |
| FCV | – | 0.5 | 0.7 | 80.0 | 0.0 | 0.0 | 0.0 | 2.0 |
| HEV | 633.4 | 1,144.5 | 1,380.1 | 1,520.0 | 19.6 | 29.6 | 33.4 | 38.0 |
| Sub-total | 650.4 | 1,173.9 | 1,439.0 | 2,800.0 | 20.1 | 30.4 | 34.8 | 70.0 |
| Conventional | 2,578.2 | 2.686.9 | 2,690.4 | 1,200.0 | 79.9 | 69.6 | 65.2 | 30.0 |
| Total | 3,228.6 | 3,860.7 | 4,129.4 | 4,000.0 | 100.0 | 100.0 | 100.0 | 100.0 |
| Exports | Volume of production (thousand) | | | | Share (%) | | | |
| | 2011 | 2015 | 2017 | 2030 | 2011 | 2015 | 2017 | 2030 |
| EV | 2.4 | 4.7 | 6.9 | 180.0 | 0.1 | 0.1 | 0.2 | 4.0 |
| PHV | 6.5 | 26.1 | 59.3 | 225.0 | 0.2 | 0.7 | 1.4 | 5.0 |
| FCV | – | 0.0 | 0.0 | 45.0 | 0.0 | 0.0 | 0.0 | 1.0 |
| HEV | 195.7 | 353.6 | 426.3 | 1,350.0 | 5.0 | 8.9 | 10.1 | 30.0 |
| Sub-total | 204.6 | 384.3 | 492.5 | 1,800.0 | 5.2 | 9.7 | 11.7 | 40.0 |
| Conventional | 3,725.3 | 3,585.7 | 3,725.9 | 2,700.0 | 94.8 | 90.3 | 88.3 | 60.0 |
| Total | 3,929.9 | 3,970.0 | 4,218.4 | 4,500.0 | 100.0 | 100.0 | 100.0 | 100.0 |
| Domestic Use and Exports | Volume of production (thousand) | | | | Share (%) | | | |
| | 2011 | 2015 | 2017 | 2030 | 2011 | 2015 | 2017 | 2030 |
| EV | 15.6 | 18.5 | 31.0 | 780.0 | 0.2 | 0.2 | 0.4 | 9.2 |
| PHV | 10.3 | 41.1 | 93.4 | 825.0 | 0.1 | 0.5 | 1.1 | 9.7 |
| FCV | - | 0.5 | 0.7 | 125.0 | 0.0 | 0.0 | 0.0 | 1.5 |
| HEV | 829.1 | 1,498.1 | 1,806.5 | 2,870.0 | 11.6 | 19.9 | 21.6 | 33.8 |
| Sub-total | 855.0 | 1,558.2 | 1,931.5 | 4,600.0 | 11.9 | 80.1 | 23.1 | 54.1 |
| Conventional | 6,303.5 | 6,272.5 | 6,416.3 | 3,900.0 | 88.1 | 80.1 | 76.9 | 45.9 |
| Total | 7,158.5 | 7,830.7 | 8,347.8 | 8,500.0 | 100.0 | 100.0 | 100.0 | 100.0 |

*Source* Values up to 2017 are compiled by the author based on statistics published on the Next-Generation Automobile Progress Center website and the JAMA website. The value for 2030 has been estimated by the author

vehicles are common in terms of electrification, they differ in fuel used and whether an internal combustion engine is present. Such characteristics are reflected in their input structures. Table 11.5 presents the input values for the unit production of each type of vehicle for the sectors whose characteristics are represented among the 106 sectors in the analysis. The inputs of the other sectors for next-generation vehicles are assumed to be the same as those of conventional vehicles.

The Chubu Region Institute for Social and Economic Research (2015) estimated the unit price of characteristic automotive parts for next-generation vehicles in 2013

**Table 11.5** Input costs for various vehicle types (unit: million yen)

| | 2017 | | | | | 2030 | | | | |
|---|---|---|---|---|---|---|---|---|---|---|
| | Conventional | HEV | PHV | EV | FCV | Conventional | HEV | PHV | EV | FCV |
| Miscellaneous ceramic, stone, and clay products | 0.0030 | 0.0030 | 0.0030 | 0.0030 | 0.7030 | 0.0030 | 0.0030 | 0.0030 | 0.0030 | 0.2000 |
| Miscellaneous electronic components | 0.0000 | 0.0037 | 0.0037 | 0.0037 | 0.0037 | 0.0000 | 0.0037 | 0.0037 | 0.0037 | 0.0037 |
| Electrical devices and parts | 0.0343 | 0.1646 | 0.1646 | 0.1036 | 0.1096 | 0.0343 | 0.1646 | 0.1646 | 0.1036 | 0.1096 |
| Applied electronic equipment and electric measuring instruments | 0.0000 | 0.0087 | 0.0110 | 0.0094 | 0.0094 | 0.0000 | 0.0087 | 0.0110 | 0.0094 | 0.0094 |
| Miscellaneous electrical machinery | 0.0239 | 0.1077 | 0.3057 | 0.8239 | 2.3077 | 0.0239 | 0.0269 | 0.1049 | 0.4239 | 0.4669 |
| Motor vehicle parts and accessories | 0.8894 | 0.8983 | 0.8983 | 0.6504 | 0.6504 | 0.8894 | 0.8983 | 0.8983 | 0.6504 | 0.6504 |
| Other intermediate sectors | 0.4837 | 0.4837 | 0.4837 | 0.4837 | 0.4837 | 0.4837 | 0.4837 | 0.4837 | 0.4837 | 0.4837 |
| Total of Intermediate inputs | 1.4342 | 1.6696 | 1.8699 | 2.0776 | 4.2674 | 1.4342 | 1.5888 | 1.6691 | 1.6776 | 1.9236 |
| Gross value added | 0.2148 | 0.1856 | 0.3975 | 0.1555 | 0.7209 | 0.2148 | 0.2320 | 0.3921 | 0.2806 | 0.3782 |
| Domestic production at producer's price | 1.6490 | 1.8551 | 2.2674 | 2.2330 | 4.9883 | 1.6490 | 1.8208 | 2.0613 | 1.9582 | 2.3018 |
| Domestic production at purchaser's price | 2.4000 | 2.7000 | 3.3000 | 3.2500 | 7.2600 | 2.4000 | 2.6500 | 3.0000 | 2.8500 | 3.3500 |

*Source* Prepared by the author

and 2030, then aggregated them into the corresponding sections of the IOT and calculated the input. The values in Table 11.5 are essentially the same as these estimates, with several revisions for new information that subsequently became available.

Table 11.6 depicts the information on costs of batteries, fuel cells, and hydrogen storage systems in 2017 and 2030, extracted from the Sumitomo Mitsui Banking Corporation (2017), METI, New Automotive Strategies Meeting (2018), and METI Hydrogen and Fuel Cell Strategy Council (2019). In 2017, engine and related parts accounted for 27.6% of domestic shipments of auto parts for assembling manufacturers, and we assume in this study that the automotive parts for EVs and FCVs will be reduced by this proportion. This cost information is reflected in the inputs, and the purchaser price in 2030 is assumed to reflect the reduction in major costs in Table 5.

By multiplying the production and export volumes of various vehicles in Table 11.4 by each unit cost and the producer prices of the corresponding vehicles in Table 11.5, the production values, export values, and input values were obtained for each vehicle. In the following, we undertake two simulations. The first case involves sales and production only for the domestic market in Japan for 2017 and 2030, as indicated in Table 11.7. The second simulation considers not only domestic sales and production but also exports. Table 11.7 summarizes the production value and input structure of the two simulations; the left side is Case 1, and the right side is Case 2.

In Case 1, domestic sales and production in the automotive sector were 7131.3 billion yen in 2017 and 7342.3 billion yen in 2030, an increase of 211 billion yen. The commercial margin and transportation costs are 3247.7 billion yen and 3343.7 billion yen, respectively, giving the domestic product at the purchaser's price of 10,379 billion yen and 10,686 billion yen. In Case 2, exports were added to Case 1. The production value of the automobile sector was 14,216.1 billion yen in 2017 and 15,172.5 billion yen in 2030. However, the commercial margin and transportation cost are assumed only for the domestic market and are the same as in Case 1.

Electrification of automobiles increases the input of parts related to the core technology of electrification, but it does not require an internal combustion engine to

**Table 11.6** Cost changes of batteries, fuel cell systems, and hydrogen storage for next-generation vehicles

| Type of vehicle | HEV | | PHV | | EV | | FCV | |
|---|---|---|---|---|---|---|---|---|
| Year | 2017 | 2030 | 2017 | 2030 | 2017 | 2030 | 2017 | 2030 |
| Price of battery (10,000 yen/kWh) | 2.7 | 1 | 2.7 | 1 | 2.7 | 1 | 2.7 | 1 |
| Storage capacity (kWh) | | 1.3 | | 8.8 | | 40 | | 1.3 |
| Cost of battery (10,000 yen) | 4 | 1 | 23.8 | 8.8 | 108 | 40 | 4 | 1 |
| Fuel cell system (10,000 yen) | – | – | – | – | – | – | 220 | 44 |
| Hydrogen storage system (10,000 yen) | – | – | – | – | – | – | 70 | 20 |

*Source* The relevant information is extracted from Sumitomo Mitsui Banking Corporation (2017), METI, Automotive New Era Strategy Conference (2018), and METI, Hydrogen and Fuel Cell Strategy Council (2019)

**Table 11.7** Assumed input value for the automobile sector (unit: billion yen, %)

| | Case 1 | | | | Case 2 | | | |
|---|---|---|---|---|---|---|---|---|
| | 2017 | 2030 | Difference | Changing rate | 2017 | 2030 | Difference | Changing rate |
| Miscellaneous ceramic, stone and clay products | 12.9 | 27.8 | 14.9 | 0.14 | 25.6 | 50.2 | 24.6 | 0.14 |
| Miscellaneous electronic components | 5.3 | 10.3 | 5.0 | 0.05 | 7.2 | 17.0 | 9.8 | 0.06 |
| Electrical devices and parts | 327.5 | 461.0 | 133.5 | 1.29 | 535.8 | 836.3 | 300.5 | 1.72 |
| Applied electronic equipment and electric measuring instruments | 12.6 | 26.2 | 13.6 | 0.13 | 17.1 | 42.5 | 25.4 | 0.15 |
| Miscellaneous electrical machinery | 244.7 | 424.2 | 179.5 | 1.73 | 403.4 | 646.0 | 242.6 | 1.39 |
| Motor vehicle parts and accessories | 3,679.3 | 3,413.9 | −265.4 | −2.56 | 7,433.8 | 7,376.3 | −57.5 | −0.33 |
| Other intermediate sectors | 1,997.2 | 1,934.7 | −62.6 | −0.60 | 4,037.5 | 4,111.1 | 73.6 | 0.42 |
| Total of Intermediate inputs | 6,279.6 | 6,298.0 | 18.4 | 0.18 | 12,460.4 | 13,079.4 | 619.0 | 3.54 |
| Gross value added | 851.7 | 1,044.3 | 192.5 | 1.85 | 1,755.8 | 2,093.1 | 337.3 | 1.93 |
| Domestic production at producer's price | 7,131.3 | 7,342.3 | 210.9 | 2.03 | 14,216.1 | 15,172.5 | 956.4 | 5.48 |
| Trade margins and transportation charges | 3,247.7 | 3,343.7 | 96.1 | 0.93 | 3,247.7 | 3,343.7 | 96.1 | 0.55 |
| Domestic production at purchaser's price | 10,379.0 | 10,686.0 | 307.0 | 2.96 | 17,463.8 | 18,516.3 | 1,052.4 | 6.03 |

*Source* Prepared by the author

produce EVs and FCVs, which reduces the input of automobile components. This tendency is observed, especially in Case 1.

However, an increase in final demand leads to an increase in the input of various goods and services required for automobile production, which results in expanding production. This tendency is remarkable in Case 2 and is expected to delay the spread of electrifying passenger cars exported compared to domestic use.

To analyze the impact of the electrification of automobiles on the regional economy, we used an inter-municipal IOT for Aichi Prefecture. When conducting a simulation analysis based on the assumptions in Table 11.7, there remains the problem of regional allocation of the final demand assumed. Here, sales of passenger cars for the domestic market are allocated to each municipality based on the (supplying and producing) regional composition ratio of the automobile sector in the final demand of the inter-municipal IOT. Regarding commercial margins and transportation costs, retail margins are allocated according to the municipalities that purchase automobiles, and wholesale margins and transportation costs are allocated in proportion to the regionally allocated automobile demand. In addition, export value is apportioned based on the export composition ratio of the automobile sector in each municipality.

## 11.4 Impact on Municipal Economies

Case 1 focuses on the domestic market, assuming that the electrification rate of passenger cars is 70% in 2030, of which 15% comprises EVs and 2% FCVs, which do not require an internal combustion engine. The production value of the automobile sector is projected to increase by 210.9 billion yen, from 7131.3 billion yen in 2017 to 7342.3 billion yen in 2030. Production in 2030 will increase by 2.96% from that in 2017.

The impact on the regional economy is the result of combining the increasing effect of the final demand and the shift effect of the input structure due to the diffusion of electrification. Even though demand is derived from the expansion of automobile demand, if demand for automobile parts related to internal combustion engine production declines greatly due to electrification in regions with a high production share, regional production may possibly decrease there.

Table 11.8 shows the impact of electrified vehicles on the municipal economy for Case 1. The top four rows of the table indicate the total final demand and its total production-induced value, which is broken down to the production-induced value in the ROJ and Aichi Prefecture. The regional breakdown of Aichi Prefecture follows downward. The next six are divided into six areas in Aichi Prefecture. Lines 11 and below present the effect of the top 30 out of 54 municipalities in 2017 with the highest production in Aichi Prefecture.

The first two columns of Table 11.8 are the production-induced values in 2017 and 2030. The third column is the difference between the two. The fourth and fifth columns show the effects of the input coefficient changing factor and the final demand

**Table 11.8** Impact of the spread of electrified vehicles on the municipal economy (Case 1)

| Case 1 | | (1) 2017 production-induced value (billion yen) | (1) 2030 production-induced value (billion yen) | (3) 2017–2030 difference (billion yen) | (4) Input coef-ficient changing effect (billion yen) | (5) Final demand changing effect (billion yen) | (6) Ratio (=(3)/(1): %) | (7) Ratio (=(4)/(1): %) | (8) Ratio (=(5)/(1): %) |
|---|---|---|---|---|---|---|---|---|---|
| | Final demand, total | 10,379.0 | 10,686.0 | 307.0 | – | – | 2.96 | – | – |
| | Production-induced value, total | 26,633.1 | 26,756.6 | 123.5 | −654.7 | 778.2 | 0.46 | −2.46 | 2.92 |
| | (Multiplier) | 2.57 | 2.50 | | | | | | |
| | Rest of Japan | 21,211.7 | 21,404.1 | 192.4 | −428.8 | 621.2 | 0.91 | −2.02 | 2.93 |
| | Aichi Prefecture | 5,421.3 | 5,352.5 | −68.9 | −225.9 | 157.1 | −1.27 | −4.17 | 2.90 |
| 5 | Nishi-Mikawa area | 3,453.8 | 3,404.8 | −49.1 | −149.1 | 100.0 | −1.42 | −4.32 | 2.90 |
| 1 | Nagoya City | 623.7 | 618.9 | −4.8 | −22.9 | 18.1 | −0.77 | −3.68 | 2.90 |
| 6 | Higashi-Mikawa area | 613.1 | 605.0 | −8.1 | −25.9 | 17.8 | −1.32 | −4.22 | 2.90 |
| 4 | Chita area | 397.4 | 385.0 | −12.4 | −23.9 | 11.4 | −3.13 | −6.00 | 2.87 |
| 2 | Owari area | 280.6 | 285.8 | 5.2 | −3.1 | 8.3 | 1.85 | −1.09 | 2.94 |
| 3 | Ama area | 52.7 | 53.1 | 0.4 | −1.1 | 1.5 | 0.78 | −2.14 | 2.93 |
| 5 | Toyota City | 2,241.6 | 2,220.4 | −21.2 | −86.3 | 65.0 | −0.95 | −3.85 | 2.90 |
| 1 | Nagoya City | 623.7 | 618.9 | −4.8 | −22.9 | 18.1 | −0.77 | −3.68 | 2.90 |
| 6 | Tahara City | 352.9 | 349.0 | −3.9 | −14.1 | 10.2 | −1.10 | −4.00 | 2.90 |
| 5 | Okazaki City | 323.4 | 326.6 | 3.2 | −6.3 | 9.5 | 1.00 | −1.93 | 2.93 |
| 5 | Kariya City | 248.9 | 246.7 | −2.2 | −9.5 | 7.2 | −0.89 | −3.80 | 2.90 |

(continued)

**Table 11.8** (continued)

| Case 1 | | (1) 2017 production-induced value (billion yen) | (1) 2030 production-induced value (billion yen) | (3) 2017–2030 difference (billion yen) | (4) Input coef-ficient changing effect (billion yen) | (5) Final demand changing effect (billion yen) | (6) Ratio (=(3)/(1): %) | (7) Ratio (=(4)/(1): %) | (8) Ratio (=(5)/(1): %) |
|---|---|---|---|---|---|---|---|---|---|
| 5 | Anjo City | 182.2 | 177.1 | −5.2 | −10.4 | 5.2 | −2.84 | −5.71 | 2.87 |
| 5 | Nishio City | 153.9 | 144.3 | −9.6 | −13.9 | 4.3 | −6.23 | −9.05 | 2.83 |
| 4 | Tokai City | 139.6 | 136.3 | −3.4 | −7.4 | 4.0 | −2.42 | −5.30 | 2.88 |
| 6 | Toyohashi City | 120.6 | 117.5 | −3.1 | −6.6 | 3.5 | −2.60 | −5.47 | 2.88 |
| 5 | Miyoshi City | 114.6 | 107.7 | −7.0 | −10.2 | 3.2 | −6.08 | −8.91 | 2.83 |
| 5 | Hekinan City | 110.1 | 104.3 | −5.8 | −8.9 | 3.1 | −5.23 | −8.07 | 2.84 |
| 6 | Toyokawa City | 101.2 | 100.4 | −0.8 | −3.8 | 2.9 | −0.80 | −3.71 | 2.90 |
| 4 | Obu City | 83.0 | 78.4 | −4.6 | −7.0 | 2.4 | −5.55 | −8.39 | 2.84 |
| 4 | Handa City | 61.4 | 58.9 | −2.5 | −4.3 | 1.8 | −4.13 | −6.99 | 2.86 |
| 4 | Chita City | 55.8 | 54.8 | −1.1 | −2.7 | 1.6 | −1.90 | −4.78 | 2.89 |
| 2 | Komaki City | 50.1 | 50.7 | 0.6 | −0.9 | 1.5 | 1.20 | −1.73 | 2.93 |
| 5 | Koda Town | 38.3 | 38.7 | 0.4 | −0.7 | 1.1 | 1.01 | −1.92 | 2.93 |
| 2 | Kasugai City | 37.3 | 38.5 | 1.2 | 0.1 | 1.1 | 3.18 | 0.22 | 2.96 |
| 2 | Ichinomiya City | 29.2 | 29.3 | 0.2 | −0.7 | 0.9 | 0.53 | −2.40 | 2.92 |
| 5 | Takahama City | 24.9 | 23.8 | −1.1 | −1.8 | 0.7 | −4.46 | −7.31 | 2.85 |
| 2 | Seto City | 23.9 | 25.1 | 1.1 | 0.4 | 0.7 | 4.72 | 1.73 | 2.98 |
| 2 | Inazawa City | 23.9 | 24.2 | 0.4 | −0.3 | 0.7 | 1.48 | −1.46 | 2.94 |

(continued)

**Table 11.8** (continued)

| Case 1 | | (1) 2017 production-induced value (billion yen) | (1) 2030 production-induced value (billion yen) | (3) 2017–2030 difference (billion yen) | (4) Input coef-ficient changing effect (billion yen) | (5) Final demand changing effect (billion yen) | (6) Ratio (=(3)/(1): %) | (7) Ratio (=(4)/(1): %) | (8) Ratio (=(5)/(1): %) |
|---|---|---|---|---|---|---|---|---|---|
| 6 | Shinshiro City | 21.5 | 21.6 | 0.1 | −0.5 | 0.6 | 0.49 | −2.43 | 2.92 |
| 4 | Higashiura Town | 18.4 | 18.1 | −0.3 | −0.8 | 0.5 | −1.69 | −4.59 | 2.89 |
| 4 | Taketoyo Town | 17.9 | 17.7 | −0.2 | −0.7 | 0.5 | −1.26 | −4.15 | 2.90 |
| 2 | Oguchi Town | 17.3 | 18.9 | 1.6 | 1.1 | 0.5 | 9.21 | 6.16 | 3.05 |
| 3 | Tobishima Village | 16.8 | 16.5 | −0.3 | −0.8 | 0.5 | −1.83 | −4.72 | 2.89 |
| 6 | Gamagori City | 16.1 | 15.6 | −0.4 | −0.9 | 0.5 | −2.58 | −5.46 | 2.88 |
| 5 | Chiryu City | 15.9 | 15.3 | −0.6 | −1.1 | 0.5 | −3.93 | −6.79 | 2.86 |
| 4 | Tokoname City | 15.9 | 15.6 | −0.3 | −0.8 | 0.5 | −1.90 | −4.79 | 2.89 |

*Source* Calculated by the author

changing factor, respectively. The sixth, seventh, and eighth columns show the ratio of the overall effect and two separate factors to the 2017 value, respectively.

Production, induced by the final demand of 10,379.0 billion yen in 2017, increased to 26,633.1 billion yen, which is 2.57 times the final demand. Of this, the ROJ obtains 21,211.7 billion yen, and Aichi Prefecture receives 5421.3 billion yen. Within Aichi Prefecture, the Nishimikawa area, which has the largest concentration of automobile and automotive parts industries, obtains 3453.8 billion yen, followed by Nagoya City with 623.7 billion yen, the Higashimikawa area with 613.1 billion yen, the Chita area with 397.4 billion yen, the Owari area with 280.6 billion yen, and the Ama area with 52.7 billion yen.

At the municipal level, Toyota City has the largest concentration in the automobile industry, at 2241.6 billion yen, followed by the cities of Nagoya with 623.7 billion yen, Tahara with 352.9 billion yen, Okazaki with 323.4 billion yen, Kariya with 248.9 billion, Anjo with 182.2 billion yen, Nishio with 153.9 billion yen, and Tokai with 139.6 billion yen. Except for Nagoya City, the municipalities dominated by the automobile industry and the automotive parts industry gain a large amount of production inducement.

In 2030, the production inducement against the final demand of 10,686 billion yen will increase 2.5 times the final demand of 26,756.6 billion yen. Of this, the ROJ obtains 21,404.1 billion yen, and Aichi Prefecture acquires 5352.5 billion yen. Similarly, within the prefecture, the Nishimikawa area obtains the largest production-induced value at 3404.8 billion yen, followed by Nagoya City at 618.9 billion yen, the Higashimikawa area at 605.0 billion yen, the Chita area at 385 billion yen, the Owari area at 285.8 billion yen, and the Ama area at 53.1 billion yen.

For municipalities, Toyota City obtains the largest amount of induced production at 2220.4 billion yen, followed by the cities of Nagoya at 618.9 billion yen, Tahara at 349.0 billion yen, Okazaki at 326.6 billion yen, Kariya at 246.7 billion yen, Anjo at 177.1 billion yen, Nishio at 144.3 billion yen, and Tokai at 136.3 billion yen.

Consequently, the difference between the production-induced values in both years is 123.5 billion yen in total. For the ROJ, the amount increases by 192.4 billion yen, while for Aichi Prefecture, it decreases by 68.9 billion yen. Within Aichi Prefecture, the Nishimikawa area decreases by 49.1 billion yen, the Chita area by 12.4 billion yen, the Higashimikawa area by 8.1 billion yen, and Nagoya City by 4.8 billion yen, while the Owari and Ama areas increase conversely by 5.2 billion yen and 400 million yen, respectively. The reason for such a difference in direction and magnitude for those areas is that the overall effect consists of two varied factors: a shift in the input structure for the electrification of automobiles and expanding final demand.

Therefore, we examined each factor obtained by decomposing the overall effect on the production-induced value according to Eq. (11.12). The increase in final demand is 307.0 billion yen, as shown at the beginning of column (3) of Table 11.8. If there is no change in the input structure, the production-induced value increases by 778.2 billion yen (see column 5). This represents a 2.92% increase over the 2017 production-induced value (see column 8). In addition, the corresponding production-induced value of each region and municipality in columns (5) and (8) is proportional to the scale, and the increase is about 2.9%.

Next, looking at the input coefficient changing factor obtained by keeping the final demand constant in columns (4) and (7), the production-induced value decreases by 654.7 billion yen. Changes in the input structure owing to the electrification of automobiles lead to an increase in demand for core components, such as motors and batteries, while a shift in the input structure results in a decrease in demand for components related to internal combustion engines. If the effect of the latter is large in each region and municipality, the production-induced value decreases.

The induced production of the ROJ decreases by 428.8 billion yen and in Aichi Prefecture by 225.9 billion yen. Within the prefecture, the Nishimikawa area loses 149.1 billion yen of production, Nagoya City 22.9 billion yen, the Higashimikawa area 25.9 billion yen, and the Chita area 23.9 billion yen. The Owari area loses 3.1 billion yen, and the Ama area loses 1.1 billion yen.

For municipalities, Toyota City has the largest decrease of 86.3 billion yen, followed by the cities of Nagoya at 22.9 billion yen, Tahara at 14.1 billion yen, Nishio at 13.9 billion yen, Anjo at 10.4 billion yen, Miyoshi at 10.2 billion yen, Kariya at 9.5 billion yen, Hekinan at 8.9 billion yen, Tokai at 7.4 billion yen, Obu at 7 billion yen, Toyohashi at 6.6 billion yen, Okazaki at 6.3 billion yen, Handa at 4.3 billion yen, Toyokawa at 3.8 billion yen, and Chita at 2.7 billion yen.

Looking at the ratio of the production-induced difference to the value in 2017 (see column 7), Toyota City, which has a large effect, decreases by 3.85%, followed by a decrease in the cities of Nishio of 9.05%, Miyoshi of 8.91%, Obu of 8.39%, and Hekinan of 8.07%. Handa of 6.99%, Anjo of 5.71%, Toyohashi of 5.47%, Tokai of 5.30%, Chita of 4.78%, Tahara of 4.00%, Kariya of 3.80%, Toyokawa of 3.71%, Nagoya of 3.68%, and Okazaki City of 1.93%. It is evident that municipalities in the Nishimikawa area, where automobile and automotive parts production is large, have a significant reduction effect.

In Case 2, the production of export passenger cars of 4.5 million vehicles is considered in addition to the production of domestic passenger cars of Case 1 of 4 million vehicles (see Table 11.9). It is assumed that the electrification rate of vehicles to be exported is 40% (including 4% for EVs and 1% for FCVs), which is lower than that for domestic use. The total is 8.5 million units, and the electrification rate is 54.1% (9.2% for EVs and 1.5% for FCVs). The lower electrification rate and the relatively lower diffusion rate of EVs and FCVs result in the input coefficient changing factor being lower than that in Case 1, although the final demand-increasing effect is large.

In 2017, the final demand was 17,463.8 billion yen, and the production-induced value was 48,239.6 billion yen, 2.76 times the final demand. The ROJ obtained 37,884.8 billion yen, and Aichi Prefecture 10,390.8 billion yen. Within the prefecture, the Nishimikawa area obtained 6758.2 billion yen, the Higashimikawa area 1184.4 billion yen, Nagoya City 1109.5 billion yen, the Chita area 759.2 billion yen, the Owari area 486.7 billion yen, and the Ama area 92.8 billion yen.

Meanwhile, the final demand in 2030 will be 18,516.3 billion yen, and the production inducement amount will be 50,371.8 billion yen; the ROJ will have 39,624.6 billion yen, and Aichi Prefecture will have 10,747.2 billion yen. The Nishimikawa area will acquire 6985.4 billion yen, the Higashimikawa area 1225 billion yen,

**Table 11.9** Impact of the spread of electrified vehicles on the municipal economy (Case 2)

| Case 2 | | (1) 2017 production-induced value (billion yen) | (1) 2030 production-induced value (billion yen) | (3) 2017–2030 difference (billion yen) | (4) Input coefficient changing effect (billion yen) | (5) Final demand changing effect (billion yen) | (6) Ratio (=(3)/(1): %) | (7) Ratio (=(4)/(1): %) | (8) Ratio (=(5)/(1): %) |
|---|---|---|---|---|---|---|---|---|---|
| | Final demand, total | 17,463.8 | 18,516.3 | 1,052.4 | - | - | 6.03 | - | - |
| | Production-induced value, total | 48,239.6 | 50,371.8 | 2,132.2 | −899.8 | 3,032.1 | 4.42 | −1.87 | 6.29 |
| | (Multiplier) | 2.76 | 2.72 | | | | | | |
| | ROJ | 37,848.8 | 39,624.6 | 1,775.8 | −584.7 | 2,360.5 | 4.69 | −1.54 | 6.24 |
| | Aichi Prefecture | 10,390.8 | 10,747.2 | 356.4 | −315.1 | 671.6 | 3.43 | −3.03 | 6.46 |
| 5 | Nishi-Mikawa area | 6,758.2 | 6,985.4 | 227.2 | −214.4 | 441.6 | 3.36 | −3.17 | 6.53 |
| 6 | Nagoya City | 1,184.4 | 1,225.0 | 40.5 | −36.3 | 76.9 | 3.42 | −3.07 | 6.49 |
| 1 | Higashi-Mikawa area | 1,109.5 | 1,149.3 | 39.8 | −28.8 | 68.6 | 3.58 | −2.60 | 6.18 |
| 4 | Chita area | 759.2 | 773.2 | 14.0 | −34.5 | 48.5 | 1.85 | −4.54 | 6.39 |
| 2 | Owari area | 486.7 | 517.4 | 30.7 | 0.5 | 30.2 | 6.31 | 0.11 | 6.21 |
| 3 | Ama area | 92.8 | 96.9 | 4.1 | −1.6 | 5.7 | 4.45 | −1.73 | 6.18 |
| 5 | Toyota City | 4,397.7 | 4,560.3 | 162.6 | −125.6 | 288.2 | 3.70 | −2.86 | 6.55 |
| 1 | Nagoya City | 1,109.5 | 1,149.3 | 39.8 | −28.8 | 68.6 | 3.58 | −2.60 | 6.18 |
| 6 | Tahara City | 692.5 | 717.2 | 24.7 | −20.6 | 45.4 | 3.57 | −2.98 | 6.55 |
| 5 | Okazaki City | 621.8 | 652.8 | 31.0 | −9.7 | 40.7 | 4.98 | −1.56 | 6.54 |
| 5 | Kariya City | 483.8 | 501.7 | 17.9 | −13.6 | 31.5 | 3.71 | −2.81 | 6.52 |

(continued)

**Table 11.9** (continued)

| Case 2 | | (1) 2017 production-induced value (billion yen) | (1) 2030 production-induced value (billion yen) | (3) 2017–2030 difference (billion yen) | (4) Input coefficient changing effect (billion yen) | (5) Final demand changing effect (billion yen) | (6) Ratio (=(3)/(1): %) | (7) Ratio (=(4)/(1): %) | (8) Ratio (=(5)/(1): %) |
|---|---|---|---|---|---|---|---|---|---|
| 5 | Anjo City | 355.0 | 365.5 | 10.5 | −12.7 | 23.2 | 2.96 | −3.57 | 6.53 |
| 5 | Nishio City | 304.9 | 304.3 | − 0.6 | −20.2 | 19.7 | −0.18 | −6.63 | 6.45 |
| 4 | Tokai City | 271.5 | 278.5 | 6.9 | −10.7 | 17.6 | 2.56 | −3.92 | 6.48 |
| 5 | Miyoshi City | 227.7 | 227.5 | − 0.2 | −14.9 | 14.7 | −0.10 | −6.55 | 6.46 |
| 6 | Toyohashi City | 226.7 | 232.4 | 5.7 | −8.7 | 14.4 | 2.51 | −3.85 | 6.36 |
| 5 | Hekinan City | 216.0 | 217.0 | 1.0 | −12.9 | 13.9 | 0.48 | −5.96 | 6.44 |
| 6 | Toyokawa City | 193.7 | 200.8 | 7.1 | −5.4 | 12.5 | 3.68 | −2.78 | 6.46 |
| 4 | Obu City | 163.3 | 163.8 | 0.5 | −10.0 | 10.5 | 0.33 | −6.11 | 6.44 |
| 4 | Handa City | 118.4 | 119.9 | 1.4 | −6.2 | 7.6 | 1.20 | −5.20 | 6.40 |
| 4 | Chita City | 99.8 | 102.0 | 2.3 | −3.9 | 6.1 | 2.26 | −3.88 | 6.14 |
| 2 | Komaki City | 91.2 | 96.6 | 5.4 | −0.5 | 5.8 | 5.88 | −0.50 | 6.38 |
| 5 | Koda Town | 73.2 | 77.4 | 4.1 | −0.7 | 4.8 | 5.62 | −0.95 | 6.57 |
| 2 | Kasugai City | 62.3 | 67.0 | 4.7 | 0.9 | 3.8 | 7.59 | 1.49 | 6.10 |
| 5 | Takahama City | 48.3 | 48.8 | 0.5 | −2.6 | 3.1 | 1.00 | −5.41 | 6.41 |
| 2 | Ichinomiya City | 46.6 | 48.4 | 1.8 | −0.9 | 2.7 | 3.86 | −1.87 | 5.73 |

(continued)

**Table 11.9** (continued)

| Case 2 | | (1) 2017 production-induced value (billion yen) | (1) 2030 production-induced value (billion yen) | (3) 2017–2030 difference (billion yen) | (4) Input coefficient changing effect (billion yen) | (5) Final demand changing effect (billion yen) | (6) Ratio (=(3)/(1): %) | (7) Ratio (=(4)/(1): %) | (8) Ratio (=(5)/(1): %) |
|---|---|---|---|---|---|---|---|---|---|
| 2 | Seto City | 42.3 | 46.4 | 4.1 | 1.4 | 2.7 | 9.69 | 3.25 | 6.43 |
| 2 | Inazawa City | 41.8 | 44.1 | 2.3 | −0.3 | 2.6 | 5.55 | −0.66 | 6.21 |
| 6 | Shinshiro City | 40.7 | 43.0 | 2.3 | −0.3 | 2.7 | 5.70 | −0.83 | 6.53 |
| 4 | Higashiura Town | 35.2 | 36.1 | 1.0 | −1.3 | 2.3 | 2.71 | −3.73 | 6.43 |
| 4 | Taketoyo Town | 33.8 | 34.8 | 1.0 | −1.2 | 2.2 | 2.95 | −3.42 | 6.37 |
| 3 | Tobishima Village | 31.6 | 32.5 | 0.9 | −1.1 | 2.0 | 2.81 | −3.55 | 6.36 |
| 2 | Oguchi Town | 31.4 | 36.2 | 4.8 | 2.7 | 2.1 | 15.31 | 8.49 | 6.82 |
| 5 | Chiryu City | 29.8 | 30.1 | 0.3 | −1.6 | 1.9 | 1.06 | −5.22 | 6.28 |
| 6 | Gamagori City | 29.5 | 30.1 | 0.6 | −1.2 | 1.8 | 2.04 | −4.20 | 6.24 |
| 2 | Nisshin City | 28.9 | 29.3 | 0.5 | −1.3 | 1.8 | 1.64 | −4.58 | 6.22 |

*Source* Calculated by the author

Nagoya City 1149.3 billion yen, the Chita area 773.2 billion yen, the Owari area 517.4 billion yen, and the Ama area 96.9 billion yen.

The difference in final demand between 2017 and 2030 is an increase of 1052.4 billion yen, while the production inducement increases by 2132.2 billion yen; that for Aichi Prefecture increases by 356.4 billion yen; and that for the ROJ by 1775.8 billion yen. Within Aichi Prefecture, the Nishimikawa area increased by 227.2 billion yen, the Higashimikawa area by 40.5 billion yen, Nagoya City by 39.8 billion yen, the Chita area by 14 billion yen, the Owari area by 30.7 billion yen, and the Ama area by 4.1 billion yen. Unlike Case 1, the production-induced value increases in all six areas of Aichi Prefecture.

Decomposing the change of the production-induced value into two factors, namely, the input coefficient changing factor and the final demand changing factor. On the one hand, the latter is 3032.1 billion yen, which means a 6.29% increase from the 2017 production-induced value. On the other hand, the input coefficient changing factor is 899.8 billion yen, a decrease of 1.87% from the 2017 value. In the ROJ, the decrease is 584.7 billion yen, and in Aichi Prefecture, it is 315.1 billion yen. For the six areas, the decrease is 214.4 billion yen in the Nishimikawa area, 36.3 billion yen in the Higashimikawa area, 28.8 billion yen in Nagoya City, 34.5 billion yen in the Chita area, and 1.6 billion yen in the Ama area, but 500 million yen increase in the Owari area.

Turning to the change in input structure by municipality in column (4), the decrease in Toyota City is 125.6 billion yen, followed by the cities of Nagoya at 28.8 billion yen, Tahara at 20.6 billion yen, Nishio at 20.2 billion yen, Miyoshi at 14.9 billion yen, Kariya at 13.6 billion yen, Hekinan at 12.9 billion yen, Anjo at 12.7 billion yen, Tokai at 10.7 billion yen, Obu at 10 billion yen, Toyohashi at 8.7 billion yen, Okazaki at 9.7 billion yen, Handa at 6.2 billion yen, Toyokawa at 5.4 billion yen, and Chita at 3.9 billion yen.

As a percentage of the 2017 production-induced value, Toyota City, which has the largest amount, decreased by 2.86%, followed by Nagoya City at 2.60%. Some municipalities have a larger reduction than these two cities, including the cities of Nishio at 6.63%, Miyoshi at 6.55%, Obu at 6.11%, Hekinan at 5.96%, Handa at 5.20%, Tokai at 3.92%, Chita at 3.88%, Toyohashi at 3.85%, and Anjo at 3.57%.

Compared with the effect of the input coefficient changing in Case 2, Case 1 has a large electrification diffusion rate, which has a relatively large negative effect on the municipal economy. The electrification of automobiles, especially the further spread of EVs and FCVs, may further reduce the amount of induced production in municipalities with large automobile parts production.

Thus far, we have compared the relative size of the effect against the amount of municipal production induced by the expected vehicle demand. However, this has an impact on the production induced in each municipality. Instead, Fig. 11.3 illustrates the effect of the electrification of vehicles on the overall production of each municipality. The production reduction rate is the largest at 0.80% in Miyoshi City, followed by 0.68% in Nishio City, 0.53% in Obu City, and 0.45% in Hekinan City, which indicates that a dominant impact on municipalities appears in the Nishimikawa area.

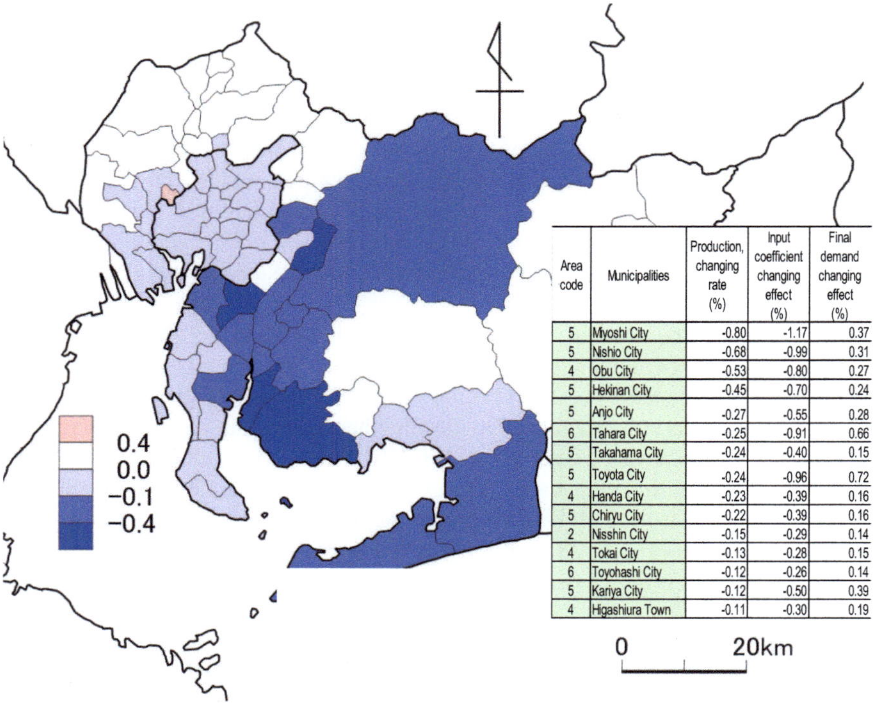


| Area code | Municipalities | Production, changing rate (%) | Input coefficient changing effect (%) | Final demand changing effect (%) |
|---|---|---|---|---|
| 5 | Miyoshi City | -0.80 | -1.17 | 0.37 |
| 5 | Nishio City | -0.68 | -0.99 | 0.31 |
| 4 | Obu City | -0.53 | -0.80 | 0.27 |
| 5 | Hekinan City | -0.45 | -0.70 | 0.24 |
| 5 | Anjo City | -0.27 | -0.55 | 0.28 |
| 6 | Tahara City | -0.25 | -0.91 | 0.66 |
| 5 | Takahama City | -0.24 | -0.40 | 0.15 |
| 5 | Toyota City | -0.24 | -0.96 | 0.72 |
| 4 | Handa City | -0.23 | -0.39 | 0.16 |
| 5 | Chiryu City | -0.22 | -0.39 | 0.16 |
| 2 | Nisshin City | -0.15 | -0.29 | 0.14 |
| 4 | Tokai City | -0.13 | -0.28 | 0.15 |
| 6 | Toyohashi City | -0.12 | -0.26 | 0.14 |
| 5 | Kariya City | -0.12 | -0.50 | 0.39 |
| 4 | Higashiura Town | -0.11 | -0.30 | 0.19 |

**Fig. 11.3** Impact of the spread of electrified vehicles on the municipal economy (Case 1). *Source* Created by the author, using the MANDARA supporting system for geographic information analysis (http://ktgis.net/mandara/)

Besides Nagoya City, there is also a negative effect on cities in the Higashimikawa and Chita areas.

## 11.5 Concluding Remarks

Aichi Prefecture has benefited from the growth of the automobile-related industry. However, a major challenge for each municipality is to figure out how to achieve sustainable economic growth against future declining populations. Aichi is no exception, certainly from a long-term perspective.

In this study, we analyzed the effects of automobile electrification on the regional economy using inter-municipal input–output analysis in Aichi Prefecture. The electrification of automobiles not only has an expanding effect with the introduction of core components for electrification, such as motors, batteries, and power units, but also has a reducing effect by reducing the need for internal combustion engines and related components in the case of EVs and FCVs. A major trend appears to be a shift in demand, with an increase in intermediate inputs in the electrical machinery sector and a decrease in intermediate inputs in the automotive parts sector. Overall, the effect on the region depends on the type of automobiles that will become popular.

We estimate the diffusion rate of next-generation vehicles in 2017 and 2030, measure the production-inducing effect, and examine the difference between the two as the economic effect on the region. Consequently, in the case of domestic-use automobiles, if the electrification rate in 2030 is 70%, including 15% for EVs and 2% for FCVs, Aichi Prefecture will reduce induced production by 68.9 billion yen in 2030 compared to that of 2017. This can be broken down into an increase in the final demand-changing effect of 157.1 billion yen and a decrease in the input coefficient-changing effect of 225.9 billion yen.

The change in the input structure of automobile production has a significant impact on Aichi Prefecture, especially in the Nishimikawa area where automobile production is concentrated, and on municipalities like Toyota City and surrounding municipalities, such as the cities of Nishio, Miyoshi, Obu, and Hekinan. These cities, where automobile and automotive parts-related companies are concentrated, are projected to experience a substantial reduction effect.

Export demand is expected to have a lower electrification rate than domestic demand, and the diffusion of EVs and FCVs is also expected to be lower. However, the electrification of automobiles and the diffusion of EVs and FCVs are a long-term trend that will continue after 2030. If global warming countermeasures are strengthened, the electrification of automobiles and the spread of EVs may be accelerated. Thus, it is necessary to consider how the regional economy responds to such shifts in demand.

## References

Chubu Region Institute for Social and Economic Research. 2015. Influence of Next Generation Mobility on the Industries in Chubu Region (in Japanese).

Fujikawa, K., and W. Jiayang. 2017. Economic and environmental impact of renewable energy - An application of input-output analysis. *The Ritsumeikan Economic Review* 65 (4): 619–630 (in Japanese).

Ishikawa, Y. 2004. A three-region interregional input-output model using non-survey technique. *Journal of Japan Society of Civil Engineers* 758 (4–63): 45–55 (in Japanese).

Kimura, S. 2019. Impact of the next-generation vehicle on Chubu region: Analysis of the interregional input–output table of Chubu region. *Sango Renkan (Business Journal of PAPAIOS)* 26 (1): 80–98 (in Japanese).

Mase, Takayuki. 2019. Estimation of the electric vehicle sector in the input–output table and simulation analysis of the increase in the share of electric vehicle production. Central Research Institute of Electric Power Industry, *Social Economics Research Institute Discussion Paper* SERC18001 (in Japanese).

METI, Automotive New Era Strategy Conference. 2018. *Automotive new era strategy conference: Interim report* (in Japanese). https://www.meti.go.jp/shingikai/mono_info_service/jidosha_shin jidai/pdf/20180831_01.pdf

METI, Hydrogen and Fuel Cell Strategy Council. 2019. Roadmap for hydrogen and fuel cell strategies: Action plans of industry, academia and government for realizing a hydrogen society (in Japanese).

Osawa, J., and M. Nakano. 2015. A model of the economic ripple effect caused by spread of clean energy vehicles. *Bulletin of the JSME* 81 (823): 1–14 (in Japanese).

Shibusawa, H., and T. Sugawara. 2011. Evaluating the economic impacts of the production of the new generation automobiles with a technological innovation. *Regional Studies* 41 (1): 127–146 (in Japanese).

Sogo Giken Co., Ltd. 2019. *Automotive industry forecast for 2030* (in Japanese).

Sumitomo Mitsui Banking Corporation. 2017. The future of automotive and related industries (in Japanese).

Tsukamoto, T., N. Komiyama, and J. Nemoto. 2018. Construction of inter-regional input-output table among all municipalities in Aichi Prefecture and analysis on spatial interdependence between municipalities. *Sango Renkan (Business Journal of PAPAIOS)* 26 (1): 1–20 (in Japanese).

Wang, J. 2016. Economic and environmental effects of introduction of renewable power sources: An application of scenario input-output analysis to China. *Sango Renkan (Business Journal of PAPAIOS)* 24 (1): 35–48 (in Japanese).

Yamada, M. 1995. Estimation of Mie Prefecture inter-regional input-output table. *Sango Renkan (Business Journal of PAPAIOS)* 5 (4): 52–67 (in Japanese).

Yamada, M. 2015. Construction of a Multi-regional Input-Output Table for Nagoya Metropolitan Area, Japan. *Journal of Economic Structures* 4 (11): 1–18.

Yamada, Mitsuo, and Yuichi Owaki. 2012. Estimation of 2005 inter-regional input-output table of four-regions within Aichi Prefecture. Chukyo University, *Institute of economics discussion paper* No. 1205 (in Japanese).

Yamada, M., and Y. Horiuchi. 2015. Comparison of inter-regional input-output tables for Mie Prefecture from 1985 to 2010. *Sango Renkan (Business Journal of PAPAIOS)* 23 (1–2): 15–28 (in Japanese).

Yamada, M., K. Fujikawa, and Y. Umeda. 2019. Scenario input–output analysis on the diffusion of fuel cell vehicles and alternative hydrogen supply systems. *Journal of Economic Structures* 8 (4): 1–22.

Yoshioka, Kanji, and Mikio Suga. 1997. Applications of input-output approach in environmental analysis - A study of scenario Leontief inverse. Economic and Social Research Institute, Cabinet Office, Japan, *Economic Analysis*, 154 (in Japanese).

# Chapter 12
# Economic Contribution of Small and Medium-Sized Enterprises' Production to the Regional Economy

## 12.1 Introduction

A prominent issue in Japan is that the declining population with a low birthrate and aging will reduce the vitality of society, and such local economies will stagnate and shrink. In response to the issue, the national and local governments are working on regional economic revitalization policies.

Production fluctuation in the regional economy depends not only on the consumption-demand change caused by the population reduction in that region but also on the population decline in other regions. If the impact of the latter is greater than the former, the economy may stagnate even if the population does not decrease significantly. In Chap. 10, we discuss the impact of the declining consumption demand due to the population reduction on the municipal economy by using the inter-municipal input–output model of Aichi Prefecture.

So far, Aichi's economy has developed along with the growth of the automobile industry. To realize a carbon–neutral society by 2050, it is important to transition from conventional vehicles using fossil fuels to next-generation vehicles that do not rely on them. In Chap. 11, we discuss the impact of automobile electrification on the municipal economy, which manufactures mainly engine-related automobile parts. New business development with the manufacturing technology of the automobile parts industry is required.

For the development of the municipal economy, it is important that SMEs continue to play an active role in the local economy. In this chapter, we discuss how to measure the regional contribution of the SME's production to the regional economy. The contribution of SMEs to the local economy is not limited to the direct added value and job creation that they bring. It is important to understand how individual SMEs affect the local economy through raw material procurement and their product sales. This is related to measuring the production ripple effects of SMEs' production activities through the input–output analysis.



M. Yamada, *Multi-Regional Input–Output Analysis of the Japanese Economy*,
https://doi.org/10.1007/978-981-97-9041-8_12

The input–output analysis of SMEs mainly includes studies such as Kaneko (1990), Shimoda et al. (2005), and Ishiro (2007) using IOTs by size, which divides individual sectors by company size, such as large companies and SMEs. However, here we will focus on calculating and visualizing the economic contribution that SMEs bring to the local economy. Furthermore, for the development of companies, sharing information about their contributions to the local community is important. It also has the potential to be applied as a method to measure the effects that various business support policies have on the local economy. No research from this perspective has been found.

The "HEM" is known as a tool for measuring the degree of influence that the economic activities of specific sectors in IOTs have on the economy. If the targeting SMEs can be appropriately separated into one sector, it will be possible to measure the regional contribution of this enterprise by applying this method. Here, we extend this method and introduce a new tool to be called the "Hypothetical insertion method (HIM)" that measures economic contribution by inserting the production activities of SMEs rather than extracting the production activities of specific sectors from IOTs.

However, in the case of an existing company rather than a new company, unless the company's production activities in the reference year are deducted from the IOT, the calculated value may be overestimated. Therefore, after discussing the appropriate way to measure the regional contribution of SMEs, we measure the economic contribution of SMEs' production activities to the regional economy, taking Nishio City in Aichi Prefecture as a case study. We also measure two kinds of regional contribution: "backward linkage" by applying this method to the Leontief model and "forward linkage" by applying this method to the Ghosh model.

Section 12.2 summarizes the research on input–output analysis related to regional revitalization in Japan, and Sect. 12.3 discusses an analytical model for measuring the regional economic contribution of SMEs. In Sect. 12.4, with the cooperation of four SMEs located in Nishio City, we conduct a questionnaire survey on their production activities and attempt to measure their economic contribution to the local economy. Section 12.5 summarizes the analytical results.

## 12.2 Preceding Research on the Input–output Analysis of Regional Revitalization

In recent years, input–output analysis of regional revitalization has been increasing in municipalities. Based on the idea of EBPM (evidence-based policy-making), many municipalities are trying their regional revitalization projects. The Regional Economic Analysis System (RESAS) is an easy tool to grasp the current state of income circulation and industrial structure in municipalities and extract their issues. Various municipality-based data are maintained in RESAS, in which municipal regional incomes and IOTs have been developed, making it possible to grasp the income circulation of municipalities. However, to evaluate the ripple effects of various policies proposed by municipalities, it is necessary to create each municipal-based IOT (Heiho and Kikuchi, 2021).

Many of the municipal activation measures in regional revitalization are based on the export base model. This model regards export-based industries that mainly export outside the region, and others as local industries that support the regional economy, with the former earning income from other regions and the latter circulating that income within the region. Therefore, regional revitalization measures will focus on creating such export-based industries and on fostering non-export-based industries that will enable the circulation of income within the region.

Based on this theory, Miura (2018) applied Osaka Prefecture's IOT to extract export-based industries from the perspective of production scale, export-production ratio, labor productivity, and production ripple effects within the region. Osaka Prefecture has identified the "Commerce sector" and other industries such as "Other office services," "Real estate agencies and rental services," "Goods rental and leasing services," and "Advertising services" as core industries. Additionally, using Shizuoka Prefecture's IOT, Takase (2016a) attempts to grasp the region's core industries from the index of power of dispersion, the production inducement coefficient due to exports, and the regional contribution index by the HEM.

On a municipal basis, Okuma et al. (2019) constructed an IOT for Minami-Sanriku Town, Miyagi Prefecture, and analyzed the economic effects of biogas and related businesses. By using the generated biogas to generate electricity and produce liquid fertilizer, it was possible to replace the chemical fertilizers imported into the agricultural sector and waste disposal services that have been outsourced. They concluded that the projects had increased the degree of resource circulation within the region.

These are analyzed using an intra-regional IOT that focuses on each specific region. The smaller the area, the more economic transactions there are with other regions, which lowers the self-sufficiency rate of the area. An interregional IOT must be required to accurately assess such leakage of demand between regions.

Ishikawa-Nakamura (2018), taking Fuji City as an example, created an interregional IOT from the Fuji City IOT and the national IOT. Explicitly considering the workplace and residence of employees in the consumption endogenous model, they analyzed the economic effects of a regional revitalization project. Even if income is generated in a certain region, it will be difficult to increase consumption demand within the region when many employees obtaining it commute from outside the region. In that case, the induced production in the region will not increase. This indicates that an economic effect analysis based on intra-regional IOTs that does not consider such effects may result in overestimation. In addition, Ishikawa (2019) improved the method of constructing this interregional input–output model.

This chapter evaluates the regional contribution of SMEs in Nishio City using an interregional IOT, which captures interdependence between Nishio City and other municipalities. We apply an extended model of the HEM to evaluate the regional contribution of SMEs, in which we consider not only the backward linkage effect through raw material procurement but also the forward linkage effect through product sales. The next section examines such an analytical model.

## 12.3 Analytical Model

The purpose of this chapter is to examine the method of measuring the degree of SME's contribution to the regional economy. In this section, we discuss our analytical model.

### *12.3.1 Hypothetical Extraction Method*

"Hypothetical Extraction Method (HEM)" measures inter-industrial linkage or the importance of industries in an IOT to other industries. This method finds how the ripple effect of the economy changes when one sector is extracted from an IOT by considering that the transaction between that sector and the others is interrupted.

Considering the case of extracting the n-th sector (hereinafter, the sector to be extracted shows "2" and the others "1"), the IOT is expressed as follows:

$$\begin{bmatrix} \mathbf{x}_1 \\ x_2 \end{bmatrix} = \begin{bmatrix} \mathbf{A}_{11} & \mathbf{a}_{12} \\ \mathbf{a}_{21} & a_{22} \end{bmatrix} \begin{bmatrix} \mathbf{x}_1 \\ x_2 \end{bmatrix} + \begin{bmatrix} \mathbf{f}_1 \\ f_2 \end{bmatrix} \tag{12.1}$$

$$\begin{bmatrix} \mathbf{x}_1 \\ x_2 \end{bmatrix} = \begin{bmatrix} \mathbf{I} - \mathbf{A}_{11} & -\mathbf{a}_{12} \\ -\mathbf{a}_{21} & 1 - a_{22} \end{bmatrix}^{-1} \begin{bmatrix} \mathbf{f}_1 \\ f_2 \end{bmatrix} = \begin{bmatrix} \mathbf{B}_{11} & \mathbf{b}_{12} \\ \mathbf{b}_{21} & \mathbf{b}_{22} \end{bmatrix} \begin{bmatrix} \mathbf{f}_1 \\ f_2 \end{bmatrix} \tag{12.2}$$

Here, we extract the n-th sector.

$$\begin{bmatrix} \mathbf{x}_1^* \\ 0 \end{bmatrix} = \begin{bmatrix} \mathbf{A}_{11} & 0 \\ 0 & 0 \end{bmatrix} \begin{bmatrix} \mathbf{x}_1^* \\ 0 \end{bmatrix} + \begin{bmatrix} \mathbf{f}_1 \\ 0 \end{bmatrix} \tag{12.3}$$

$$\begin{bmatrix} \mathbf{x}_1^* \\ 0 \end{bmatrix} = \begin{bmatrix} \mathbf{I} - \mathbf{A}_{11} & \mathbf{0} \\ \mathbf{0} & 1 \end{bmatrix}^{-1} \begin{bmatrix} \mathbf{f}_1 \\ 0 \end{bmatrix} = \begin{bmatrix} (\mathbf{I} - \mathbf{A}_{11})^{-1} & \mathbf{0} \\ \mathbf{0} & 1 \end{bmatrix} \begin{bmatrix} \mathbf{f}_1 \\ 0 \end{bmatrix} = \begin{bmatrix} \mathbf{B}_{11}^* & \mathbf{0} \\ \mathbf{0} & 1 \end{bmatrix} \begin{bmatrix} \mathbf{f}_1 \\ 0 \end{bmatrix} \tag{12.4}$$

The ripple effect change caused by extracting the n-th sector is obtained by the difference between (12.2) and (12.4).

$$\begin{aligned} \begin{bmatrix} \mathbf{x}_1^* \\ 0 \end{bmatrix} - \begin{bmatrix} \mathbf{x}_1 \\ x_2 \end{bmatrix} &= \begin{bmatrix} \mathbf{B}_{11}^* & \mathbf{0} \\ \mathbf{0} & 1 \end{bmatrix} \begin{bmatrix} \mathbf{f}_1 \\ 0 \end{bmatrix} - \begin{bmatrix} \mathbf{B}_{11} & \mathbf{b}_{12} \\ \mathbf{b}_{21} & b_{22} \end{bmatrix} \begin{bmatrix} \mathbf{f}_1 \\ f_2 \end{bmatrix} \\ &= \begin{bmatrix} (\mathbf{B}_{11}^* - \mathbf{B}_{11})\mathbf{f}_1 - \mathbf{b}_{12} f_2 \\ -\mathbf{b}_{21}\mathbf{f}_1 - b_{22} f_2 \end{bmatrix} \end{aligned} \tag{12.5}$$

By aggregating the Eq. (12.5), the total amount of the production change in the economy can be obtained.

$$\begin{bmatrix} \mathbf{e}_1' & 1 \end{bmatrix}\left(\begin{bmatrix} \mathbf{x}_1^* \\ 0 \end{bmatrix} - \begin{bmatrix} \mathbf{x}_1 \\ x_2 \end{bmatrix}\right) = -\mathbf{e}_1'(\mathbf{B}_{11} - \mathbf{B}_{11}^*)\mathbf{f}_1 - \mathbf{b}_{21}\mathbf{f}_1 - \mathbf{e}_1'\mathbf{b}_{12}f_2 - b_{22}f_2 \quad (12.6)$$

Here, the first term is the effect of the multiplier change of the remaining n-1 sectors due to the removal of the n-th sector, and the second term is the effect of the n-1 sector's final demand on n-th sector production. The third term is the ripple effect of the n-th sector on the production of the remaining n-1 sectors, and the fourth term is the effect of the n-th sector on its own production.

However, a one-to-one correspondence between the sectors in the IOT and the targeted individual companies does not necessarily exist, and there may be cases where there are multiple companies in one sector, or conversely, one company engages in production activities across multiple sectors. Therefore, certain modifications are required to measure the regional contribution of individual companies' production activities.

If sector 2 in Eq. (12.2) consists of multiple companies, it is conceivable to separate the company as sector 3 and then set the activity portion of the company to 0. At that time, the IOT will increase by one sector to become (n + 1) sectors, and Eqs. (12.2) and (12.3) are modified as follows:

$$\begin{bmatrix} \mathbf{x}_1 \\ x_2 \\ x_3 \end{bmatrix} = \begin{bmatrix} \mathbf{I} - \mathbf{A}_{11} & -\mathbf{a}_{12} & -\mathbf{a}_{13} \\ -\mathbf{a}_{21} & 1 - a_{22} & -a_{23} \\ -\mathbf{a}_{31} & -a_{32} & -a_{33} \end{bmatrix}^{-1} \begin{bmatrix} \mathbf{f}_1 \\ f_2 \\ f_3 \end{bmatrix} \quad (12.2')$$

$$\begin{bmatrix} \mathbf{x}_1^* \\ x_2^* \\ 0 \end{bmatrix} = \begin{bmatrix} \mathbf{I} - \mathbf{A}_{11} & -\mathbf{a}_{12} & \mathbf{0} \\ -\mathbf{a}_{21} & 1 - a_{22} & 0 \\ \mathbf{0} & 0 & 1 \end{bmatrix}^{-1} \begin{bmatrix} \mathbf{f}_1 \\ f_2 \\ 0 \end{bmatrix} \quad (12.3')$$

Here, because sector 2 is divided into two, it would be necessary to display that sector differently from the sector before division, but to avoid complications, the two sectors after division are represented as 2 and 3.[1]

If the production activities of the targeting SME can be separated appropriately, the production of the company in the base year included in the IOT can be calculated based on Eqs. (12.5), (12.2'), and (12.3'), and thus, it would be possible to measure the regional contribution.

[1] When a SME produces the products across multiple sectors, consider sector 2 before division as a matrix consisting of multiple corresponding sectors, extract the activities of the company, and aggregate them into one sector, which is set as sector 3 after the division. In addition, for the analysis with explicitly multiple activities, it is sufficient to reread the vector notation of the targeting SME into matrix notation, and the model can be easily extended.

### *12.3.2 Hypothetical Insertion Method*

Next, we consider measuring the regional contribution of a new SME entering a region rather than an existing company. In this case, the IOT for the base year does not include the production activities of the company in question. Therefore, instead of deducting the vertical cost structure and horizontal sales channel structure that represent the company's production activities, they are newly added. A possible method would be to revise the IOT, calculate the difference in the production-induced amount between the two situations, and evaluate the company's contribution to the region based on that change. Formally, this method does not remove specific sectors from the IOT but adds new sectors that are not in the IOT, and here we refer to this as the "Hypothetical Insertion Method (HIM)."

The HIM is expressed as follows: First, the base n-sector IOT is expressed as follows: Here we set 0 at the position of the (n + 1)-th sector to be added.

$$\begin{bmatrix} \mathbf{x} \\ 0 \end{bmatrix} = \begin{bmatrix} \mathbf{A} & \mathbf{0} \\ \mathbf{0} & 0 \end{bmatrix} \begin{bmatrix} \mathbf{x} \\ 0 \end{bmatrix} + \begin{bmatrix} \mathbf{f} \\ 0 \end{bmatrix} \tag{12.7}$$

$$\begin{bmatrix} \mathbf{x} \\ 0 \end{bmatrix} = \begin{bmatrix} \mathbf{I}-\mathbf{A} & \mathbf{0} \\ \mathbf{0} & 1 \end{bmatrix}^{-1} \begin{bmatrix} \mathbf{f} \\ 0 \end{bmatrix} = \begin{bmatrix} (\mathbf{I}-\mathbf{A})^{-1} & \mathbf{0} \\ \mathbf{0} & 1 \end{bmatrix} \begin{bmatrix} \mathbf{f} \\ 0 \end{bmatrix} = \begin{bmatrix} \mathbf{B} & \mathbf{0} \\ \mathbf{0} & 1 \end{bmatrix} \begin{bmatrix} \mathbf{f} \\ 0 \end{bmatrix} \tag{12.8}$$

Then, add the production activities of the SMEs (represented by the subscript "4") as the (n + 1) sector.

$$\begin{bmatrix} \mathbf{x}^{**} \\ x_4 \end{bmatrix} = \begin{bmatrix} \mathbf{A} & \mathbf{a}_{\mathbf{n}4} \\ \mathbf{a}_{4\mathbf{n}} & a_{44} \end{bmatrix} \begin{bmatrix} \mathbf{x}^{**} \\ x_4 \end{bmatrix} + \begin{bmatrix} \mathbf{f} \\ f_4 \end{bmatrix} \tag{12.9}$$

$$\begin{bmatrix} \mathbf{x}^{**} \\ x_4 \end{bmatrix} = \begin{bmatrix} \mathbf{I}-\mathbf{A} & -\mathbf{a}_{\mathbf{n}4} \\ -\mathbf{a}_{4\mathbf{n}} & 1-a_{44} \end{bmatrix}^{-1} \begin{bmatrix} \mathbf{f} \\ f_4 \end{bmatrix} = \begin{bmatrix} \mathbf{B}^{**} & \mathbf{b}_{\mathbf{n}4} \\ \mathbf{b}_{4\mathbf{n}} & b_{44} \end{bmatrix} \begin{bmatrix} \mathbf{f} \\ f_4 \end{bmatrix} \tag{12.10}$$

Taking the difference between Eqs. (12.8) and (12.10),

$$\begin{bmatrix} \mathbf{x}^{**} \\ x_4 \end{bmatrix} - \begin{bmatrix} \mathbf{x} \\ 0 \end{bmatrix} = \begin{bmatrix} \mathbf{B}^{**} & \mathbf{b}_{\mathbf{n}4} \\ \mathbf{b}_{4\mathbf{n}} & b_{44} \end{bmatrix} \begin{bmatrix} \mathbf{f} \\ f_4 \end{bmatrix} - \begin{bmatrix} \mathbf{B} & \mathbf{0} \\ \mathbf{0} & 1 \end{bmatrix} \begin{bmatrix} \mathbf{f} \\ 0 \end{bmatrix} \tag{12.11}$$

Aggregating this gives

$$\begin{bmatrix} \mathbf{e}' & 1 \end{bmatrix} \left( \begin{bmatrix} \mathbf{x}^{**} \\ x_4 \end{bmatrix} - \begin{bmatrix} \mathbf{x} \\ 0 \end{bmatrix} \right) = \mathbf{e}'(\mathbf{B}^{**} - \mathbf{B})\mathbf{f} + \mathbf{b}_{4\mathbf{n}}\mathbf{f} + \mathbf{e}'\mathbf{b}_{\mathbf{n}4} f_4 + b_{44} f_4 \tag{12.12}$$

The first term of the Eq. (12.12) is the effect of the multiplier change of the n sectors' final demand because of the new entry of the SMEs. The second term is the production ripple effect on the new firm owing to the final demand of the n sector, and the third term is the induced effect on the n sector due to the procurement of raw materials brought by the final demand production of the new company. The fourth term is the ripple effect on its own sector. If the firm produces only intermediate goods, $f_4 = \mathbf{0}$, the third and fourth terms will also be zero. In that case, the ripple effect is measured by the first and second terms.

The impact of a new firm's production activities can be calculated by exogenizing the firm's production and generating a ripple effect on other sectors through its raw material procurement ($\mathbf{x}^{**} = \mathbf{B}\mathbf{a}_{n4}x_4$) (Miller and Blair, 2009). This corresponds to the value before the aggregation of the third term on the right side of Eq. (12.12) if the company does not sell intermediate goods ($\mathbf{a}_{4n} = \mathbf{0}$, $a_{44}=0$). Equation (12.12) calculates the regional contribution that endogenously considers the sales of intermediate goods, even if the company sells the final goods.

When this method is applied to existing companies, even though the added company already exists in the target year of the IOT, production activities at the base time are not deducted. In this case, the production-ripple effect might become an excessive estimation.

### 12.3.3 Modified Hypothetical Insertion Method

Next, consider the case of measuring the regional contribution of production activities at a time different from the base year of the IOT for existing companies rather than new ones. The production activities of the company that differ from the base year can be treated in the same way as the production activities of a new company in the "3.2 Hypothetical Insertion Method." The difference is that a certain amount of production activity is carried out in the base year; therefore, removing this effect is necessary. This can be done by using the IOT for the base year, where the production activities of the company can be properly separated as one sector, and by setting this as 0 as the standard for comparison. Using the notation of Eq. (12.2'), Eq. (12.8) becomes

$$\begin{bmatrix} \mathbf{x}_1 \\ x_2 \\ x_3 \\ 0 \end{bmatrix} = \begin{bmatrix} \mathbf{I} - \mathbf{A}_{11} & -\mathbf{a}_{12} & -\mathbf{a}_{13} & \mathbf{0} \\ -\mathbf{a}_{21} & 1 - a_{22} & -a_{23} & 0 \\ -\mathbf{a}_{31} & -a_{32} & 1 - a_{33} & 0 \\ \mathbf{0} & 0 & 0 & 1 \end{bmatrix}^{-1} \begin{bmatrix} \mathbf{f}_1 \\ f_2 \\ f_3 \\ 0 \end{bmatrix} \tag{12.18'}$$

Here, sector 3 represents the activities of the company in the IOT for the base year, and the formula (12.16), which is the IOT extracted by setting sector 3 as 0, can be used as the production-induced amount for the base year.

$$\begin{bmatrix} \mathbf{x}_1 \\ x_2 \\ 0 \\ 0 \end{bmatrix} = \begin{bmatrix} \mathbf{I} - \mathbf{A}_{11} & -\mathbf{a}_{12} & \mathbf{0} & \mathbf{0} \\ -\mathbf{a}_{21} & 1 - a_{22} & 0 & 0 \\ 0 & 0 & 1 & 0 \\ 0 & 0 & 0 & 1 \end{bmatrix}^{-1} \begin{bmatrix} \mathbf{f}_1 \\ f_2 \\ 0 \\ 0 \end{bmatrix} \tag{12.8''}$$

Furthermore, if the new production activities of the company are expressed as sector 4, then Eq. (12.10) becomes,

$$\begin{bmatrix} \mathbf{x}_1^{**} \\ x_2^{**} \\ 0 \\ x_4 \end{bmatrix} = \begin{bmatrix} \mathbf{I} - \mathbf{A}_{11} & -\mathbf{a}_{12} & \mathbf{0} & -\mathbf{a}_{14} \\ -\mathbf{a}_{21} & 1 - a_{22} & 0 & -a_{24} \\ 0 & 0 & 1 & 0 \\ -\mathbf{a}_{41} & -a_{42} & 0 & 1 - a_{44} \end{bmatrix}^{-1} \begin{bmatrix} \mathbf{f}_1 \\ f_2 \\ 0 \\ f_4 \end{bmatrix} \tag{12.10'}$$

By calculating the corresponding Eq. (12.11) based on Eqs. (12.8") and (12.10'), it is possible to measure the regional contribution after removing the influence of the company's production activities in the base year.

This modified HIM deducts the production activities of target companies in the base year. When analyzing the regional contributions of many companies, it is necessary to revise the IOT for the base year each time. Each economic structure used as the base of comparison is different, and the calculations are complicated. Therefore, if there is no significant difference in the results between when the company's production activities in the base year are deducted and when they are not, the HIM, that does not deduct them may be useful. This point will be discussed in Sect. 12.4.

### *12.3.4 Leontief Model and Ghosh Model*

The production-induced effect on the final demand in the HEM or the HIM with the Leontief inverse matrix measures the ripple effect of production through raw material procurement, which is the backward linkage effect. Conversely, the forward linkage effect can be measured by the ripple effect based on the Ghosh model, which assumes the stability of the allocation coefficient of the intermediate goods transaction.

Because the stability of the allocation coefficients in the Ghosh model is not as dependable as the stability of the input coefficients in the Leontief model, the Ghosh model has not been used as much as the Leontief model thus far. Recently, the Ghosh model was applied to cases measuring the economic impact of natural disasters and the linkage effect of the supply chain of production parts.[2] Furthermore, Takase (2016b) considered the application of the hypothetical sampling method using the Ghosh model as one of the indicators of industrial connectivity in the regional economy. Here, we apply the model together as one method of measuring the ripple effect downstream in the supply chain.[3]

---

[2] Shimoda and Fujikawa (2012) used the Ghosh model to measure the effects of the Great East Japan Earthquake.

[3] Dietzenbacher (1997) demonstrates that the production-induced effect of exogenous value-added in the Ghosh model can be interpreted as the price-induced effect in the Leontief model. In this case, the ripple effect calculated by the Ghosh model is based on price changes. This point must be kept in mind when interpreting the measured regional effects.

The contribution of the SMEs to the local economy through raw material procurement can be measured by applying the HEM/HIM method to the Leontief model (12.13), while the effect of product sales on the other industries can be measured by applying the HEM/HIM to the Ghosh model (12.14).

$$\mathbf{x} = (\mathbf{I} - \mathbf{A})^{-1}\mathbf{f} = (\mathbf{I} + \mathbf{A} + \mathbf{A}^2 + \cdots)\mathbf{f} = \mathbf{B}\mathbf{f} \tag{12.13}$$

$$\mathbf{x}' = \mathbf{v}'(\mathbf{I} - \mathbf{G})^{-1} = \mathbf{v}'(\mathbf{I} + \mathbf{G} + \mathbf{G}^2 + \cdots) = \mathbf{v}'\mathbf{H} \tag{12.14}$$

Here, the Ghosh inverse matrix, **H**, has the following relation with the Leontief inverse matrix, **B** (see Miller and Blair, 2009).

$$\mathbf{H} = (\mathbf{I} - \mathbf{G})^{-1} = \hat{\mathbf{x}}^{-1}(\mathbf{I} - \mathbf{A})^{-1}\hat{\mathbf{x}} = \hat{\mathbf{x}}^{-1}\mathbf{B}\hat{\mathbf{x}} \tag{12.15}$$

Thus, we can calculate the Ghosh inverse matrix, **H**, from the Eq. (12.15) when the Leontief inverse matrix **B** is obtained. Here, $\hat{\mathbf{x}}$ means a rectangular matrix of the production vector. We have $\mathbf{A}\hat{\mathbf{x}} = \hat{\mathbf{x}}\mathbf{G}$, because the distribution coefficient is defined as $\mathbf{G} = \left[g_{ij}\right] = \left[x_{ij}/x_i\right]$.

Applying the HIM to the Ghosh model, we get four equations from (12.16) to (12.19) as the difference in production-induced amounts using the notation corresponding to (12.8), (12.10), (12.11), and (12.12) in the Leontief model,

$$\begin{bmatrix} \mathbf{x} \\ 0 \end{bmatrix}' = \begin{bmatrix} \mathbf{v} \\ 0 \end{bmatrix}' \begin{bmatrix} \mathbf{I} - \mathbf{G} & \mathbf{0} \\ \mathbf{0} & 1 \end{bmatrix}^{-1} = \begin{bmatrix} \mathbf{v} \\ 0 \end{bmatrix}' \begin{bmatrix} \mathbf{H}^{**} & \mathbf{0} \\ \mathbf{0} & 1 \end{bmatrix} \tag{12.16}$$

$$\begin{bmatrix} \mathbf{x}^{**} \\ x_4 \end{bmatrix}' = \begin{bmatrix} \mathbf{v} \\ v_4 \end{bmatrix}' \begin{bmatrix} \mathbf{I} - \mathbf{G} & -\mathbf{g}_{n4} \\ -\mathbf{g}_{4n} & 1 - g_{44} \end{bmatrix}^{-1} = \begin{bmatrix} \mathbf{v} \\ v_4 \end{bmatrix}' \begin{bmatrix} \mathbf{H}^{**} & \mathbf{h}_{n4} \\ \mathbf{h}_{4n} & h_{44} \end{bmatrix} \tag{12.17}$$

$$\begin{bmatrix} \mathbf{x}^{**} \\ x_4 \end{bmatrix}' - \begin{bmatrix} \mathbf{x} \\ 0 \end{bmatrix}' = \begin{bmatrix} \mathbf{v} \\ v_4 \end{bmatrix}' \begin{bmatrix} \mathbf{H}^{**} & \mathbf{h}_{n4} \\ \mathbf{h}_{4n} & h_{44} \end{bmatrix} - \begin{bmatrix} \mathbf{v} \\ 0 \end{bmatrix}' \begin{bmatrix} \mathbf{H} & \mathbf{0} \\ \mathbf{0} & 1 \end{bmatrix} \tag{12.18}$$

Aggregating the Eq. (12.18), we get the following equation,

$$\left( \begin{bmatrix} \mathbf{x}^{**} \\ x_4 \end{bmatrix}' - \begin{bmatrix} \mathbf{x} \\ 0 \end{bmatrix}' \right) \begin{bmatrix} \mathbf{e} \\ 1 \end{bmatrix} = \mathbf{v}'(\mathbf{H}^{**} - \mathbf{H})\mathbf{e} + \mathbf{v}'\mathbf{h}_{n4} + v_4\mathbf{h}_{4n}\mathbf{e} + v_4 h_{44} \tag{12.19}$$

The first term is the effect of a new entry of a specific firm through changes in the multipliers in other n sectors, and the second term is the ripple effect that the added value of n sectors has on the sales of the entering firm. The third term is the ripple effect that the added value of the entering firm has on the sales of other n sectors, and the fourth term is the ripple effect that the entering firm has on its own sector.

**Table 12.1** Indicators regarding the size of target companies (2019)

| Companies | Capital (million yen) | Employees (Person) | Production in 2011 (Ratio to the 2019 value) |
|---|---|---|---|
| Casting product manufacturing industry/ Company A | 24.0 | 121 | 0.674 |
| Core manufacturing industry/Company B | 10.0 | 148 | 0.838 |
| Printing industry/ Company C | 49.5 | 116 | 1.000 |
| Food and beverage manufacturing industry/ Company D | 10.0 | 40 | 0.728 |

*Source* Created by the author

## 12.4 Regional Contribution of the SMEs in Nishio City

Here, we will measure the regional contribution of a small company's production activities, using SMEs in Nishio City as an example. We use the 2011 Nishio City interregional IOT as the reference IOT. This IOT is based on the 2011 Aichi Prefecture inter-municipal IOT with 64 municipals and 106 sectors, which is explained in Chap. 6. We recompile regions in the table to integrate 54 municipals into three regions: Nishio City, the ROA Prefecture, and the ROJ.

Here, based on the results of a survey[4] that we conducted with the cooperation of four SMEs in Nishio City, we estimated the input structure (columns) and sales channel composition (rows) that describe the production activities of each company as one sector of the IOT. Then, using the HIM that we propose, we insert the production activity of one SME in the Nishio City IOT and measure the regional contribution from two aspects: raw material procurement and product sales.

Table 12.1 presents the capital, number of employees, and ratio of 2011 production to 2019 for the four companies.

Here, we will measure both the regional contribution through raw material procurement using the Leontief model and the regional contribution through product sales using the Ghosh model. Furthermore, because all four target companies already existed in the base year of 2011, we also conducted an evaluation using the modified HIM that deducted production activities in 2011, and we compared their results.

[4] We conducted a survey to obtain basic information for the construction of the regional contribution indices of SMEs. The target of the survey was SMEs certified as the "Regional Future Leading Companies" by METI, and we selected four companies among five companies that applied. The target period of the survey, in principle, was taken as the longest accounting period, including 2019, before the spread of COVID-19. The survey items are the company's sales amount, direct material costs, cost of sales, detailed items of sale, general administrative expenses, and employees, referring to the "Input Structure Survey" of the IOT, Japan. Regional sales information by product is also included to obtain the output structure of the company.

### *12.4.1 Characteristics of the Four SMEs' Production*

The features of the four SMEs' production activities are described in the following section:

(1) Casting product manufacturing company, A

Nishio City has many companies that manufacture automobile parts, and Company A is a SME that manufactures engine-related casting products. Table 12.2 displays Company A's sales composition ratio by item and region. Automobile parts account for 83.48% of sales, and the company also manufactures industrial machinery parts, construction machinery parts, water pump parts, and electric appliance parts. In addition, 80.8% of auto parts are delivered within Aichi Prefecture. The regional share of industrial machinery parts is 8.3% in Nishio City, 48.4% in Aichi Prefecture, and 43.3% outside Aichi Prefecture. The main raw materials for Company A are scrap steel and casting cores. Scrap steel is supplied from a wide range of areas inside and outside Aichi Prefecture, and the core mold is generally procured from core manufacturing companies in Nishio City.

(2) Core manufacturing company, B

Company B is an SME that specializes in manufacturing mold cores[5] (see Table 12.2). Sales shares of the products are 46.5% in Nishio City, 38.7% in Aichi Prefecture, and 14.8% outside Aichi Prefecture. It has three factories in Nishio City, Toyota City in Aichi Prefecture, and Takaoka City in Toyama Prefecture. The production ratio of the factory in Nishio City is 57.5%. The total values of the company are shown in the table. Here, we focus on the factory in Nishio City. Therefore, after dividing the production activities into three regions—Nishio City, Aichi Prefecture, and outside the prefecture—we estimated the input amount for each region, considering each establishment's production, sales, and procurement by region.

From our interviews with Company B about the sales destinations of its production in each factory, we found that the factories in Toyota City and Takaoka City deliver to neighboring factories, respectively. If 100% of the products are sold within the region for these two factories, we establish that the rest is delivered by the factory in Nishio City, and the regional ratio of sales destinations has been determined.

(3) Printing company, C

Company C is an SME that operates a variety of businesses centered on the printing industry, including information and communication services, advertising, and event planning. Looking at the composition of sales in Table 12.2, about 70% are printing-related, with leaflet printing at 38.48%, other printed matter at 30.93%, BPO[6] at 3.96%, web-related at 5.21%, Community-related at 8.30%, and other at

[5] A "core" in casting is a mold that is used separately from the main mold in the process of making the hollow part of the casting.

[6] BPO (Business Process Outsourcing) is the outsourcing of part of the business process in corporate activities. Indirect operations such as personnel affairs, general affairs, accounting, and information systems, as well as logistics operations and manufacturing operations, are covered.

**Table 12.2** Production items of each company and the regional shares of sales (2019)

| | Production item | Sales | Regional share of sales (%) | | | | |
|---|---|---|---|---|---|---|---|
| | | Share (%) | Nishio City | ROA | ROJ | Exports | Total |
| Casting product manufacturing industry/ Company A | 1 Automobile parts | 83.5 | 0.0 | 80.8 | 19.2 | 0.0 | 100.0 |
| | 2 Industrial machinery parts | 10.0 | 8.3 | 48.4 | 43.3 | 0.0 | 100.0 |
| | 3 Construction machinery parts | 1.2 | 0.0 | 0.0 | 100.0 | 0.0 | 100.0 |
| | 4 Water pump parts | 0.6 | 0.0 | 100.0 | 0.0 | 0.0 | 100.0 |
| | 5 Electric appliance parts | 0.9 | 0.0 | 0.0 | 100.0 | 0.0 | 100.0 |
| | 6 Others | 3.9 | 9.2 | 68.1 | 22.7 | 0.0 | 100.0 |
| | Total | 100.0 | 1.2 | 75.5 | 23.3 | 0.0 | 100.0 |
| Core manufacturing industry/ Company B | 1 Mold cores | 99.5 | 46.5 | 38.7 | 14.8 | 0.0 | 100.0 |
| | 2 Others | 0.5 | 0.0 | 100.0 | 0.0 | 0.0 | 100.0 |
| | Total | 100.0 | 46.3 | 39.0 | 14.7 | 0.0 | 100.0 |
| Printing industry/ Company C | 1 Leaflet printing | 38.5 | 20.0 | 70.0 | 10.0 | 0.0 | 100.0 |
| | 2 Other printed matter | 30.9 | 30.0 | 60.0 | 10.0 | 0.0 | 100.0 |
| | 3 BPO | 4.0 | 30.0 | 60.0 | 10.0 | 0.0 | 100.0 |
| | 4 Web-related | 5.2 | 20.0 | 70.0 | 10.0 | 0.0 | 100.0 |
| | 5 Community-related business | 8.3 | 90.0 | 10.0 | 0.0 | 0.0 | 100.0 |
| | 6 Others | 13.1 | 20.0 | 60.0 | 20.0 | 0.0 | 100.0 |
| | Total | 100.0 | 29.3 | 60.2 | 10.5 | 0.0 | 100.0 |
| Food and beverage manufacturing industry/ Company D | 1 Matcha | 69.5 | 5.0 | 25.0 | 62.0 | 8.0 | 100.0 |
| | 2 Sencha | 10.0 | 20.0 | 75.0 | 5.0 | 0.0 | 100.0 |
| | 3 Hojicha | 1.3 | 3.0 | 15.0 | 67.0 | 15.0 | 100.0 |
| | 4 Matcha latte | 0.9 | 5.0 | 20.0 | 25.0 | 50.0 | 100.0 |
| | 5 Matcha bean paste | 0.7 | 2.0 | 18.0 | 80.0 | 0.0 | 100.0 |
| | 6 Others | 17.5 | 20.0 | 40.0 | 40.0 | 0.0 | 100.0 |
| | Total | 100.0 | 9.1 | 32.4 | 52.3 | 6.2 | 100.0 |

*Source* Made from the survey data for the corresponding company

13.12%. Looking at the sales destination area, Nishio City is 29.3%, Aichi Prefecture is 60.2%, and outside the prefecture is 10.5%. Sales of Community-related businesses are concentrated in Nishio City.

Table 12.3 presents the ratio of sales destination industries for each production item of Company C obtained through interviews. Flyers are focused on the construction and retail trades. All BPOs and community-related businesses are local governments. We estimated the sales composition of Company C from the information on the product ratios in Table 12.3 and the regional shares of sales destinations in Table 12.2.

(4) Food and beverage manufacturing company, D

Company D is an SME that manufactures and sells food and beverages centered on matcha products.[7] Looking at the composition of sales in Table 12.2, matcha is at 69.53%, sencha at 10.04%, hojicha at 1.28%, matcha latte at 0.91%, matcha bean paste at 0.73%, and others at 17.52%. Looking at the sales destination area ratio, Nishio City is at 9.1%, Aichi Prefecture is at 32.4%, outside the prefecture is 52.3%, and export is at 6.2%.

Table 12.4 shows the composition of Company D's sales by item obtained through interviews. According to it, there are three types of sales: wholesale to other food manufacturers and retailers, retail sales at their own stores, and sales at an attached coffee shop. Wholesale sales include both intermediate goods that are used as raw materials for other products and final goods that are sold through other retail stores.

Through a questionnaire survey, we determined the production value, cost of sales, and direct material costs for each company's production item and calculated the input amount of detailed items for the cost of sales and selling, general, and administrative expenses according to the sector classification of the IOT. Here, the characteristics of the item appear depending on the content of the direct material costs.

Next, we converted these input amounts from purchaser price evaluation to producer price evaluation using the margin rate in the IOT and then estimated the input amount by the sales amount of each company's main products.

Then, the estimated sectoral inputs were apportioned by region using the regional procurement ratios of major raw materials obtained from the questionnaire and, for other sectors, the trade coefficients from the IOT. Finally, by aggregating the inputs by sector in the IOT, you can obtain input amounts by region and sector.

Company A belongs to "casting and forging products," and Company B is included in "other ceramic and clay products." Company C provides products of "printing, prepress, and bookbinding," "video, audio, and textual information production," "advertising," and "other business services." Company D provides "food products," "beverages," "commerce," and "beverage services." By further aggregating the data, the values of companies C and D can be obtained.

The output value of Company A and Company B can be divided using the share of customers for each sales item in the questionnaire. Company C's production value

[7] Matcha, sencha, and hojicha are all types of green tea. Matcha is finely powdered tencha, which is made by drying the sprouts of tea grown in a covered tea garden without rubbing. Sencha is made by steaming tea leaves cultivated in an open-air tea garden with ample sunlight and then drying them while rubbing them. Hojicha is made by roasting tea, which is not used as sencha, over high heat to bring out its aroma.

**Table 12.3** Company C's sales destination ratio by item (%, 2019)

| | Construction | Manufacturing | Information and communication | Transportation and postal services | Retail | Hotel and restaurant | Other personal services | Local government | Total |
|---|---|---|---|---|---|---|---|---|---|
| Leaflet printing | 10.0 | 0.0 | 0.0 | 0.0 | 90.0 | 0.0 | 0.0 | 0.0 | 100.0 |
| Other printed matter | 10.0 | 20.0 | 5.0 | 5.0 | 30.0 | 10.0 | 20.0 | 0.0 | 100.0 |
| BPO | 0.0 | 0.0 | 0.0 | 0.0 | 0.0 | 0.0 | 0.0 | 100.0 | 100.0 |
| Web-related | 10.0 | 10.0 | 0.0 | 10.0 | 30.0 | 10.0 | 30.0 | 0.0 | 100.0 |
| Community-related business | 0.0 | 0.0 | 0.0 | 0.0 | 0.0 | 0.0 | 0.0 | 100.0 | 100.0 |

*Source* Made from the survey data for the corresponding company

**Table 12.4** Company D's sales share by products and sales structure for each item

| Production item | Sales | Sales structure (%) | | | | |
|---|---|---|---|---|---|---|
| | Share (%) | Wholesale (inter-mediate goods) | Wholesale (final goods) | Attached coffee shop | Retail sales | Total |
| 1 Matcha | 69.53 | 66.8 | 3.2 | 5.0 | 25.0 | 100.0 |
| 2 Sencha | 10.04 | 10.0 | 10.0 | 5.0 | 75.0 | 100.0 |
| 3 Hojicha | 1.28 | 45.0 | 15.0 | 0.0 | 40.0 | 100.0 |
| 4 Matcha latte | 0.91 | 54.0 | 6.0 | 0.0 | 40.0 | 100.0 |
| 5 Matcha bean paste | 0.73 | 100.0 | 0.0 | 0.0 | 0.0 | 100.0 |
| 6 Others | 17.52 | 18.0 | 2.0 | 40.0 | 40.0 | 100.0 |
| Total | 100.00 | 52.4 | 3.8 | 11.0 | 32.8 | 100.0 |

*Source* Made from the survey data for the corresponding company

was estimated on a pro-rata basis based on the sales amount by item and industry in Table 12.3, and for detailed sectors, it was estimated on a pro-rata basis using the intermediate goods transaction amount of the corresponding sector in the IOT.

For Company D, the sales amount by department was estimated using the ratios by item and sales format in Table 12.4. Regarding wholesale and retail store sales of Company D, from the sales amount by sales format shown in Table 12.4, the production margin corresponding to the wholesale margin and retail margin is calculated using the commercial margin rate in the IOT. We used the calculated amount as the production for the commercial sector and added the rest to the manufacturing sector.

In applying the HIM, input and output amounts aggregated for each firm are used. In addition, when applying the modified HIM that deducts production activities in the base year, the value by sector corresponding to the company's main items in 2019 is subtracted by the value adjusted proportionally to the scale of production value in 2011.[8]

## 12.4.2 Regional Contribution of Each SME

Table 12.5 displays the influence of each company's production and sales activities on regional production value using the HIM and modified HIM, the backward linkage

[8] Normally, it would be necessary to obtain basic data during the questionnaire survey to estimate the production value of each company in 2011 and the corresponding sectoral input and sectoral output, but this would be difficult because of the heavy burden on respondents. Therefore, here we asked only for the production value for 2011, assumed that input and output values were proportional to 2019, and calculated the base year value that should be deducted from the IOT. See Table 1 for the ratio of production scales for both years.

effect through raw material procurement using the Leontief model, and the forward linkage effect using the Ghosh model. The upper half of the table is the value of HIM when the production activities of the company in the base year are not deducted, and the lower half is the value of modified HIM when the production activities of the company in the base year are deducted. Each of them is divided into three parts, and the first six lines of "regional multiplier" represent the ratio of regional production-induced value to the company's production value, and the next six lines of "regional composition ratio" display the ratio of each region to the domestic total.

Finally, there are four rows for "Regional Contribution." (1) The national contribution is the value of the "total" in regional multipliers, which shows the magnitude of the impact each company's production activities have on other sectors through raw material procurement and product sales nationwide. The higher the number, the greater the influence on the whole country. (2) The regional contributions use the Nishio City total value of the "composition ratio by region." The larger this value, the greater the relative contribution to Nishio City. In addition, (3) and (4) calculate the ratio of the forward linkage effect to the backward linkage effect of national contribution and regional contribution, respectively. If this value is greater than 1, the effect through sales is greater than the effect through procurement. If we consider the effect nationwide, the ripple effect through sales is greater than the ripple effect through procurement because the closer the company is to the upstream side of a product's supply chain, the shorter the path upstream and the longer the path downstream.

Comparing the top half of Table 12.5 based on the HIM and the bottom half based on the modified HIM after deducting the production activities of the target SME in the base year, it can be seen that the corresponding numbers are almost the same because the production scale of the target SMEs is not large compared to the Nishio City economy. Below, we will focus on the content of the calculation results obtained using the simpler HIM.

The scatter diagram in Fig. 12.1 depicts each company's contribution to the nation on the horizontal axis and its contribution to the region, Nishio City, on the vertical axis. The two contributions of each company are displayed separately: backward linkage effects through raw material procurement and forward linkage effects through product sales. Further to the right of the diagram, the greater the contribution to the nation, and the higher the location, the greater the contribution to Nishio City.

Looking at the figure, first, the backward linkage effect for all four companies is about double the effect on the whole country, and the effect on Nishio City is about 50–65%, which is just over half of the production; hence, there is slight variation among the companies. However, there is a significant difference between the four companies regarding the forward linkage effect. Companies A and B contribute 3–4 times as much to the national market, but conversely, their contribution to Nishio City is 30–40%, affecting production in a wide area. On the contrary, the contribution of companies C and D to the nation is smaller, at 2.66 times and 1.68 times, respectively, and conversely, the contribution to Nishio City is larger, at 49.80% and 61.89%, respectively.

**Table 12.5** Comparison of the regional contribution of SMEs' production and sales

| | | | Casting product manufacturing company A | | Core manufacturing company B | | Printing company C | | Food and beverage manufacturing company D | |
|---|---|---|---|---|---|---|---|---|---|---|
| | | | BL | FL | BL | FL | BL | FL | BL | FL |
| Evaluation using HIM (Add each company's production activities without subtracting base year activities) | Regional multiplier (SME concerned = 1.0) | SME concerned | 1.00 | 1.00 | 1.00 | 1.00 | 1.00 | 1.00 | 1.00 | 1.00 |
| | | Rest of Nishio city | 0.22 | 0.03 | 0.25 | 0.88 | 0.10 | 0.33 | 0.06 | 0.04 |
| | | ROA | 0.41 | 1.31 | 0.52 | 0.83 | 0.42 | 0.92 | 0.38 | 0.19 |
| | | ROJ | 0.24 | 1.00 | 0.31 | 1.18 | 0.53 | 0.42 | 0.49 | 0.45 |
| | | Total | 1.88 | 3.34 | 2.08 | 3.89 | 2.05 | 2.66 | 1.93 | 1.68 |
| | | Nishio City, total | 1.22 | 1.03 | 1.25 | 1.88 | 1.10 | 1.33 | 1.06 | 1.04 |
| | Regional share (%) | SME concerned | 53.22 | 29.90 | 48.08 | 25.69 | 48.69 | 37.56 | 51.73 | 59.39 |
| | | Rest of Nishio city | 11.95 | 0.90 | 12.13 | 22.61 | 4.86 | 12.23 | 3.18 | 2.50 |
| | | ROA | 21.83 | 39.19 | 25.07 | 21.40 | 20.55 | 34.52 | 19.55 | 11.25 |
| | | ROJ | 12.99 | 30.01 | 14.71 | 30.30 | 25.90 | 15.68 | 25.54 | 26.86 |
| | | Total | 100.00 | 100.00 | 100.00 | 100.00 | 100.00 | 100.00 | 100.00 | 100.00 |
| | | Nishio City, total | 65.18 | 30.80 | 60.22 | 48.30 | 53.55 | 49.80 | 54.91 | 61.89 |
| | Regional contribution indices | (1) Nationwide contribution | 1.88 | 3.34 | 2.08 | 3.89 | 2.05 | 2.66 | 1.93 | 1.68 |
| | | (2) Regional contribution | 65.18 | 30.80 | 60.22 | 48.30 | 53.55 | 49.80 | 54.91 | 61.89 |

(continued)

**Table 12.5** (continued)

| | | | Casting product manufacturing company A | | Core manufacturing company B | | Printing company C | | Food and beverage manufacturing company D | |
|---|---|---|---|---|---|---|---|---|---|---|
| | | | BL | FL | BL | FL | BL | FL | BL | FL |
| | | (3) FL/BL ratio of nationwide contribution | | 1.78 | | 1.87 | | 1.30 | | 0.87 |
| | | (4) FL/BL ratio of regional contribution | | 0.47 | | 0.80 | | 0.93 | | 1.13 |
| Evaluation using midified HIM (Add each company's production activities with subtracting base year activities) | Regional multiplier (SME concerned = 1.0) | SME concerned | 1.00 | 1.00 | 1.00 | 1.00 | 1.00 | 1.00 | 1.00 | 1.00 |
| | | Rest of Nishio city | 0.22 | 0.03 | 0.25 | 0.88 | 0.10 | 0.33 | 0.06 | 0.04 |
| | | ROA | 0.41 | 1.31 | 0.52 | 0.83 | 0.42 | 0.92 | 0.38 | 0.19 |
| | | ROJ | 0.24 | 1.00 | 0.31 | 1.18 | 0.53 | 0.42 | 0.49 | 0.45 |
| | | Total | 1.88 | 3.34 | 2.07 | 3.89 | 2.05 | 2.66 | 1.93 | 1.68 |
| | | Nishio City, total | 1.22 | 1.03 | 1.25 | 1.88 | 1.10 | 1.33 | 1.06 | 1.04 |
| | Regional share (%) | SME concerned | 53.22 | 29.90 | 48.26 | 25.69 | 48.74 | 37.57 | 51.73 | 59.40 |
| | | Rest of Nishio city | 11.95 | 0.90 | 11.88 | 22.61 | 4.83 | 12.23 | 3.18 | 2.50 |
| | | ROA | 21.83 | 39.19 | 24.87 | 21.40 | 20.50 | 34.49 | 19.55 | 11.25 |
| | | ROJ | 12.99 | 30.01 | 14.99 | 30.30 | 25.92 | 15.71 | 25.54 | 26.85 |

(continued)

**Table 12.5** (continued)

| | | | Casting product manufacturing company A | | Core manufacturing company B | | Printing company C | | Food and beverage manufacturing company D | |
|---|---|---|---|---|---|---|---|---|---|---|
| | | | BL | FL | BL | FL | BL | FL | BL | FL |
| | | Total | 100.00 | 100.00 | 100.00 | 100.00 | 100.00 | 100.00 | 100.00 | 100.00 |
| | | Nishio City, total | 65.18 | 30.80 | 60.14 | 48.30 | 53.58 | 49.80 | 54.91 | 61.90 |
| | Regional contribution indices | (1) Nationwide contribution | 1.88 | 3.34 | 2.07 | 3.89 | 2.05 | 2.66 | 1.93 | 1.68 |
| | | (2) Regional contribution | 65.18 | 30.80 | 60.14 | 48.30 | 53.58 | 49.80 | 54.91 | 61.90 |
| | | (3) FL/BL ratio of nationwide contribution | 1.78 | | 1.88 | | 1.30 | | 0.87 | |
| | | (4) FL/BL ratio of regional contribution | 0.47 | | 0.80 | | 0.93 | | 1.13 | |

*Source* Calculated by the author

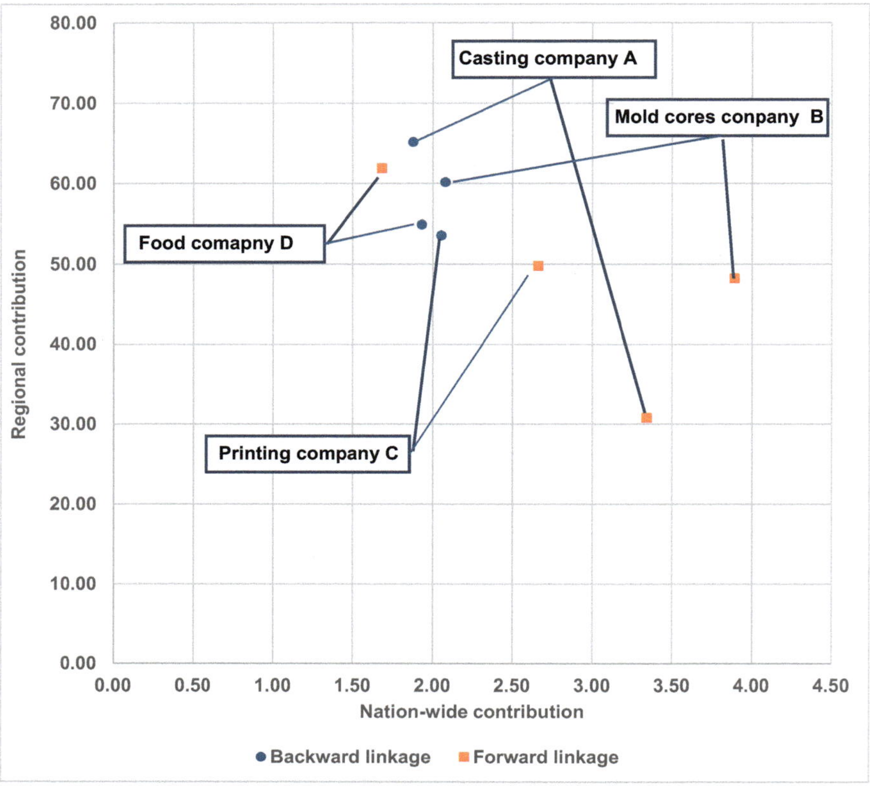


**Fig. 12.1** Nation-wide contribution index and regional contribution index of each company. *Source* Created by the author

This is related to differences in the characteristics of the products and services handled. Companies A and B have an impact on a wider range of regions and industries through the production and sale of automobile parts, whereas companies C and D have a market for food, printing, and information services, a significant percentage of which covers Nishio City and Aichi Prefecture. Considering the supply-chain relationship, in the process of supplying resources and raw materials to produce final goods, companies A and B produce and supply products that are located further upstream, while companies C and D produce and supply products that are located further downstream.

Next, we will compare the ratios of the backward linkage effect to the forward linkage effect for the above-mentioned indicators of national contribution and regional contribution, respectively. To express the relative position of the supply chain, if this value is greater than 1 for the national contribution, the forward linkage is considered to be greater than the backward linkage and is located further upstream.

The scatter diagram in Fig. 12.2 shows the positions of four companies, with the horizontal axis representing the forward/backward linkage ratio of national contribution and the vertical axis representing the forward/backward linkage ratio of regional contribution.

Looking at the figure, the impact of the three companies specializing in intermediate goods production (Companies A, B, and C) on a national basis is attributed to the larger forward linkage effect, and conversely, the contribution to Nishio City is because of the larger backward linkage effect. Relatively speaking, this means that in terms of product sales, demand is captured from the national market and more is returned to the local area in the procurement of raw materials.

However, food and beverage manufacturing company D produces not only intermediate goods but also final goods. In terms of contribution to the nation, the backward linkage effect is relatively larger than the forward linkage effect, and raw materials are procured from a wide area. Nevertheless, the contribution to Nishio City is that the forward linkage effect is relatively larger than the backward linkage

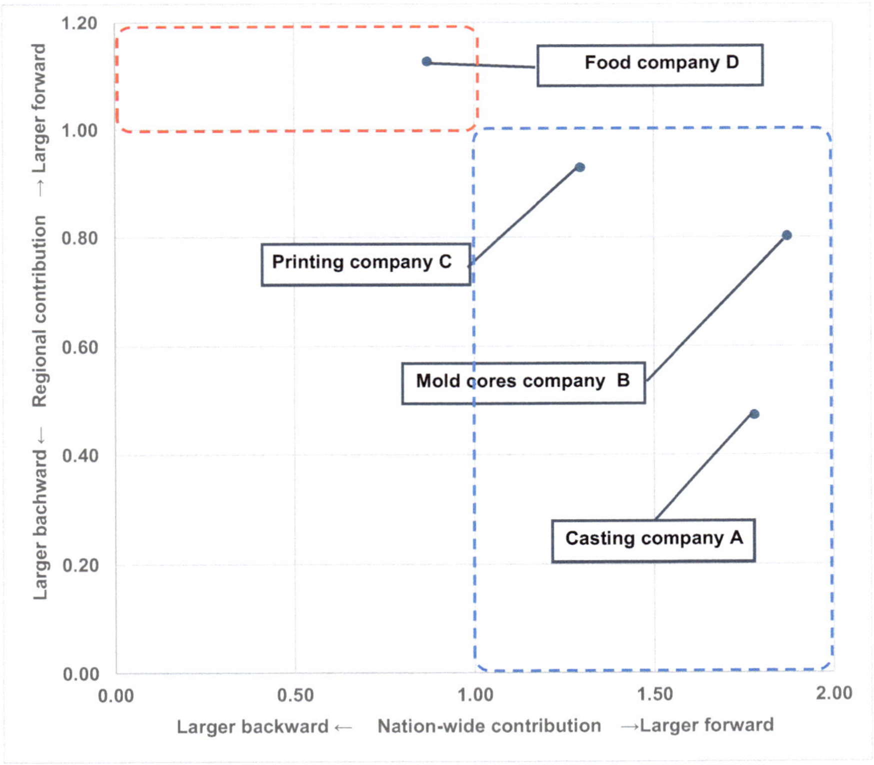


**Fig. 12.2** Relative relationship between forward and backward linkages of each firm's contribution index. *Source* Created by the author

effect, and it can be seen that the contribution in terms of product sales targeted at markets near the local area is larger.

## 12.5 Concluding Remarks

To sustainably develop the local economy, it is expected that energetic SMEs will play an active role. Therefore, it is important to calculate and visualize the economic contribution that these SMEs make to the local regional economy. Here, we proposed an analysis tool called the "HIM," which is an extension of the "HEM," one of the analytical methods for input–output analysis. We estimated the production activities of one company using the input structure (column) and sales channel structure (row) of the IOT and measured the change in the production ripple effect brought about by adding them to the existing IOT.

This method was applied to the Leontief model to measure regional contribution through the "backward linkage effect" from raw material procurement for production and regional contribution through the "forward linkage effect" from product sales by applying it to the Ghosh model. However, in the case of existing companies, the production activities of the companies are included in the IOT. If the activities are not deducted, the estimates might be overestimated. Therefore, here we performed calculations both with and without deducting the company's production activities from the IOT and verified the extent of the difference. The results revealed that almost no differences existed in the following indicators for companies whose production scale was not large compared to the economic scale analyzed here.

We summarized regional contributions into two evaluation axes. One is the degree of contribution to the nation as the ratio (multiplier) of the national production value to the production value of the company in question. The other measure was the contribution to the region as the ratio of Nishio City's production value to the national production value. Consequently, the difference between the four companies is greater in the degree of contribution through product sales (forward linkage effect) than in the contribution through raw material procurement (backward linkage effect). As for the backward linkage effect, more than half of the production was a local contribution to Nishio City. Differences in forward linkage effects are thought to be related to the characteristics of the products and services handled. Furthermore, when considering the supply chain relationship, companies A and B produce and supply products that are located further upstream in the supply chain, while companies C and D produce and supply products that are located downstream.

For the three companies specializing in intermediate goods production (Companies A, B, and C), the forward linkage effect is larger in terms of national contribution, but conversely, the backward linkage effect is larger in terms of regional contribution. This means that in terms of product sales, demand is captured from the national market and more is returned to the local area in the procurement of raw materials, and these industries function as export-based industries. However, food and beverage manufacturing company D produces not only intermediate goods but also final goods.

In terms of national contribution, the backward linkage effect is larger, and in terms of regional contribution, the forward linkage effect is larger. The contribution of raw materials procured from a wide area and sales targeted at local markets is greater.

In this chapter, we measured the degree of regional contribution in production, but expansion to evaluation based on added value, final demand, and employment is also important. Evaluation of the changes in regional contribution based on a company's future business plan is another opportunity. In this study, although the regional contribution was evaluated based on the 2011 Nishio City regional IOT, updating the IOT also remains. Furthermore, like the HEM, the HIM proposed here has a methodological issue as the IOT after the change (extraction or insertion) is not balanced. This time we compared four companies from different industries, but evaluating the regional contribution of more companies will help verify the validity of the method. We have asked the four companies that cooperated with us to consider whether the results of measuring their degree of regional contribution can be utilized in future business development. A follow-up is important from the perspective of regional revitalization. These points remain future issues.

## References

Heiho, Aya, and Yasunori Kikuchi. 2021. Creating a flow chart based on the historical record of the construction and application of the regional input-output tables in municipalities. *Journal of Life Cycle Assessment, Japan* 17 (3): 174–192 (in Japanese).

Shimoda, Mitsuru, Kiyoshi Fujikawa, and Takatoshi Watanabe. 2005. Japan's Industrial Structure as seen from the input-output table by company size. *Sango Renkan (Business Journal of PAPAIOS)* 13 (3): 52–65 (in Japanese).

Ishikawa, Yoshifumi, and Ryohei Nakamura (2018) Spatial Incidence Analysis of Economic Impacts: An Extended Input-Output Approach, *Papers presented at the 54th Annual Meeting of the JSRSAI* (in Japanese).

Ishikawa, Yoshifumi (2019) "General-purpose inter-regional input-output model for the analysis on effect of regional revitalization policies," RIETI Discussion Paper Series 19-J-062, pp.1–19 (in Japanese).

Ishiro, Taku. 2007. Industrial network structure in Kanagawa Prefecture: Through the creation of an input-output table by company size of Kanagawa Prefecture from 1985 to 2000. *Sango Renkan (Business Journal of PAPAIOS)* 15 (2): 57–70 (in Japanese).

Miura, Tsuyoshi. 2018. Regional analysis and utilization of input-output tables. *The Review of Economics and Business Management (Kwansei Gakuin University)* 45: 1–10 (in Japanese).

Miller, R.E., and P.D. Blair. 2009. *Input-output analysis: Foundations and Extensions*, Cambridge University Press.

Okuma, Kazuhiro, Yuta Endou, and Akira Matsumoto. 2019. Empirical Analysis on Economic Effects of Recycling-Oriented Regional Development Measures: Construction and Application of Minamisanriku Town's Input-Output Table. *Sangyo Renkan (Business Journal of PAPAIOS)* 27 (1): 14–25 (in Japanese).

Takase, Koji. 2016b. Indicators of inter-industry linkages and identification of major industries in regional economies. *Shizuoka University Economics Research* 20 (4): 87–107 (in Japanese).

Takase, Koji (2016a) Grasp of basic industries by input-output model. In Takayuki Yamashita ed. *Handbook of Regional Economic Analysis: Regional revitalization learned from the Shizuoka model*, Koyo Shobo, Kyoto (in Japanese).

# Chapter 13
# Concluding Summary and the Remaining Future Directions

## 13.1 Concluding Summary

Input–output analysis is widely used as a useful tool for analyzing and resolving various economic issues. In recent years, there has been growing interest not only in intra-regional IOTs that cover a single region but also in interregional IOTs that cover multiple regions. The production activities of a regional economy are not limited to the region in question, and the smaller the regional unit being targeted, the greater the relationship with other regions becomes in both the procurement of raw materials and the sale of products. Interregional IOTs can measure such interregional linkage structures.

This book summarizes the author's research on the creation and application of IOTs for regional economies in Japan, focusing on interregional IOTs that cover multiple regions. The book consists of two parts: six chapters on the creation of interregional IOTs and five chapters that use the created interregional IOTs to analyze various economic issues.

In the former, we first organized the structure of Japan's regional IOTs using three axes: time, region, and scope (Chap. 2). Starting with the national IOT, the time axis includes the development of updated tables and connection IOTs in different years. On the regional axis, we can see that there are four hierarchical levels, including the national table: regional IOTs that divide the country into multiple regions, prefectural IOTs that divide the country into 47 prefectures, and small-region IOTs or municipal IOTs that divide prefectures into multiple small regions or cities, towns, and villages. On the scope axis, there is a division into independent regional IOTs and interregional IOTs that integrate multiple regions.

In Japan, IOTs for several prefectures were developed at roughly the same time as the national table. It was only after the 1990 tables that IOTs for each prefecture were completed. Prior to that, the development of regional IOTs for regions under the jurisdiction of the METI contributed to the development of regional IOTs in Japan.



M. Yamada, *Multi-Regional Input–Output Analysis of the Japanese Economy*,
https://doi.org/10.1007/978-981-97-9041-8_13

However, the METI stopped compiling such regional IOTs after the 2005 table, and since then, the importance of prefectural IOTs has increased.

We also summarized the outline of the compilation of regional IOTs in comparison with the national table and confirmed that, in compiling regional IOTs, it is important to estimate the production value by sector and final demand items, especially the estimation of imports and exports by sector. Furthermore, we compared the aggregated values of the prefectural IOTs with the values of the national table for the 2011 IOTs and confirmed that the discrepancy rate in the aggregated values of production is less than one percent (Chap. 3). However, when comparing production values and net exports by sector, we found some sectors with a large error rate. The regional IOTs developed by the METI were compiled to ensure they matched the national table when aggregated, but with the prefectural IOTs, no mechanism for making such adjustments is available, which is an issue.

Next, we discussed how to create the Chubu region IOT, which is one of the inter-prefectural IOTs (Chap. 4). The Chubu region is a region comprising nine prefectures: Toyama, Ishikawa, Fukui, Nagano, Gifu, Shizuoka, Aichi, Mie, and Shiga, located between Tokyo and Osaka. The IOTs of these nine prefectures and the ROJ are integrated into a single IOT. Therefore, it is necessary to estimate interregional trade between the nine prefectures and the other regions by sector. Here, we estimated based on the MLIT's Interregional Net Freight Flow Survey and other data. The interregional trade coefficient obtained from the survey was used to integrate each table into an interregional IOT; hence, estimating interregional trade is the most crucial factor. The MLIT's Interregional Net Cargo Flow Survey is a three-day survey; hence, there are issues with the stability of inter-prefectural trade volume. The CFS, conducted in conjunction with the compilation of the METI regional IOTs, is another option for estimating annual trade volumes, but with METI ceasing to compile IOTS, there are issues regarding the continuity of this statistical survey.

Although primary statistics on inter-prefectural trade, which are essential in compiling an inter-prefectural IOT, are available for commodities, the information on trade related to services is limited. Additionally, in compiling an interregional IOT for small regions or municipalities within a prefecture, estimates of trade between them are required; however, the corresponding primary statistics are not available except for Hokkaido. In such cases, non-survey methods must be used. Here, we examined one such estimation method, the gravity-RAS method (Chap. 5). In this case, we used the Aichi Prefecture IOT as a basis to create an interregional IOT that breaks the prefecture down into four small regions and estimates trade between the four regions within the prefecture. Gravity parameters are estimated based on the interregional trade data by sector in the 2005 METI Interregional Input–Output Table, and the results are compared with the case where a priori parameters are given.

Next, as an example of an IOT between small regions within a prefecture, the creation of an inter-municipal IOT in Aichi Prefecture was discussed (Chap. 6). Interregional trade between municipalities within the prefecture was estimated by applying the gravity-RAS method discussed in Chap. 5. As the validity of the estimated interregional trade cannot be verified, here we examined the validity of the inter-municipal linkages calculated from the production spillover effects of the created IOT.

At the end of Part 1, we discussed the merging of intra-prefectural small-region IOTs covering multiple neighboring prefectures (Chap. 7). Ideally, we would create an inter-municipal IOT for each prefecture, link them, and create an inter-municipal IOT spanning multiple prefectures. However, to reduce the amount of work, we combined municipalities, created an interregional IOT for each prefecture, and linked them. Specifically, we created an interregional IOT for Aichi, Gifu, and Mie Prefectures, dividing them into 14 regions in total. This revealed that by breaking down the IOTs for each prefecture—which are divided by administrative district—into small regions and then merging them into an interregional IOT spanning multiple prefectures, we can obtain a tool to analyze regions based on economic connections rather than administrative districts such as prefectures.

In Part 2, we conducted several applied analyses of the interregional IOT we created. In Chap. 8, we conducted a multiplier decomposition of the Chubu region interregional IOT discussed in Chap. 4. By calculating the amount of production induced by final demand in each prefecture, we confirmed a mutual dependency centered on Aichi Prefecture within the Chubu region based on the relationship of inter-prefectural spillover. Additionally, the production value of each prefecture generally increased from 2011 to 2015. However, when this was decomposed into a technological factor owing to changes in input coefficients and market factors because of changes in the final demand, we found that the technological factor decreased and that the market factor increased. Despite the increase in final demand, the demand for intermediate goods is decreasing, which is thought to be related to the high added value of produced goods and services and the expansion of the service economy, as well as the progress in the globalization of intermediate goods procurement. Moreover, by decomposing the production-induced multiplier into intra-prefectural multipliers, spillover multipliers (within the Chubu region and outside the Chubu region), as well as feedback multipliers and comparing the changes between the two years, we found that the production multiplier has decreased, mainly because of a decrease in the feedback effect on the Chubu Region. Here too, the increasing globalization of intermediate goods procurement and the increasing regionalization of domestic procurement are thought to be related to the situation.

In Chap. 9, using the MRIOT for small areas of the three prefectures in the Tokai region discussed in Chap. 7, we considered the economic distance calculated by the APL from the perspective of establishing metropolitan areas. Metropolitan areas can be defined by population flow, such as commuting rates, or by the physical distance, but economic distance should also be an option. Here, we used Dietzenbacher's APL index to examine whether it corresponds to the aforementioned criteria for setting metropolitan areas. It was revealed that the APL of each region is generally negatively related to its respective physical distance, and when a diagram was drawn based on the average propagation length of each region centered on Nagoya City, the closer the region is to Nagoya City, the closer the economic distance indicated by the index is. However, this relationship is not perfect, and for example, in the Chusei and Iga regions of Mie Prefecture, the physical distance is farther, but the economic distance is closer than in the surrounding areas, which leaves room for further investigation.

The three chapters following Chap. 10 are applied studies using the inter-municipal IOT of Aichi Prefecture. Chapter 10 examines how the decline in household consumption demand in a society with a declining population affects the regional economy. A declining population directly reduces the consumption demand in the region, which has a negative impact on the region's production. However, when considering the supply of products that satisfy consumption demand on a regional basis, there is supply not only from the region itself but also from other regions, and in the case of a municipal basis, the latter has a larger impact.

The target prefecture, Aichi, is an area where manufacturing is developing, centered on the automobile industry, and the demand for employment is large. Compared to other regions, the population decline is small, and a significant decline is not expected in the future. For this reason, the decline in consumption demand is relatively small, and therefore the impact on the region's production is expected to be small. However, the population decline in areas other than Aichi Prefecture is relatively large, and therefore this has a negative impact on Aichi Prefecture's production. For this reason, although the decline in consumption demand within the region is not large, it is necessary to consider the impact of the decline in consumption demand in other regions.

As mentioned above, Aichi Prefecture is a region that has developed mainly around the automobile industry. Currently, the automobile industry is one of the important industries that lead the Japanese economy. However, the automobile industry has been facing a once-in-a-century transformation in recent years, and it has been pointed out that the role of automobiles in the transformation of mobility services may change in the future. Electrification is also progressing as a response to global warming. Here, we focused on the electrification of automobiles and analyzed the impact that the shift from conventional automobiles powered by gasoline engines to EVs has brought about, such as a decrease in automobile parts related to gasoline engines and an increase in electro-mechanical parts such as batteries and motors, and its impact on the local economy through changes in the subcontracting structure of automobile parts. In the case of Aichi Prefecture, automobile assembly plants are located mainly in Toyota City and its neighboring regions, and automobile parts factories are located mainly in the Nishimikawa region surrounding them, and we found that electrification has a negative impact on production in cities in the Nishimikawa region.

Chapter 12 provides an applied study on the regional contribution of production activities of SMEs. The impact of a specific sector on the regional economy can be analyzed using HEM. Setting the row and column of a specific sector in the IOT to zero means that there is no production activity in that sector; hence, the impact of that sector can be determined by taking the difference between the amount of induced production when that sector is present and when it is not. If the sector is a single company, we can use this to evaluate the regional contribution of the specific company. In this chapter, we assumed that a specific company participates in production as a new sector, and we proposed a HIM that adds a new sector, contrary to the HEM. The company in question may not only be new, but it may also be an existing company. In that case, it is necessary to deduct the production activity of the existing company from the IOT; hence, we examined different variations of this method.

In fact, we conducted a questionnaire survey on the production activities of four SMEs located in Nishio City. We used an interregional IOT and compiled municipalities from the inter-municipal IOT of Aichi Prefecture into three regions: Nishio City, the ROA Prefecture, and the ROJ. We conducted an impact analysis for the companies using HIM.

In this study, the impact of backward linkages on raw material procurement for the company's production activities was calculated using the Leontief model, and the impact of forward linkages on product sales was calculated using the Ghosh model. Regional contributions were evaluated by using two indicators: the national market contribution using the multiplier of the induced production amount, and the local contribution calculated as the impact ratio on the local economy of Nishio City.

We found that the three companies belonging to the manufacturing industry made a large contribution to the national market in terms of product sales and a large contribution to the local economy in terms of raw material procurement, while one company that manufactures and sells food and beverages had a relatively large impact on the local economy in terms of product sales, but procured raw materials from a relatively wide area. There have been few studies that have examined methods for evaluating the regional contribution of companies. We believe that the application of the HIM proposed in this chapter could be one of them.

## 13.2 Future Directions Remaining

This book is a compilation of the author's research on interregional IOTs, and it is not a comprehensive introduction to research on regional IOTs in Japan. Therefore, it should be noted that it might be missing other important research perspectives on interregional IOTs in the Japanese economy.

Additionally, as depicted in Table 13.1, the data on interregional IOTs used in this book does not necessarily cover the same years. At the time of drafting this book, the latest year for the prefectural IOTs that formed the basis of this research was 2015, and updating the intermunicipal IOTs to match these IOTs remains a future task.

Furthermore, the parameter estimation of the gravity model discussed in Chap. 5 is based on the interregional trade data by sector in the METI interregional IOT, which covers nine regions nationwide. As the METI interregional IOT has not been compiled since then, parameter estimation for subsequent years has not been performed, and the same estimates have been used. Therefore, it is an important task to create alternative interregional trade data for newer years and estimate the parameters of the gravity model.

Despite these remaining challenges, we believe that we have been able to provide some resolutions to the issues in compiling interregional IOTs and to develop methods of applying interregional IOTs to solve the problems of the current Japanese regional

**Table 13.1** Characteristics of the input–output table used in this book and related data

| Name of data | Year | Region | Sector | Chapter |
|---|---|---|---|---|
| IOT of each prefecture | 2011 | 47 prefectures | 80 | 3 |
| Chubu Region IOT | 2011, 2015 | Nine prefectures (Toyama, Ichikawa, Fukui, Nagano, Gifu, Shizuoka, Aichi, Mie, and Shiga) | 104 | 4, 8 |
| METI's interregional IOT | 2005 | 9 regions of METI | 186 | 5 |
| Tokai Region MRIOT | 2005 | 14 areas in 3 prefectures | 186 | 7, 9 |
| Aichi Prefecture multi-municipal IOT | 2011 | 54 municipalities in Aichi Prefecture | 106 | 6, 10, 11, 12 |

*Source* Compiled by the author

economy: regional revitalization in a society with a declining population and the harmonization between solving global warming and developing regional economies.

## References

Ashiya, T., and H. Goto. 2015. Analysis of the economic ripple effects of regional economic zones based on the inter-regional input-output table estimated for the seven-regions in Hyogo Prefecture. *Sango Renkan (Business Journal of PAPAIOS)* 22 (3): 106–114 (in Japanese).

Dietzenbacher, E. 1997. In vindication of the Ghosh model: A reinterpretation as a price model. *Journal of Regional Science* 37:629–651.

Dietzenbacher, E., and I. Romero. 2007. Production chains in an interregional framework: Identification by means of average propagation lengths. *International Regional Science Review* 30 (4): 362–383.

Ghosh, A. 1958. Input-output approach in an allocation system. *Economica* 25:58–64.

Ihara, T., S. Xuemei, and C. Yantian. 2015. On the construction of the Chubu region inter-regional input-output table. *Sango Renkan (Business Journal of PAPAIOS)* 22 (3): 91–105 (in Japanese).

Input-Output Department Director's Meeting. 2007. *Basic guidelines for constructing 2005 input-output tables* (in Japanese).

Input-Output Department Director's Meeting. 2013. *Basic guidelines for constructing 2011 input-output tables* (in Japanese).

Input-Output Department Director's Meeting. 2017. *Basic guidelines for constructing 2015 input-output tables* (in Japanese).

Ishiro, T. 2012. The analysis of interregional specialization in Kanto region: The compilation of Kanto interregional input-output table and the verification of inducement effect in Tokyo to Kanto or other region. *Ryutsu Keizai University Review* 47 (3): 95–114 (in Japanese).

Japan Auto Parts Industries Association. 2010–2017. *Survey of auto parts shipment trend* (in Japanese).

Japan Automobile Manufacturers Association. 2019. *Japan Automobile Industry 2019* (in Japanese).

Leontief, W. 1936. Quantitative input and output relations in the economic system of the United States. *Review of Economics and Statistics* 18 (3): 105–125.

Leontief, W. 1986. *Input-output economics*, 2nd ed. Oxford University Press.
METI. 2009. *Basic manual for METI 2005 regional input-output tables* (in Japanese).
MIC. 2009. *2005 Input-output tables, explanatory report* (in Japanese).
MIC. 2020. *2015 Input-output tables, explanatory report* (in Japanese).
MIC. 2008. *Basic guidelines for creating regional input-output tables* (in Japanese).
Next Generation Vehicle Promotion Center. 2017. Research report on clean energy vehicles (in Japanese). http://www.cev-pc.or.jp/chosa/pdf/H28_chosa_1_honpen.pdf
Shimoda, M., and K. Fujikawa. 2012. Input-output analysis model and supply constraints caused by the Great East Japan Earthquake. *Sango Renkan (Business Journal of PAPAIOS)* 20 (2): 133–146 (in Japanese).
Toyota Motor Corporation. 2019. Toward the spread of EVs (in Japanese). https://global.toyota/jp/newsroom/corporate/28416855.html
Yamada, Mitsuo. 2020a. Construction of inter-municipal input-output tables and its application–Based on the 2011 Aichi Prefecture input-output table. *Chukyo Economic Review* 31: 9–36 (in Japanese).
Yamada, Mitsuo. 2020b. Electrification of automobiles and the Aichi Prefecture economy. In: Chapter 4 in Mitsuo Yamada and Junya Masuda (eds.) *Econometric modeling of globalization and regional economies*, 119–151. Tokyo: Keiso Shobo, (in Japanese).
Yamada, M. 2022. Impact of consumption fluctuations under population decline on the municipal economy of Aichi Prefecture. *Sangyo Renkan (Business Journal of PAPAIOS)* 30 (1): 1–15 (in Japanese).
Yamada, M. 2023. Inter-regional input-output analysis of the regional contributions of small and medium-sized enterprises: A case study of Nishio City, Aichi Prefecture. *Sangyo Renkan (Business Journal of PAPAIOS)* 31 (1): 42–56 (in Japanese).

MIX
Papier aus verantwortungsvollen Quellen
Paper from responsible sources
FSC® C105338

If you have any concerns about our products,
you can contact us on
**ProductSafety@springernature.com**

In case Publisher is established outside the EU,
the EU authorized representative is:
**Springer Nature Customer Service Center GmbH**
**Europaplatz 3, 69115 Heidelberg, Germany**

Printed by Libri Plureos GmbH
in Hamburg, Germany